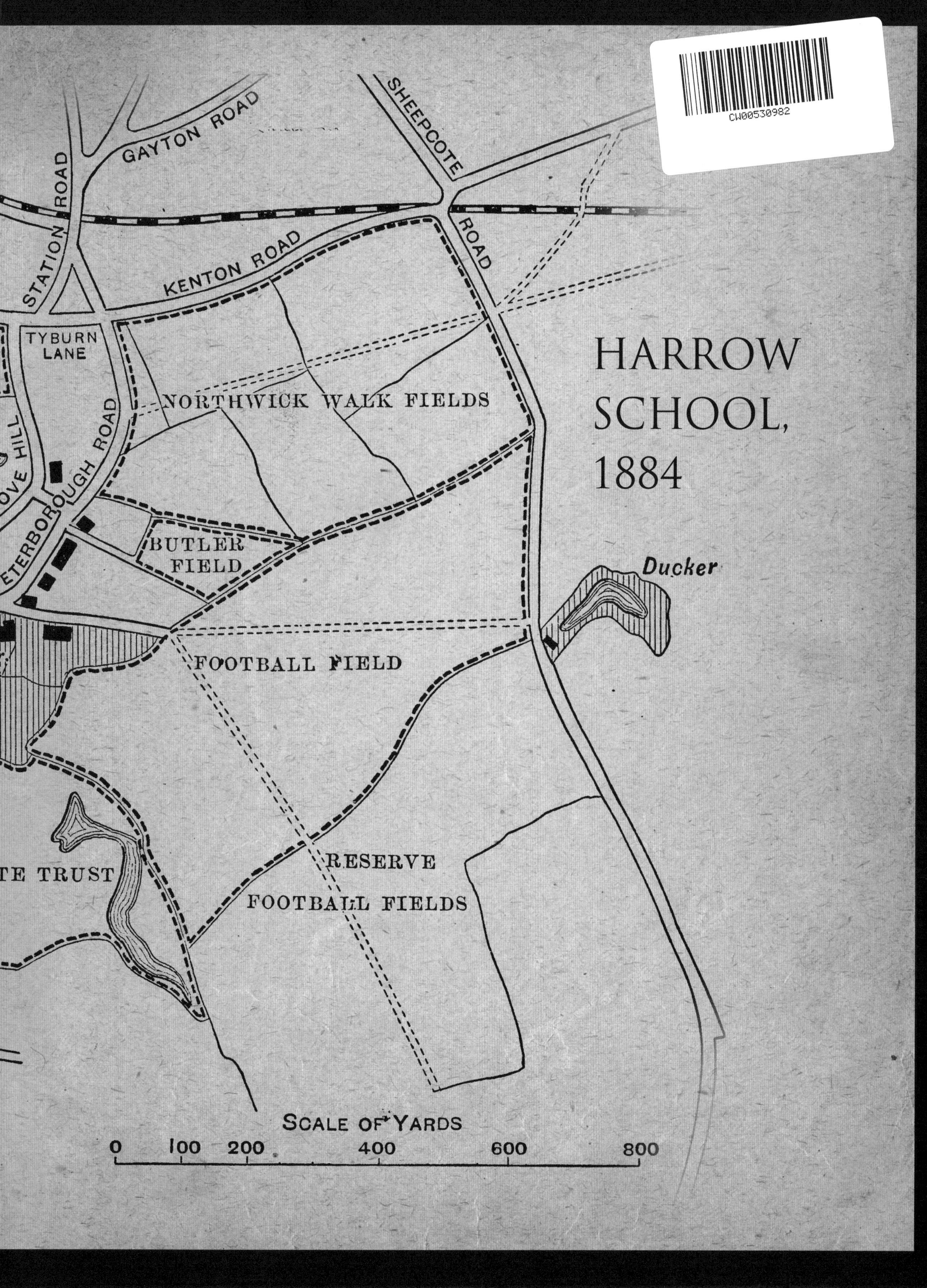
HARROW
SCHOOL,
1884
GAYTON ROAD
SHEEPCOTE
ROAD
STATION ROAD
KENTON ROAD
TYBURN
LANE
NORTHWICK WALK FIELDS
PETERBOROUGH ROAD
GROVE HILL
BUTLER
FIELD
Ducker
FOOTBALL FIELD
RESERVE
FOOTBALL FIELDS
TE TRUST
SCALE OF YARDS
0
100
200
400
600
800
CW00530982

The Timeline History of

HARROW SCHOOL

1572 to the Present

The Timeline History of

HARROW SCHOOL

1572 to the Present

DALE VARGAS

FOREWORD: RT HON LORD BUTLER OF BROCKWELL KG GCB CVO

WORTH PRESS

THE TIMELINE HISTORY OF HARROW SCHOOL

First published in 2010 by Worth Press Limited, on behalf of Harrow School.

World publishing rights Worth Press Limited, www.worthpress.co.uk

ISBN: 978-1-84931-023-9

All surplus profits from the sale of this title will go to the Harrow Development Trust.

Publisher's note:
Every effort has been made to ensure the accuracy of the information presented in this book. The Publisher will not assume liability for damages caused by inaccuracies in the data and makes no warranty whatsoever expressed or implied. The Publisher welcomes comments and corrections from readers, emailed to info@worthpress.co.uk, which will be considered for incorporation in future editions. Likewise, every effort has been made to trace copyright holders and seek permission to use illustrative and other material. The Publisher wishes to apologise for any inadvertent errors or omissions and would be glad to rectify these in future editions.

Proofreading: Kirsty Shanahan
Page design and layout: Arati Devasher, www.aratidevasher.com

Printed and bound by IMAGO in China.

CONTENTS

Comprehensive appendices containing further details are online at **www.harrowassociation.com**

FOREWORD

I LIKE TIMELINES. WHEN my old friend and housemate, Dale Vargas, and I were at school the foundation of history teaching was that every child should learn by heart the names and dates of every king and queen of England since the Norman conquest – "Willy, Willy, Harry, Steve and so on" is history as I first remember it.

The teaching of history has now become more imaginative – "what did it feel like to live in Tudor England?" – and, I hope, less anglo-centred. But I have always been glad to have had the timeline of the English kings planted in my juvenile memory because, whenever I have come across the date of some event elsewhere in the world – the Spanish invasion of Central America, for example, or the Thirty Years War – I have had some point of reference with what was going on in my own country. Over the years, history has become for me a wider and more comprehensive timeline.

So, as soon as I heard of the project, proposed by Ken Webb, to produce a timeline history of Harrow School, I immediately ordered a copy. I should have known better. The response from Dale Vargas was not a copy of the book, then still work in progress, but an invitation to write a foreword. The compensation has been to see the book in its early stages. It contains not only a fascinating and, to my eye, brilliantly designed overall timeline but chapters on the chronological development of a very wide range of aspects of the School. These, despite Dale Vargas's disclaimer in his introduction, seem to me remarkably comprehensive. It will be hard for any Harrovian, whatever aspect of the School meant most to him, not to find a chapter that covers it. And the chapters are accompanied by a fascinating selection of historic illustrations and photographs.

As Dale Vargas says, this book is a bran tub to be dipped into, not read continuously. It is history made visual and easily digestible. It adds a new and very enjoyable dimension to previous histories of the School. As such, it is not the least of the many services Dale Vargas has done for Harrow.

RT HON LORD BUTLER
OF BROCKWELL, KG GCB CVO
August 2010

Facing page: The Old Schools, c1860

INTRODUCTION

THERE HAVE BEEN many successful books written about Harrow, most recently a collection of reminiscences, *Portrait of a School*, edited by Robert Dudley, and Dr Christopher Tyerman's scholarly *A History of Harrow School*. I make no apology for adding to this collection because the *Timeline History* is essentially different: its closest ancestor is ED Laborde's *Harrow Yesterday and Today*, published in 1948 and out of print for more than half a century.

When Ken Webb, whose idea the Timeline series is, approached me to write the text for a Timeline history of the School, I had some reservations as I am no historian. My only qualification for writing a book such as this is my intimate knowledge of the School as pupil and Master, a relationship lasting nearly sixty years. Even so, when I embarked on these essays I became fully aware of the whole swathes of School life of which I remained totally ignorant. I am grateful therefore to the many people – Masters, former Masters and Old Harrovians – who have helped me to cultivate these barren areas. I especially wish to thank Ross Beckett, Kirsty Shanahan and Rob Dudley, whose knowledge of the School, of the English language and of what constitutes a readable piece of prose, have been invaluable. I would also like to thank my wife, Krystyna, for her encouragement and advice. Most of all I am grateful to Christopher Tyerman, who has allowed me to plunder his *A History of Harrow School*, picking out choice pieces here and there, and has cast a critical eye over several of the essays; he has also contributed the essay on 'Governors and Governance', of which he has an unequalled knowledge.

I hope therefore that readers will find this book informative, interesting and occasionally entertaining. I expect that it will appeal largely to those who have spent time on the Hill either as teachers or learners, but I hope that others, interested in education in general and its development at a school that has achieved renown across the world, will also find something in it for them. I have attempted to make the text intelligible to the general reader but, in case of the occasional lapse, there is a glossary in the essay, 'Harrow Speak'.

I do not expect this book to be read as a narrative from page 1 to page 253 – it is much more likely that the reader will turn in the first instance to topics of personal interest and dip into the Timeline itself for reference. As you will see from the Contents, I have tried to cover each aspect of the School by sections under separate headings (although the classification in several cases is disputable). Each topic is summarised in a short essay, a bite sized nugget that I hope will be easily digestible. The original intention was to have an appendix, which would contain much factual information, useful for reference but turgid reading, but as the text grew by over 50% from its expected length, this became impractical. The appendix will now appear online. This has the advantage of being adaptable, errors can be corrected and lists can be updated; the disadvantage is that some readers – a small minority nowadays, I think – do not have access to the internet.

In spite of this expansion I am conscious of numerous omissions and I fear that some of these may

be areas of School life that were very important to some readers: for example I have not included any Societies, except to list them in the appendix. Thus there is nothing on the Marmots, that very popular climbing and mountaineering society, the Chess and Bridge Clubs that have thrived for many years, and such high profile prize competitions as the Lady Bouchier Reading Prize and the Fox Talbot Photography Prize, which have attracted both distinguished competitors and adjudicators. Where these omissions have caused disappointment, I apologise.

I am also aware of some other serious omissions: I would like to have written about House Matrons, who have played a huge part in the lives of generations of Harrovians, but the lack of material beyond a few random reminiscences has prevented me from being able to do them justice. The School's gardens, grounds and trees, all often taken for granted, but a source of wonder to many visiting the Hill, deserved to be mentioned. And the shopkeepers: Mr Caddy and Mr Richards, the haircutters at Rosemary Upton's; Mr Trundle at Gieves; Jim Crook of the Hill; Mr Chatham, the shoemaker, who wore a morning coat every day well into the 1950s; Mrs Dave at the Post Office... These and many other characters were institutions to generations of Harrovians and are fondly remembered. Alas, there has not been space.

A couple of further notes: I have kept a 'thirty year rule' on observations of a personal or professional nature. Thus, for example, I have not commented on Head Masters who have retired since 1980: this may have left their career summaries looking rather meagre. I have also referred to Harrow "School" and "Masters" thus, other schools and masters being all in lower case. This is for clarification rather than any misplaced sense of superiority.

I suppose this book is really a tribute to the many friends I have made at and through Harrow; to the Masters who taught me, mostly no longer with us, to my contemporaries in the School, to my colleagues as a beak, to my pupils, especially those who were in The Head Master's House in my time as House Master, and to others more recent, who are friends of my son, Ashley. I treasure these relationships and consider myself very fortunate to have been associated with such a great School.

DALE VARGAS
Harrow 2010

Looking from Church Hill towards the Head Master's House, c1830

1572 | 1575 | 1590 | 1600 | 1610 | 1620

NO. OF BOYS

GOVERNORS APPOINTED

1572 Sir Gilbert Gerard – 1592 • William Gerard – 1583 • John Page – 1623 • Thomas Reding – 1586

1586 William Gerard – 1609 • Henry Page – 1615

1591 William Greenhill (OH) – 1613

1592 Sir Thomas Gerard – 1617

1604 Richard Page – 1642

1609 Sir Gilbert Gerard Bt – 1669

1613 Dudley, 3rd Baron North – 1666

1615 Thomas Page – 1648

1617 Edward Claxton – 1654

Left: John Lyon, the founder

SCHOOL EVENTS

1572 John Lyon's Charter granted by Queen Elizabeth I

1578 John Lyon gave land in St John's Wood to the Governors

1582 John Lyon gave a farm in St John's Wood to the Governors

1591 John Lyon's Orders, Statutes and Rules framed

1592 Death of John Lyon

Left: Joan Lyon, wife of John Lyon

1615 Earliest pupil recorded: Macharie Wildblud

BUILDINGS & GROUNDS

1608 Work begun on the School House

1615 School House ready

HEAD MASTERS & ASSISTANT MASTERS

1608 Head Master: **Anthony Rate** (evidence unreliable)

1611 Head Master: **Mr Bradley** (evidence unreliable)

1615 Head Master: **The Rev William Launce** • Usher: The Rev Thomas Launce – 1636

1621 Head Master: **The Rev Robert Whittle**

AN EXTRACT FROM JOHN LYON'S CHARTER

Elizabeth, by the grace of God Queen of England, France and Ireland, Defender of the Faith, etc.

To all whom these presents may concern, greeting.

"Whereas our beloved subject John Lyon of Preston in the parish of Harrow on the Hill in our County of Middlesex, a yeoman inspired by divine grace with the instinct of charity, has resolved to found, create and forever to establish anew in the town of Harrow on the Hill in our County of Middlesex a certain grammar school with one schoolmaster and one usher for the perpetual education, training and instruction of boys and youths of the said parish and generously to endow and maintain two scholars in our University of Cambridge and also two scholars in our University of Oxford; and has determined to repair and mend at his own very great expense certain highways between Edgware and London as well as other places; and to undertake further works of devotion and piety for the very great benefit and encouragement of the scholars applying themselves to learning in the said parish; thereby offering a very good example to all other to imitate the like hereafter; and also for the common profit of all our subjects;

We grant and ordain, by our special favour and from sure knowledge and of our own accord, on behalf of ourself, our heirs, our successors, upon the humble petition of the same John Lyon ...that there be and shall be established forever hereafter with our permission a Grammar School in the said town of Harrow on the Hill, which shall be called the Free Grammar School of the said John Lyon..."

Left: This statue of Queen Elizabeth I is placed in a niche of the wall of the south tower of Speech Room. It was brought from Ashridge Park in Hertfordshire in 1925 and is a memorial to Lord Claud Hamilton (OH)

CURRICULUM & ACADEMICS

1623 Books costing £1.10.4 added to library

SCHOOL SPORTS

OTHER ACTIVITIES

WORLD EVENTS

1600 East India Company founded

1603 Queen Elizabeth I died; James VI of Scotland became James I of England

1607 Gunpowder Plot thwarted • First permanent settlement in the New World established at Jamestown

1609 Shakespeare's sonnets were published

1610 Galileo discovered the movement of planets and confirmed Copernicus' theory that the sun is the centre of the solar system

1617 Mayflower sailed to Massachusetts where the Pilgrim's Fathers' colony was established

1630 | 1640 | 1650 | 1660 | 1670

1642 Daniel Waldo – 1661

1648 Sir Francis Gerard 2nd Bart – 1680

1653 William Greenhill – 1667

1654 John Page – 1667

1661 Daniel Waldo – 1691

1666 Edward Fenn – 1670

1667 Sir Edward Waldo – 1707; Thomas Smith – 1687

1669 William Page – 1690

1670 John Anderson – 1672

1672 Sir Gilbert Gerard – 1682

1630 Earliest 'foreigner' recorded: Hammond Claxton

1646 William Hide given lease of a house (on the site of the present Head Master's) by the Governors

1655 Governors petitioned in the Court of Chancery for increased funds for road maintenance

1674 First Contio Latina recorded. Orator: J Dennis

1645 Hearth in School Room

1651 Sun dial positioned

1654 Sun dial replaced by clock

1661 School Room re-panelled

1676 School clock upgraded to pendulum

1628 Head Master: **The Rev William Hide**

1636 Usher: William Ponder – 1638

1638 Usher: Gilbert Bamford – 1661

1650 Head Master permitted to live off the School premises

1661 Head Master: **The Rev Thomas Jonson**

1662 Usher: Mr Blithe – 1665

1665 Usher: Thomas Martin (1665); Usher: Thomas Robinson – 1700

1669 Head Master permitted to marry. Appointment: **The Rev William Horne**

1646 Curriculum at this time: Cicero, Ovid, Horace, Virgil, Homer

1650 Head Master introduced lessons in writing for free scholars • Dames' school founded for teaching poor children to write

1627 1st 'Founder Exhibitioner' to Oxford: Robert Ashwell

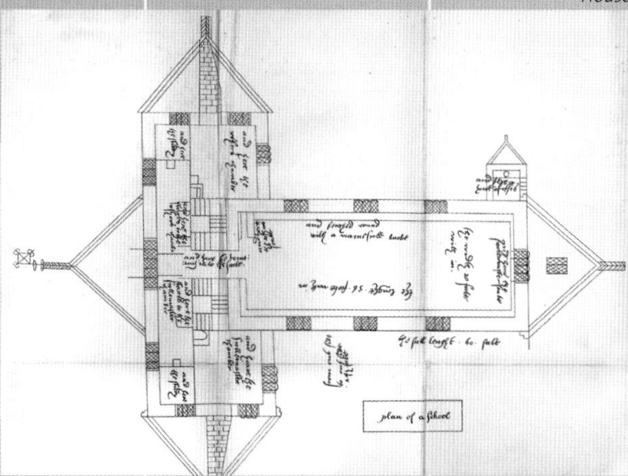

Below: The plan of the School House

Right: The School House

1628 William Harvey discovered the working of the human heart

1642 Civil War began

1649 King Charles I was executed; Oliver Cromwell became Lord Protector

1660 Restoration of the monarchy: Charles II

1665 The Great Plague of London

1666 The Great Fire of London

1667 *Paradise Lost* by John Milton published

1680 | 1690 | 1700 | 1710 | 1720

NO. OF BOYS

1682 120

1721 140 including 40 free scholars

GOVERNORS APPOINTED

1680 Sir Charles Gerard 3rd Bart

1683 William Fenn (OH) – 1701

1687 Sir Cheke Gerard 5th Bart – 1701

1690 Edmund Waldo (OH) – 1707

1690 Samuel Finch – 1698

1698 Richard Page – 1715

1701 Sir Francis Gerard 4th Bart – 1704

1702 Warwick Lake – 1713

1704 John Page – 1715

1707 Sir Thomas Francklyn 3rd Bart – 1728; Rev Peter Waldo (OH) – 1745

1713 James Brydges, 1st Duke of Chandos – 1740

1715 Sir John Rushout 4th Bart – 1775; William Bucknall (OH) – 1742

1717 John Page – 1727

1727 Thomas Graham – 1734

1728 Francis Herne (OH) – 1777

SCHOOL EVENTS

1709 John Lyon Trust financial crisis; Dame system suspended

1720 Contio discontinued

1728 Contio reinstated. Orator: Kentish

Right: The resignation letter of Head Master The Rev Thomas Thackeray, in 1760

Gentlemen

As I am prevented by sickness from attending at your present meeting, I take this method of acquainting you, that I intend to leave the School at Bartholomewtide next.
Permit me to return my thanks to those Gentlemen from whom I have received favours; & to subscribe myself

Their much Obliged
Humble Servant
Thos Thackeray

Harrow May 3d. 1760.

BUILDINGS & GROUNDS

1680 Purchase of piece of land adjoining School Yard

1682 School Yard levelled

1686 Head Master established in house at peppercorn rent

1691 Vane & red lion erected on top of gable of School building

1725 Burglary from School Room: seal stolen

1728 Lion on School building given collar • Lion on School building gilded

HEAD MASTERS & ASSISTANT MASTERS

1685 Head Master: **The Rev William Bolton**

1691 Head Master: **The Rev Thomas Bryan**

1722 Usher: The Rev James Cox – 1730 • Usher permitted to marry

Left: Records of the Silver Arrow shooting contest which began in 1684

CURRICULUM & ACADEMICS

1700 Usher: John Le Hunte – 1705

1701 Usher: John Hooker (OH) – 1721

1728 New term dates introduced: holiday of one month at Christmas, one at Whitsun

Below: W Jones, later Sir William Jones, philologist

SCHOOL SPORTS

1684 First reference to the Silver Arrow archery contest

1697 Silver Arrow presented for competition

OTHER ACTIVITIES

1697 Performance of *Sophonistra* or *Hannibal's Overthrow*

WORLD EVENTS

1685 James II became King

1687 *Principia Mathematica* by Isaac Newton published

1688 James II deposed

1689 William III & Mary II ruled jointly

1702 Queen Anne became Queen • First daily newspapers published in Britain

1704 Duke of Marlborough defeated Franco-Bavarian army at Blenheim

1707 Union of England and Scotland declared

1711 St Paul's Cathedral rebuilt by Christopher Wren

1713 The Treaty of Utrecht ended the war of Spanish succession

1714 King George I became King

1717 Triple Alliance signed with France & Netherlands

1721 Robert Walpole (Whig) became de facto first Minister in England • Bach composed *Brandenburg Concertos*

1727 George II became King

1730 1740 1750 1760 1770

1738 13 Free Scholars

1739 14 Free Scholars

1740 11 Free Scholars

1746 130

1760 80

1761 250

1769 236

1770 238

1771 232

1774 205

1775 207

1776 242

1779 220

1734 James Lightbourn – 1738

1738 Daniel Graham – 1761

1740 Henry, Marquess of Carnarvon – 1745

1742 John Bucknall (OH) – 1797

1745 Lancelot Lake – 1751

1747 The Rev Francis Saunders – 1777

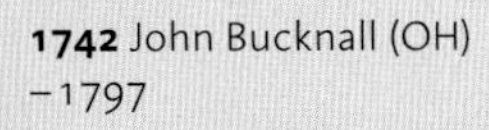

Left: J Banks, later Sir Joseph Banks, botanist

1761 Sir John Rushout, 5th Bart, later 1st Baron Northwick (OH) – 1801

1774 Richard Page – 1803

1775 James Brydges – 1790

1777 James, 3rd Viscount Grimston – 1810 • Rev Walter Williams – 1811

Below: Head Master The Rev Thomas Thackeray

1734 School bell placed

1746 Old House opened for boarders under Dr Samuel Glasse

1749 Addition of playing field below School Yard

1752 Action brought against Governors by Trustees of the Road Fund

1770 All boys were boarders • Number of Monitors increased to 4

1771 Petition objecting to appointment of Dr Heath as Head Master • Number of Monitors increased to 6 • Three Speech Days introduced

1772 Appointment of a Clerk to Governors

1777 Protests at timing of Bills

1770 Mr Anthony Tassoni built a dancing school

1772 Large extension to Head Master's House built

1775 Governors first took out insurance on school buildings • Fire damage to School House (Old Schools)

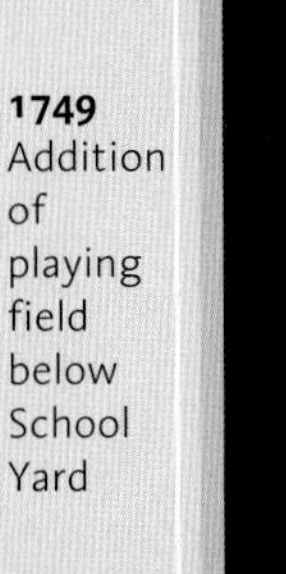

Below: Head Master The Rev Robert Carey Sumner

1730 Usher re-named Under Master • Under Master: The Rev Francis Saunders – 1732

1731 Head Master: **The Rev James Cox**

1732 Usher: The Rev William Charles – 1743

1743 Under Master: William Saunders (OH) – 1747

1746 Head Master James Cox absconded with many debts after period of drunken negligence • Head Master: **The Rev Thomas Thackeray**

1747 Under Master: The Rev William Cox (1747) • Under Master: The Rev William Prior – 1765

1748 Writing Master: Mr Henry Reeves – 1768

1760 Head Master: **The Rev Robert Carey Sumner** • Dancing Master: Mr Anthony Tassoni

1765 Under Master: The Rev Richard Wadeson – 1789

1767 Assistant Master: Dr Samuel Parr – 1771

1768 Master's Assistant: The Rev David Roderick (OH) – 1771 • Under Master's Assistant: The Rev Joseph Drury – 1785 • Writing Master: Mr Henry "Quilley" Reeves – 1819

Right: Dr Samuel Parr

1770 French Master: M. Jacques Butticaz – 1805 • Writing Master: Mr Bernadin (1770) • French Master; Mr Elasore (1770) • Dancing Master: Mr Richard Blake – 1793 • Drawing Master: Mr Tasoni (1770)

1771 Head Master: **The Rev Benjamin Heath** • Assistant Master: The Rev Thomas Bromley – 1808

1774 Assistant Master: The Rev Glover – 1780(?) • Assistant Master: The Rev Cooke – 1780(?)

1779 Dancing Master: Mr Dominic Velloni

1759 Holiday periods changed to Christmas, Easter & August

Left: The cricket ground, in 1840

Right: Head Master The Rev Benjamin Heath

1750 Cricket being played at this time on the 'Bowling Green' at top of Sudbury Hill

1775 VI Form introduced

1771 Cricket established (or earlier)

1772 Silver Arrow abolished

1738 Methodist Society formed by John & Charles Wesley

1739 War declared on Spain (War of Jenkin's Ear)

1744 Marylebone Cricket Club formed; Laws of Cricket formulated

1746 Jacobite Rebellion ended with Battle of Culloden

1752 Gregorian Calendar adopted • Benjamin Franklin invented the lightning conductor

1755 Samuel Johnson's English Dictionary published • Earthquake in Lisbon, Portugal

1756 England declared war on France (Seven Years War)

1757 Robert Clive defeated the Nawab of Bengal at Plassey

1759 The British annexed Quebec

1760 George III became King

1770 Captain Cook discovered Australia

1773 The 'Boston Tea Party' • First Governor-General of India appointed

1775 American War of Independence started

1776 American Declaration of Independence signed

1780 – 1790 – 1800 – 1805

No. of Boys

1780 189 · 1785 149 · 1786 153 · 1787 150 · 1788 149 · 1789 132

1790 131 · 1791 116 · 1792 130 · 1793 122 · 1794 124 · 1795 119 · 1796 134 · 1797 141 · 1798 192 · 1799 204

1800 225 · 1801 274 · 1802 324 · 1803 348 · 1804 307

1805 262 · 1806 257 · 1807 215 · 1808 234 · 1809 220

Governors Appointed

1790 Thomas Villiers, 2nd Earl of Clarendon – 1821

1797 Samuel Moody – 1823

1801 John, 2nd Baron Northwick – 1859

1803 William Page – 1824

Left: The Hon RH Fitzgibbon, later 3rd Earl of Clare

Above: Pie House off West Street

School Events

1787 Governors opened bank account with Denne & Co

1791 Custos: D Peachey appointed

1800 Act of Parliament enforced payments for upkeep of roads • Lower Forms moved upstairs in the Old Schools

1803 Upkeep of Harrow & Edgware Roads transferred to local authorities

1804 Visit of George III

1805 Court of Chancery ruling confirmed that endowment funds could only be used for the teaching of Classics

1808 Monitors found to be caning pupils. Rebellion ensued

Below: A view of Harrow School, 1802

Below: Sheridan's Stables on the site of the Leaf Schools

Buildings & Grounds

1787 Governors acquired Dancing School (also used as Speech Room)

1799 Major refurbishment of School House

1803 Roxeth Common enclosed. School received a share in return for loss of rights.

1809 Duckpuddle used for swimming

Left: John, 2nd Earl of Clare, later Governor of Bombay

Head Masters & Assistant Masters

1785 Head Master: **The Rev Dr Joseph Drury** • Assistant Master: The Rev Mark Drury – 1826

1789 Under Master: The Rev Mark Drury

1790 Assistant Master: The Rev William Roberts

1791 Assistant Master:The Rev Edmund (?) Outram – 1795(?)

1792 Assistant Master: Mr Benjamin Evans – 1833

1793 Dancing Master: Mr James Webb – 1828

Left: Head Master Dr George Butler

1804 Payment to Masters clear of income tax

1805 Head Master: **Dr George Butler** • Mr Henry Reeves appointed Writing Master & School Librarian • French Master: M. Briod

1806 House Master of The Abbey: The Rev Henry Drury

Curriculum & Academics

1780 Introduction of Shell Form between IV and V Forms

Left: Spencer Perceval, son of the OH Prime Minister of the same name, assassinated in 1812

School Sports

1780 Fencing by this time an established activity

Left: The Rev Henry Drury

1804 Messrs Angelo appointed to teach Fencing

1805 First recorded cricket match v Eton at Lord's

Other Activities

Right: Lord Byron, poet and adventurer

World Events

1780 First Derby horse race run at Epsom

1781 James Watt invented the steam engine

1783 The Treaty of Paris concluded the American War of Independence

1788 Penal colony set up in New South Wales

1789 George Washington became first President of the United States • French Revolution began

1796 Vaccination for smallpox was discovered by Edward Jenner

1798 Income tax introduced

1799 Napoleon came to power in France

1800 Act of Union (Ireland and Britain)

1801 First census held in Britain

1802 Factory Act • War re-declared with France

1804 First steam-powered locomotive built • Spain declared war on Britain

1805 Nelson's fleet defeated Spanish & French at Battle of Trafalgar

1806 Carbon paper patented

1807 Slave Trade Act abolished slavery in Britain

1809 Spencer Perceval's (OH) Tory ministry

1810 1815 1820 1825

1810 192 · 1811 184 · 1812 193 · 1814 236 · 1815 183 · 1816 287 including 3 Free Scholars · 1817 268 · 1818 246 including 10 Free Scholars · 1819 243 · 1820 247 · 1821 249 · 1823 238 · 1824 248 · 1825 238 including 17 Free Scholars · 1826 198 · 1827 163 · 1828 129 · 1829 118

1810 John Gray – 1828

1811 John, 1st Marquess of Abercorn – 1818

Left: The Rev Joseph Cunningham, Governor 1818–1862

1817 Custos: D Peachey retired; H Hope appointed

1818 Rev Joseph Cunningham – 1862

1819 Custos: H Hope retired; G Hoare appointed

1823 George, 4th Earl of Aberdeen – 1860

1824 Charles Hamilton – 1834 • Col Mark Beaufoy – 1827

1825 Further Court of Chancery confirmation of ruling of 1805

1827 The Rev John Roberts – 1841

1828 Joseph Neeld (OH) – 1836

1811 Proceedings against Governors for mismanaging Trust. Judgement in favour of Governors

Above: View from The Park post-1819

1820 Old School building completed. (Old) Speech Room opened

1826 The Rev WJJ Drury & Rev Mark Drury absconded leaving debts

1810 Sixth Form Ground enclosed by railings

1811 High Street (later Moretons) opened by The Rev WJJ Drury

1818 The Abbey (later Druries) enlarged by The Rev Henry Drury • New wing added to School House (Old Schools)

1819 The Rev SE Batten purchased the Manor House, renamed The Grove • Old Schools opened by Lord Clarendon June 3; Lion & ornament removed & lost

1821 School Yard enlarged • Cupola replaced: larger bell & new clock

1823 First attempt to drain the Sixth Form Ground

1825 Construction of Duckpuddle

1826 Extension of Old Schools • House in the High Street, later named Moretons, pulled down and re-built

1827 'Night fagging' outlawed

1827 Sixth Form Ground levelled

1828 The Rev W Oxenham rebuilt High Street

1829 Number of Speech Days reduced to two

Below: The Head Master's House, 1815

Above: Mr JF Marillier

Above: The Rev W Oxenham

1811 House Master of High Street: The Rev WJJ Drury

1819 Assistant Master (Mathematics): Mr JF Marillier • The Rev SE Batten opened The Grove as a boarding house

1826 6 Assistant Masters • Under Master: Mr Benjamin Evans • House Master of High Street: The Rev W Oxenham • Writing Master: Mr Jacob Marillier

1829 Head Master: **The Rev Charles Thomas Longley**

Above: The Old Schools, c1819

Left: Head Master The Rev CT Longley

1820 Current teaching arrangements: VI, Lower VI & III in the Fourth Form room; V in the Governors' room (Old Schools 2); Upper VI in the south chamber (OS4); Shell in the Cock Loft (on 2nd floor) • Head Master introduced prizes for Latin & Greek verse

1821 Governors' Prizes introduced

1824 Lyon Scholarships awarded by written exam

1826 Peel Medal for Latin prose endowed • John Sayer endowed scholarship to Caius College, Cambridge

1828 Leaving Scholarship examination introduced

1829 First Leaving Scholarship awarded to CT Cunningham • Head Master forbidden to take private pupils • Termly exams (trials) introduced

1818 Cricket XI beat Eton at Lord's by 13 runs

1822 Cricket XI beat Eton at Lord's by 87 runs

1823 Leith's (Dame's House) v The School at cricket; cricket & rackets fagging regular practice • First professional cricket coach appointed: John Anderton

1825 Cricket v Winchester at Lord's played for first time

1828 *The Harrovian* first published

1811 George, Prince of Wales, became Regent • Luddites began protests against introduction of machinery

1812 War with America began • Prime Minister Spencer Perceval (OH) assassinated • Lord Liverpool formed Tory government

1814 Napoleon abdicated

1815 Duke of Wellington's victory at Waterloo ends Napoleonic Wars

1818 Charities Commission established

1820 King George IV became King

1825 Financial crash

1829 Metropolitan Police Act • First Oxford v Cambridge boat race

1830 | 1835 | 1840

NO. OF BOYS

1830	1831	1832	1833	1834	1835	1836	1837	1838	1839	1841
162	219	240	255	243	218	176	169	154	150	121

GOVERNORS APPOINTED

1834 James, 1st Duke of Abercorn – 1885

1836 George, 1st Baron Wolverton – 1871

1841 Rt Hon Thomas Sotheron-Estcourt (OH) – 1870

SCHOOL EVENTS

1838 HM reforms fagging. Term Harroviensis or 'Harrovian' coined

1840 Induction of Monitors ceremony in Chapel: presentation of keys

Above: The Park was bought in 1831

Below: The Head Master's House on fire

Below: The Rev BH Drury

BUILDINGS & GROUNDS

1831 Flambards bought by Rev WW Phelps, renamed The Park

1832 A cricket pavilion built on VI Form Ground

1833 The Grove burned down and re-built

1838 The Head Master's House burned down

1839 Dr Wordsworth's Chapel completed

HEAD MASTERS & ASSISTANT MASTERS

1830 House Master of The Grove: The Rev BH Kennedy

1831 House Master of The Park: The Rev WW Phelps

1833 Under Master: The Rev Henry Drury

1836 Head Master: **The Rev Christopher Wordsworth**

1837 House Master of The Grove: The Rev TH Steel

1839 Head Master became Chaplain • House Master of The Park: The Rev JW Colenso

1840 Dancing Master, Mr Webb, retired (no pupils)

1841 House Master of The Abbey: The Rev BH Drury

Left: The Rev WW Phelps

Right: The Rev TH Steel

Left: Head Master The Rev Christopher Wordsworth

CURRICULUM & ACADEMICS

1830 School timetable reorganised (see page 108)

1837 Maths introduced to main curriculum

1838 Reorganisation of curriculum • Weekly Masters' meetings instituted • Alex Beresford-Hope Prize for Greek Prose founded

1840 Form Masters appointed • Richard Gregory scholarship & medal for Latin prose endowed • Joseph Neeld endowed 2 scholarships

SCHOOL SPORTS

1830 House colours began to be introduced

1832 Sixth successive & heaviest defeat by Eton at Lord's: by inns & 156 runs • Football match, The Head Master's & The Grove v The Rest. House colours (inc. caps) worn.

1833 Cricket XI beat Eton at Lord's by 8 wickets

1834 Cricket XI beat Eton at Lord's by 13 runs; R Broughton took 13 wickets

1836 Cricket XI beat Eton at Lord's by 9 wickets

OTHER ACTIVITIES

1836 *The Harrow Magazine* first published

WORLD EVENTS

1830 King William IV became King • Manchester to Liverpool railway begins operation

1832 The Great Reform Bill giving the vote to a million people became law

1833 Slavery Abolition Act passed • Factory Act banning child labour became law

1834 Lord Melbourne (Whig), Duke of Wellington (Tory) and Robert Peel (OH, Conservative) form governments • Palace of Westminster destroyed by fire

1837 Queen Victoria became Queen • London to Bath and London to Birmingham railway lines opened

1839 1st Opium War with China began • First Henley Royal Regatta

1840 Queen Victoria married Prince Albert • Penny postage introduced • Grammar Schools Act passed

1841 Robert Peel's (OH) 2nd Conservative ministry

1842 93 · **1843** 89 · **1844** 73 · **1845** 123 including 14 Free Scholars · **1846** 190 · **1847** 270 · **1851** 396

Left: Brothers G Hoare and S Hoare, both Custos of the School

Right: The visit of Prince Albert to the School, 1854

1842 Founder's Day introduced on 3 October, anniversary of John Lyon's death

1843 Contention over 'free scholars'

1844 Number of Speech Days reduced to one

1848 Custos: G Hoare retired; S Hoare appointed • Visit of Queen Victoria

1853 Philathletic Club formed

1854 Visit of HRH Prince Albert • 10-15 Monitors

1844 The Head Master's House re-opened

1845 Second attempt to drain the Sixth Form Ground • Improvements to Ducker started • Chapel organ installed

1846 West Acre bought by Rev G Townsend Warner

1847 West Acre opened as Large House

1848 High Street (later renamed Bradbys) built by the Rev H Keary

1850 Two uncovered rackets courts built below the Milling Ground • Water pumped into Ducker from well at Sheepcote Farm instead of feed from dyke

1851 Ducker caretaker's cottage built

1853 Water closets introduced to sanitary systems • Further drainage to VI Form Ground • Mr F Rendall built Grove Hill

1854 Building of new Chapel begun.

Below: Mr GF Harris

1842 House Master of The Park: Mr GF Harris

1845 Head Master: **The Rev Dr Charles John Vaughan** • Six Assistant Masters • House Master of The Grove: The Rev JN Simkinson

Above: Head Master CJ Vaughan

Left: The Rev BF Westcott

Left: The Rev EH Bradby

1852 House Master of High Street North: The Rev BF Westcott

1853 House Master of High Street South: The Rev EH Bradby

1854 House Master of West Acre: The Rev SA Pears • House Master of West Acre: The Rev EH Vaughan • House Master of Grove Hill: The Rev F Rendall

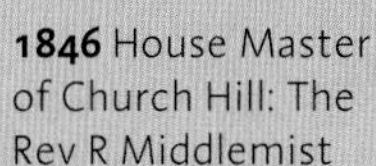

1844 House Master of The Grove: The Rev R Shilleto

1846 House Master of Church Hill: The Rev R Middlemist • House Master of West Acre: The Rev G Townsend Warner

1849 House Master of High Street North: The Rev H Keary

Right: The Rev JN Simpkinson

1851 Neeld Medal for Mathematics donated • Earl Spencer Scholarship endowed • Army Class formed

1852 Beriah Botley medal & Viscount Ebrington medal for Modern Languages donated

Right: Arthur Haygarth, later cricket historian

1842 Cricket XI beat Eton at Lord's by 65 runs

1843 Cricket XI beat Eton at Lord's by 20 runs

1848 Cricket XI beat Eton at Lord's by 41 runs; TD Platt took 13 wickets

1849 Goose Match (cricket) first played • Cricket XI beat Eton at Lord's by 77 runs; R Hankey took 14 wickets

1851 Speckled straw hat first worn by Flannels • Cricket XI beat Eton at Lord's by 8 wickets

1852 Cricket XI beat Eton at Lord's by 71 runs

1853 Philathletic Club formed to manage games • Cricket v Winchester became a 'home & away' fixture • Cricket XI beat Eton at Lord's by 98 runs • Football moved to east side of the Hill

Left: Francis Hawkins, later Sir Francis, a Governor

Left: GO Trevelyan, later scholar, historian and a Governor

1846 The Debating Society established

1842 First Opium War ended • Sewing machine patented • Ether used as anaesthetic for the first time

1844 First electric telegram sent • Safety match invented • Nitrous oxide first used as anaesthetic by Horace Wells

1845 Irish potato famine • Rubber band invented.

1846 2nd Opium War with China began

1849 Abolition of the Corn Laws

1850 Irish potato famine ends

1851 The Great Exhibition in Hyde Park

1852 Earl of Aberdeen's (OH) Peelite/Whig ministry

1853 Crimean War began

1854 Coal gas street lighting introduced • Charge of the Light Brigade immortalised by poet Tennyson

NO. OF BOYS	1855	1856	1857	1858	1859	1860	1861	1862	1863
	436	419	432	453	476	477	484	482 including 32 Free Scholars	472

GOVERNORS APPOINTED

Left: Interior of the new Chapel, completed in 1855

Above: JE Bourchier, Head of School, commemorated by the Bourchier prizes

1859 George, 3rd Baron Northwick (OH) – 1887

1861 George, 4th Earl of Clarendon – 1870

1862 James, 2nd Earl of Verulam (OH) – 1892; Chairman 1871–88

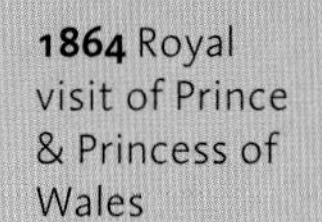

Below: The Vaughan Library

SCHOOL EVENTS

1857 New Chapel consecrated by Dr Tait, Bishop of London • Foundation stone of Memorial Aisle laid by Gen Sir William Fenwick Williams, Bt

Right: Viscount Palmerston

1861 Foundation stone of Vaughan Library laid by Viscount Palmerston

BUILDINGS & GROUNDS

1855 Chapel completed • New Schools built • Gas supply to Harrow

1858 Crimean Memorial aisle added to Chapel • Organ placed in Chapel

1862 Crown & Anchor public house purchased as house for Custos

1864 Royal visit of Prince & Princess of Wales

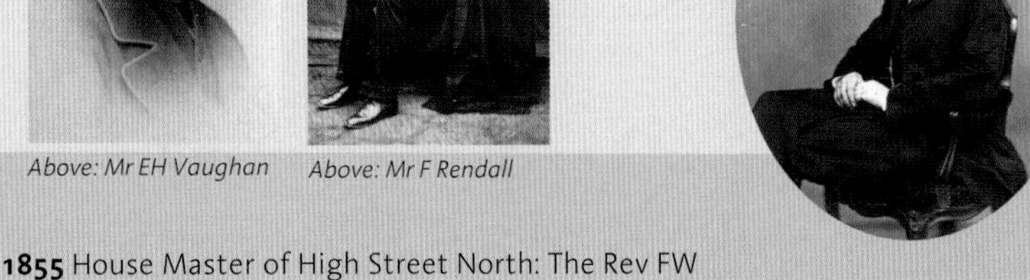

Above: Mr EH Vaughan

Above: Mr F Rendall

Right: The Rev FW Farrar

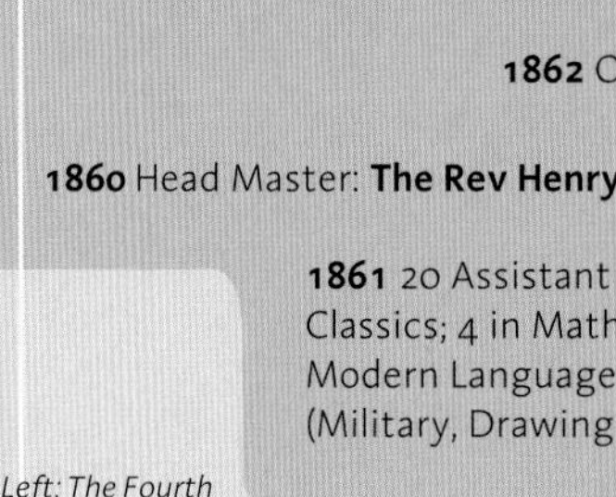

Left: Head Master The Rev Henry Montagu Butler

1863 Garlands built by Mr RB Hayward • Rifle Corps Armoury created below the Old Schools Vaughan Library opened • First sanatorium built

1864 Covered rackets court, 3 Eton Fives, 4 Rugby Fives courts built • The Abbey pulled down and rebuilt; renamed Druries

HEAD MASTERS & ASSISTANT MASTERS

1855 House Master of High Street North: The Rev FW Farrar • House Master of The Grove: The Rev TH Steel

1859 21 Assistant Masters

Above: Mr CF Holmes

Left: The Fourth Form Room from the Illustrated London News, 1862

1862 Organist appointed: Mr John Farmer

1860 Head Master: **The Rev Henry Montagu Butler**

1861 20 Assistant Masters: 14 in Classics; 4 in Mathematics; 2 in Modern Languages; 3 Extra Masters (Military, Drawing and Fencing)

1864 Head Master of Druries: Mr CF Holmes • House Master of High Street: The Rev EH Bradby

CURRICULUM & ACADEMICS

1855 Introduction of the learning of French for all and German for some

1859 Remove Form created (between Shell & V Forms)

1860 Walter Beaumont prize for Scripture donated

1863 Joseph Jones medal for Latin Elegiac Verse donated • Botfield Scholarship endowed • William Oxenham Prize for Greek & Latin Epigrams donated

SCHOOL SPORTS

1855 Cricket XI beat Eton at Lord's by an innings and 66 runs

1857 Cricket XI beat Eton at Lord's by 10 wickets

1858 Cricket XI beat Eton at Lord's by an innings and 7 runs

1859 Cricket XI beat Eton at Lord's by an innings and 48 run (8th successive victory)

1860 AWT Daniel scored 112* v Eton at Lord's

1861 Public School Shooting Competition for Ashburton Challenge Shield began

1863 Rifle Corps revived

1864 VI Form football game introduced • Cricket XI beat Eton at Lord's by an innings and 66 runs • Shooting team won the Ashburton Challenge Shield

Left: GO Trevelyan, Head of School 1856, historian & scholar

OTHER ACTIVITIES

1857 Music Society founded by Capel Henry Berger

1859 HSVRC founded as company of 18th Middlesex RVC • *The Triumvirate* published (up to 1861)

1862 Shooting team won the Ashburton Challenge Shield

1864 First Harrow Song *Io Triumphe* written: words by Brooke Westcott, music by John Farmer

WORLD EVENTS

1855 *Daily Telegraph* newspaper founded • Viscount Palmerston's (OH) Whig ministry

1856 Crimean War ended

1857 Treaty of Paris ends Crimean War • Victoria Cross instituted

1859 Charles Darwin publishes *The Origin of Species* • Viscount Palmerston's (OH, Liberal) 2nd ministry

1860 2nd Opium War ends

1861 Clarendon Commission formed to reform the public schools

1862 Start of American Civil War

1863 First section of London Underground Railway opened

1864 Clarendon Report published

1867 455 · 1870 533 · 1871 562 · 1872 577 · 1873 539 · 1874 540

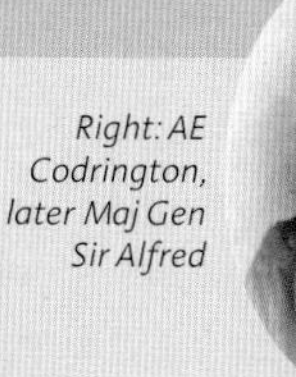

Right: AE Codrington, later Maj Gen Sir Alfred

Above: Charles Gore, later Bishop of Oxford

Above: AN 'Monkey' Hornby, later captain of England at both rugby and cricket

1870 John, 5th Earl Spencer (OH) –1908; Chairman 1888–1908 • William Stone (OH) –1897

1871 Rt Hon Montague Bernard –1882 • Rt Rev Brooke Westcott –1901 • Charles Roundell (OH) –1901 • Sir John Wickens –1873 • John Tyndall FRS –1892

Below: Harrow High Street, c1870

1874 Francis Hawkins –1908

1865 Druries opened

1867 The Knoll opened as a Small House

1868 *Harrow Glee Book* published

1869 First Roman Catholic boys admitted

1870 Monitor appointments reformed to recognise 'leadership'

1871 Celebration of Tercentenary (a year early); visit of Prince & Princess of Wales • Opening of John Lyon Memorial Fund

1865 Spire added to Chapel

1866 New Side of The Head Master's House built • Six acres of land acquired for the Philathletic ground • Ducker bridge built.

1867 Sanatorium built on south side of the Hill

Left: Mr HE Hutton

1872 First *Harrow School Song Book* published • Metropolitan (Kilburn & Harrow) Road Act passed • School Bill moved from Fourth Form Room to School Yard

1874 School regulations included 'conscience clause' allowing religious freedom • Foundation stone of Speech Room laid by the Duke of Abercorn

1865 Military Master: Major Griffiths RA

1866 House Master of West Acre: Mr WH Bull

1867 First Science Master appointed: Mr George Griffith

1868 Position of Lower Master abolished • House Master of High Street: Mr AG Watson

1869 House Master of The Park: Rev FW Farrar • Vaughan Librarian: Mr G Masson

Left: AJ Webbe, Captain of Cricket

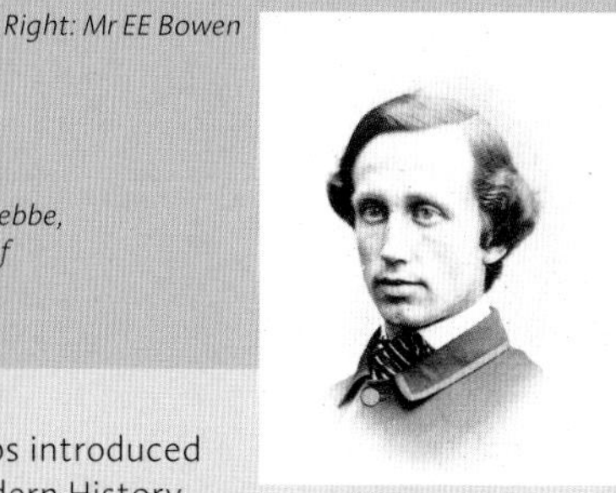
Right: Mr EE Bowen

1870 The Knoll expanded into large House • Hillside built as a Small House

1873 Old Music School built

1874 New Gymnasium opened • New Science Schools opened

1870 House Master of High Street: Mr HE Hutton • House Master of The Knoll: Mr R Boswell-Smith • Appointed Master of the Modern Side: Mr EE Bowen • 26 Assistant Masters: 16 in Classics, 5 in Mathematics, 1 in Natural Science, 2 in Modern Languages, 2 on the Modern Side; 4 Extra Masters (Drawing, 2 Music, Fencing)

1871 House Master of The Park: Mr RB Hayward

Right: MC Kemp, Public Schools Rackets Champion

1865 Entrance Scholarships introduced • Bourchier prizes for Modern History & English Literature • Natural Science introduced

1867 FW Farrar published "Essays on a Liberal Education"

1869 Institution of Modern Side • Lord Charles Russell medal for Shakespeare donated

1870 39 boys in Modern Side • Charles Leaf Scholarship donated • Clayton Memorial Scholarship for Modern Studies donated

1871 Douglas Anderson Scholarship donated.

1873 Cyril Flower Prizes for French & German donated

1874 Leaving Scholarships suspended • Modern Side entrance examination introduced • Three closed Baring Scholarships endowed

1865 Harrow Football rules published • Cricket XI beat Eton at Lord's by an innings and 51 runs • RJH Jones won the Spencer Shooting Cup • Shooting team won the Ashburton Challenge Shield

1868 'Superannuation' introduced

Above: Mr R Boswell-Smith

Above: Mr RB Hayward

1866 RJH Jones won the Spencer Shooting Cup • Cricket XI beat Eton at Lord's by an innings and 136 runs. WB Money got a 'hat trick' • Shooting team won the Ashburton Challenge Shield again

1867 'Silver Arrow' House shooting competition on full range with rifles • Shooting team won the Ashburton Challenge Shield for 4th successive year

1868 Cricket XI beat Eton at Lord's by 7 wickets

1869 Shooting team won the Ashburton Challenge Shield

1870 CES Emery won the Spencer Shooting Cup • Shooting team won the Ashburton Challenge Shield

1871 GA Webbe & AA Hadow won Public Schools Rackets Championships

1872 GA Webbe & AA Hadow won Public Schools Rackets Championships

1873 PF Hadow & FD Leyland won Public Schools Rackets Championships • Cricket XI beat Eton at Lord's by 5 wickets

1874 FD Leyland & CW Kemp won Public Schools Rackets Championships

1865 Scientific Society founded • *Harrow Almanack* first published (up to 1939)

1867 Song *Willow the King* (EE Bowen, J Farmer) written and dedicated to the Hon R Grimston & the Hon F Ponsonby

1869 *The Harrovian* published again (up to 1872)

1872 *Forty Years On* written: words by Edward Bowen, music by John Farmer

1865 Public School Bill introduced (passed in 1868)

1869 Endowed Schools Act passed • Suez Canal opened

1870 (Forster) Elementary Education Act

1871 Royal Albert Hall opened

1872 First Football Association Cup competition played

Right: HF Blaine, cricket and football XIs, later KC and Attorney-Gen, Transvaal

1875 | 1880

NO. OF BOYS	1875	1876	1877	1878	1879	1880	1881	1882	1883	1884
	533	508	511	513	513	529	542	557	547	539

GOVERNORS APPOINTED

Above: The Science Schools

Right (from l to r): Stanley Baldwin, later Prime Minister; John Galsworthy, later novelist; FS Jackson, later Sir Stanley, captained England at cricket and was Governor of Bengal

1882 Professor Henry Pelham (OH) – 1907

Right: The Museum Schools

SCHOOL EVENTS

1876 John Lyon School founded • Science Schools came into use • Limitation on number of Monitors removed

1877 'Cricket Bill' introduced

1880 Jewish House opened under Dr Joseph Chotzner

1881 First Bursar appointed: Mr AC Tosswill

1882 Harrow Mission Fund started

1883 Mr MG Glazebrook appointed Bursar • Part of John Lyon's estate sold

1884 John Lyon's Stautes discovered in the chest in the Fourth Form Room • Harrow School Songs published

BUILDINGS & GROUNDS

1875 Chapel terrace created

1876 Workshops opened

Above: Eustace Crawley, Public Schools Rackets Champion

Above: The Rev JA Cruikshank

1877 Speech Room opened

1880 Four more Eton Fives courts built

Left: Mr J Stogdon

1881 House in the High Street enlarged by Mr HE Hutton; renamed Moretons • The Grove modernised by Mr EE Bowen to provide single rooms • Ducker enlarged: sheds & seats added

1883 Lower chapel terrace created • VI Form cricket pavilion built • Canopies installed over chancel stalls in Chapel

1884 Phil Ground enlarged by 3 acres in memory of the Hon Robert Grimston • Field House given to the School by Lord Bessborough & William Nicholson

HEAD MASTERS & ASSISTANT MASTERS

Above: Spencer Gore, later a distinguished artist

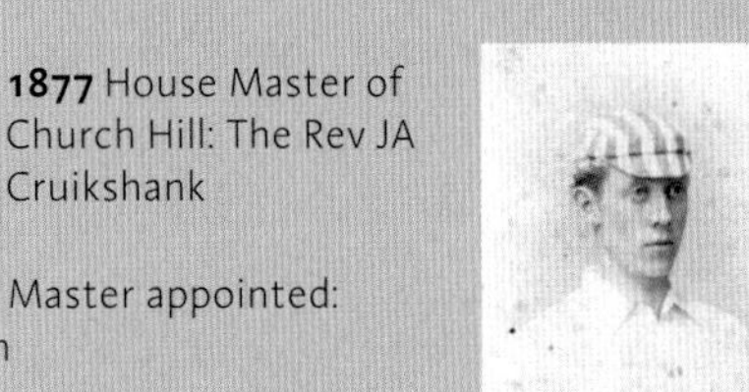

1877 House Master of Church Hill: The Rev JA Cruikshank

1876 2nd Science Master appointed: Mr Sydney Lupton

Left: HE Crawley, Public Schools Rackets Champion

1880 House Master of West Acre: Mr J Stogdon • 30 Assistant Masters: 18 in Classics, 4 in Mathematics, 2 in Natural Science, 2 in Modern Languages, 4 on the Modern Side; 4 Extra Masters (Drawing, Music, Gymnasium and Fencing) • Head Master's Secretary appointed: Mr W Moss

1881 House Master of Grove Hill: Rev WD Bushell • 70 boys in Modern Side

CURRICULUM & ACADEMICS

1875 VI Form Oxford & Cambridge Certificate of Proficiency Examination introduced

1876 Viscount Strangford Geography prizes donated

1878 Lady Bourchier English Reading Prizes

1877 George Briscoe-Eyre Music prizes donated

1881 William Roundell Scholarship for Modern Studies endowed

1882 Frederick Ponsonby Scholarship for Modern Studies donated

Below: EM Butler, Public Schools Rackets Champion, captain of cricket & football, later Harrow Master

SCHOOL SPORTS

Left: Football XI, 1878

1875 Shooting team won the Ashburton Challenge Shield

1876 HE Meek & LK Jarvis won Public Schools Rackets Championships

1878 Cricket XI beat Eton at Lord's by 20 runs

1879 MC Kemp & the Hon FR de Moleyns won Public Schools Rackets Championships • AG Foulkes won the Spencer Shooting Cup • Shooting team won the Ashburton Challenge Shield

1880 MC Kemp & EM Hadow won Public Schools Rackets Championships • Cricket XI beat Eton at Lord's by 95 runs

1881 EM Hadow & AF Kemp won Public Schools Rackets Championships • Cricket XI beat Eton at Lord's by 112 runs

1882 RH Pemberton & AC Richards won Public Schools Rackets Championships

1883 HE Crawley & CD Buxton won Public Schools Rackets Championships

1884 Athletic sports held on a 'field beyond Ducker' • EM Butler & CD Buxton won Public Schools Rackets Championships

OTHER ACTIVITIES

1878 *The Harrovian* published again (up to 1881)

1883 *Harrow Notes* published (up to 1888) • Harrow Mission founded

WORLD EVENTS

1876 Queen Victoria proclaimed Empress of India • Metropolitan Railway line opened • Telephone invented

1877 First Lawn Tennis Championship played at Wimbledon, won by Spencer Gore (OH)

1878 Gramophone patented

1879 Electric light bulb invented • Peterborough Road opened as a public highway

1880 1st Boer War began • Extension of the Metropolitan Railway line to Harrow on the Hill

1881 1st Boer War ended • Education Act provided free elementary education

1884 Greenwich meridian chosen for longitude zero

1885	1886	1887	1888	1889	1890	1891	1892	1893	1894
524	516	525	552	578	594	599	597	610	630

1885 Matthew, 1st Viscount Ridley (OH) – 1904

1887 Rt Hon Sir George Trevelyan Bt (OH) – 1900

Above: JH Titchener, Custos

Left: Mom Chow Bovaradej, later a Minister in Siamese government

1892 Dr Walter Leaf (OH) – 1923 • Sir Archibald Geikie FRS – 1922

1885 Formation of Harrow Park Trust • *Harrow School & its Surroundings* (Thornton) published • Custos: S Hoare retired; JH Titchener appointed

1886 The Butler Museum opened

1888 Mr Robert Somervell appointed Bursar

1890 Alperton & part of Preston Farm of John Lyon estate sold

1893 Harrow Park Trust bought Druries from Mr CF Holmes

1894 Prince & Princess of Wales' 3rd visit • *Harrow School Register* (1st edition) published

1891 New Music School built • The field north of VI Form Ground (later named Bessborough Ground) leased to the School • Six more Eton Fives courts built

1885 New Chapel organ installed • Football fields purchased in memory of Dr Montagu Butler

1888 Newlands built by Mr FE Marshall

1886 Museum Schools built

1887 Additions made to The Park by Mr GH Hallam

1890 Name-carving by boys in Fourth Form Room stopped

1892 Machine shop added to Workshops

1893 Elmfield built; boys transferred from High Street • Gift received of further 1½ acres to Philathletic Ground

1894 Football fields drained for first time • Buxton Pavilion built on Philathletic Ground

1889 Further 30 acres bought on east side of the Hill • Two more Eton Fives courts built

1885 Head Master: **The Rev Dr JEC Welldon** • 25 Assistant Masters of whom five were ordained

Left: Head Master the Rev JEC Welldon

Below (from l to r): Mr Eaton Faning, the Rev ECE Owen, Mr GH Hallam, Mr G Griffith

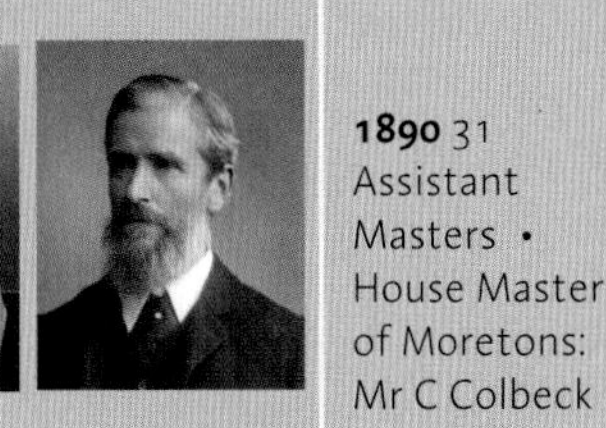

1890 31 Assistant Masters • House Master of Moretons: Mr C Colbeck

1891 House Master of Church Hill: Mr JC Moss

1892 Mr William Egerton Hine appointed Art Master

1887 House Master of Druries: Mr G Griffith • House Master of The Park: Mr GH Hallam

1888 Vaughan Librarian: Mr BP Lascelles

1889 House Master of Newlands: Mr FE Marshall • Introduction of a pension fund for Masters

1893 House Master of High Street: Mr JWW Welsford • House Master of Elmfield: Mr HOD Davidson • Mr EE Bowen resigned as Head of Modern Side

Above: WL Spencer-Churchill, later Prime Minister

Above: Mr HOD Davidson

Left: Mr BP Lascelles

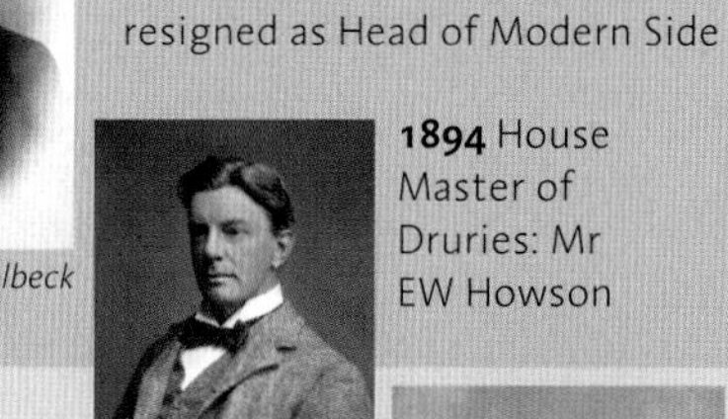

Above: Mr C Colbeck

1894 House Master of Druries: Mr EW Howson

Above: Mr EW Howson

1886 WdeL Winter passed 1st into Royal Military Academy, Woolwich

Left: Harrow Masters, Summer term, 1885

1887 CW Firebrace passed 1st into Royal Military College, Sandhurst

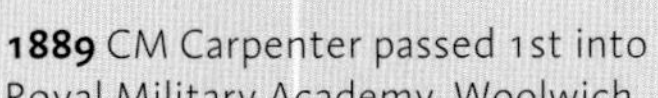

1889 CM Carpenter passed 1st into Royal Military Academy, Woolwich

Above: Mr JW Welsford

1888 Reorganisation of School & curriculum

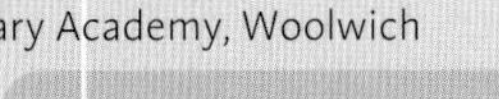

1890 AHM Butler & WFG Wyndham won Public Schools Rackets Championships • J Oppenshaw was Foil Champion in the Public Schools Fencing Championships

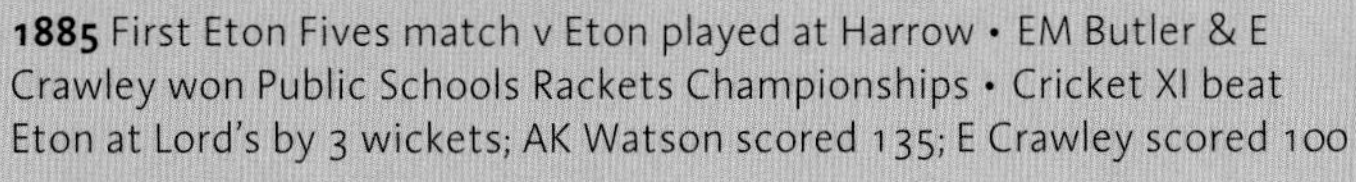

1885 First Eton Fives match v Eton played at Harrow • EM Butler & E Crawley won Public Schools Rackets Championships • Cricket XI beat Eton at Lord's by 3 wickets; AK Watson scored 135; E Crawley scored 100

Above: Mr FE Marshall

1886 Athletic sports held on the New Recreation Ground, Pinner Road • LH Crake won the Spencer Shooting Cup • P Ashworth & RD Cheales won Public Schools Rackets Championships (fifth win in succession)

1888 Cricket XI beat Eton at Lord's by 156 runs; RB Hoare scored 108 • WTC Poole won the Public Schools' Gymnastics Competition

Left: Chandos Leigh, the first OH to fall in the Great War

1889 Cricket XI beat Eton at Lord's by 9 wickets • Public Schools Shooting championships moved from Wimbledon to Bisley

1891 Cricket XI beat Eton at Lord's by 7 wickets • JA Halliday was Heavyweight Champion & SP Druce was Lightweight Champion in the Public Schools' Boxing Competition

1893 WS Rome was Middleweight Champion in the Public Schools' Boxing Competition

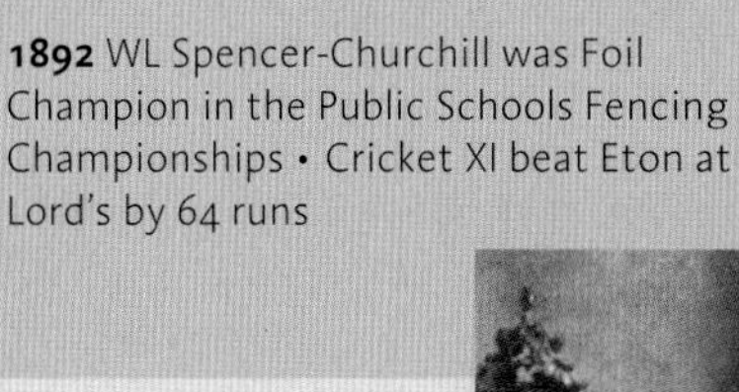

1892 WL Spencer-Churchill was Foil Champion in the Public Schools Fencing Championships • Cricket XI beat Eton at Lord's by 64 runs

1885 Song *Three Yards* written (EW Howson, J Farmer) dedicated to EM Butler (capt of football 1884)

Left: Mr J Farmer

1887 Song *Ducker* written (EW Howson, E Fanning)

1888 *The Harrovian* published regularly from this date

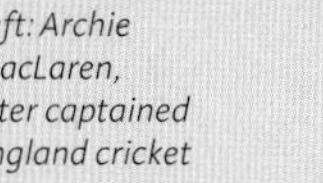

Left: Archie MacLaren, later captained England cricket team

Right: WL Spencer-Churchill was Foil Champion in the Public Schools Fencing Championships

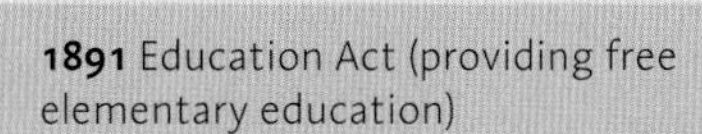

1891 Education Act (providing free elementary education)

1895 **1900**

NO. OF BOYS

1895	1896	1897	1898	1899	1900	1901	1902	1903	1904
625	631	620	611	587	594	584	590	575	563

GOVERNORS APPOINTED

1897 Arthur, 1st Viscount Peel (OH) – 1904

Left: Prince Ibrahim Hassan of Egypt

Left: The King of Siam's visit, 1897

1900 Rt Hon Lord George Hamilton GCSI (OH) – 1924; Chairman 1908-1924

1901 Very Rev Henry Montagu Butler DD (OH) – 1917 • William Chawner – 1908

1904 Sir Kenelm Digby GCB (OH) – 1916

Right: Mr (later Sir Percy) Buck

SCHOOL EVENTS

1895 Fund raised for the improvement of the cricket fields • Monitors' Room created

1896 A new edition of *Harrow School Songs* published

1897 Central Barnet part of the John Lyon estate sold

1898 Hopkinson's, the School's bankers, collapsed • Harrow School (Howson & Townsend Warner) published

1901 Bradbys re-opened as a Large House • *Harrow Register* (2nd edition) published

1902 Foundation stones of Chapel transepts laid by Field Marshal Lord Roberts

1903 Jewish House closed; boys integrated into other Houses • Additions to the Chapel consecrated by the Bishop of London • Land Purchase Fund opened to buy land on the eastern side of the Hill

BUILDINGS & GROUNDS

1895 Fields between Kenton Rd & Northwick Park acquired

1896 Art Schools built • Installation of electric light begun • Museum Schools built • Ducker Cottage replaced by brick building

1897 Reredos and additions to the chancel in Chapel in memory of Dr Vaughan

1898 Electric lighting installed in Chapel

1899 Memorials to Dr Vaughan in Chapel unveiled

Left: The visit of Field Marshal Roberts, 1902

1901 The Copse bequeathed to the School by EE Bowen

1902 North & South transepts added to Chapel in memory of 55 OHs lost in Boer War

1903 New porches, organ gallery & spiral staircase erected in Chapel

1904 Maulden Farm (Bedfordshire) part of John Lyon's estate sold

1904 50-yard Morris tube rifle range built off Garlands Lane

HEAD MASTERS & ASSISTANT MASTERS

1895 First Modern Side Head of School appointed: AC Pigou

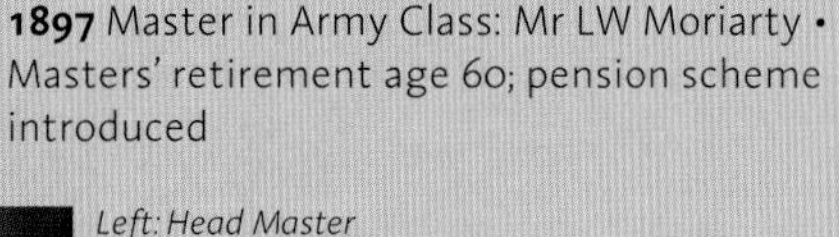

1897 Master in Army Class: Mr LW Moriarty • Masters' retirement age 60; pension scheme introduced

1900 42 Assistant Masters

Left: Head Master Dr Joseph Wood

1899 Head Master: **The Rev Dr Joseph Wood** • House Master of Grove Hill: Mr E Graham • Chaplain: The Rev WD Bushell

1901 House Master of The Grove: Mr WG Guillemard • House Master of The Knoll: Mr EEC Owen • Director of Music: Mr Percy Buck

1903 The House Master of Moretons: The Rev FC Searle

1904 House Master of Moretons: Mr MC Kemp • House Master of West Acre: Mr R Somervell • Master in Army Class: Mr G Townsend Warner

Above: Mr MC Kemp

Right: The Rev FC Searle

Right: Mr WG Guillemard

Left: Mr Robert Somervell

CURRICULUM & ACADEMICS

1900 Cricket XI beat Eton at Lord's by 1 wicket • AJ North & CE Wood won the Public Schools Cadet Shield for Shooting • FJV Hopley was Heavyweight Champion in the Public Schools' Boxing Competition

1903 Rugby replaced soccer in the Spring term • R Gorrell-Barnes played cricket for the Public Schools XI • DR Brandt was Lightweight Champion in the Public Schools' Boxing Competition • GA Phelps & LM MacLean won Public Schools Rackets Championships

SCHOOL SPORTS

1895 JH Stogdon & AS Crawley won Public Schools Rackets Championships • RLC Hobson won the Spencer Shooting Cup • GP Gore was Middleweight Champion in the Public Schools' Boxing Competition

1897 LF Andrewes & WFA Rattigan won Public Schools Rackets Championships

1898 Cricket XI beat Eton at Lord's by 9 wickets; TGO Cole scored 142 • WFA Rattigan & LF Andrewes won Public Schools Rackets Championships

1901 Cricket XI beat Eton at Lord's by 10 wickets

1899 FE Bray won the Spencer Shooting Cup

1902 GA Phelps & C Browning won Public Schools Rackets Championships • Cricket XI beat Eton at Lord's by 8 wickets • AJ North won the Spencer Shooting Cup • FJV Hopley was Heavy-weight Champion in the Public Schools' Boxing Competition

1904 EH Crake & RE Eiloart unbeaten at Eton Fives for 3 years.

OTHER ACTIVITIES

1896 Soccer introduced in the spring term • JH Stogdon scored 124 v Eton at Lord's • RF Vibart was Heavy-weight Champion in the Public Schools' Boxing Competition

Right: Champion Shooting Pair, 1899

Right: Michael Falcon, later captain of cricket at Cambridge

WORLD EVENTS

1895 X-rays discovered

1896 First Modern Olympic Games opened in Athens

1897 Queen Victoria's Diamond Jubilee

1899 2nd Boer War began • School leaving age raised to 12

1901 Death of Queen Victoria; Edward VII becomes King

1902 2nd Boer War ended • Education Act introduced fee-paying grammar schools with some free places • Local Education Authorities introduced

1905	1906	1907	1908	1909	1910	1911	1912	1913	1914
549	557	578	579	558	543	523	536	501	504

1905 Most Rev Randall Davidson (OH) – 1929

1907 Charles Heberden (OH) – 1913

1908 Francis Pember (OH) – 1945; Chairman 1924-42 • Rt Hon Frederick Huth Jackson (OH) – 1921 • The Rev Thomas Fitzpatrick – 1925

1913 Alfred Godley (OH) – 1925

1905 Visit of King Edward VII & Queen Alexandra

Left: Head Master Welldon greeting King Rama V of Siam, 1902

1908 Harrow Association formed for former pupils of the School

1910 Governors Finance Committee formed

1911 Board of Education Inspection • *Harrow School Register* (3rd edition) published

1912 Mr E Graham's House re-named Rendalls • Visit of King George V & Queen Mary

1913 Endowment Fund opened

Right: King George V inspecting the HSOTC

Below: Sir Arthur F Hort

Left: MC Bird, 'double centurion' at Lord's in 1907, later played cricket for England

1911 Construction of gravel parade ground & cinder running track. • Six old Eton fives courts roofed; new block of 8 covered & 3 open courts built.

Below: Jawaharlal Nehru, later Prime Minister of India

Left: RC Joynson Hicks, later Viscount Brentford

1905 254 acres beyond Ducker Road, Sheepcote & Hemstall fields acquired

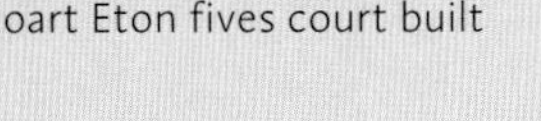

1907 Steps from Chapel terrace built • Crake Eiloart Eton fives court built

1913 Extension to Art Schools built • Roxeth Farm purchased and added to Philathletic Ground • Richardson (V.1) pavilion built on the Philathletic Ground

1906 Further building additions to The Park • Cloister of Old Schools became Armoury for HSVRC

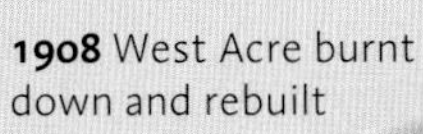

1908 West Acre burnt down and rebuilt

1914 Science Schools extended for Chemistry

Left: MCH Colyer-Fergusson, football XI 1908

Right: Mr CG Pope

Left: Mr Archer Vassall

Left: Head Master Dr Lionel Ford

1905 House Master of High Street: Mr G Townsend Warner • House Master of Newlands: Sir AF Hort, Bt

1906 House Master of Druries: Mr NK Stephen • House Master of The Park: Mr EM Butler

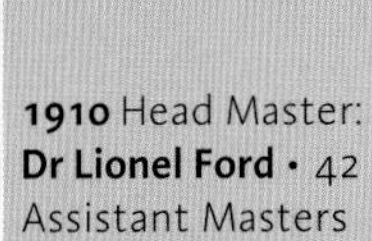

1910 Head Master: **Dr Lionel Ford** • 42 Assistant Masters

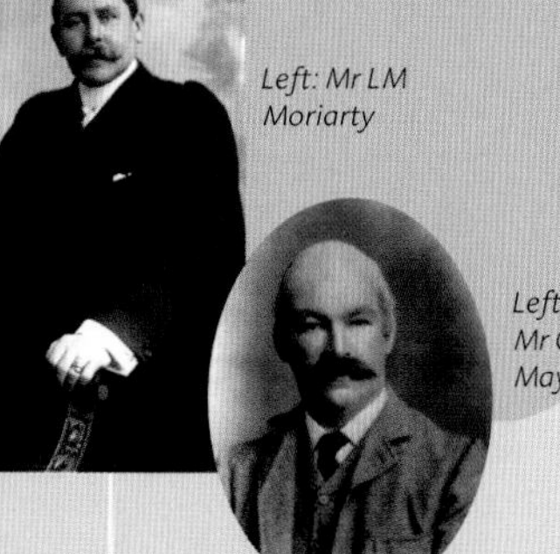

Left: Mr LM Moriarty

Left: Mr CHP Mayo

1907 House Master at The Head Master's: Mr CA Werner

1908 House Master of The Grove: Mr LM Moriarty

1909 House Master of The Knoll: Mr CHP Mayo

1911 House Master of West Acre: Mr WG Young

1912 House Master of Church Hill: Mr CG Pope

1913 House Master of Elmfield: Mr A Vassall

1914 House Master at The Head Master's: Mr CW Moorsom • Vaughan Librarian: Mr CAA Du Pontet • Officer commanding HSOTC: Maj EW Freeborn

1907 8 Scholarships, 2 Exhibitions gained at Oxford & Cambridge

Right: CAG Fitch, commemorated by the Alex Fitch Room

Above: EH Crake, captain of cricket 1905-06

1909 8 Scholarships, 3 Exhibitions gained at Oxford & Cambridge

1911 Boys take School Certificate for first time

1913 Abolition of 'pupil room' system • New timetable introduced

1905 Soccer returned; rugby continued informally. • Shooting team won the Ashburton Challenge Shield • MAC Halliday won the Public Schools' Gymnastics Competition

1907 Cricket XI beat Eton at Lord's by 79 runs; MC Bird, scored 100 not out and 131 v Eton at Lord's in 1907, later played cricket for England • GdeCE Findlay won the Spencer Shooting Cup • GF Earle played cricket for the Public Schools XI

1908 FWW Baines was Sabre Champion in the Public Schools Fencing Championships • Cricket XI beat Eton at Lord's by 10 wickets

1909 AH Lang played cricket for the Public Schools XI • Shooting team won the Ashburton Challenge Shield

1910 Shooting team won the 'Rapid Fire' Shooting Cup at Bisley • OB Graham played cricket for the Public Schools XI

1911 KA Stewart was Foil Champion Public Schools Fencing Championships • LA de Jongh played cricket for the Public Schools XI

1912 CHB Blount scored 137 v Eton at Lord's • G Wilson scored 173 v Eton at Lord's • Swimming team won Public Schools 4x50m freestyle relay (Bath Cup)

1913 ET Buller played cricket for the Public Schools XI

1914 G Wilson played cricket for the Public Schools XI • JL Vaughan won 1st prize in the Public Schools' Boxing Competition

Above (clockwise from top left): KE de Jongh, cricketer; FA Leaf, later Harrow Master; RE Eiloart, Fives player; Hon Rupert Anson, cricketer

1908 Officer Training Corps established

1909 EF Brown awarded Organ Scholarship at Brasenose College, Oxford

Right: Guy Butler, Olympic Gold medallist

1910 George V became King

1908 Ford Motor Company launched its first car

1912 Liner *Titanic* sank

1914 World War I (The Great War) began • Panama Canal opened

No. of Boys

1915	1916	1917	1918	1919	1920	1921	1922	1923	1924
466	480	505	526	580	596	608	624	630	634

Governors Appointed

1916 Thomas, 3rd Earl of Lichfield (OH) – 1918

1918 Walter, 1st Viscount Long of Wraxall (OH) – 1924; Chairman 1924 • George Tallents (OH) – 1924

1920 Butler memorial dedicated by Bishop Gore (OH) • Cecil Goodden (OH) appointed Bursar

1922 Edward, 1st Baron St Just (OH) – 1941 • Sir Hugh Anderson FRS (OH) – 1927

1923 Col the Rt Hon Sir Francis Stanley Jackson GCSI GCIE (OH) – 1927

1924 Gen Lord Horne, (Henry, 1st Baron Horne of Stirkoke) GCB KCMG (OH) – 1929

Right: CS Crawley, Public Schools Rackets Champion

Left: HJL Gorse, Head of School, later Harrow Master

Left: The Rt Hon Sir Francis Stanley Jackson

School Events

Left: The Grove

1917 War Memorial Fund opened

1918 Governors form General Purposes Committee • 2917 served, 690 wounded, 644 killed in The Great War

1919 New Sanatorium appeal opened • House in High Street re-named Bradbys

1921 New Chapel organ dedicated by Rt Rev Randall Davidson (OH), Archbishop of Canterbury • Foundation stone of War Memorial Building laid

1922 A "Complete Edition" of *Harrow School Songs* published

1924 Custos: JH Titchener retired; JE Hayward appointed

Buildings & Grounds

1915 Church Hill closed; boys transferred to The Grove

1917 2½ acres added to Philathletic Ground

1918 Memorial Chapel created in the Crypt of the School Chapel

1919 North Tower of Speech Room completed

1920 Moretons, Nos 7,12,14,16,32,34 High Street purchased • Pulpit and windows in north aisle of Chapel in memory of Dr HM Butler • Electric lighting installed in Chapel

Left: Mr HJ Hollingsworth

1922 Shops between top of West Street & Druries demolished • Science Schools extended for Physics • Further 2½ acres added to Philathletic Ground

1924 New Schools extended • Further 2½ acres added to Philathletic ground (Apcar bequest) • Miniature shooting range built • King Charles's Well plaque erected

Head Masters & Assistant Masters

1915 House Master of The Grove: Mr CG Pope

1916 House Master of High Street: Mr TW Holme

Above: Mr AW Siddons

Above: Mr B Middleditch

Left: Mr TW Holme

1919 House Master of Bradbys: Mr EW Freeborn • House Master of The Park: Mr B Middleditch • House Master of Rendalls: Mr AW Siddons

1920 House Master of The Knoll: Mr JH Hollingsworth • 39 Assistant Masters; 6 Extra Masters (2 Music, 2 Art, Gymnasium, Workshop)

1921 House Master of Moretons: Mr A Wyatt-Smith

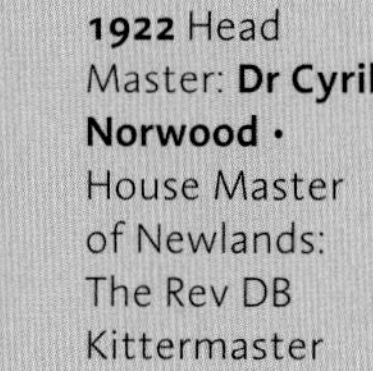

Right: Mr A Wyatt-Smith

1922 Head Master: **Dr Cyril Norwood** • House Master of Newlands: The Rev DB Kittermaster

Below: Head Master Dr Cyril Norwood

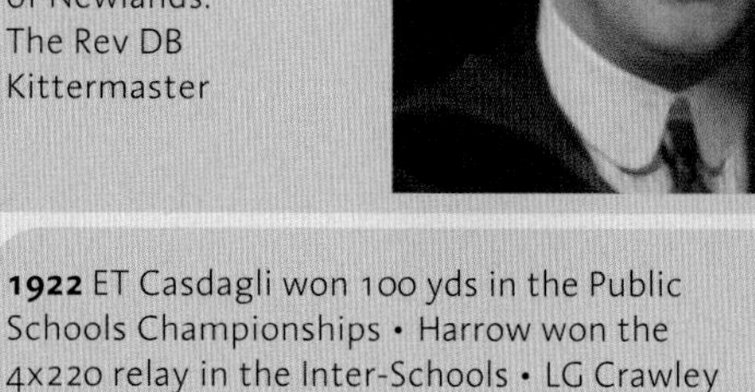

Curriculum & Academics

1917 7 Scholarships, 3 Exhibitions gained at Oxford & Cambridge • Distinction between Classics & Modern Sides abolished

1918 DA Blyth passed 1st into Royal Military College, Sandhurst, with Prize Cadetship

1920 Creation of specialist VI Form began

School Sports

1919 HEL Rose won the Spencer Shooting Cup

1921 LG Crawley scored 103 v Eton at Lord's • CT Bennett & HJ Enthoven played cricket for the Public Schools XI • The Bowling Fund formed to provide professional cricket coaching

1922 ET Casdagli won 100 yds in the Public Schools Championships • Harrow won the 4x220 relay in the Inter-Schools • LG Crawley played cricket for the Public Schools XI

1923 PH Stewart-Brown scored 102* v Eton at Lord's and played for the Public Schools XI

1924 JC Butterworth played cricket for the Public Schools XI

Other Activities

Below (from l to r): Prince Jafar of Persia; Cecil Beaton, later photographic designer; C Bertram Mills, later circus proprietor

Right: LG Crawley, later golfer and journalist

World Events

1916 Battle of the Somme

1917 Russian Revolution

1918 The Great War ended • Education Act made education up to age 14 obligatory • School Certificate Examination introduced

1921 Cadet Force compulsory for boys aged over 15

1922 First BBC transmission

1923 Stanley Baldwin's (OH) first Conservative ministry

1924 Stanley Baldwin's (OH) 2nd ministry • King George V made first radio broadcast to the nation • British Empire Exhibition opened at Wembley

1925	1926	1927	1928	1929	1930	1931	1932	1933	1934
641	647	659	663	666	660	622	631	617	603

1925 Rt Hon Leopold Amery, CH (OH) – 1955 • Professor James Butler (OH) – 1962 • Lawrence, 2nd Marquess of Zetland GCSI GCIE (OH) – 1942 • Sir Arthur Pickard-Cambridge DLitt LLD FBA – 1952

Right: Sir Walter Monckton

1927 Rt Rev Frederick Hicks DD (OH) – 1942

1929 Professor Archibald Hill ScD FRS – 1933

1930 Sir Walter Monckton KCMG KCVO KC (OH) – 1947 • Stanley, 1st Earl Baldwin of Bewdley KG (OH) – 1945

1934 Professor Hamilton Hartridge ScD FRS (OH) – 1944

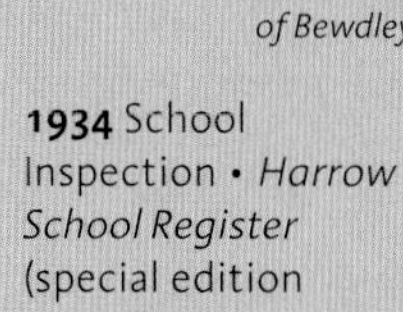

Above: Stanley, 1st Earl Baldwin of Bewdley

1925 Governors purchased West Acre from the Stogdon family • Monitors escapade scandal

Above: Bill Deedes, later journalist

1926 Opening of War Memorial building by Rt Rev Randall Davidson (OH), Archbishop of Canterbury • New Monitors' and Philathletic Club rooms created in War Memorial building • Birching abolished

Above: The War Memorial building

Right: (from l to r) JD Profumo, later Cabinet Minister; GWR Monckton, later Maj-Gen Viscount; M Tindall, captain of cricket, later Harrow Master

Right: (from l to r) MA Clarke from Melbourne, School Monitor; PM Studd, captain of cricket & rugby, later Sir Peter, Lord Mayor of London; ET Pelham, 'triple blood', later stockbroker

1934 School Inspection • *Harrow School Register* (special edition 1571-1800) published • Hegan bequest of watercolour collection

1929 Visit of Duke (later King George VI) and Duchess of York • Head Master defined 'bounds'

1932 Governors purchased Bradbys • Football grounds named Julian, Upper Reding, Hemstall, Sheepcote & Ducker

1925 The Bowling Shed built with two indoor cricket nets • 300 yard shooting range opened beside Ducker • Parade ground converted to asphalt with hard tennis courts

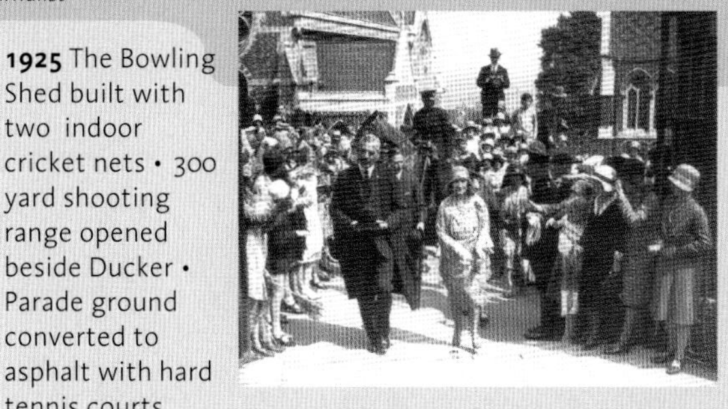

Left: The visit of the Duke and Duchess of York, 1929

1930 Further draining of the football fields • Grounds of Sanatorium leased as playing fields to Lower School of John Lyon • Operating theatre at the Sanatorium equipped

1933 Boyer Webb Pavilion built in memory of Charles & John Boyer Webb killed in WWI • A further two acres adjacent to the Park Lake donated

1934 Science Schools lecture room added

1929 Remaining shops on Church Hill replaced by steps and terracing • Bowden House on Sudbury Hill purchased as Sanatorium • Nicholson Ground bought by Bessborough Trust, presented to the School, re-named Bessborough Ground

1926 Alex Fitch Room given to the School • Additional land by the Park Lake purchased

1930 51 Assistant Masters; 2 Art, 2 Music Masters • House Master of The Grove: Mr TEJ Bradshaw

1934 Head Master: **Mr Paul Vellacott** • House Master of Druries: Mr JW Moir • House Master of Rendalls: Mr J Bostock • House Master of Bradbys: Mr OG Bowlby • House Master at The Head Master's: The Rev HJL Gorse • Officer commanding HSOTC: Maj EF Housden

1925 House Master of Druries: Mr CWM Moorsom • House Master at The Head Master's: Mr J Bostock • Master of the Army Class: Mr A Wyatt-Smith • Chaplain: The Rev EM Venables • Organisation Master: The Rev JW Coke-Norris

1931 Organisation Master: Mr JW Moir

1926 House Master of West Acre: Mr FA Leaf

1928 House Masters' term fixed at 15 years • Director of Music: Mr RS Thatcher

Above (l to r): Rev EM Venables, Mr EVC Plumtre, Mr John Bostock, Mr CWM Moorsom, Mr JW Coke Norris

1929 House Master of Moretons: Mr AP Boissier • Vaughan Librarian: Mr EVC Plumtre

Above: Head Master Dr Paul Vellacott

1932 House Master of The Park: The Rev EM Venables • House Master of The Knoll: Mr RM Baldwin • Chaplain: The Rev GH Woolley

1933 House Master of Elmfield: Mr CR Browne • Careers Master: Dr ED Laborde

1925 Sir Edward Hulton endowed the History Library

1931 AN Bray won a Prize Cadetship at RAF Cranwell

1933 Careers Master appointed

1934 6 Scholarships, 4 Exhibitions gained at Oxford & Cambridge

1925 AC Raphael & NM Ford won Public Schools Rackets Championships • AW Hill won the half-mile, AC Wills won the mile in the Public Schools Sports • Harrow won the sprint medley, the 4x220 and the distance medley in the Public Schools Relay Races • Shooting team won the Snap Shooting Cup at Bisley

1930 WM Welch & JFM Lightly won Public Schools Eton Fives Championships • AS Lawrence played cricket for the Public Schools XI

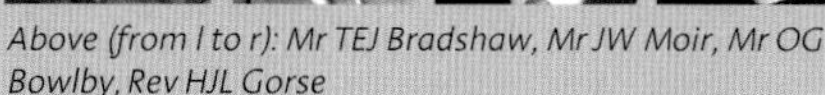

Above (from l to r): Mr TEJ Bradshaw, Mr JW Moir, Mr OG Bowlby, Rev HJL Gorse

1926 AM Crawley played cricket for the Public Schools XI

1927 Rugby adopted as major game in Autumn term • WO'B Lindsay played cricket for the Public Schools XI

Above: Rugby XV, 1927

1928 WO'B Lindsay & DAM Rome played cricket for the Public Schools XI

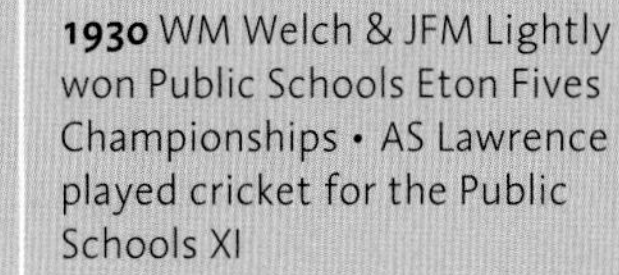

Right: EL de Rothschild, later merchant banker

1931 R Pulbrook & JFM Lightly won Public Schools Rackets Championships • FR Covington played cricket for the Public Schools XI

1933 JAS Collins & AH Henderson won Public Schools Eton Fives Championships • M Tindall played cricket for the Public Schools XI

1929 WM Welch & HG de Grey-Warter won Public Schools Eton Fives Championships • DAM Rome played cricket for the Public Schools XI

1932 R Pulbrook & JH Pawle won Public Schools Rackets Championships • R Pulbrook scored 104 v Eton at Lord's • M Tindall played cricket for the Public Schools XI

1934 JH Pawle played cricket for the Public Schools XI

1928 Alexander Fleming discovered Penicillin

1927 First 'talking' film made • First solo flight across the Atlantic

1929 Wall Street crash was the beginning of the 'great depression'

1931 Headmasters' Conference founded for Principals of Public Schools

1933 Adolph Hitler became German Chancellor

Above: Michael Denison, actor

1935 – 1940

NO. OF BOYS	1935	1936	1937	1938	1939	1940	1941	1942	1943	1944
	588	574	551	531	493	391	322	302	314	374

GOVERNORS APPOINTED

Below: Mr RAB Bruce Lockhart

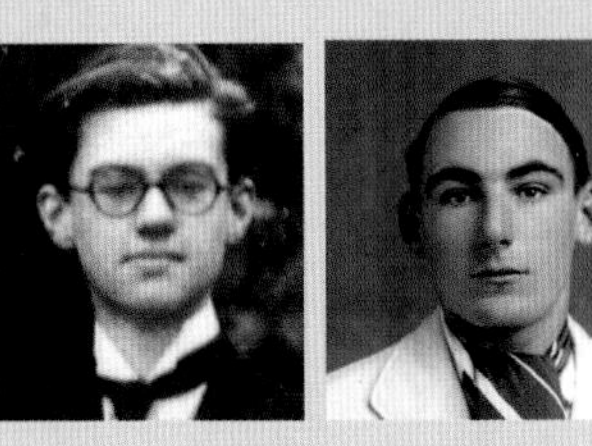

Left (from l to r): John Mortimer, later QC and writer; MT Turnbull, Head of School

1939 Col the Rt Hon Sir Francis Stanley Jackson GCSI GCIE (OH) – 1947 Chairman 1942-46 • William, 7th Earl of Radnor KCVO (OH) – 1946 • Gerald Rivington (OH) – 1969; Chairman 1953-1964

1942 Robert Thompson (OH) – 1966 • Capt Guy Jackson (OH) – 1947 • Thomas Blackwell (OH) – 1943

1943 Col Lord Templemore (Arthur, 4th Baron Templemore) KCVO (OH) – 1948 • Thomas Tallents (OH) – 1947

1944 Professor Sir Charles Ellis PhD FRS (OH) – 1969 • Rt Hon Sir Donald Somervell (OH) – 1960; Chairman 1947

Above: Sir Donald Somervell

SCHOOL EVENTS

1936 CJ Hegan (OH) presented watercolours collection to the School

Right: West Acre

1938 Philip Ledward appointed Bursar

1939 Farming begins as part of the 'Dig for Victory' campaign

1939 West Acre closed

1940 Incendiary bombs land on Speech Room • First visit of Mr Winston Churchill to Songs • Newlands closed

1942 Rendalls and Bradbys closed • Malvern College arrived at Harrow in May

BUILDINGS & GROUNDS

Below: Mr ED Gannon

1936 Leaf Schools built • 'Modern' water cleaning introduced at Ducker • Two standard squash rackets courts built

Above: Head Master Mr AP Boissier

Above: Head Master Dr RW Moore

Above: Speech Room on fire, 1940

1944 Mr SG Patterson appointed first Director of School Farm • More firebomb damage

1944 Fields beyond Ducker Road (Northwick Park Golf Club) sold

HEAD MASTERS & ASSISTANT MASTERS

1935 House Masters' status became 'salaried with capitation grant' • Mr AW Siddons elected President of The Mathematical Association • Heads of Subjects appointed • Head of Mathematics: Mr AW Siddons • Head of History: Mr LW Henry • Head of Science: Mr WH Barrett • Head of Classics: Mr JW Moir • Head of Modern Languages: Mr H Cooper • Organisation Master: Mr PH Boas

1936 House Master of The Grove: Mr LW Henry • Head of Geography: Dr ED Laborde

1937 House Master of Newlands: Mr FWT James • Director of Music: Mr HMcL Havergal

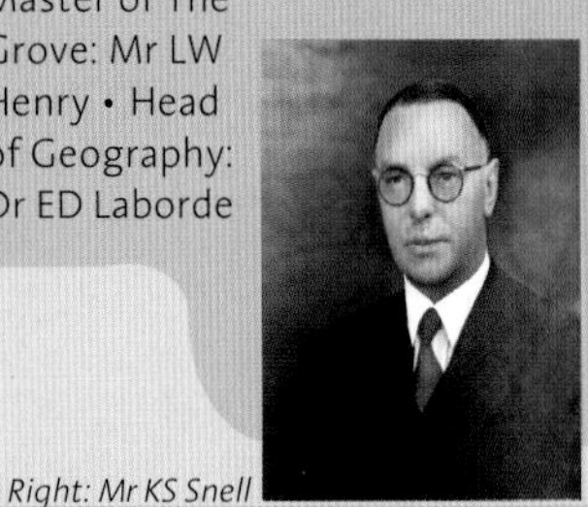

Right: Mr KS Snell

1938 Head of Mathematics: Mr KS Snell • House Master at The Head Master's: Mr WH Stevenson

1939 Head Master: **Mr AP Boissier** • House Master of Druries: Mr ED Gannon

Above: Mr WH Stevenson

1940 34 Assistant Masters; 4 Music Masters

1941 House Master of Druries: Mr KS Snell

Above (from l to r): David Drew, later music journalist; LC Wilson, killed in an air crash in 1954, commemorated by scholarships

1942 Head Master: **Dr RW Moore** • House Master of The Park: Mr WH Stevenson • House Master at The Head Master's: Mr PH Boas • House Master of Moretons: Mr OG Bowlby

1943 Chaplain: The Rev PHM Bryant • Organisation Master: Mr JW Moir • Careers Master: Mr JW Moir

Left: Mr Winston Churchill with Dr Moore, 1942

1944 House Master of The Grove: The Rev HJL Gorse • Head of English: The Rev HL Harris • Careers Master: Dr ED Laborde • Officer commanding HSJTC: Maj JW Thompson

CURRICULUM & ACADEMICS

Below (from l to r): A McCorquodale, ran in 1948 Olympic Games; PC Boissier, son of AP, later master at Sherborne; DCH McLean, Head of School

1943 4 Open Scholarships, 6 Exhibitions gained at Oxford & Cambridge • PEC Berger and HRM Mirehouse gained Special Entry to the Royal Navy

1944 AN Derrick gained Special Entry to the Royal Navy

SCHOOL SPORTS

1935 PM Studd scored 100* v Eton at Lord's and played cricket for the Public Schools XI • MACP Kaye played cricket for the Public Schools XI • Rugby: RF Dennis, EDE Reed played for English Public Schools; RJ Pollock Morris for Scottish Public Schoolboys • DA Blair won the Scottish Boys' Open Golf Championship

1936 AD Collins & PI Firmston-Williams won Public Schools Eton Fives Championships • SOF Bateman was equal first in the foil in the Public Schools Fencing Championships

Above: 'Bimby' Holt, captain of cricket, later Chairman of Governors

Below: CC Blount, cricketer, later merchant banker

1937 RAA Holt scored 111 v Eton at Lord's and played for the Public Schools XI • C Powell-Cotton played rugby football for the English Public Schools

1938 WCA Grey captained the Scottish Boys International Golf team

1939 Cricket XI beat Eton at Lord's by 8 wickets (first victory since 1908); E Crutchley scored 115 • AOL Lithgow played cricket for the Public Schools XI

1940 DF Henley played cricket for the Public Schools XI

OTHER ACTIVITIES

1940 Officer Training Corps became Junior Training Corps (along with all public schools)

1941 Shakespeare play series begins

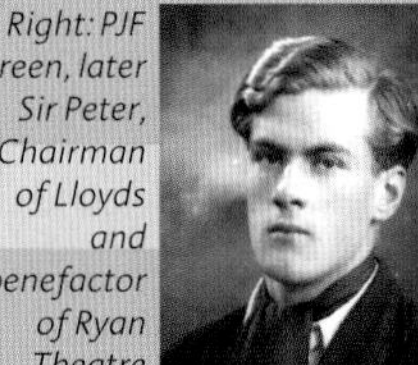

Right: PJF Green, later Sir Peter, Chairman of Lloyds and benefactor of Ryan Theatre

1939 Last issue of *The Harrow Almanack*

WORLD EVENTS

1935 Stanley Baldwin's (OH) 3rd ministry (National Conservative Government)

1936 King George V died • King Edward VIII abdicated. George VI became King • Spanish Civil War began

1939 Hitler invaded Poland and World War II began • Spanish Civil War ended • Nuclear fission discovered

1940 Winston Churchill (OH) became Prime Minister (All-party Coalition)

1941 Japanese attacked US fleet at Pearl Harbour; US enters the war

1942 Beveridge Report led to birth of the welfare state

1944 Fleming Report; (Butler) Education Act • D-Day: Allied forces liberate France

1945	1946	1947	1948	1949	1950	1951	1952	1954
400	441	487	509	525	533	535	569	584

Left: Newlands (the extension on the left was added in 1960s)

1947 Samuel, 1st Viscount Templewood GCSI GBE (OH) – 1948 • Rev Ian White-Thomson (OH) – 1962 • Malcolm, 1st Baron McCorquodale of Newton KCVO (OH) – 1952 • Cosmo Crawley (OH) – 1952 • Maj-Gen Sir Allan Adair, Bart CB DSO (OH) – 1952

1948 Sir Lancelot Royle KBE (OH) – 1962 • Sir Alfred Hurst KBE CB – 1962 • Robert Dickinson (OH) – 1958

1950 Dudley, 3rd Marquess of Aberdeen(OH) – 1965

Right: King Hussein of Jordan

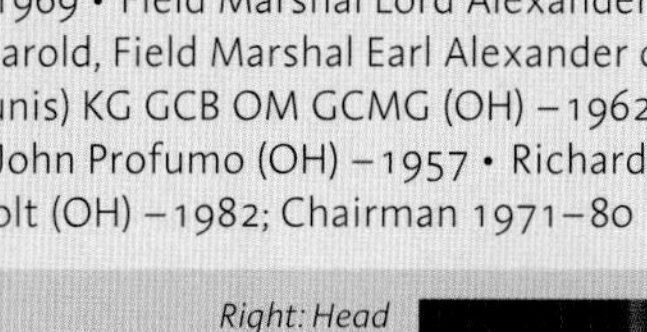

1952 Christopher Seton-Watson – 1969 • Field Marshal Lord Alexander (Harold, Field Marshal Earl Alexander of Tunis) KG GCB OM GCMG (OH) – 1962 • John Profumo (OH) – 1957 • Richard Holt (OH) – 1982; Chairman 1971–80

Below: Field Marshal Earl Alexander

1945 344 Old Harrovians were killed in World War II

1946 Malvern College returned to Malvern in June. Rendalls, Bradbys & Newlands re-opened • Custos: JE Hayward retired; BC Burton appointed • 5 Middlesex scholars admitted each year

Left (from l to r): Rendalls, Bradbys

1948 *Harrow School Yesterday & Today* (Laborde) published

1949 *Harrow School Register* (5th edition) published

1949 Memorial to fallen in WWII added to War Memorial

1951 AJ Knott appointed Bursar • School Inspection

Above (from l to r): CA Strang, Public Schools Rackets Champion; JP Lemmon, History scholar, later Harrow Master; C Collett, later Sir Christopher, Lord Mayor of London

Right: Head Master Dr RL James

1946 Northwick Lodge (Small House) closed

1947 Garlands & Hillside (Small Houses) closed

1950 41 Assistant Masters • Head of Geography: Mr OG Bowlby • Careers Master: Mr R Loverock • Head of Modern Languages: Dr JBC Grundy

Below: Mr PH Boas, Mr RdeWK Winlaw & Mr JW Thompson at CCF camp, 1939

1946 House Master of Bradbys: Mr JW Thompson • House Master of Rendalls: Mr GR McConnell • House Master of Newlands: Mr JW Greenstock • Head of English: Mr ARD Watkins • Director of Music: Mr HJ McCurrach

1951 Head of Geography: Mr JM McSwiney • Officer commanding HSCCF: Maj BED Cooper

1947 House Master of West Acre: Mr PH Boas • House Master at The Head Master's: Mr RH Dahl • Head of History: Mr CA Lillingston • Head of Science: Mr MC Nokes • Head of Latin: Mr PH Boas • Head of Modern Languages: Mr LD Stewart

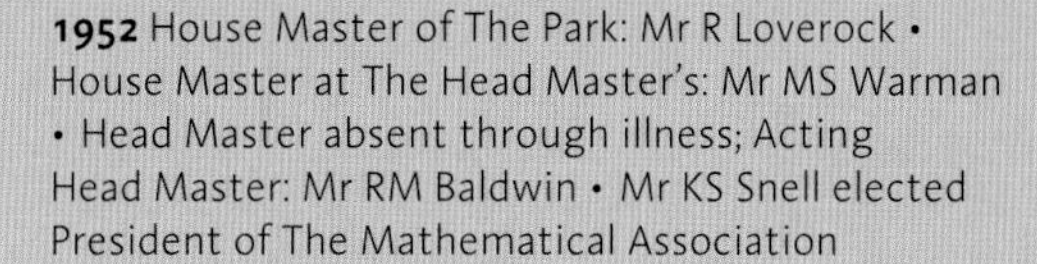

1952 House Master of The Park: Mr R Loverock • House Master at The Head Master's: Mr MS Warman • Head Master absent through illness; Acting Head Master: Mr RM Baldwin • Mr KS Snell elected President of The Mathematical Association

1945 Chaplain: The Revd PHM Bryant

Above (from l to r): Mr ARD Watkins, Mr CA Lillingston, Mr GR McConnell

1948 House Master of Elmfield: Mr ARD Watkins • House Master of The Knoll: Mr EM de M Malan • Head of Modern Languages: Mr H Cooper • Head of English: The Rev HL Harris • Officer commanding HSCCF: Maj JB Morgan

1949 Head of Mathematics: Mr JB Morgan

Right (from l to r): Mr MS Warman, Mr JB Morgan, Mr JW Greenstock

1953 The Head Master, Dr RW Moore, died at Harrow • Head Master: **Dr RL James** • Careers Master: Mr CD Laborde

1954 Organisation Master: Mr KS Snell • House Master of Moretons: Mr JB Morgan

1951 General Certificate of Education introduced

Right: Mr RM Baldwin

1946 HM Saxton awarded the Palmer Scholarship at St Mary's Hospital

Left: King Faisal of Iraq with his House Master, Mr OG Bowlby

1947 DV Dawe gained Special Entry to the Royal Navy

1947 GR Simmonds & RKFC Treherne-Thomas won Public Schools Rackets Championships • The Bowling Fund combined with Field House Club to become the Harrow School Cricket Fund

1952 Cricket XI beat Eton at Lord's by 7 wickets • CRJ Hawke played cricket for the Public Schools XI

1954 Unbeaten rugby XV • CA Strang & RB Bloomfield won Public Schools Rackets Championships; RB Bloomfield won the Singles (Foster Cup) • Cricket XI beat Eton at Lord's by 9 wickets • ARB Neame played cricket for the Public Schools XI

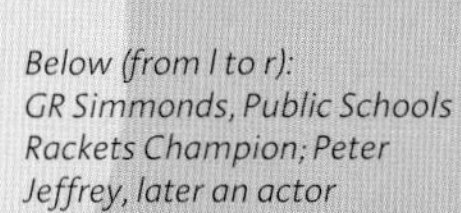

Below (from l to r): GR Simmonds, Public Schools Rackets Champion; Peter Jeffrey, later an actor

1948 DW Taylor & TAM Pigott won Public Schools Rackets Championships

1949 Rugby XV failed to score a point • RG Marlar played cricket for the Public Schools XI

Left (from l to r): J Sunley, later benefactor; T Gold Blythe, Head of School; PE de la Billiere, later Gen Sir Peter

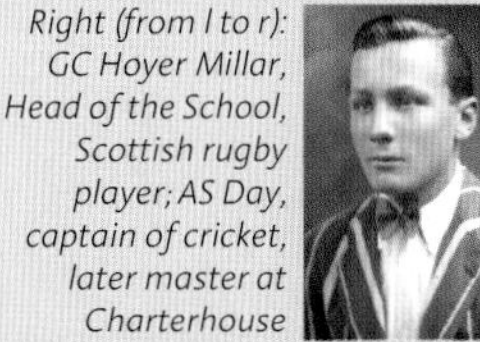

Right (from l to r): GC Hoyer Millar, Head of the School, Scottish rugby player; AS Day, captain of cricket, later master at Charterhouse

1946 RJA Askew awarded Choral Scholarship at Corpus Christi College, Cambridge

1951 JG Francke awarded Choral Scholarship at St Catharine's College, Cambridge • RSO Rees awarded Choral Scholarship at Caius College, Cambridge • AB Champniss awarded Organ Scholarship at Oriel College, Oxford • M Kok awarded Choral Scholarship at Trinity College, Cambridge

1954 MR Tubbs awarded Choral Exhibition at Corpus Christi College, Cambridge

1945 World War II ended • First atomic bombs dropped on Hiroshima and Nagasaki • Creation of the United Nations • Winston Churchill (OH) led caretaker government

1946 Antibiotics became generally available • National Health Act

1947 British withdrawal from India; India and Pakistan become independent states

1951 Winston Churchill's (OH) 3rd Conservative ministry

1952 Death of King George VI

1953 Coronation of Queen Elizabeth II • Structure of DNA discovered

1954 Food rationing ended

NO. OF BOYS	1955	1956	1957	1958	1959	1960	1961	1962	1963	1964
	592	592	600	619	631	643	638	656	648	668

GOVERNORS APPOINTED

1955 George Phillips CBE (OH) – 1965

1957 William Williams (OH) – 1971

1958 Charles Stuart (OH) – 1981

1961 Hon Sir Basil Nield CBE (OH) – 1971

1962 Malcolm, 1st Baron McCorquodale KCVO (OH) – 1971; Chairman 1964–71 • Robert Dickinson (OH) – 1967 • Rt Hon Sir John Hobson QC (OH) – 1967 • Lawrence, 3rd Marquess of Zetland (OH) – 1972 • William Cargill Thompson PhD (OH) – 1978

Left: Mr SL Parsonson

Right: Queen Elizabeth II with Dr James, 1957

Right: King Faisal of Iraq inspecting guard of honour. Behind are Maj BED Cooper and Mr GC Rivington, Chairman of Governors

SCHOOL EVENTS

1955 Visit of King Faisal (OH)

1960 Visit of Jawaharlal Nehru

1961 Harrow Trust launched appeal for £250,000

1963 Arthur Reid appointed Bursar

Above (from l to r): Mr AL Warr, Mr RB Venables, Mr CD Laborde

Right: Visit of Jawaharlal Nehru (OH)

BUILDINGS & GROUNDS

1958 Extension built on to Elmfield

1959 Boarding Houses extension programme continued: The Grove and Moretons

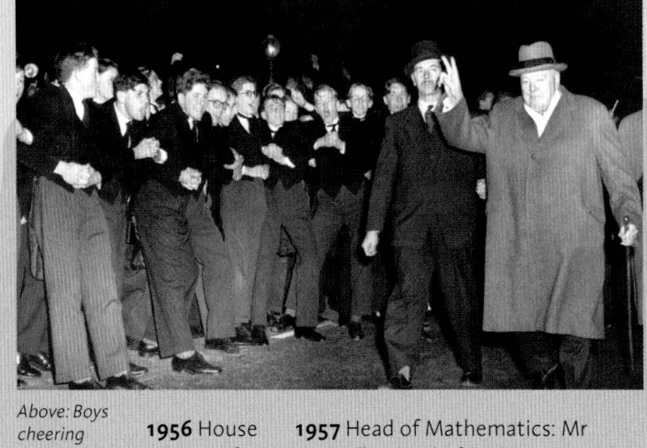

Above: Boys cheering Sir Winston Churchill after Songs

HEAD MASTERS & ASSISTANT MASTERS

1956 House Master of Druries: Mr CA Lillingston

1957 Head of Mathematics: Mr KS Snell • Head of Science: Mr GH Locket • Head of Geography & Economics: Mr JM McSwiney • Vaughan Librarian: The Rev HL Harris

Above (from top to bottom): Mr AA Bishop; Mr SG Patterson

1958 House Master of The Grove: Mr SG Patterson • Head of Science: The Rev HJL Gorse • Mr GRG Parrott appointed Director of School Farm • Head of Chemistry: Mr AA Bishop • House Master of Elmfield: Mr JM McSwiney

1960 54 Assistant Masters • House Master of The Park: Mr CD Laborde • House Master of Bradbys: Mr M Tindall • Organisation Master: Mr JF Leaf • Careers Master: Mr JA Strover • Officer commanding HSCCF: Maj AA Bishop

1961 House Master of Newlands: Mr MS Warman • House Master of Rendalls: Mr AL Warr • Head of Mathematics: Mr GR McConnell • House Master at The Head Master's: Mr RW Ellis • Chaplain: The Rev ML Hughes

1962 50 Assistant Masters plus 6 music & art staff • House Master of West Acre: Mr J Webster • Mr GR McConnell appointed MBE (Mil) • Director of Physical Education: Mr DC McNeill

Left: Mr M Tindall

1963 House Master of The Knoll: Mr RB Venables

1964 Head of Mathematics: Mr SL Parsonson • Officer commanding HSCCF: Maj JGK Ingram

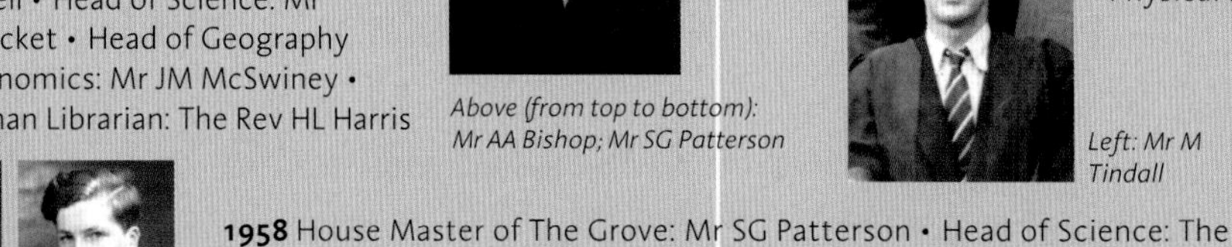

Above (from l to r): J Hermon-Taylor, later Professor of Medicine; FER Butler, Head of School, later Lord Butler, Cabinet Secretary and Chairman of Governors; CPG Blackwell, later founder of Island Records; NW Bethell, later Lord Bethell MEP

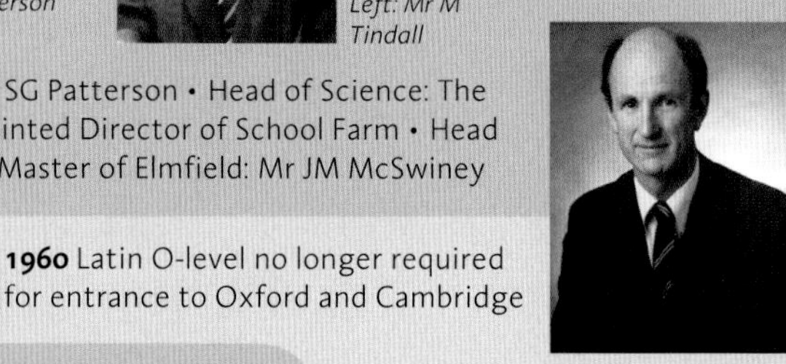

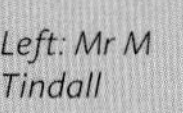

Left: Mr JF Leaf

CURRICULUM & ACADEMICS

1956 5 Open Scholarships, 5 Exhibitions gained at Oxford & Cambridge

Right: AJ Nash and AC Butler in Julius Caesar, 1968

1960 Latin O-level no longer required for entrance to Oxford and Cambridge

1962 11 Open Scholarships, 2 Exhibitions gained at Oxford & Cambridge

1964 Economics A-level introduced • 9 Open Scholarships, 2 Exhibitions gained at Oxford & Cambridge

SCHOOL SPORTS

1955 ARB Neame got a 'hat trick' in the cricket match v Eton at Lord's and played for the Public Schools XI

1956 JM Parker played cricket for the Public Schools XI

1958 School Shooting team won The Country Life Competition

1959 BS Raper played cricket for the Public Schools XI

1960 Cricket XI beat Eton at Lord's by 124 runs

1961 Cricket XI beat Eton at Lord's by an innings and 12 runs

1962 Rowing becomes a School sport • RCS Titchener-Barrett played cricket for the Public Schools XI

1963 RJ Pelham played cricket for the Public Schools XI

OTHER ACTIVITIES

Left (from l to r): JM Parker, captain of cricket & football; GD Massy, cricketer and rackets player, killed in flying accident, 1966; CRL Guthrie, Head of School, later Gen Lord Guthrie; JDC Vargas, Head of School, later Harrow Master; the Hon TP Anson, later Earl of Lichfield, Patrick Lichfield, photographer

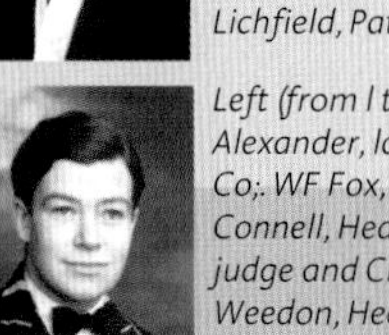

Left (from l to r): The Hon Brian Alexander, later MD of the Mustique Co;. WF Fox, later James Fox, actor; MB Connell, Head of School, later Sir Michael, judge and Chairman of Governors; MJH Weedon, Head of School and cricketer; KM Carlisle, later Sir Kenneth, Under Secretary of State

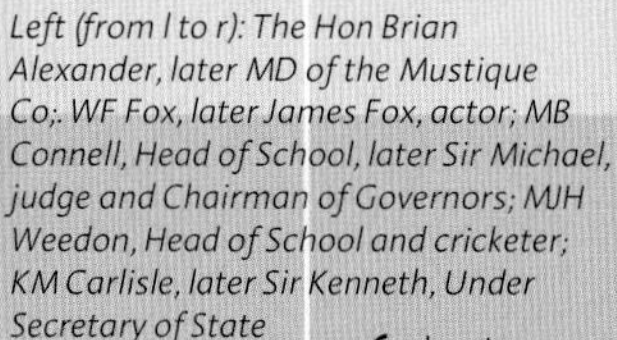

Above (from l to r): SP Welfare, later television producer; JQ Greenstock, later Sir Jeremy, UK Ambassador to UN; GR Gilbart-Smith, Mathematics scholar, later master at Tonbridge; PR Dunkels, cricketer, later QC; DB Buik, later financier & broadcaster; BS Raper, Head of School & captain of cricket

WORLD EVENTS

1957 First Russian rocket launched into space

1960 Last conscripts for National Service called up

1961 First man in space

1963 President Kennedy assassinated in Texas, US

1964 Labour Party published intent to abolish Public Schools in manifesto

1965 — 1970

1965	1966	1967	1968	1969	1970	1971	1972	1973	1974
670	691	689	698	697	709	716	714	711	719

1965 The Very Rev Ian White-Thomson (OH) – 1970 • Sir Peter Green (OH) – 1985

1966 Kenneth Carlisle (OH) – 1976

1967 Sir Donald Cameron of Lochiel KT CVO (OH) – 1977

1968 Robert, Baron Allan of Kilmahew (OH) – 1977

1969 Sir Peter Allen (OH) – 1982 • Sir Randle Baker Wilbraham, Bt (OH) – 1978

1970 Rev Canon Patrick Gilliat (OH) – 1975

1971 Sir Peter Studd GBE KCVO (OH) – 1980 • Sir (John) Val Duncan (OH) – 1975

1972 Alastair McCorquodale (OH) – 1982 • His Hon Judge Lawrence Verney (OH) – 1987

Right: Richard Curtis, Head of School, later writer for film and television

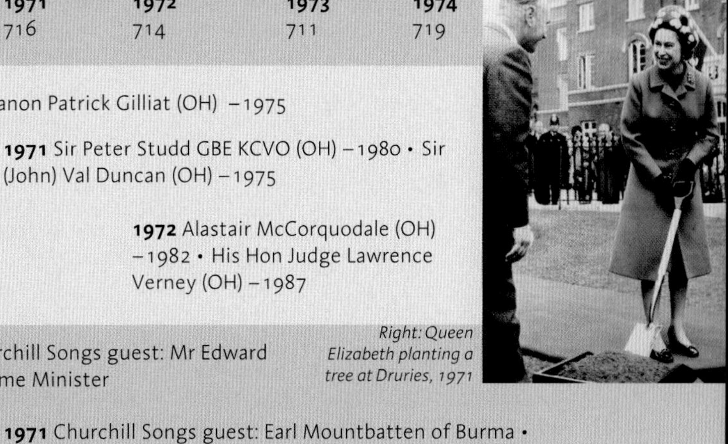

Right: Queen Elizabeth planting a tree at Druries, 1971

1967 Churchill Memorial Appeal funded a boy per year • Lady Churchill guest at Songs • Opening of Harrow Club W10 • Bomb explosion at The Knoll

1970 Churchill Songs guest: Mr Edward Heath, Prime Minister

Above (from l to r): Peter Webster, Head of School; Vernon Sankey, later a Governor; Tim Bentinck, later Earl of Portland, an actor

1968 Mr Harold Macmillan guest at Churchill Songs • Custos: BC Burton retired; SG Wilkinson appointed

1969 Churchill Songs guest: Sir Alec Douglas-Home • Quatercentenary Appeal launched

1971 Churchill Songs guest: Earl Mountbatten of Burma • *Harrow Register* (6th edition) published • Visit of HM Queen Elizabeth II & Prince Philip: Physics Schools plaque unveiled

Right: Head Master Mr BMS Hoban

1972 Physics Schools built • Dutch Elm disease destroyed over 300 trees on the estate • Middlesex scholar scheme ended • Churchill Songs guest: Lord "Rab" Butler

1973 Churchill Songs guest: Lord Carrington • Michael Starkey appointed Bursar

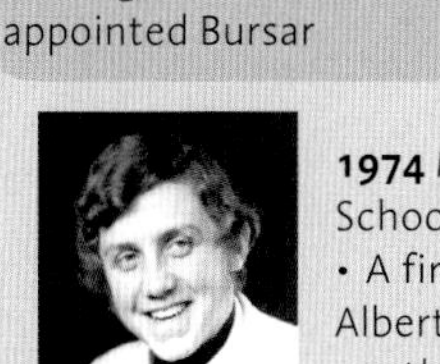

Above: Huw Jenkins, Head of School

1974 Mathematics Schools building began • A fire at The Grove • Albert Hall Songs for 100th anniversary of Churchill's birth • IRA bomb at Peterborough Cottage

1965 Boarding Houses extension programme continues • New Rackets Court built

Right (from left to right): Mr CD Sumner, Mr MG Balme, Mr EA Escritt

1965 Head of Latin: Mr AT Davis • Head of Geography: Mr CD Laborde • Head of Economics: Mr JM McSwiney

Below: PTE Massey and RC Paterson in Coriolanus, 1964

1966 Head of English: Mr JP Lemmon • Head of Science: Mr AA Bishop • Mr GR McConnell appointed Senior Master • Salaried House Tutors introduced • Head of Latin: Mr MG Balme • Head of Economics: Mr MT Wright

1967 Head of Classics: Mr MG Balme • Head of Geography: Mr EA Escritt • Head of Business Studies: Dr JS Dugdale • Vaughan Librarian: Mr CH Shaw • Mr Ned Holdaway retired after 46 years as Head Gardener • House Master at The Head Master's: Mr GRR Treasure • CSM Moores and RSM Jukes awarded British Empire Medal for services to CCF • Director of Music: Mr JH Winstanley

1968 Head of History: Mr DJ Parry • Chaplain: The Revd BA Boucher • Organisation Master: Mr MW Pailthorpe • Mr JB Morgan appointed Second Master • House Master of Druries: Mr JF Leaf

1969 House Master of Moretons: Mr CD Sumner

1970 63 Assistant Masters • Head of Economics: Mr AJD Rees • Careers Master: Mr DJ Humphrey

1971 Head Master: **Mr BMS Hoban** • Organisation Master: Mr J Jeremy • Second Master: Mr MS Warman • Officer commanding HSCCF: Maj Sir Alan Outram

1972 House Master of Newlands: Mr MG Balme • Head of Classics: Mr MS Warman

1973 Retirement age for Masters raised to 62 • House Master at The Head Master's: Mr CH Shaw • House Master of Rendalls: Mr AA Bishop • Vaughan Librarian: Mr JHW Morwood • Chaplain: The Rev BA Boucher • House Master of The Grove: Mr GRR Treasure • Head of History: Mr AH Beadles • Head of Science: Mr MR Etheridge

1974 Head of Geography: Mr EJH Gould • Organisation Master: Mr DJ Parry • Head of Chemistry: Mr TG Hersey • House Master of Bradbys: Mr J Jeremy • House Master of The Park: Mr JGK Ingram

1965 School inspection

Above (from l to r): RS Crawley, cricket & rackets player, killed in flying accident, 1988; JR Hodgkinson, captain of cricket, later barrister; JA Stenhouse, later professor of music

1967 5 Open Scholarships, 6 Exhibitions gained at Oxford & Cambridge • Business Studies introduced in the Sixth Form • Politics introduced in the Sixth Form

1968 7 Open Scholarships, 7 Exhibitions gained at Oxford & Cambridge • 'New Group' formed for less able O-level candidates

1969 University Liaison Master appointed

1970 8 Open Scholarships, 6 Exhibitions gained at Oxford & Cambridge

1971 9 Open Scholarships, 6 Exhibitions gained at Oxford & Cambridge

1970 NE McCorquodale played rugby for English Schools

Above: EJD Clarke, captain of cricket & rugby, later preparatory school headmaster

1974 Nuffield Physics introduced • Political Studies introduced • Business Studies terminated

1965 Cricket XI beat Eton at Lord's by 48 runs

Below (from l to r): RJ Pelham, Head of School & captain of cricket; DJL Fitzwilliams, rugby lion, later investment banker & Governor

1967 AJ Higginson (capt) & JC Mountain played for England Schoolboys Rugby XV. RS Crawley won Foster Cup at Queen's

1968 AP Webster played cricket for the Public Schools and MCC Schools XIs • Cricket XI beat Eton at Lord's by 7 wickets

1969 Harrow won the National Schools' Coxed Fours Cup for rowing

1970 JL Suter awarded Organ Scholarship at Magdalen College, Oxford

1971 M Thatcher & JAN Prenn won Public Schools Rackets Championships; M Thatcher won Singles (Foster Cup)

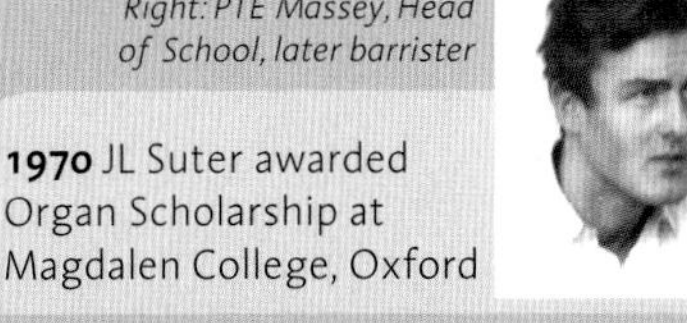

Right: PTE Massey, Head of School, later barrister

1973 Golf team won the Gerald Micklem Trophy • JCC Matthews played rugby for English Schools

1973 Compulsory CCF ended • JS Joseph awarded Organ Scholarship at Exeter College, Oxford

1974 Golf team won the Gerald Micklem Trophy • Cricket XI beat Eton at Lord's by 8 wickets • All victorious rugby XV

1965 Royal Commission on Public Schools report

1966 Royal Commission on Public Schools report • England won the Football World Cup

1967 First successful heart transplant

1968 Newsome Report: Public Schools Commission's first report published

1969 Neil Armstrong landed on the Moon • Abolition of capital punishment in United Kingdom

1970 Northwick Park Hospital opened

1972 Bloody Sunday in Londonderry

1973 School leaving age raised to 16

1974 Labour Party re-published intent to remove charitable status from Public Schools

1975 – 1980

No. of Boys

1975	1976	1977	1978	1979	1980	1981
716	724	740	743	737	742	740

Governors Appointed

1975 Thomas Blackwell (OH) – 1982 • Geoffrey Simmonds (OH) – 1994 • (Frederick E) Robin Butler CVO (OH) – 1991; Chairman 1988-91

1976 Rt Rev Michael Mann (OH) – 1990; Chairman 1980-88 • Roger Boissier CBE (OH) – 1996 • Sir Evelyn de Rothschild (OH) – 1995 • Alexander Macdonald-Buchanan – 1986

1977 Donald Lindsay CBE – 1982 • John Findlay (OH) – 1982

1978 John Hopkins – 2002 • Anthony Beresford – 1983

Right: SJ Sebag-Montefiore, later historian & novelist

1979 Nicholas Owen (OH) – 1996

1980 Mary, Baroness Soames DBE – 1996

Left (from top to bottom): RNP Hadow, captain of rugby & football, later explorer; Alain de Botton, History scholar and later, writer; NJM Patrick, later engineer & astronaut

School Events

1975 Churchill Songs guest: Rt Hon Julian Amery

1976 Sidney Patterson appointed Bursar. • Churchill Songs guest: Lady Soames • Central List for Admissions introduced

1977 Churchill Songs guest: Sir John Colville (OH)

1978 Churchill Songs guest: Rt Hon Anthony Grant • Sixth Form Social Club, funded by American Old Harrovians, opened in the former Hill Restaurant

1979 Churchill Songs guest: Lord Joseph (OH) • 3 Masters' daughters admitted for first time

1981 Mr MT Liddiard appointed Bursar. • Churchill Songs guest: Rt Hon Michael Heseltine

Buildings & Grounds

Right: The Old Speech Room Gallery

Left: The Knoll

1975 School 9-hole golf course begun

1976 Shepherd Churchill Dining Hall built • Old Speech Room Gallery opened • Mathematics Schools opened

1977 Shepherd Churchill Hall opened • School golf course built

1978 VI Form Club opened

1981 Garlands sold • New Knoll opened • House refurbishment begins with The Grove

Head Masters & Assistant Masters

1975 Head of Physics: Mr AG Bagnall • Head of Biology: Mr M Thain

1976 House Masters' term reduced to 12 years • House Master of Bradbys: Mr AWD Sankey • Director of Music: Mr RJ Drakeford • Head of Physics: Mr AG Bagnall • Organisation Master: Mr J Jeremy • Director of Music: Mr RJ Drakeford

1977 House Master of West Acre: Mr DJ Parry • Careers Master: Dr FW Dalton

1978 House Master of The Knoll: Mr SL Parsonson • Head of Mathematics: Dr FW Dalton • Director of Workshops: Mr PR Francis • Careers Master: Mr DPK Gaunt

1979 Second Master: Mr RB Venables • House Master of Druries: Sir AJ Outram Bt • House Master at The Head Master's: Mr EJH Gould • Head of Classics: Mr JHW Morwood • Head of Geography: Mr EA Escritt • Officer commanding HRC: Maj JR Beckett

1980 72 Assistant Masters • Head Master absent for the summer term through illness. Acting Head Master: Mr RB Venables • Head Master ceased to be House Master of The Head Master's House • House Master of The Head Master's: Mr EJH Gould • Head of Economics: Mr MT Bruce Lockhart

1981 Head Master: **Mr IDS Beer**

Left: Head Master Mr IDS Beer

Curriculum & Academics

Below: RC Compton, Head of School & captain of football, later Chairman of Governors

Left: DJG Thomas, U14, U16 & U19 National Squash Rackets Champion

1981 6 Open Scholarships, 5 Exhibitions gained at Oxford & Cambridge

School Sports

1975 Cricket XI beat Eton at Lord's by an innings and 151 runs (greatest margin of victory); MK Fosh scored 161* • MK Fosh played cricket for MCC Schools XI & England Young Cricketers • MK Fosh played rugby for English Schools

1976 AC Pigott won the Rackets Singles Championship (Foster Cup) • RM Tindall scored 151 v Eton at Lord's

1977 Athletics: JJ Espir represented UK in 3000m • Squash team won the National Schools Championships

1978 TMH James scored 112* v Eton at Lord's • DJH Thomas played squash for England U19 • CP Varley won an England Vest in the English Schools Athletics Championships

1979 DJG Thomas & MJL Paul won Public Schools Rackets Championships • Squash V won the Premier National Tournament for Schools

1980 Harrow Lawn Tennis Club relocated to School courts

Other Activities

Left: CN Black and MS Dryden in The Merchant of Venice, 1976

1981 ES Jume'an was the Individual Champion in the Public Schools Gymnastics Championships

World Events

1975 Microsoft Computer Company formed

1976 Education Act introduced 'comprehensive education' leading to the demise of most grammar schools

1979 Margaret Thatcher (Conservative) became first woman Prime Minister

1981 IBM marketed the first personal computer • Assisted Places scheme introduced (not Harrow) • Clementine Churchill Hospital, Sudbury Hill, opened

1982	1983	1984	1985	1986	1987	1988	1989
731	736	732	755	764	772	774	765

1982 (Robert) Jeremy Catto DPhil – 2001 • Sir Richard Baker Wilbraham Bt (OH) – 1991 • Lt Gen Sir John Akehurst KBE CBE – 1997; Chairman 1991–97 • Hugh Woodcock – 1992 • (Francis) Robson Fisher – 1987 • Sir John Clark (OH) – 1993 • Professor Michael Edwards JP PhD – 2004

1983 Sir Michael Connell QC (OH) – 2002; Chairman 1997-2002

Left: The visit of the Queen Mother, 1985

1986 The Duchess of Abercorn – 1999 • Gerald, 6th Duke of Westminster (OH) – 1991

1987 Brigadier Paul Orchard-Lisle CBE TD DL – 1999 • Roger Ellis CBE – 1997 • Sir Richard Norman KBE FRS – 1993

Right: The opening of the Churchill Schools by Sir Herman Bondi

1982 Churchill Songs guest: Lord Hailsham • Lyon Services founded

1983 Churchill Songs guest: Rt Hon Margaret Thatcher, Prime Minister • Custos: SG Wilkinson retired; AL Arnold appointed

1984 Churchill Songs guest: HM King Hussein of Jordan (OH)

1985 Churchill Songs guest: HM Queen Elizabeth, the Queen Mother • *Harrow Register* (7th edition) published

1986 Churchill Songs guest: HM Queen Elizabeth II • Chemistry Schools opened by Professor Richard Norman

1987 Churchill Songs guest: HRH The Duke of Kent

1988 Churchill Schools opened by Sir Herman Bondi, Master of Churchill College, Cambridge • Churchill Songs guest: Lord Callaghan

1989 Churchill Songs guest: Lord Jenkins • Crypt Chapel rededicated by Rt Rev Michael Mann (OH).

1982 Peel House built as residence for the Head Master

Above: CWD Laing, Head of The Head Master's House

1984 Drama Studio opened below the Science Schools • A farm building converted into a Multiple Sclerosis Therapy Unit

Left: Queen Elizabeth II at Churchill songs, 1986

1985 Sports Hall & swimming Pool opened • Ducker closed

1986 Chemistry Schools renovated

1987 Churchill Schools (Design Technology, IT and Geography) built

1988 Fire in the Shepherd Churchill Hall • Shepherd Churchill Room extended following the fire • Chapel stonework cleaned; Crypt re-ordered

Left: Mr MT Bruce Lockhart

1982 Head of Modern Languages: Mr J Jeremy • Head of Design & Technology: Mr A Jaggs • Chaplain: The Revd R Christian

1983 House Master of The Head Master's: Mr JDC Vargas • House Master of Elmfield: Mr JR Beckett • Head of History: Mr CH Shaw • Head of Geography: Mr NW Thorne • Head of Drama: Mr MG Tyrell • Director of Art: Mr JAR Braham

1984 House Master of Moretons: Mr GM Attenborough • Joint Heads of Economics: Mr MES Smith, Mr B Hurl • Mr AG Bagnall appointed Leader of British Physics Olympiad

1985 House Master of Newlands: Mr MC Greenstock • Vaughan Librarian: Mr AHM Thompson • Director of Music: Mr RH Walker

1987 Head of Biology: Mr RD Burden

Below: Chaplain, The Rev James Power

1988 House Master of The Grove: Mr PAG Stilwell • House Master of Rendalls: Mr JFEC Gates • House Master of Bradbys: Mr JA Smith • Head of Science: Mr TG Hersey • Head of Chemistry: Dr IW Farrell

1989 Senior Masters' salary scale introduced • House Master of The Park: Mr RG Collins • House Master of West Acre: Mr AS Lee • Chaplain: The Rev JE Power • Head of Religious Studies: The Rev PJE Jackson • Chaplain: The Revd John Inge • Vaughan Librarian: Mr PD Hunter

1982 Parents' evenings introduced • 6 Open Scholarships, 4 Exhibitions gained at Oxford & Cambridge

1983 7th term entry to Cambridge abolished • 4 Open Scholarships, 7 Exhibitions gained at Oxford & Cambridge

1985 Entry awards to Oxford & Cambridge abolished

1986 GP Ward won the Royal Society of Chemistry award for the best A-level examination

1987 General Certificate of Education and Certificate of Secondary Education replaced by the General Certificate of Secondary Education • Entry to the School became September only

1988 Spanish introduced to the curriculum

1982 Cricket match v Eton at Lord's reduced to one day

1984 DG Dick & SO'N Segrave won Public Schools Rackets Championships • Cricket v Eton at Lord's drawn for 7th year in succession • JE Ironside-Smith shot for the British Cadet Rifle Team v Canada

1985 All victorious rugby XV

1986 Archery re-introduced as a minor sport

1987 AJD Dury represented English Public Schools on golf tour to United States

1988 HDM Poncia was Epée Champion in the Public Schools Fencing Championships • DP Hopley played rugby for England Under-19 XV

1989 JE Rutland won Gold Medal in the Under-19 British Gymnastics Championships

1982 OH Lewis-Barclay awarded Choral Scholarship at Selwyn College, Cambridge

1983 DJF Pailthorpe, Helena Gaunt & JP Gibbon selected for National Youth Orchestra • DJF Pailthorpe, Helena Gaunt & PH Ricketts won the National Chamber Music Competition for Schools

1984 HJ Wickham awarded Choral Scholarship at New College, Oxford • ATK Pitcairn awarded Choral Scholarship at Selwyn College, Cambridge

1985 D Koyama selected for the National Youth Orchestra

Right: HM King Hussein of Jordan and Queen Noor as guests at Churchill Songs, 1984

1988 Rachell Sutton selected for National Youth Orchestra • NJ Robinson awarded a Scholarship to the Royal College of Music

1982 Falklands War

1986 Chernobyl nuclear reactor exploded

1988 Education Reform Act

1989 Tiananmen Square massacre in Beijing • Fall of Berlin Wall

No. of Boys

1990 768 · **1991** 779 · **1992** 776 · **1993** 803 · **1994** 784 · **1995** 784

Governors Appointed

1990 John Hignett (OH) – 2000

Left: PM Beckwith, captain of football, later Governor and benefactor

1991 Rt Rev Noel Jones CB – 2001 • Ian Angus (OH) – 2001 • Peter Beckwith (OH) –

1993 Peter Siddons (OH) – 2008; Chairman 2002-08

1994 Professor DM Mingos BSc DPhil FRS – 2004 • Hubert Reid (OH) – 2001 • Gillian Baker – 2004

Right: (from l to r) Prince Rashid Bin El Hassan, Crown Prince Hassan Bin Talal, the late King Hussein Bin Talal of Jordan, Prince Hamzah Bin Al Hussein on Speech Day 1994.

School Events

1990 Fiftieth anniversary of first Churchill visit: Songs at Royal Albert Hall; guest Lady Soames

1991 Churchill Songs guest: Mr Douglas Hurd • Harrow School Road Trust became John Lyon's Charity

1992 Churchill Songs guest: Gen Sir Peter de la Billiere (OH) • Peter Beckwith Scholarship Scheme began

1993 Churchill Songs guest: Mr Ray Seitz, US Ambassador in London • LA Herner killed in a motor accident on Peterborough Road

1994 Churchill Songs guest: Lord Deedes (OH) • Ryan Theatre opened

1995 Full time Development Director, AJD Rees appointed • Churchill Songs guest: Sir Leon Brittan

Buildings & Grounds

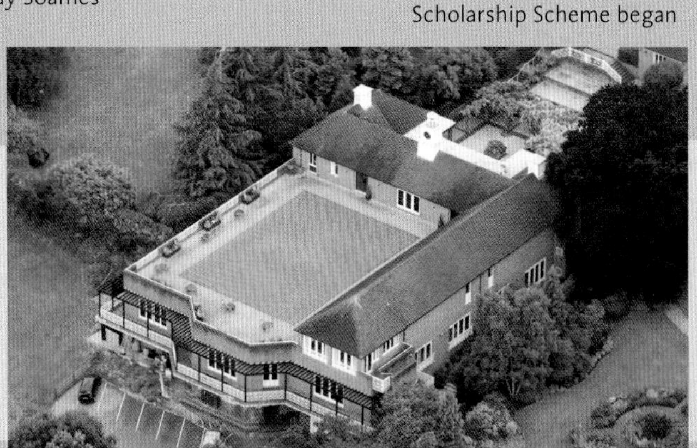

Right: The Shepherd Churchill Hall

1993 Extensive improvements made to kitchens and serving area of Shepherd Churchill Hall

Below (from l to r): Mr PJ Bieneman, Mr PA Cartledge, Mr ME Smith

Head Masters & Assistant Masters

1990 House Master of The Knoll: Mr AHM Thompson • Head of English: Mr CJ Deacon • Head of History: Dr CJ Tyerman

1991 Head Master: **Mr NR Bomford** • House Master of Druries: Mr DR Elleray • Colonel JR Beckett awarded OBE for services to CCF • Mr RM Uttley awarded OBE for services to rugby football • Head of Biology: Mr PJ Bieneman • Head of Geography: Mr ML Mrowiec

Left: Head Master Mr NR Bomford

1992 Director of Studies: Mr MJ Duncan

1993 Head of General Studies: Mr PA Cartledge

Right: Mr DR Elleray

1994 Head of Modern Languages: Mr D Swift • Head of Strings (Music): Mr DN Burov • Mr AA Bishop awarded OBE for services to science education

1995 Head of Economics: Mr ME Smith • House Master of The Head Master's: Mr JPM Baron • House Master of Elmfield: Dr JE Holland

Curriculum & Academics

1992 Academic league tables introduced

1994 A-level Theatre Studies introduced

Left: Sneh Khemka and BTC Cumberbatch in Richard III, 1993

1995 7th term entry to Oxford abolished

School Sports

Below: Col JR Beckett OBE

1991 CBJ Danby won Public Schools' Rackets (Foster Cup)

1992 HStJR Foster won Public Schools' Rackets (Foster Cup) • HStJR Foster scored 102* v Eton at Lord's • Harrow won the Schools Eton Fives Three-pair Competition

1994 RMW Norris & NR Shaw won the Schools Eton Fives Championships • FHH Waters played rugby for England U19

Other Activities

1991 GJ Crouch awarded Choral Scholarship at Trinity College, Cambridge

Below: Toby Dantzic in Richard III

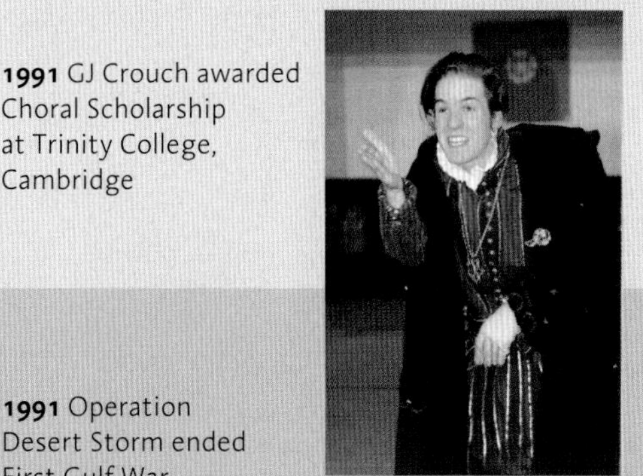

1993 AJ Walker awarded Organ Scholarship at St John's College, Cambridge

1994 JM Stuttard selected for National Youth Orchestra

1995 JA Cotton awarded Choral Scholarship at Magdalen College, Oxford

Right: JH Blount, later James Blunt, musician

World Events

1990 First Gulf War began • Reunification of Germany

1991 Operation Desert Storm ended First Gulf War

1996 773

1997 767

1998 793

1999 798

794

1996 David Salisbury (OH) – 1999 • Forbes Singer – 2005 • Nicholas Stuart (OH) –

1997 Duncan Fitzwilliams (OH) – 2008 • Richard Compton (OH) – ; Chairman 2008 – • Dr Anne Longley – 2007 • Lt-Gen Timothy Granville-Chapman KCB CBE

1998 Thomas Walduck (OH) – 2008

1999 Hon Irene Danilovich – 2001 • John Strachan –

John Hayes (OH) –

Millennium Songs at the Royal Albert Hall; guest: The Lady Soames • *A History of Harrow School* (Tyerman) published • Sir John Beckwith sports scholarships introduced • Outstanding talent scholarships introduced

1996 Churchill Songs guest: HRH Prince Al Hassan, Crown Prince of Jordan (OH) • John Lyon's Charity funded VI Form scholarship

1997 Nicholas Shryane appointed Bursar • Douglas Collins appointed Development Director • Churchill Songs guest: Sir Robin Butler (OH)

1998 First School website launched • Development Board formed • Harrow International School Bangkok founded • Churchill Songs guest: The Lady Soames • Custos: AL Arnold retired; RB Thompson appointed

1999 Churchill Songs guest: Viscount Montgomery of Alamein • Lyon Services renamed Harrow School Enterprises Ltd

Above: Millennium Songs at the Royal Albert Hall in 2000

1996 Bowling Shed re-built and equipped for cricket practice

1997 Overflow House: The Foss closed; Gayton House opened • Extension to Gayton House

Right: The original building of Harrow International Schools, Bangkok

1999 Speech Room organ restored • 68 High Street purchased to become part of Bradbys • Cabling laid for Information Technology links between buildings • The Grove refurbished

Major refurbishment of Vaughan Library completed • Drainage of upper part of Philathletic Ground • Electronic scoreboard erected on the Sixth Form Ground

Below: Mr SP Berry

Left: Mr MJM Ridgway

1996 Head of Classics: Miss JP Affleck • House Master of Moretons: Mr SP Berry

1997 Head of Biology: Mr MJM Ridgway • House Master of Newlands: Mr RD Burden

1998 Head of Mathematics: Dr PG Davies • Director of Studies: Dr IW Farrell • Roman Catholic Chaplain: The Rev AR Wadsworth

1999 Head Master: **Mr BJ Lenon** • Full-time Librarian appointed: Mrs Margaret Knight • Head of Physics: Dr IR Gray • Director of Boarding: Mr DR Elleray

93 Assistant Masters, 10 of whom were female • Head of General Studies: Mr AD Todd • House Master of Rendalls: Mr ML Mrowiec • Head of History: Dr DA Luckett • House Master of The Grove: Mr PJ Bieneman • Head of Chemistry: Dr ER Sie • Senior Tutor: Dr CJ Tyerman • Head of Business Studies: Mr DJ Atkins • House Master of Bradbys: Mr PG Dunbar • House Master of Rendalls: Mr KM Wilding • Officer commanding HRC: Maj JL Ing

Above: Mr PG Dunbar

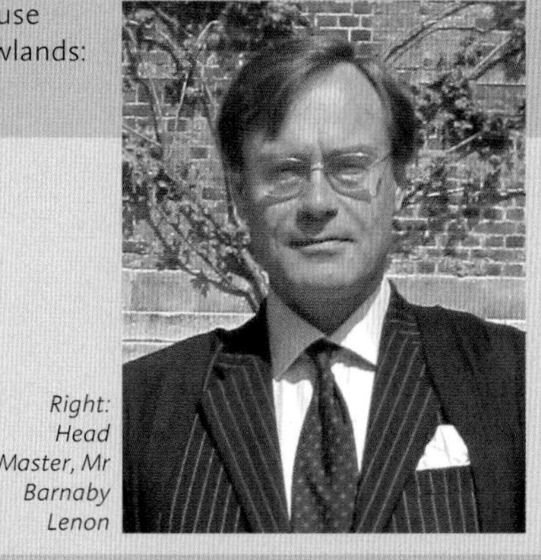

Right: Head Master, Mr Barnaby Lenon

1999 Master appointed for 'special learning needs' • A-level league tables introduced • Harrow placed 126th in *Daily Telegraph* A-level table

Modular A-level established for all subjects • Early GCSE for able students re-introduced • Harrow placed 68th in *Daily Telegraph* A-level table • Business Studies re-introduced as an A-level subject

Left: The Philathletic Ground

1998 Association football given major game status

1999 Golf team won Gerald Micklem Trophy • TG Dunbar & RJ Wilcox won Public Schools Rackets Championships; TG Dunbar won Foster Cup

Cricket match v Eton at Lord's changed to 'limited overs'. Harrow won by 19 runs • Golf team won Gerald Micklem Trophy • TG Dunbar & PR Dunbar won the Schools Eton Fives Championships • OE Craven & TG Dunbar won Public Schools Rackets Championships • Cowdrey Cup introduced for cricket competition with Charterhouse, Eton, Radley, Tonbridge & Wellington

1996 GH Walker awarded Choral Scholarship at St John's College, Cambridge • OJH Gooch awarded Organ Scholarship at Magdalene College, Cambridge

1997 CEP Lyon awarded Choral Scholarship at St John's College, Cambridge

1998 Leadership training courses established for Monitors

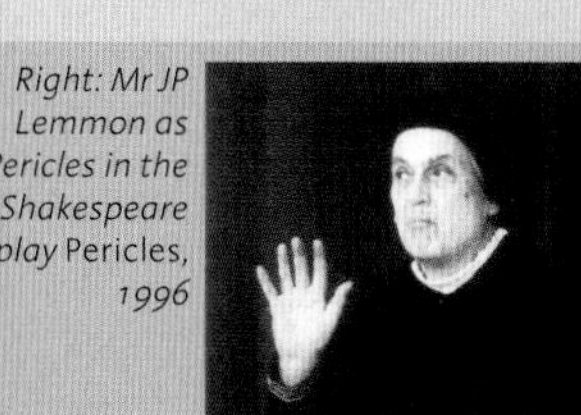

Right: Mr JP Lemmon as Pericles in the Shakespeare play Pericles, 1996

1997 Hong Kong transferred to China • Tony Blair's 'New Labour' ministry • Princess Diana killed in car crash in Paris

1998 Good Friday Agreement in Northern Ireland

Right: Monitors' training courses were established in 1998: WJB Davies, Head of Rendalls

	2001	2002	2003
NO. OF BOYS	789	797	799
GOVERNORS APPOINTED	William Massey QC (OH) – • Professor David Womersley PhD – • Simon Doggart – • Vernon Sankey (OH) –	David Salisbury (OH) – 2007 • Jane Forman Hardy – • Dr Owain Arwel Hughes – 2008 • Dr Mark Billinge – 2007	(Christopher) Toby Hoare (OH) – • Kevin Gilbert FCA –
SCHOOL EVENTS	Churchill Songs guest: Gen Lord Guthrie of Craigiebank (OH)	*Harrow Register* (8th edition) published • Custos: RB Thompson retired; KJ Sincock appointed • Churchill Songs guest: Sir Jeremy Greenstock (OH)	Churchill Songs guest: Ms Rebecca Stevens
BUILDINGS & GROUNDS	Assault course upgraded	Richardson (V.1) pavilion restored • Upper Reding grounds levelled and drained	New choir stalls in Chapel • South Transept of Chapel dedicated as a Lady Chapel • Two all-weather pitches laid on football fields
HEAD MASTERS & ASSISTANT MASTERS	House Master of The Park: Mr PD Hunter • Head of Science: Dr IR Gray • Head of Information Technology: Mr NJ Marchant • House Master of West Acre: Mr ME Smith • Head of Economics: Mr DJ Atkins • Head of Religious Studies: Miss AL Wall • Examinations Officer: Mr PJ Evans • Organisation Master: Mr MT Bruce Lockhart	House Master of The Knoll: Mr CJ Farrar-Bell • House Master of The Head Master's: Mr WJ McKinney • Head of Geography: Mr KM Wilding • Head of History: Mr AD Todd	Head of Economics: Mr CS Tolman • Head of General Studies: Mr CD Barry • Head of Business Studies: Mr RB Corthine
CURRICULUM & ACADEMICS	Harrow placed 58th in *Daily Telegraph* A-level table • Physical Education introduced as an A-level subject	Harrow placed 59th in *Daily Telegraph* A-level table • Pre-Common Entrance tests introduced	Harrow placed 51st in *Daily Telegraph* A-level table
SCHOOL SPORTS		Rugby XV all-victorious • JS Wellwood played rugby for Wales U19 XV • TWV French played rugby for England U18 XV	PR Dunbar & JC Bone won Public Schools Rackets Championships
OTHER ACTIVITIES		JG Kennerley awarded Organ Scholarship to Jesus College, Cambridge	
WORLD EVENTS	9/11 terrorist attack on the World Trade Center in New York • War in Afghanistan began		Allied invasion of Iraq • England won the Rugby Union World Cup Tournament

Above: Mr PD Hunter

Below: Endurance training on the upgraded assault course

Right: Songs, 2003

Above: SDR Liddle, Head of School

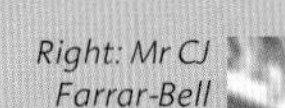
Right: Mr CJ Farrar-Bell

Right: Rugby XV, 2002

Above: Eton v Harrow at Lord's, 2002

Right: The Music Schools (right), built in 1890: the recording studio, the small brick building in the front left corner of the picture, was added in 2007

2004

799

Edward Gould – • Crispin Odey (OH) –

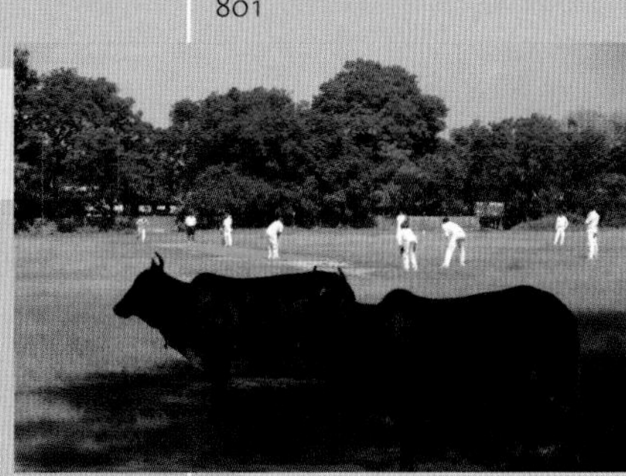

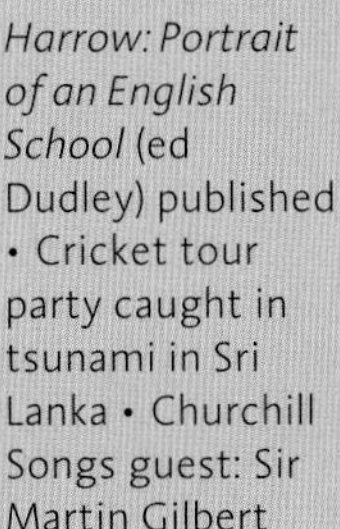

Left: Soccer on the Astroturf pitch

Harrow: Portrait of an English School (ed Dudley) published • Cricket tour party caught in tsunami in Sri Lanka • Churchill Songs guest: Sir Martin Gilbert

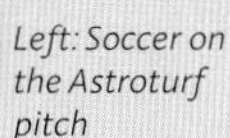

New athletics track built. Parade Ground relocated below rifle range • The Bookshop closed. School Shop opened in West Street • Conference Room opened behind the School Shop • Music Schools recording studio built • Astroturf football pitch came into play • Extension to The Knoll built

Left: The Tartan athletics track

Second Master re-named Deputy Head (Mr ML Mrowiec) • Head of Statistics: Mr I Hammond • Head of Geography: Mr AK Metcalfe

Head of Italian: The Rev AR Wadsworth • Harrow placed 55th in *Daily Telegraph* A-level table • Critical Thinking became an A-level subject

Above: Fr Andrew Wadsworth

Above: Dr E-R Sie

Harrow football moved to Hemstall fields • JC Bone won the Foster Cup for Rackets

Left: Harrow football on the Hemstall fields

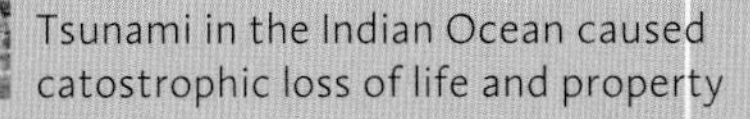

Tsunami in the Indian Ocean caused catastrophic loss of life and property

2005

801

Left: The cricket XI play at Dambulla in Sri Lanka

Sir Neil Chalmers –2010 • Harriet Crawley –

Harrow International School Beijing founded • Development Trust launched the 'Three Yards Fund' • 200th anniversary of cricket match v Eton at Lord's • Churchill Songs guest: Lady Williams of Elvel

Sunley Field (VI Form Ground Rugby & Soccer) opened • Photography Studio created • Beckwith tennis courts opened • VI Form cricket pavilion refurbished • Dove Cottage pulled down and replaced by new terrace

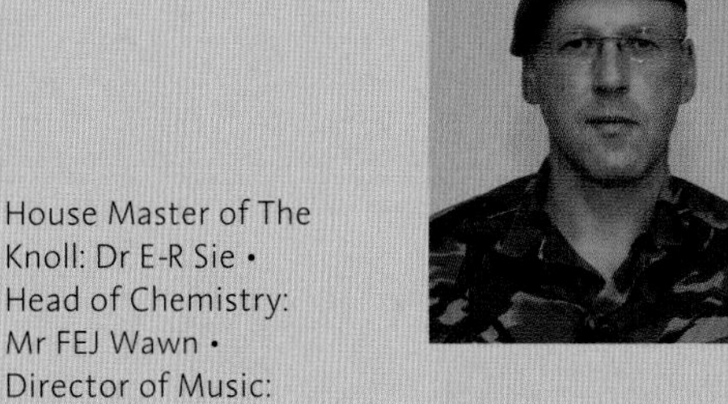

Right: Maj MP Stead

House Master of The Knoll: Dr E-R Sie • Head of Chemistry: Mr FEJ Wawn • Director of Music: Mr DN Woodcock

Photography became an A-level subject • Musical Technology became an A-level subject • Harrow placed 42nd in *Daily Telegraph* A-level table • Mathematics changed from GCSE to IGCSE • Pre-Common Entrance tests computerised

WBD Fortune & JC Bone won Public Schools Rackets Championships; Fortune won the Foster Cup • Cricket XI beat Eton at Lord's by 7 wickets & had an unbeaten season • All Harrow football played on Hemstall and Sheepcote fields • EMN Martins played football for the Independent Schools FA XI • Harrow football relegated to minor games status

Suicide bomb attacks in London

2006

John Batting FFA (OH) –

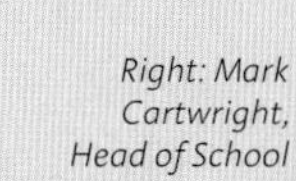

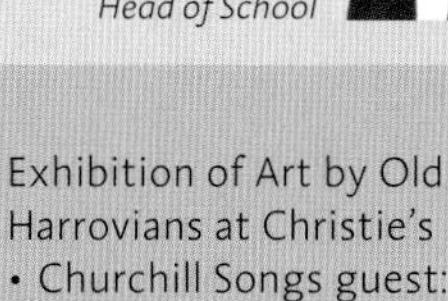

Right: Mark Cartwright, Head of School

Exhibition of Art by Old Harrovians at Christie's • Churchill Songs guest: Mr Robert Hardy

Flannels boards in the VI Form pavilion updated

Right: Biennial inspection 2003

House Master of Moretons: Mr PJ Evans • Officer commanding HRC: Maj MP Stead • Examinations Officer: Mr BJD Shaw

Harrow placed 32nd in *Daily Telegraph* A-level table

Cricket XI beat Eton at Lord's by 23 runs • GR Querl and GS Ballance played cricket for Zimbabwe U19 in the World Cup

Below: Harrow Cricket XI, 2006

2007

NO. OF BOYS

801

GOVERNORS APPOINTED

Professor Graham Furniss PhD – • Matthew Fosh MSI (OH) –

Right: Modern Languages Schools

SCHOOL EVENTS

Harrow Association Centenary Songs at the Royal Albert Hall; speaker Lord Butler of Brockwell (OH)

BUILDINGS & GROUNDS

Leaf Gallery opened on the ground floor of Leaf Schools; Leaf Schools refurbished as Art Schools extension • Modern Languages Schools opened • New kitchens built in the Shepherd Churchill Hall • The Knoll Games Room extension built

HEAD MASTERS & ASSISTANT MASTERS

House Master of Elmfield: Mr MJ Tremlett • Director of Design Technology: Mr SM Griffiths • House Master of The Head Master's: Mr AR McGregor • Head of Mathematics: Mr I Hammond • Head of Photography: Mrs FEG Corthine • Examinations Officer: Mr SA Harrison • Head of Art: Mr JC Cockburn • Head of History of Art: Miss RL Fulton • Organisation Master: Mr GH White • Head of Sculpture & Pottery: Mr IA Stroud • Head of Classics: Mr BJD Shaw • Head of Wind Instruments & Commercial Music: Mr S McWilliam • Head of Modern Languages: Mr NC Hulme

Left: (clockwise from top left): Mr BJD Shaw, Mr MJ Tremlett, Mr AR McGregor, Mr NC Hulme

CURRICULUM & ACADEMICS

Mandarin became an alternative to Latin • History changed from GCSE to IGCSE • Harrow placed 25th in *Daily Telegraph* A-level table

SCHOOL SPORTS

Left: Harrow v Eton at Lord's

SA Northeast & RG Querl won Public Schools Rackets Championships; SA Northeast won Foster Cup • Cricket XI beat Eton at Lord's by 95 runs; SA Northeast 115 • Cricket XI won the Cowdrey Cup for the third successive year.

OTHER ACTIVITIES

EJL Symington won an Organ Scholarship to Keble College, Oxford

WORLD EVENTS

Gordon Brown's Labour ministry

2008

NO. OF BOYS

801

GOVERNORS APPOINTED

Professor David Wallace CBE FRS FREng – • Hon Robert Orr-Ewing (OH) – • Dominic Creran ARCS Cphys – • Susan Whiddington –

Right: Daniel Draper, Head of School

SCHOOL EVENTS

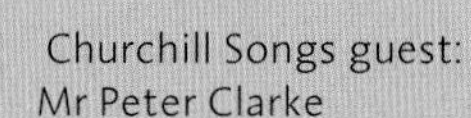
Churchill Songs guest: Mr Peter Clarke

BUILDINGS & GROUNDS

Mezzanine floor in Art School converted into the Pasmore Gallery • New serveries built in Shepherd Churchill Hall • Installation of computers in boys' rooms begun

Right: The new serveries in the Shepherd Churchill Hall

HEAD MASTERS & ASSISTANT MASTERS

Head of Physics: Mr CD Barry • Head of Chemistry: Dr AF Worrall • Head of Biology: Mr NS Keylock • Director of Sport: Mr JJ Coulson • Head of English: Mr JN James • Head of Photography: Mr DRJ Bell • Examinations Officer: Mr JA Hanson • Head of Government & Politics: Dr DR Wendelken

CURRICULUM & ACADEMICS

Harrow placed 28th in *Daily Telegraph* A-level table

Below (from l to r): Mr NS Keylock, Mr JA Hanson

SCHOOL SPORTS

Cricket XI beat Eton at Lord's by 8 wickets (GS Balance 119*) & had an unbeaten season • SA Northeast played cricket for England U19

Above: SA Northeast, Captain of cricket

OTHER ACTIVITIES

EA Philips won a Scholarship to the Royal Academy of Music • STJ Lau won an Organ Scholarship to Trinity College, Oxford • RRCK Opoku won an Academical Clerkship to Christ Church, Oxford

Above: STJ Lau, Organ Scholar

WORLD EVENTS

Bank failures started world economic recession

Left: Jasper Jolly, Head of School

810

Rear Admiral GM Zambellas –

Agreement reached to open Harrow International School Hong Kong in 2012 • Churchill Songs guest: Mr Andrew Roberts • Swine flu epidemic

Above: Lyon's House

Philathletic ground relaid • Further restoration of the Speech Room organ • Work begun on Lyon's House • Major tree-planting programme completed on Philathletic ground • New pitches on the Philathletic Ground named Jackson, MacLaren, Hornby, Grimston & Walker

Field House Club refurbished • Lyon's House opened • Extension to the Sports Centre built • Cooke Data-logging Suite opened in the Physics Schools in memory of Mr GD Cooke, Director of Computing, 1999-2007

Below (clockwise from top left): Dr DR Wendelken, Mr Simon Taylor, Dr NDA Kemp, Mr EW Higgins

Above: Maj N Page

Above: Mr AK Metcalfe

House Master of Newlands: Mr EW Higgins • Director of Boarding: Mr PG Dunbar • House Master of Bradbys: Dr DR Wendelken • House Master of Druries: Mr MJM Ridgway • Head of Modern Languages: Mr N Page • Head of Government & Politics: Dr NDA Kemp • Head of Art: Mr SN Taylor • Officer Commanding HRC: Maj N Page

House Master of Lyon's House: Mr AK Metcalfe • Head of Science: Dr AF Worrall • Head of Geography: Mr RJ O'Donoghue • Head of Italian: Mr JS Webb • Roman Catholic Chaplain: The Rev SP Seaton

Right: ELS Lee, Organ Scholar

Spanish became an alternative to French for some boys on entry • Harrow placed 32nd in *Daily Telegraph* A-level table • Modular GCSEs begin • Biology, Chemistry, Modern Languages move from GCSE to IGCSE • A-level reduced from 6 to 4 modules

A* grade introduced at A-level

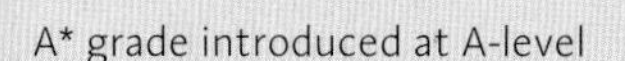

Swimming team won the Public Schools 4x50m freestyle relay (Bath Cup) • CC Stidson-Nott & AM Fedoricow played rugby for Scotland U19 • VML Vunipola played rugby for England U19 • ME Doughty played football for the England Independent Schools U19

CF Nagle won the Foil in the Independent Schools' Fencing Championships • AC Smith played cricket for Hong Kong in the Under 19 World Cup Tournament • Swimming team won the Public Schools 4x50m freestyle relay (Bath Cup) • Cricket XI beat Eton at Lord's by 5 wickets; YM Sert scored 105 not out

Above: The Harrow XI celebrating on the balcony at Lord's, 2010

Left: FA Lashmar

FA Lashmar selected for National Youth Orchestra

DH Wong won an Organ Scholarship at Downing College, Cambridge • DJ Lewis and S Popat gained places in the National Youth Choir of Great Britain • EPB Smith won a Choral Scholarship at University College, Oxford • GW Thomas won a Choral Scholarship to Jesus College, Cambridge • ELS Lee won an Organ Scholarship to Robinson College, Cambridge

Barack Obama became first black US President

Ash cloud from volcanic eruption in Iceland grounded all commercial aircraft for 6 days • Conservative-Liberal coalition government formed

THE FOUNDER: WHO WAS JOHN LYON?

FOR MANY YEARS THE belief at the School was that John Lyon was a 'yeoman farmer': "Lyon of Preston, Yeoman John…" wrote Edward Bowen in the School Song written in 1869. A yeoman was one notch up from a peasant but certainly not gentry, although how that squared up with his considerable property holding is not clear.

We know little about John Lyon. He was clearly a man of substance who had built up his wealth to make himself, below the gentry, the richest citizen in a prosperous area. Apart from his considerable possessions in Middlesex, he had property in Bedfordshire, Hertfordshire and Essex. John Lyon was probably born in 1514 and lived and farmed in the hamlet of Preston, a property that had come into his family in 1393. In 1562 he headed the rental list of the parish and is known to have collected local subsidies for support of national defences against Spain and the Low Countries in 1567. In 1580 he became 'bailiff and parish officer'.

Researches in the 1880s revealed that Lyon, if not one of the gentrified class, certainly had good connections: his cousin had been Lord Mayor of London in 1554 and he had close associations with the Gerrard family, who lived in a house on the site of The Park. Sir Gilbert Gerrard, Queen Elizabeth's Attorney-General, was the most important person living in the area. He was joint Treasurer of Gray's Inn with Sir Nicholas Bacon. In 1559 Bacon wrote the rules for St Alban's Grammar School, which were almost identical to those for John Lyon's school – surely no coincidence. It is very likely that Gerrard was the moving agent in the granting to John Lyon of the Charter – a privilege not lightly conferred in Tudor days.

A sketch of John Lyon's farmhouse at Preston. The farm was sold for building development in the 1890s

Another important person living nearby was Dr Caius, the Founder of Caius College, Cambridge, resident in Ruislip. The close connection between the College and Harrow School in the early years of the existence of these two institutions suggests more than a casual relationship.

Lyon appears to have had no aspirations to social status. We know that he died childless (although the brass on his tomb suggests that a child may have predeceased him) and that he left his estate, after the death of his widow, to providing a free education for thirty boys of the parish and for the upkeep of the Harrow and Edgware roads to central London. As Christopher Tyerman explains, this was not unusual at the time and several other grammar schools of the period have a similar foundation. Nor was the provision for road maintenance unusual as access to the city was important both for commercial and social traffic. It is estimated that a farm cart would have taken a full day to make the journey at that time.

The further information we have is piecemeal. We know that he travelled from Preston to Harrow fairly regularly – often enough to have made arrangements for accommodation and the stabling of his horses. We know that, during his lifetime, he made financial provision for boys of the parish to be apprenticed

... his cousin had been Lord Mayor of London in 1554 and he had close associations with the Gerrard family, who lived in a house on the site of The Park.

to tradesmen. And we also know that the cost of his benefaction, the endowment for the building of the school, for the employment of the school master, for the free education of his scholars and for the upkeep of the roads – not to mention provision for his widow – stretched his resources to the very limit.

We know John Lyon's image from the brass in St Mary's Church and the more lifelike depiction of the stained glass window in Chapel. We know what he did, but he remains a distant, misty figure, more legend than reality. His philanthropy has ensured that his name will live on – at least here on Harrow Hill.

The Chapel window depicting the Founder, John Lyon and his wife, Joan

GOVERNORS AND GOVERNANCE

THE ROYAL CHARTER OF 1572 establishing the Free Grammar School of John Lyon in the town of Harrow on the Hill made careful provision for its administration and finance. A 'free school' did not mean that education was free or that it was free from church control. Rather it indicated that the management of the school's funds was vested in an independent autonomous corporation with 'perpetual succession'. In Harrow's case, a new charitable trust, which was to enjoy tax relief up to £100 p.a., was created, presided over by a board of five named 'Keepers and Governors'. They were to receive the lands and property donated to the School by John Lyon during the founder's and his wife's lifetimes and thereafter to manage the trust's estates and fulfil the requirements of the statutes. Income from the trust's property was divided into two. Receipts from Lyon's land in Middlesex and Hertfordshire were to be spent on building and maintaining the School; those from his land in Marylebone and Kilburn were reserved for the upkeep of the roads from Edgware and Harrow to London. It was explicitly forbidden for income from the Road Trust, as the latter became known, to be used for the School. This stipulation caused generations of Governors much bother and frustration, from a law suit in 1611 challenging their use of Road Trust money in building the original schoolhouse until 1991, when at last the old trust was broken and the new John Lyon's Charity was established to provide funds for charitable purposes in the boroughs through which the Harrow Road passes.

The Charter of 1572 and the statutes of 1591 did not envisage the Governors managing the School. This was the preserve of the Head Master. From 1615, when the School opened, until 1874, when new statutes came into force, there were two separate, parallel systems of administration. The Head Master ran the School, dealt with the finances it generated, hired staff, and admitted pupils, including lucrative fee-paying 'foreigners' and later the increasingly ubiquitous boarders. Whatever he or his staff made above the Head Master's statutory stipend of £26 13s 4d (the formal salary until the 1870s), they kept. The Governors, on the other hand, administered the Lyon estates and trusts, disbursed the income on capital expenditure for the School or the roads, chose leaving scholars and apprentices, and, most importantly, appointed Head Masters. They remained tightly constrained by the statutes, which were regularly reiterated during legal challenges to their administration, notably in a long chancery case in 1810 concerning the rights of parishioners to free education.

Governors tended to be drawn from important local families or local landowners, many of whom had contacts or employment in London, or at court; the Gerrards, Pages and Norths of the sixteenth and seventeenth centuries; the Lakes, Waldos, Bucknalls and Rushouts of the eighteenth; the Northwicks, Clarendons, Grimstons and Abercorns of the nineteenth. Nepotism and cronyism were at the core of the fabric of the system. It was usual for the Vicar of Harrow (for much of the time one of the two or three richest livings in England) to be a Governor, as were successive Norths and Rushouts as Lords of the Manor, most of whom lived where The Grove now stands. Some Governors were influential by virtue of their careers: Gilbert Gerrard, Elizabeth I's Attorney General, who had eased the path of the Charter in 1572, or James Brydges, later Duke of Chandos, a Governor 1713–40, who made a huge fortune as Paymaster General for Marlborough's wars in the early eighteenth century and probably initiated the Governors' investment in the new forms of finance, with the first purchase of Government Bonds (1716/17). Others possessed local clout and, through longevity, asserted a potent force in deliberations: Sir Gilbert Gerrard, great-nephew of the Elizabethan Attorney General, Governor 1609–70; Sir John Rushout (1715–75) and his grandson the second Baron Northwick (1801–59); the Rev JW Cunningham, known by the boys, unoriginally, as 'Old Slybacon' (1818–61). Their meetings, held in the Governors' Room in the Old Schools (now OS2), were usually confined to receiving the audit of accounts and treating themselves to a good dinner. Until 1801, they acted as their own receivers and auditors, only then employing a professional firm. Only in 1802 did they appoint a clerk to the Governors, a solicitor, Francis Fladgate; there have only been eight since.

The most significant moments when the Governors' responsibilities impinged directly on the School were elections or dismissals (1669; 1746) of Head Masters. Occasionally, the Governors' choice proved historically significant. In 1669 the appointment of William Horne from Eton set the pattern for the next century when Harrow rose in eminence in deliberate imitation of its older rival. In 1771, the election of Benjamin Heath instead of the 'local boy made good', Samuel Parr, caused a riot, in which one Governor's carriage was destroyed and another's windows were smashed, but it confirmed the School's national perspective. Occasionally, the Governors were in conflict with the Heads, as with Robert Sumner in the late 1760s and, more seriously, with Christopher Wordsworth in the early 1840s, over the issue of parishioners' rights. By then, the paradox of a national school masquerading as a local one and the inappropriateness of the Elizabethan statutes to the running of a large boarding public school had reached breaking point.

The Public Schools Act of 1868 radically altered both statutes and organisation in recognition of the actual status and nature of a large public school. By 1874, the old board of Governors and trust had been swept away; a new governing body, although it assumed the old title of Keepers and Governors, was both different in composition and charged with very different responsibilities. The reformed Governing Body comprised ten members, half from the old body and five appointed by different interest groups: the universities of Oxford and Cambridge, the Royal Society, the Lord Chancellor and the Head and Assistant Masters. The vexatious matter of parishioners' rights was resolved by the creation of the Lower School of John Lyon (1876). For the first time the Governors were placed in charge of the finances of the whole School, from fee receipts

The Keepers & Governors, 1974; Chairman Mr 'Bimby' Holt

The Governors in 1983; Chairman: The Rt Rev Michael Mann (above); The Governors in 1998; Chairman: Sir Michael Connell (below)

to paying staff salaries. A School Fund was created, administered by the Head Master who was now paid a realistic salary in compensation for losing control of fee income. He remained in executive control of the School and formed the only official conduit between the Governors and the teaching staff. Slowly, by virtue of buying up the boarding houses, the Governors exerted direct control over House Masters, culminating in the 1935 scheme that gradually did away with House Masters' hotelier freehold. By the beginning of the twentieth century the Governors, although not necessarily any more visible within the School, were involved in all aspects of the institution, from the fabric and finances to the education and management. As a sign of the new financial regime, a bursar was appointed for the first time in 1881 to assist with the management of the School Fund.

The fundamental task of the Governors is to ensure the solvency of the School, always a delicate matter as Harrow never enjoyed the sort of endowments some other competitors did, being heavily reliant on fee income and extraordinary fundraising initiatives. Increasingly, from the 1880s, the Governors' portfolio was extended by a series of trusts created to purchase land for the School on the Hill to save it from alternative development and to channel the proceeds of ever more frequent appeals to Old Boys, a tactic pioneered by George Butler for the new Old Schools in 1820 and his son Monty for Speech Room in the 1870s. In addition, there was a raft of major donations to absorb and manage, such as the Bowen legacy of 1901, the Shepard (sic) Churchill bequest of 1916, the massive Apcar Reversion of 1936 and the Peter Beckwith grant for assisted places in 1992. From 1955, the Governors were able by law to invest up to two thirds of trust income without restriction.

Governors continued to be drawn from the ranks of Old Harrovians: bankers, lawyers, academics, public servants, members of the armed forces, clerics and, although decreasingly from the mid-twentieth century, politicians. They rarely disturbed routine School life except in moments of perceived crisis, such as the Night Club scandal of 1924, when Governors converged on the Hill in a rush of impotent activity, or the financial impasse of 1938–42 when plans were laid to remove the then nearly bankrupt School from Harrow entirely. Otherwise, Governors tended to be distant, more available in clubland than on the Hill. This did not stop them musing on a vast range of School matters; some important, such as the dismissal of House Masters, the allocation of certain scholarship funds, the curriculum or the admissions of girls and day boys; others perhaps less so, such as the shade of blue in 'bluers', school heraldry, the introduction of rugby football (fiercely opposed by many in 1927) or changing fashions in playing cricket.

This image of remote, often somewhat dusty Olympians only on parade for the Contio, changed radically from the 1970s, partly as a result of the financial crises of that decade, and partly because of the lengthy and intense simultaneous redevelopment and refurbishment of the School buildings, including the erection of a central feeding block, new form rooms and, most recently, a whole new House. A group of active and engaged younger Governors took the lead in refashioning the conduct of business and relations with the School. Numbers of Governors were steadily increased, from the original 10 of 1874 to 15 in 1939, 20 in 1974 and 25 in 1997. This in part reflected the diverse tasks required, but also indicated a wider recruitment and greater sensitivity to their clients and the world outside, new members including non-Old Harrovians, parents and women as well as the more usual cohort of Old Boys. If the central task of building up an impregnable Endowment Fund remained much the same, increasingly the Governors adopted a consciously business model that included holiday letting as well as overseas ventures alongside more or less continuous appeals to sustain the traditional nature of the School and provide more bursaries to encourage the widest possible range of access. Although the formal link with the staff continued to be the Head Master, who remains the absolute effective chief executive of the educational and pastoral aspects of the School, direct relations, communication and contact between Governors and the teaching staff improved immeasurably. By the early twenty-first century, although still professionally aloof and still responsible for all significant strategic and financial issues, the Governors were engaged and familiar figures within the School community in ways their predecessors could scarcely have imagined.

Governors in 2002; Mr Peter Siddons became Chairman later that year

THE HEAD MASTERS

Author's Note: At various times the titles 'Schoolmaster', 'Master', 'Headmaster' and 'Head Master' have been used. I have adopted the current form. I have applied a 'thirty year rule' to observations of a personal and professional nature; thus these are restricted to Head Masters who retired before 1980.

Anthony Rate, Head Master 1608–11, was previously a private tutor in the family of William Gerrard, a Governor of the School. An entry in the Parish Register reads: "Buried, Anthony Rate, schoolmaster at Flambards, elected schoolmaster at the free schole." Mr Rate was not a graduate of Oxford or Cambridge.

(Either Thomas or Henry) Bradley was Head Master from 1611 to 1615; it is not known whether he was Thomas Bradley, scholar of Trinity College, Cambridge, or Henry Bradley of The Queens' College, Oxford with BA from Brasenose and MA from Oriel.

The Rev William Launce, Head Master 1615–21, left almost no trace in the School records. The main achievement during his time was the building of an elaborate brick and timber 'house of office'. Subsequently he became Vicar of Harrow and Rector of St Edmund the King, Lombard Street.

The Rev Robert Whittle, Head Master 1621–28, was a graduate of Magdalene College, Cambridge, and a scholar of Emmanuel College. He supplemented the Governors' provision of a library with books and it is known that at least three of his pupils proceeded to Cambridge.

The Rev William Hide, Head Master 1626–61, was either William Hyde of Jesus College, Cambridge or William Hide of St John's College, Cambridge. He is credited with establishing the School on firm and lasting foundations. He spent money on books and organised the teaching of reading to local children by Dames, while at the same time accepting fee-paying pupils into the School.

The Rev Thomas Jonson, Head Master 1661–68, was probably educated at St Paul's and Trinity College, Cambridge. He seems to have disappeared unexpectedly: "He went suddenly to Lincoln on the Monday following Nov 2, 1688". His subsequent career has not been traced.

The Rev Dr Thomas Martin, Head Master 1668–69, was removed from the headmastership after six months with no reason given in the Governors' Minutes. As he died insane in 1674, that may have had something to do with his departure.

The Rev William Horne, Head Master 1669–85, was educated at Eton (where his father had been Head Master) and was a scholar of King's College, Cambridge. He has been described as an "active, zealous man", whose tenure of office was very successful. He increased the numbers by attracting 'foreigners' (see *Boarding Houses,* page 51), spent money on books and encouraged the purchase of land adjoining the School Yard as a playing field. He was the first 'school master' to secure Governors' permission to marry, a practice that was already in place at Eton.

The Rev William Bolton, Head Master 1685–91, was educated at St John's College, Oxford, and took an MA at King's College, Cambridge. "He presided over a period of quiet success". He published two sermons in 1684 extolling the Stuarts.

The Rev Thomas Bryan, Head Master 1691–1730, educated at Eton, was a scholar of King's College,

Cambridge. His tenure, lasting 39 years, was a period of prosperity – at least at first. He was greatly assisted by George Brydges, Duke of Chandos, being a Governor. Chandos induced many of the nobility and other Whig supporters to send their sons to Harrow. Bryan restored the Contio and divided the School year into two 'halves'.

The Rev Dr James Cox, Head Master 1730–46, was educated at Merton College, Oxford. He had been Mr Bryan's Under Master since 1721 and married his daughter; it was a disastrous appointment. The School deteriorated during his time and he was ultimately dismissed because "he has for a great while last past lived a Disorderly, Drunken Idle Life and neglected the care of the School, by which means it is very much decreased and did on or about Easter Week abscond on account of his great Extravagance and running into Debt more than he is able to pay, therefore for these his misdoings we are of opinion that he shall be displaced from being Schoolmaster and declare the same to be void."

The Rev Dr Thomas Thackeray, Head Master 1746–60, was educated at Eton and King's College Cambridge. He was formerly Lower Master at Eton but resigned after a disagreement with the Head Master. As the Prince of Wales's Chaplain, he had a wide circle of friends among the nobility and was able to persuade many of them to send their sons to Harrow; this caused some displeasure among the local residents. However he is credited for "completely retrieving the position of the School" after the disastrous headmastership of Dr Cox. He was described by a pupil as "benign and humane", by the School historian, Christopher Tyerman, as "suave, likeable and literate". Later in his tenure, discipline became slack, resulting in a serious reduction in the number of boarders: at the end of his time there were just 80 boys in the School.

The Rev Dr Robert Carey Sumner, Head Master 1760–71, was educated at Eton and was a scholar of King's College, Cambridge. According to Tyerman, he was "one of the greatest Harrow Head Masters". He was responsible for a great rise in the level of scholarship and established a Monitors' library. Behaviour at Harrow (and at many similar schools) was very bad around this time: drinking, gambling, bullying and fighting were rife. One of the problems was that many of the boarding house keepers were independent and would not, or could not, impose discipline on their charges. Dr Sumner established disciplinary control of all boys, including those lodged in boarding houses. This prompted a row with Dr Glasse, an influential man who had allowed his pupils special privileges. Sumner replaced Glasse, creating new boarding houses with Dames in charge. The number of monitors was increased to six in 1771.

The Rev Benjamin Heath, Head Master 1771–85, was educated at Eton and King's College, Cambridge. His election caused a riot by those pupils favouring the appointment of Dr Samuel Parr, Sumner's righthand man and the local hero. However he dealt with the insurrection effectively and was commended for his firmness. He was an enthusiastic flogger, known by the boys as "Black Ben". A contemporary remarked, "Dr Heath seems to be a well behaved man and reckoned very severe in his school; this I think an advantage". He established a VI form for advanced boys under his tuition, but made no other notable educational changes. He abolished the archery competition which had become disorderly and replaced it with three 'speech days'. Heath's firm rule and wise direction laid a foundation the results of which became clearly visible in the time of his successor. Dr Heath was unmarried.

The Rev Dr Joseph Drury, Head Master 1785–1805, was educated at Westminster and a scholar of Trinity College, Cambridge. He had previously been an Assistant Master at Harrow from 1768, and ran the School as a family business. His wife was a sister of Dr Heath and his brother-in-law, Thomas

Bromley, was a Master who ran a boarding house; his nephew Mark Drury became Under Master and he also appointed Henry Drury, his eldest son, to the teaching staff. Dr Drury took the School to unprecedented numbers and social distinction. He was a 'networker' but appears to have been liked and admired, for all his suave friendliness and studied charm. One of the reasons for his popularity among the boys was that he was disinclined to punish personally. However he delegated beating to monitors and the barbarity of earlier regimes was not diminished.

The Rev George Butler, Head Master 1805–29, was a scholar and Fellow of Sidney Sussex College, Cambridge, and a Senior Wrangler. His was an unpopular appointment with the boys, who preferred Mark Drury, nephew of Butler's predecessor. A plot to blow him up in The Head Master's House was averted when the perpetrators were persuaded that an explosion would destroy the name boards carved by their predecessors. Dr Butler promoted scholarship, introduced 'copies' (see *"Harrow-Speak"*, page 100) and increased the number of prizes. Many 'men of letters' were trained by him, but numbers fell off towards the end of his time. He subsequently became Dean of Peterborough.

The Rev Charles Thomas Longley, Head Master 1829–36, was educated at Westminster and Trinity College, Cambridge. Good natured and good mannered, he was described by a former pupil as "well bred and courteous". To others he appeared polite, pompous, aloof and intellectual. He was certainly no disciplinarian and had little concept of the growing needs of education. The boys called him "Jacob" after his pet parrot. For him Harrow was a stepping stone to greater things: he was appointed Bishop of Ripon in 1836; of Durham in 1856; Archbishop of York in 1860 and of Canterbury in 1862.

The Rev Christopher Wordsworth, Head Master 1836–45, was educated at Winchester College and Trinity College, Cambridge, where he was Senior Classic. Numbers declined to 69 boys in 1844 but Wordsworth laid the foundations on which his successors were to build. He added Mathematics to the curriculum in 1837, abolished many abuses such as excessive fagging, and built the first School Chapel. Subsequently he became Bishop of Lincoln.

The Rev Charles John Vaughan, Head Master 1845–59, was educated at Rugby School and Trinity College, Cambridge where he was Senior Classic. Tactful, dignified and charming, he was an able administrator who achieved disruption without friction. He increased the size of the School from 69 in 1845 to 466 in 1859. He reformed the monitorial system and built a new, bigger Chapel, paying for the chancel out of his own pocket. One of the greatest elements in his success was his ability to attract men of quality to his teaching staff. Among his appointments were BF Westcott, FW Farrar, SA Pears, EH Bradby – a future bishop and three future headmasters. Dr Vaughan is thought to have been the victim of blackmail over an alleged incident involving a boy, this being the reason for his refusal of the several bishoprics he was offered. He eked out his days as Master of the Temple 1864–94 and Dean of Llandaff 1879–97.

Dr Henry Montagu Butler (OH) was Head Master from 1860 to 1885. The son of Head Master, George Butler, he was educated at Harrow and was a scholar of Trinity College, Cambridge. One of Dr Vaughan's brightest pupils, he was appointed at the age of 26. He continued Vaughan's work in building up the School's reputation as a scholastic establishment. Christopher Tyerman wrote, "Butler presided over one of the great powerhouses of the late nineteenth century British

Establishment during a headmastership that defined Harrow's reputation, character and standing." He was in many ways like a schoolboy himself: eager, earnest and energetic. He enjoyed the company of his pupils and could communicate with them on topics of mutual interest from classics to cricket. He forged a new quasi-religious, quasi-secular cult of 'The School', one that famously found voice in the songs of Edward Bowen and John Farmer. Later Dr Butler became Master of Trinity College, Cambridge.

The Rev James Welldon, Head Master 1885–1898, was educated at Eton, and was a scholar and Fellow of King's College Cambridge. He had been Master of Dulwich College. The School continued to prosper under him and a new boarding house, Newlands, was opened in 1889. Dr Welldon greatly accelerated the process of modernisation: he reorganised the academic structure of the School and reformed the curriculum. He, like his immediate predecessors, believed in the power of the pulpit, communicating with his pupils by sermons. He exuded a self-confidence that bordered on arrogance and was a more popular Head Master with the boys, with whom he communicated well, than with his staff, whom he rarely consulted or took advice from. He was known as "Porker" by the boys. Subsequently he became Bishop of Calcutta. He was unmarried.

The Rev Joseph Wood, Head Master 1899–1910, educated at Manchester Grammar School and Balliol College, Oxford, had previously been Head Master of Tonbridge. He was an elegant, old fashioned scholar of the old school. He had good looks and manners, and a large private income. Appointed at the age of 57, for him the headmastership was akin to a retirement job. He tried to maintain a high standard of classical scholarship, but ensured that his duties were lighter than those of his predecessors: he relied heavily on his Assistant at The Head Master's House, and had a Chaplain. Christopher Tyerman wrote, "He displayed all the symptoms of a man enjoying an unexpected boost to his standing at the end of a worthy but less than outstanding schoolmaster's career". He was a generous benefactor to the School.

The Rev Dr Lionel Ford, Head Master 1910–25, was educated at Repton and was a scholar of King's College, Cambridge. A classical scholar, cricketer, Cambridge golf 'blue' and former President of the Union, he had previously been Head Master of Repton. He was a man of massive self-confidence (and hubris) but devoted to Harrow and popular with the boys. His foremost interest was the education of his pupils. He made numerous improvements, abolishing 'pupil room' (see *Academic Curriculum,* page 106), introducing optional studies to the VI form and removing the distinction between Classical and Modern sides. Ford was also a builder and the centre of the School was transformed in his time. However he was not a good communicator, especially with adults, and he was a poor public speaker. One of his great delights was the piggery he kept at the bottom of The Head Master's House garden. He was later Dean of York.

Dr Cyril Norwood, Head Master 1926–34, was educated at Merchant Taylors' School and St John's College, Oxford, where he gained 'firsts' in 'Mods' and 'Greats'. He was a civil servant before becoming Headmaster of Bristol Grammar School. He had the manner and habits of an austere Olympian mandarin, an administrator rather than a teacher, a theorist rather than a form room practitioner, an educational pundit. He

was very keen on 'team effort' and deplored acclaim of the individual. He was responsible for rugby becoming the major winter game at Harrow. Appreciating the importance of games in boys' lives at school, he was the first Head Master actively to recruit teaching staff with sporting expertise. There were suggestions that he never really liked Harrow – and that it was mutual. Harrow snobs condemned him as a plebeian; he was nicknamed "Boots". Dr Norwood was knighted in 1938.

Dr Paul Vellacott CBE, Head Master 1934–39, was educated at Marlborough College and Peterhouse, Cambridge. A history scholar, formerly a Cambridge don, he was intelligent and stylish, calm, precise and unworldly, affecting a donnish persona. He was a good public speaker; sociable and accessible. He made a point of consulting senior advisers but felt no obligation to act on their advice. He saw no virtue in obfuscation or deceit, was a plain talker and no sufferer of fools. When a financial crisis loomed in 1938–9, he managed it well. Later he was Master of Peterhouse.

Mr Arthur Paul Boissier, Head Master 1940–42, had been educated at St John's School, Leatherhead, and Balliol College, Oxford, where he was an exhibitioner and where he had gained 'blues' at both cricket and hockey. He had been an Assistant Master, teaching Mathematics, since 1919 and House Master of Moretons since 1929. Known as 'Boss', he was a wartime 'fill-in' as Head Master. He had become engaged in a long-running feud with EM Venables, House Master of The Park, who had resented Boissier's appointment as House Master of Moretons in preference to himself.

Unfortunately Boissier continued to fight these battles through his headmastership. He manoeuvred the School successfully through the difficult early days of the war but in 1941–42 only 70 names were registered and half the School had been leased to Malvern College. Staff redundancies had to be made and, not surprisingly, personal relationships became cruelly exposed. Boissier left with the other casualties.

Dr Ralph Westwood Moore, Head Master 1942–53, was educated at Wolverhampton Grammar School and Christ Church, Oxford, where he gained a 'first' in 'Mods' and 'Greats'. He had previously been Headmaster of Bristol Grammar School, but was only 36 when he arrived at Harrow. Christopher Tyerman describes his appointment as "an inspired choice". The opportunity for revival was there and Moore was its instrument. On his arrival the bill numbered 298; in his last it had grown to 566. Times were certainly hard with food-rationing and general austerity but Moore managed to make some outstanding appointments to the staff. He was a deeply religious, scrupulously honest and just man – known by the boys as "Holy Joe" – and his untimely death in post at the age of 47 was a tragedy both for his family and the School.

Dr Robert Leoline James, Head Master 1953–71, educated at Rossall and Jesus College, Oxford, was another 'double first' in Classics. He had previously been Head Master of Chigwell School and High Master of St Paul's. Known to friends as "Jimmy" but to the boys as "Jankers", Dr James was in many ways the most successful Head Master of the twentieth century. He was also fortunate in that he inherited a school that could only go up and the post-war economic revival allowed it to do so. Dr James was a small, neatly dressed man who managed to create an image beyond his stature.

He was an undemonstrative conservative, with a pathological hatred of the press, and a determination not to follow modish trends, either in education or any other arena. He trick was to appear to have time for everyone, but there was no doubting his political shrewdness, his managerial skills, his willingness to delegate and his ability to have an intimate knowledge of activity on the Hill without apparently leaving his study. Dr James, in his desire to preside over the School's 400th anniversary, probably stayed in office too long, but he was certainly a hard act to follow.

Mr Brian Michael Stanislaus Hoban, Head Master 1971–81, was educated at Charterhouse and University College, Oxford, where he was a classical scholar. He had previously been Head Master of St Edmund's Canterbury and Bradfield College. Tyerman describes him as "a scholarly thoughtful man with a gentle wit, far shrewder than his mild appearance indicated". He inherited the oppressive legacy of Dr James, which regarded all change as unnecessary and undesirable. Michael Hoban was a reformer but he met with hostility from his senior staff, who had been allowed to build their power centres under Dr James. Michael Hoban was not a politician and so was less adept at manipulating dissident forces. He was an honest, principled and affable man, who always wanted to do the right thing; this was sometimes misunderstood for weakness. His headmastership spanned a difficult economic period and he had no luck. He was perhaps also unfortunate in having a domineering Chairman of Governors and a popular but inexperienced Bursar.

Maybe he would have been a happier man had he remained a House Master at Shrewsbury, as had been his original intention, but he managed to introduce many changes to Harrow and left it a much less stuffy place than when he arrived.

Mr Ian Stafford Beer CBE, Head Master 1981–91, was educated at Whitgift and St Catherine's College, Cambridge, where he read Zoology and was a member of the University rugby teams from 1952 to 1954, being captain in his last year. He also played rugby for England in 1955. Before Harrow, Ian Beer had

been Head Master of Ellesmere College and Lancing College. He was Chairman of The Head Masters' Conference in 1980, Chairman of the Physical Education for National Curriculum Committee 1990–91, President of the Rugby Football Union 1993–94 and Chairman of the Independent Schools Council 1997–2001.

Mr Nicholas Raymond Bomford, Head Master 1991–99, was educated at Kelly College and Trinity College, Oxford, where he read History and captained the Oxford University Rifle Club. He shot for England in 1960. He had previously been Headmaster of Monmouth College and Uppingham School.

Mr Barnaby John Lenon, Head Master 1999–2011, was educated at Eltham College, Keble College, Oxford, where he read Geography, and St John's College, Cambridge, where he won the university prize for Education. He was previously Deputy Head at Highgate School and Headmaster of Trinity School, Croydon.

THE BOARDING HOUSES

"The Schoolmaster may recover, over and above the children of the inhabitants within the parish, so many foreigners as the whole number may be well taught and applied, and the place can conveniently contain, by the judgment and discretion of the Governors."

John Lyon's Statutes

THE FOUNDER'S ORIGINAL INTENTION had been to provide a classical education for thirty (later increased to forty) boys of Harrow: the free or foundation scholars. By 1651 the Master had ceased to live in the School House and in the 1670s William Horne received an increased allowance from the Governors for setting up a House to accommodate boarders. Quite soon the 'foreigners' began to outnumber the free scholars and in 1721 there were forty free scholars in a school of 144. By 1739, the number of free scholars had fallen to fourteen, by 1780 to seven or eight and in 1816 there were only three out of a school of nearly 300.

All these 'foreigners' required accommodation and for many generations, in addition to the Schoolmaster, this was provided by landladies or 'Dames'. Masters also turned to this method of supplementing their income, notably Henry Reeves, the Writing Master, in the 1750s and 1760s and Joseph Drury in the 1770s. The Head Master in particular saw boarding as a vital form of income.

Head Master William Thackeray, an Old Etonian, was a friend of the Prince of Wales and Harrow began to attract the sons of aristocratic families. Some of the grander and more prosperous were able to set up their own establishments with servants and private tutors but, to accommodate the slightly less grand, Dr Samuel Glasse, who also had friends among the nobility, set up an up-market boarding house. He also demanded special privileges for his boys until, in 1767, the Governors decided that all boys should conform to school rules. Dr Glasse closed his house.

By 1800 the growing School had ensured that almost all the Masters were taking in boarders. In 1804 Henry Drury had twelve, Messrs Bland, Roberts and Webb four or five each; even the School doctor took a few boys. The Dames' houses also expanded both in number and size, especially Mrs Leith's (on the site of the present Vicarage), which accommodated up

Druries, 1930s

Facing page: The Head Master's House, 1860

The Knoll House group, 1896. Although designated a large House in 1870, there are still just 35 boys; Mr Bosworth-Smith appears intent on making up the numbers by his own family

to thirty-five boys and survived until 1841, and Mrs Armstrong's (on the site of the War Memorial steps). A succession of extensions to **The Head Master's House**, notably by Dr Butler, had rendered it capable of holding up to 120 boys in 1818.

But these were not boarding houses in the modern sense, and transfers between houses were both easy and common. Moreover the Dames had no authority over their boarders beyond those of a landlady and there were disciplinary problems.

However a change was to take place in the next 40 years as entrepreneurial Masters began to acquire, either as owners or as tenants, some large buildings on the Hill. Towards the end of the 18th century, the Rev T Bromley had bought the Abbey; this house was enlarged by the Rev Henry Drury in 1818. His successor, Mr Holmes, rebuilt the House in 1864 and renamed it **Druries**.

In 1811 the Rev WJJ Drury opened a house, known as High Street, on the site of the Bursar's Office but absconded one night leaving massive debts to tradesmen; it was rebuilt by the Rev W Oxenham in 1828 and enlarged by Mr HE Hutton in 1881. Hutton named the House **Moretons** after two early members of the House who were relatives of his.

In 1819, the Rev SE Batten bought the Manor House, which he renamed **The Grove**. It is a building with a long and interesting history, being originally the Rectory. It had been occupied by various Archbishops of Canterbury, who were Lords of the Manor, and in 1773 it had been let to RB Sheridan's family. It was burnt down in 1833 but speedily rebuilt.

In 1831 the Rev WW Phelps purchased Flambards, the former home of the 2nd Baron Northwick, changed its name to **The Park**, and opened it as a boarding house. These were private ventures from which the School derived no financial benefit; on the other hand the opportunities for profit may have encouraged these Masters to recruit more boys for the School – and also to have made their salaries from teaching a less important issue. The Governors had also ruled that Masters had to receive the Head Master's permission to open a House.

When Dr Vaughan became Head Master in 1845, there were just 69 boys in the School in four 'large' Houses. But with numbers rising and young Masters keen to earn some money, four new 'large' Houses and several 'small' Houses were opened. These were either for boys considered to be unsuitable for immediate entry to a 'large' House, or simply as an overflow. The terms 'large' and 'small' became accepted classifications. This marked the beginning of the modern House-based federal school.

By the 1830s there were some signs of Houses achieving their own identity: House colours for games began to appear; in 1839 Phelps passed on the boarders in The Park to his successor. In 1846 Mr GT Warner bought a pair of semi-detached villas on London Road and a year later opened a House, which he named **West Acre**. Later that year Custos's Cottage between Armstrong's and Ivy House (on the site of the War Memorial) was demolished and a new House, **Church Hill**, was built by Mr Middlemist. This was extended by his successor, Mr Cruikshank, who knocked down Ivy House in 1879. In 1848 the Rev H Keary built a house on the High Street opposite The Park gates. However a legal wrangle over "ancient lights" (a curious dispute about windows) with the occupants of neighbouring Marilliers, meant that the house was not able to be occupied as a boarding house until 1864, when the building was extended and became a Large House under the Rev EH Bradby. When the House was taken over by Major EW Freeborn in 1919, he gave it the name **Bradbys**.

In 1853 Mr F Rendall built a house at the top of Grove Hill on the site of an old pond; for some years it was known as Grove Hill until Mr E Graham named it **Rendalls** in 1912. In 1867 Mr R Bosworth Smith built **The Knoll**, first as a Small House then a Large House in 1870. **Byron House** (known up to 1846 as Pond House) is thought to have been built by Head Master Thomas Bryan, and is one of the oldest houses on the Hill. It was occupied by Mr Phelps between 1828 and 1831 with about a dozen boarders. From 1849 to 1867 it was again a boarding house under Mr EH Vaughan followed by Mr AG Watson. After a period in Matthew Arnold's ownership, the house became a Small House under Mr Hallam in 1880. It no longer belongs to the School.

Mr Marshall built **Newlands** on a portion of the Harrow Park estate in 1889 and in 1893 Mr Davidson built **Elmfield** on Grove Hill and transferred the boys and traditions of Mr Watson's in the High Street to the new House. Vaughan also encouraged some Small Houses for boys (a) who were delicate, (b) for whom it was the parents' preference, and (c) waiting for a vacancy in a Large House.

Dr Vaughan himself built two houses at the top of Grove Hill in 1859, known as **Grove Hill House**. By this time there were 460 boys in the School. The Rev BF Westcott opened Grove Hill as a Small House; the southerly house was renamed The Foss by Mr Moriarty in 1915. In 1864 Mr Hayward built **Garlands**, a Small House lower down Peterborough Road from The Knoll. In 1870 Mr Rendall built a second house, **Hillside,** below his garden in Peterborough Road. It opened as a Small House under the Rev WD Bushell.

The apparent confusion of the names of the buildings with, for example, both Moretons and Bradbys being at different times known as 'High Street' and two houses being called 'Grove Hill', was avoided by referring to each by the name of the House Master. Up to the 1911 Register, Houses were known as Mr Marshall's or Mr Davidson's, abbreviated as they still are today, to initials FEM or HODD in bill books or lists.

However, the federal House system did have its problems. As some of the Houses were actually owned by absentees, negotiations for repairs and improvements were often tortuous. In the 1880s Head Master Welldon expressed his dissatisfaction with the quality of the accommodation in Houses. Mr Bowen had redesigned The Grove so that almost

When Dr Vaughan became Head Master in 1845, there were just 69 boys in the School in four 'large' Houses. But with numbers rising and young Masters keen to earn some money, four new 'large' Houses and several 'small' Houses were opened.

Top row (from left to right): The Head Master's; The Grove, 1932; Druries; The Knoll on its former site in Peterborough Road (now Masters' accommodation); Newlands (from the garden); West Acre from the garden, c1904

every boy had a single room and Mr Stogdon had endeavoured to follow suit, but such was the pressure on numbers and the reluctance of the owners (both active and absent) to spend money on such a cause that progress was slow. None the less, Harrow never went the way of many other schools that were building dormitories. There was a protracted battle over sanitary conditions in 1894.

Another difficulty was encountered when a House Master wished to pass on his House to a successor. The solution was for the School to buy the Houses. In 1885, the Harrow Park Trust was formed (investments being made mostly by Old Harrovians) to purchase The Park at the end of Mr Hayward's term of office. In 1889, Newlands became a Trust property, Druries in 1893, The Knoll and Elmfield in 1914. In 1917 the Governors took over the Trust and, in 1919 they bought Moretons and, in 1925, West Acre (which had been burned down and rebuilt in 1909). The last House to be acquired was Bradbys in 1930. These eleven Large Houses remained the School establishment until the opening of the twelfth House in 2010. Of the Small Houses, only The Foss, to be replaced by Gayton House in 1997, reopened after the war as a 'waiting' or 'overspill' House.

In spite of all being now tenants of the School, the House Masters continued to wield considerable power and were fiercely independent: for example, when School dress became 'bluer and greyers' in 1919, Mr Pope of The Grove insisted upon his boys wearing the former school dress of tailcoats until 1929. Some continued to be a thorn in the Head Master's flesh right up to the 1970s.

In 1930 the period of tenure of a House Master was fixed at fifteen years and in 1936 a new scheme was introduced whereby new House Masters surrendered financial independence in return for a fixed salary and capitation grant. Existing holders had the choice of joining the scheme or not. All but three did, and the last 'independent' House Master, Mr CR Browne, left Elmfield in 1948.

The financial difficulties of the late 1930s, followed by the outbreak of war in 1939, brought about a serious decline in numbers. In 1939 West Acre was closed; in 1940 Newlands (to be used as a temporary extension of Harrow Hospital); in 1941 Rendalls and in 1942, Bradbys. The arrival in 1942 of Malvern College,

which occupied these Houses in addition to Garlands and Deyne Court in Harrow Park, probably saved both schools from closure.

After the war, the financial situation improved, numbers increased and the closed Houses were reopened. Further increases in the 1960s led to extensions being built onto every House. The arrival of the Shepherd Churchill Hall in 1976 made a further difference: the kitchens, sculleries, food stores and staff rooms were no longer needed, creating further space for boys' rooms.

The 'new' Knoll, built in 1981, was the first phase in a refurbishment programme for all the boarding houses. With the boys of The Knoll permanently established in their new home, each House then moved into the 'Old Knoll' while its building was refurbished with new plumbing, roofing, central heating, electric wiring as appropriate. The boys returned to their Houses with mixed feelings: the carpets, butteries (where they could cook rudimentary meals) and improved décor were generally welcome, the fixed and fitted furniture less so. They regretted the demise of the old desks and chairs that had been passed down in House sales for generations, and they deplored the abolition of drapes (sheets of material such as curtains, blankets or flags, which had be used to cover the unsightly walls and crumbling plaster in earlier days). But this modernisation had been necessary; now the Houses could be used for commercial lets in the school holidays. This lengthy and expensive business took over twelve years.

In 2008, the uneasy feeling that the expansion in the numbers in each House, in particular The Head Master's whose numbers had climbed to well over 90, had not altogether been for the best, led to the realisation of the suggestion, often mooted over the years, that there should be a twelfth House. Although the economic climate appeared to be inauspicious, the Governors took the decision to go ahead with its construction: Lyon's House was built on the site of Peterborough Cottage, just above the Rifle Range in Garlands Lane in 2010. As the first House built for over thirty years, its accomodation is far superior to the other Houses. Whether this will prove to be divisive remains to be seen.

Of the other Small Houses only The Foss, later transferred to Gayton House, remains in use as an 'overflow' House for boys. Many are no longer School property, although Hillside, Grove Hill House and Deyne Court are now for staff accommodation.

(Lower row, left to right): The Park (garden side); Moretons from the garden; Bradbys, 1860; Rendalls; Elmfield, c1902; Lyon's, in Garlands Lane, opened in 2010

THE SCHOOL BUILDINGS

THE OLD SCHOOLS. JOHN Lyon's school house, now known as the Old Schools, comprised the western wing of the present building with an east side projection holding a spiral oak staircase, giving it an L-shaped footprint. The walls were of red brick with sand-coloured freestone dressings, three massive brick chimneys giving high relief to the west facade. It was designed by an architect named Sly with conservative Tudor details typical of schools of this period. The building consisted of three cellars at ground level, a school room later known as the Fourth Form Room on the first floor, three rooms on the second floor providing accommodation for the Master, and an attic known as the 'cock loft'.

By 1800 the School had outgrown its first building and Head Master George Butler decided to double its size. The architect was Charles Robert Cockerell, architect to the Dean and Chapter of St Paul's Cathedral. Cockerell, who went on to win the RIBA Gold Medal and to become President of the RIBA, is best known for the Ashmolean Museum in Oxford. Following Cockerell's design, an east wing housing a speech room (later known as Old Speech Room) was built, giving a symmetrical facade to the south, and entrance steps up to a *piano nobile* entrance were added. Above the Speech Room were three new rooms and below, a cloister. Large oriel windows were formed in the south and east walls (including one in the Fourth Form Room) and the gables were capped with Flemish style crow-steps. The roof was given a central clock tower and weathervane, and the clock numerals and hands in gold leaf on a Harrow blue face were a fitting climax to a majestic design. It was completed in 1819.

The Old Schools c1890, before the shops on Church Hill were demolished.

In 1929 the row of houses between the School Yard and the top of West Street was demolished and a grand flight of steps was created on the axis of the Old Schools entrance to lead up by easy stages from the High Street. Level terraces, with planting, lawns and clipped yew trees were formed on either side of the steps. The walls of the Yard are of the same red brick as the Old Schools, the columns topped with Portland stone capitals and classical urns. Between the columns are wrought iron railings with ornamental gates to the south and east. The vista from the High Street, up these steps to the School Yard and Old Schools, is dramatic.

Old Speech Room was converted into a gallery to the design of Alan Irvine in 1976. A mezzanine floor was built; heating and air conditioning were then installed. The Fourth Form Room remains as a prized example of a Jacobean school room, but the rest of the building now houses the History department.

Chapel. The present Chapel, which came into use in 1855, replaced Dr Wordsworth's smaller chapel, which had been on the same site since 1839. The eminent architect, Sir George Gilbert Scott, perhaps best known for his designs for St Pancras Station, the Albert Memorial and St Giles Church, Camberwell, was employed. The style is High Victorian Gothic, a development of fourteenth century Decorated Gothic. The design incorporated a nave, chancel with a larger apsidal end and two aisles. The south aisle was added a year later as a memorial to those killed in the Crimean War. The fall in ground level, allowed for a crypt chapel and vestry at the east end. The crypt was converted into a memorial chapel by Sir Charles Nicholson before the grander War Memorial was conceived.

Externally the walls are of flint with Portland stone dressings; the flint is thought by some to be inappropriate for the local geology and out of keeping with the materials used for other buildings on the Hill. The roof is of ornamental plain tiles with an ironwork design along the ridge. It is crowned by a delicate spire, sheeted in copper, with crockets along each of the ribs. This spire, though smaller than that of St Mary's Church at the highest point, contributes significantly to the silhouette of the Hill. In 1901 two transepts designed by Sir Aston Webb were added at the north and south sides of the chancel, as a memorial to those that fell in the South African War. At the same time two porches were added at the southwest and northwest corners, providing improved off-street entrances to the Chapel.

Internally the Chapel is lofty and dignified. There is an organ and choir gallery at the west end. The walls are covered in memorial plaques and the stained glass windows depict various biblical scenes, many of them themselves memorials. In 2003 the chancel was re-ordered and oak choir stalls, in keeping with the High Victorian interior, were added.

The New Schools were built at the same time as the Chapel to provide more form rooms for the expanding School. The building is situated on the north side of the Chapel where there had previously been a pond with a barn at its eastern end. Later the barn had become a dancing school. In 1855 the pond was filled in with material excavated from the foundations of the Chapel and the dancing school was demolished. The structure has been variously described as "grand Jacobean/Elizabethan with late Gothic touches around the arches and windows" and "a blend of Tudor and perpendicular". Principal features of the original were bay windows on either side of the entrance; gable ends, parapets and chimney caps characteristic of the period were modelled on an old mansion in Norfolk. The architect was Frederick Barnes of Ipswich. The building consisted of three stories, two form rooms on each and a staircase in the middle of the west front; in 1907 the bay windows were expanded into two more form rooms. In 1924 a new wing of three form rooms was added on the north side with an entrance from the terrace.

The Vaughan Library, built in memory of Head Master Dr Vaughan lies between the Chapel and The Head Master's House, set back from the High Street and fronted by a small lawn. The architect was again Sir George Gilbert Scott. It is an oblong, gable-ended building in Ruskinian Gothic style. It is built of red brick ornamented with patterns of vitrified blue and yellow, a style that became typical of Victorian Harrow. The doors and windows feature stone dressings and polychrome surrounds. The west front has buttresses, arcades and a porch. The east side is plainer but a bold oriel is a strong feature and, with the fall in the ground, the basement shows, giving additional importance to this front. There is a blind arcade of arches on Purbeck marble columns at lower level, under a *piano nobile* of pointed headed windows. At high level in the central gable there is a rose window. The tiled roof is high and steep-pitched. The foundation stone was laid by Lord Palmerston in 1861 and the library was opened two years

The New Schools, built at the same time as the Chapel, 1857

The Science Schools (left) is now used for Economics and Chemistry, and the Museum Schools for Biology: the magnificent cedar tree which, until recently dominated the lower Chapel Terrace, became unsafe and was felled in 2009. The Music Schools (right)

later. In 1998 Kenneth Reed & Associates designed a major refurbishment. The roof was stripped, with new custom-made tiles on the east side where a stunning impact was made with the juxtaposition of fresh reds and dark blues. Stonework was cleaned outside and inside to reveal delicate pinks and creams under the ubiquitous grey. New stone finials were copied from nineteenth century steel engravings. Ladder access and walkways to the upper shelves were provided, more or less doubling the accessible shelf space and clearing the centre of the building for improved study areas. A new circular staircase descends to mezzanine and lower levels, where two former form rooms have been incorporated into the library. The library is now much more suitable for modern usage.

Speech Room. In 1871 the Governors and Head Master resolved to celebrate the tercentenary of John Lyon's Charter by building a hall large enough to seat the whole School. The Head Master and Governors selected as architect William Burges, perhaps best known for his design for the restoration of Cardiff Castle. Burges was one of the greatest architects of the Victorian era, but his designs were often extravagant and strong disagreement arose over his plans for Speech Room. This caused a delay between the laying of the foundation stone in 1874 and the completion of the building in 1877. The final design was something of a compromise, not a characteristic for which Burges was renowned.

The building is semi-circular in shape, the east front being straight, following the line of the High Street. The exterior is of red brick with polychrome dressings but the two asymmetric towers were omitted from the original building. The north tower, by Sir Charles Nicholson, was added in 1919, thus realising Burges's intentions. The south tower was to have been by far the higher of the two, but doubts arose as to the possibility of the foundations bearing the weight of the proposed structure, and this tower was not completed until 1925, when its plan was modified by Sir Herbert Baker to make it fit with the design of the War Memorial building. On its completion the South Tower was given a bell to be used for summoning the School to Chapel as well as to Speech Room.

Internally the building is an amphitheatre, with steep, tiered seating. The seats face a platform with two rows of choir stalls behind. The ceiling is of timber boarding, the central part flat. Beyond is an ingenious arrangement of vaulting supported on pointed arches on fourteen paired columns, which follow the semi-circular shape of the building. The columns and arches are richly decorated in red, blue and gold. The principal windows to the auditorium are grand in scale, with semi-circular heads and an intricate design of arches and roundels. There is an organ whose console is in the well of the hall, the pipes being in the two towers.

In a niche in the external wall of the southern tower there is a statue of Queen Elizabeth I. She holds an orb and sceptre, finished in gold leaf. The statue, originally at Ashridge Park, was placed there in 1925.

Museum Schools. Lying further down the eastern slope of the hill are the Museum Schools, completed in 1886, incorporating the Butler Centre, a memorial to Head Master Montagu Butler. Another great Victorian architect was employed: Basil Champneys, best known for his design for Mansfield College, Oxford. It is built of red brick, with brick mouldings and dressings, in a spirited Shavian style, It was the first of Harrow's buildings to depart from the seriousness of High Victorian Gothic. A grand external staircase, with square terracotta balusters leading to the two upper storeys, is redolent of the Chateaux of the Loire. The top floor, now mainly used for public examinations, was formerly a museum; the rest of the building houses the Biology department. There is a superb view from the balconies and little corbelled-out oriels. For many years that to the southwest was partially obscured by a magnificent cedar tree. Sadly the tree was felled in 2009, but its removal has enabled the building to be fully enjoyed from the Chapel terrace.

Music Schools. The flourishing state of School music under the direction of John Farmer led to the building of a music school at the top of Peterborough Road, above Hillside. It was a small brick structure, now used as a lecture room and housing the Museum of Harrow Life. In 1890 what has been described as "a more commodious and well equipped building" was erected half way down the lane to the football fields, once known as Music Hill, now Football Lane. The architect was Edward Prior, later Slade Professor of Art at Cambridge and a pupil of the better known Norman Shaw. The best frontage, a large canted bay with Venetian windows, faces east. The Music Schools were opened in 1891. The building provides a concert hall, practice rooms and a band room. The acoustics are excellent. A free-standing small recording studio, designed by Kenneth Reed & Associates, was added at the east side in 2007.

Art Schools. The first part of this building was completed in 1896, with an additional wing in 1913. The exterior, designed by WC Marshall, shows Jacobean influence with Dutch gables and another fine oriel window, not unlike those in the Old Schools and the War Memorial. A low extension to the north end, to the design of S Pointon Taylor, was added in 1913 and a mezzanine floor in 1987. The building was further refurbished in 2009 to include an art gallery which is open to the public.

The War Memorial. Much smoother and more civilised than the Victorian buildings, the War Memorial takes its style from its surroundings, leaving out the trimmings but adding some Baroque detail. It comprises an oblong central block with wings of equal size and shape but slightly different orientation on the north and south sides, aligned to follow the slight change of direction of the High Street. It is arranged on two grand storeys. There are gables facing on to the High Street at each end of the building. At the centre of the High Street front is an oriel window over three arched windows at ground floor; another oriel on the south front lights the Alex Fitch Room. These reflect similar features in the Old Schools.

The main entrance is from the south and provides a ceremonial way from the High Street to Speech Room. It is faced by a broad flight of steps up to Church Hill and a spacious forecourt. The walls against Church Hill and the High Street are of flint with Portland stone dressings.

The entrance from the forecourt is through the shrine, whose walls are carved with the names of the Old Harrovians who lost their lives in the First World War, leading into a large space with steps at intervals leading up towards the level of the Speech Room. On

The Art Schools in 1900: a new wing was added in 1913, and the Art department took over the adjacent Leaf Schools in 2007

the righthand side is a second shrine commemorating the dead of the Second World War. On the left is a double staircase leading up to the Old Harrovian Room, the Masters' Room and the Alex Fitch Room, created in memory of an Old Harrovian killed in France in 1918, aged nineteen.

The Leaf Schools were designed by ALN Russell in 1936, re-using some of the brickwork from Sheridan's stables at The Grove. The northern end stands on the site of a former laundry. The first floor was added in the early 1960s. For many years the Leaf Schools housed the Modern Languages department but in 2008 it was taken over by the Art department.

The Mathematics & Physics Schools, just south of Football Lane, between the Museum Schools and the Music Schools, were constructed in 1971. It is an unassuming one and two-storey building with slated pyramid roofs. It was the first attempt at building outside the boarding houses since the Second World War, and the lack of experience shown by future users, architects and builders was all too apparent. The rooms are spacious and airy but the interiors revealed several important design faults.

The Shepherd Churchill Hall, the dining hall for the whole School, was opened in 1976.

The Shepherd Churchill Hall was designed by Dennis Lennon & Partners and built in 1976. It is approached by a slope from the High Street, flanked by two small lodges (the offices of the Estates Bursar and the Harrow Association and Harrow Development Trust) parting to two flights of steps, separated by terraced pools. At the base of the steps is a small courtyard with pergolas. The building, cleverly designed to disguise its vastness by ingenious use of the contours of the hill, has a discreetly traditional brick exterior with a big pitched roof and a central clock-turret. Inside, a further flight of steps leads to the main dining area. As a concession to the former traditional dining in Houses, the hall is split up into separate units by brick piers, thus giving the large space a more interesting flavour. The increasing use by the School and the need to improve the serving area have led to several internal revisions.

Upstairs the Shepherd Churchill Room, used for Masters' and guests' dining, was extended after a fire in 1987. Balconies and a rooftop lawn give wonderful views across the golf course to the Wembley stadium arch and central London beyond.

The Churchill Schools are neatly tucked into the north side of the hill, lying between the Leaf Schools

and The Copse. Access is from Grove Hill. It comprises Design and Technology workshops and on the lower level at the west end, the Geography School. It is a crisp, contemporary design by Kenneth Reed & Associates, with roof lights and glazed corners. It was built in 1987.

The Ryan Theatre, at the bottom of the Bill Yard steps, occupies the site of the former Workshops and backs onto the wall of the Old Gymnasium (now Squash Courts and Fencing Salle). The main benefactor was Sir Peter Green, former Chairman of Lloyd's, the insurance market, and the theatre was given his wife's maiden name. The theatre opened in 1993 after nearly eight years of delays, partly for uncertainties of funding but mainly due to planning objections, culminating in a successful appeal. It was designed by Kenneth Reed & Associates. The building, almost cubical in shape, is in stripped classical style, clad in brick, reconstituted stone and white render, and decorated with recesses and cornices; it fits well into the predominantly red brick character of the other School buildings. The fan-shaped auditorium, seating just under 400 people on two levels, provides exceptional intimacy but the back-stage facilities are generous for a small theatre. The acoustic design presented the architects with a challenge but the lead roof is an essential element in insulating the interior from the noise of aircraft on the way to Northolt and of activity in the adjacent squash courts. All School drama productions, except for Shakespeare plays, now take place in the Ryan Theatre, which is also host to some visiting performers.

The Modern Languages Schools are situated off Football Lane, on a site formerly occupied by Spinney Cottages. The building, another designed by Kenneth Reed & Associates in 2008, sits comfortably alongside Edward Prior's Music Schools of 1890. It has been designed to maintain the rhythm of both vertical and horizontal surfaces of its senior neighbour. The brick work levels, building line and height blend the new with the old, and the turrets are reflected in a contemporary way.

Inside the building, modern ventilation techniques provide even temperatures without air conditioning, good solar-shaded daylight and excellent sound-proofing.

The Ryan Theatre, built on the site of the old gymnasium and named after the late wife of Sir Peter Green, the major benefactor, was opened in 1993. The annual Shakespeare play is still performed in Speech Room

THE FOURTH FORM ROOM

IF EVER THE ATMOSPHERE of a room could cast the mind back hundreds of years, it is in the Fourth Form Room. Following John Lyon's instructions, it was completed in 1615 and occupies the whole of the first floor of the old wing of the Old Schools; entrance is on the left at the top of the steps. Although known as the Fourth Form Room, it actually began as the 'school room' and, until well into the nineteenth century, the room was the only available hall for whole School assemblies and the only indoor space for boys to go. In the ensuing centuries it has been used by many forms other than the fourth.

After 1820, when the new wing had been built, (Old) Speech Room was used for general assemblies but Bill continued to be taken in the Fourth Form Room regularly until 1872 and after that, in wet weather, until about 1890. Up to the end of the century prayers were read in it on certain days in the week. Other uses of the room were for floggings by the Head Master and public 'whoppings' by the Head of the School, both of which continued until Dr Norwood's Head Mastership in the 1920s.

The Fourth Form Room may not be the oldest school room in the country, but it is surely unique in that it has been left as it was about 150 years ago. Most schools with old buildings have modernised the interiors to become libraries or common rooms of some sort. Originally, the room was symmetrical, but this feature was lost when the oriel window was added at the south end in 1819. The lighting and heating installations were, of course, added later, and the leading of the windows on the west and north sides has been made to conform with the pattern in the oriel. A window on the right of the doorway preserves the old pattern.

The walls are wainscoted with oak up to half height, above which they are plastered and whitewashed and covered with name-boards. At one time a small door, whose existence is still marked by newer oak panels, led into the adjoining form room. At the north end is the Head Master's desk in the style of a pulpit, and at the south end the Usher's* chair and table. Parallel with the side walls are eight rows of unbacked benches, divided by gangways which run down and across the middle of the room. The modifications to this simple arrangement

Detail from the carving on the wall panels of the Fourth Form Room (right); A print of Lord Byron on the 'Peachey stone', a tomb in St Mary's churchyard where he composed the lines, "O spot of my youth..." (far right)

Facing page: The Fourth Form Room from the oriel window overlooking the School yard . Note the gas lighting installed in 1855

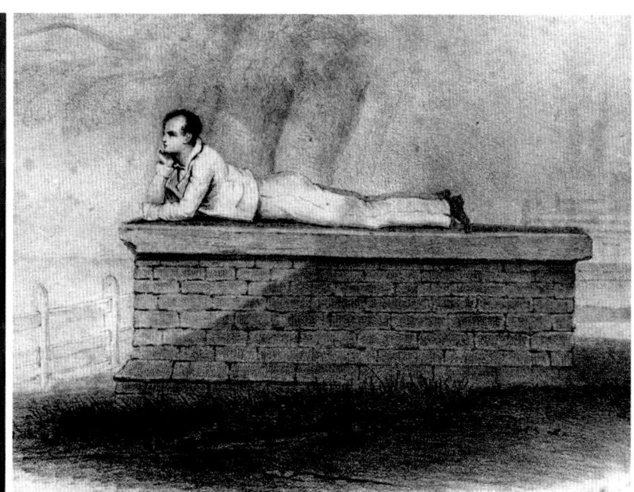

... it has been used as a set for films ... . Indeed, so well known is the scene filmed here for *The Philosopher's Stone* that some visitors refer to it as "The Harry Potter Room".

The Fourth Form Room looking south

were made towards the end of the eighteenth century as the number of Masters and pupils grew.

The Head Master's desk is provided with a metal loop for holding a taper, the only form of lighting used until the introduction of gas in 1855. On either side of his chair are cupboards which were used for holding the books and other School equipment. That on the Head Master's left was used until 1926 for keeping the birches with which offenders were beaten. The chair and table near the right of the desk probably form one of the later modifications and were used by the Head Master when overlooking exercises. On the north side of the door is the desk and seat of the Monitor of the week, whose function was to ensure that only Latin was spoken on School premises – even in the School Yard. At first the room was occupied by the whole School, but at the beginning of the nineteenth century the Sixth Form sat at the north end, and the Under Fourth and Third Forms sat at the south end, the other forms being upstairs. Prints dating from this time show the boys on the lower benches sitting with their faces to the side walls.

The modern visitor is often surprised – if not shocked – to see, near the Head Master's desk, the 'flogging stool': an actual piece of furniture, built-in for the purpose. Presumably the victim knelt on the floor and bent over it while the punishment was being administered. Flogging seems to have been a regular part of the daily routine.

The fireplace is not the original. The seventeenth century original, much more interesting and aesthetically appealing, was uncovered when the central heating system was installed in the early 1990s. Unfortunately it was promptly bricked over and presumably lost for ever. The existing fireplace is certainly substantial and one can imagine it ablaze with logs, its warmth and glow spreading across the room. Apparently that was not often the case and a report as late as 1800 describes the beginning of morning school when "a faggot smouldered for a few minutes". The chest which now stands in the fireplace was made when the School House was first built. As it was intended for keeping the Governors' muniments, it used to stand in the Governors' Room and was provided with three locks, whose keys were distributed among the Governors. At first the muniments consisted of eight books for accounts, minutes, Lyon's charter and statutes, and the Governors' seal. The chest was burgled in 1725, and the seal, which was of ivory and silver, was stolen. The archives were removed to the British Museum for cataloguing and safe-keeping in November 1883.

One of the most interesting features of the room is that of the names carved on the wainscot: this is simply graffiti. The practice seems to have been tolerated for nearly two centuries and was not outlawed until about 1847. Apparently the Head Master at that time thought that if more names were carved there was a risk of damage to those already there – an early case of vandalism later being considered as art. After this date, panels were fitted above the wainscot, and Custos, seizing the opportunity to supplement his no doubt meagre salary, carved names to order for a fee. By the 1890s these name-boards were also full, and the carving of names was transferred to the backs of chairs in the (new) Speech Room – another neat act of opportunism that enabled the School to furnish the room at the same time as giving leavers a way to leave their mark. Since then, however, a few special names, for example Winston Churchill and his brother Jack, appear to have been added.

At one time the room was the scene of the peculiar procedure known as 'Squash' or 'Squeeze', for the election of cricket keepers (i.e. captains). Percy Thornton described the scene: "The two monitors who registered votes given for rival candidates stood near the Head Master's chair, while the friends and opponents of the several would-be club-keepers occupied the space between the door and the aforesaid magisterial throne, beyond which the Squash was not allowed to extend. Within these limits, however, the battle waxed sore, and with the result of much personal discomfiture to the boys coming and going to support their House candidates for the coveted guidance of the several games of cricket, and this despite help rendered by friendly onlookers." As described, this appears to be not only undemocratic (which might be expected) but a highly unsatisfactory way of 'electing' captains.

The rooms on the second floor above the Fourth Form Room were originally built for the Head Master, Usher and Governors. The Head Master's room was at the north end, the Usher's at the south end and the Governors', which was the largest, occupied the space between them. The Head Master ceased to live there in the second half of the seventeenth century. By 1800 the Head Master's and Usher's rooms had been used as form rooms for the Fifth and Upper Fourth Forms for some years; in 1847 the Governors' room was taken over also. When the new wing was built in 1818, the whole of this floor became form rooms, except for a small room in the centre of the north end, which became the Monitors' Library between 1820 and 1863. It was superseded when the Vaughan became established.

The garret at the top of the School House, known as the Cock Loft, appears to have been in use at least since 1663, when it was ceilinged and divided into two rooms. It was certainly used as Shell form rooms by 1800 but was probably dismantled shortly after then and re-built when the extension was added. Records show that in 1855 it was used by part of the Fourth Form. One room is now the Hulton Library; the other a form room.

Today, the Fourth Form Room stands as a magnificently preserved specimen of a Tudor or Jacobean schoolroom. Along with several other School buildings, it has been used as a set for films and documentaries. Indeed, so well known is the scene filmed here for *The Philosopher's Stone* that some visitors refer to it as "The Harry Potter Room".

**Note: The senior Assistant Master has, at various times, been known as The Usher, Under Master, Senior Master, Second Master and, most recently, Deputy Head Master.*

The Old Schools in 1802 before the extension was added. The Fourth Form Room occupies the first floor

THE CHAPEL

THE INTERIORS OF MOST churches have an unmistakable atmosphere about them. Much of it is due to smell: the old country church has a musty, damp smell, a town church a bookish smell, a Catholic church a smell of incense, and so on. Many are a feast for the eyes, examples of glorious architecture, beautiful roofs, spectacular stained glass, rich carving or all of these. All usually share a sense of silence and calm. Some feel like holy places; others do not. School chapels are rather different: some of them are more welcoming than others; most of them definitely do not feel like holy places, yet there is a distinctiveness rarely found elsewhere. It is a sense of identity and of history, but more particularly continuity. When Dr Wood gave his address during the service held to commemorate the fiftieth anniversary of the consecration of the new Chapel in 1907, he said, "Cast your eyes where you may, you see nothing that is not consecrated by the most tender associations. It was not built at once, nor to one plan. Each part bears silent witness to the love and the sorrow of those who have gone. Here a window and there a window, here a screen, here a granite column, the reredos, the altar, the chancel pavement, all have individuality, all have the pathetic charm of association with a son, a brother, a friend, a colleague. Every stone is eloquent with the memories of a personal past. The Chapel is not a monument, it is a Biography."

Dr Wordsworth's Chapel, built in 1839 but replaced fifteen years later

There are some who wonder why the School should have a chapel of its own when not a hundred yards up the hill there is a spacious parish church. Those that do have missed the point that school chapels in the nineteenth century were not so much about worship as about control. Head Masters Wordsworth and Vaughan and a number of their successors saw the pulpit as their main channel of communication with their pupils – and they often disagreed with the Vicar. This was certainly the case at Harrow where the boys had attended St Mary's for nearly 250 years – although, from all accounts, the accommodation made for them was far from salubrious. An Old Harrovian of the period wrote, "One rustic, battered gallery filled up the west end of the nave and served for the Upper boys; another cavernous gallery was hitched into the north side for the Lower boys... The worship took no account of the needs and peculiarities of schoolboys".

Dr Wordsworth built a chapel (on the site of the existing building) in 1839. It was not a success. It was too small for the expanding School, but more extraordinarily it was built with a floor sloping down the hill. Dr Vaughan immediately decided to replace it, building the new chapel in stages around the old chapel: his architect was George Gilbert Scott. In 1854 a beginning was made on the chancel, funded by the Head Master himself. Before the chancel was finished, the north aisle was begun, funded by Masters and parents of boys. During

Facing page: The interior of the School Chapel Chapel, showing the reredos in memory of Dr Vaughan

St Mary's Church c1840. John Lyon had provided for sermons to be preached in the Church and the School attended Sunday services there until Dr Wordsworth built the first School Chapel in 1839.

the building works, some services were held in the parish church, others in Old Speech Room, but the additions were completed at the beginning of the autumn of 1855, and the Chapel came into use again on Founder's Day in October.

At this point there was a realisation that there should be a memorial to the twenty-two Harrovians who had lost their lives in the Crimean War 1853–56: exactly half of them were under the age of twenty-one. It was decided to build a new south aisle as a commemoration. The addition destroyed the symmetry of the building but there were stronger emotions than a need for tidiness at stake. On Speech Day, the foundation stone of the addition was laid by General Sir William Fenwick Williams, Bt. After the ceremony, the Head Master called the 'Bill of the Fallen': brass plates have been fixed under the windows to record their names. The main entrance to Chapel at this time was at the west end of the Memorial Aisle, leading straight out onto the High Street.

While all this structural work was going on, the Fifth and Sixth Forms again attended the morning service in the parish church but, at the beginning of 1857 for the first time the whole School assembled for morning chapel on Sundays. The new Chapel was consecrated by Dr Tait, Bishop of London, on All Saints' Day, November 1, 1857. From this time the old connection of the School with the parish church, apart from annual commemorations of the Founder's death, was severed.

In 1858, a new organ was installed and stained glass scenes were inserted in the chancel window. In the following four years stained glass was placed in all the other windows and Dr Vaughan's Chapel was complete. However, during the forty years that followed, a number of important additions were carried out, mainly within the building itself. The first was the erection in 1865 of a spire, placed centrally over the west end of the roof of the nave. With splendid irony, this was dedicated to the memory of the Rev William Oxenham, an Assistant Master who had strenuously opposed the addition of a spire ever since the Chapel had been built. In 1883 the canopies of the chancel stalls were erected and in 1885 a new organ installed.

On the death of Dr Vaughan in 1897, the reredos, framed in carved alabaster, panels in *opus sectile* designed by Sir Arthur Blomfield RA, a medallion portrait, and other additions to the chancel were erected to his memory. These were unveiled on Speech Day, 1899. In 1898 electric lighting was installed to replace the gas which had formerly been used. An oak staircase was built to lead to the organ gallery, and a series of tablets was placed on the walls as memorials to Old Harrovians, Assistant Masters, and friends of the School.

During the South African War of 1899–1902, fifty-five Harrovians (about one in ten of those that took part) lost their lives on active service. As a memorial to them, transepts were built at the north and south sides of the chancel. The foundation stone was laid on Speech Day, 1902 and bears the inscription: "In memory of Old Harrovians who lost their lives in the War in South Africa, this cornerstone of the new transepts was laid on July 2, 1902, by Field Marshal Earl Roberts, KG VC, Commander-in-Chief". The names of those who had given their lives in the war were inscribed in shrines placed against the east walls of the transepts. The shrines are supported by bronze figures of St Andrew, St Patrick, St George and St Michael, designed by Alfred Drury, RA, which were added in 1904.

The North Transept was for many years reserved for the use of Old Harrovian visitors and was known as the Old Harrovian Transept, but the great increase in the number in the School made it necessary in 1923 to seat boys there. The South Transept was reserved for Masters' wives and other ladies, and was popularly known as the 'Hen Coop'. The wooden pews in the transepts were removed in 1988; when seating beyond that available in the main chapel is required, for example for a 'whole school service', stacking chairs are used. In 2003, the South Transept was dedicated as a Lady Chapel and contains a Statue of Our Lady of Walsingham.

The funds raised for the transepts were found to be more than were required and the surplus was put to adding porches at the northwest and southwest corners. These were designed by Sir Aston Tebb PRA to match the rest of the Chapel. This meant that the

Chapel entrances no longer spilt straight out onto the pavement and "protected the interior from the noise and dust of the High Street". That was in 1903.

Various other alterations were made at this time. A pavement of Sicilian marble, combined with black Belgian and Dove marbles, designed by Sir Charles Nicholson, was laid in the chancel. At the west end, the main south door leads under the organ gallery which runs the whole width of the Chapel and is reached by a spiral staircase in oak. The additions were consecrated by the Bishop of London on Founder's Day, October 8, 1903.

Following the death of Dr Montagu Butler, new windows of the north aisle and a pulpit were erected as a memorial to him. The eight oak Masters' stalls, which stand against the west wall at the back of the nave, and the organ gallery were placed at the same time. The memorial was dedicated on Sunday, February 13, 1920, by Bishop Gore, one of Dr Butler's most eminent pupils. The organ, a new instrument built by Walkers to a specification by Percy Buck, was dedicated by the Archbishop of Canterbury, The Most Rev Randall Davidson (OH), on May 8, 1921.

Although no structural alterations have been made to the Chapel since 1903, in the second half of the twentieth century various changes have been made to the interior of the building, mainly due to changes in liturgical practice. In the 1990s a wooden apron was constructed at the foot of the steps to the chancel and the altar moved there. In 2002 the chancel stalls with their canopies (occupied by senior Masters at one stage) were moved back to allow a new set of carved wooden choir stalls to be fitted giving greater capacity. Made of Welsh oak, this was the work of Salisbury-based furniture maker James Winby. The Chapel Choir (once known as the 'Harmony Choir' and singing from the organ gallery) now occupies these choir stalls. A smaller wooden lectern, also the work of James Winby, has replaced the original brass lectern (which remains in the Chapel). On Sundays the Roman Catholic boys no longer walk over the Hill to the church in Roxborough Park: Mass is celebrated in Chapel, after the Anglican Eucharist. In 2000 a set of tablets representing the Stations of the Cross was purchased from the parish of St Joseph's, Grove Park, Chiswick.

The Crypt Chapel is built into the foundations of the main building. Originally used as the vestry and then a store room, it was converted in 1918 into a Chapel in memory of the 644 Old Harrovians who lost their lives in the First World War. In 1988, to coincide with the cleaning of the stonework in the main Chapel, the Crypt was re-ordered and refurbished. It was re-dedicated in June 1989 by The Right Rev Michael Mann (OH), Dean of Windsor, and former Chairman of the Governors. In 2010 a specially designed organ was installed, the gift of the Tsang family from Hong Kong.

While the Crypt Chapel is in the first instance a War Memorial, it is also a place of daily prayer and worship. The Eucharist is celebrated there daily in term, but weddings and baptisms have also taken place within its walls.

As Dr Wood said, the walls of the Chapel do indeed tell the story of the School, although it is necessarily one side of the story, and a sad side at that. The memorial tablets while sometimes the tale of a long life, triumphantly led, more often tell of grief and sorrow after the loss of a beloved son; the tablets on the west wall dedicated to boys who died while still in the School, often of diseases now preventable or curable, are particularly poignant.

The Harrow School Chapel is a Victorian treasure, the legacy of a series of Head Masters with high-minded visions for the School, the work of distinguished architects, supported by generations of generous donors. Although religious practices may have changed, few attempts have been made to modernise the building itself and it remains a totemic link with the School's past. It stands as the spiritual centre of the School, a building that, more than any other, has witnessed its joys and its sorrows.

The Chapel in 1865, showing the main entrance directly onto the High Street

THE SPEECH ROOM

THE SPEECH ROOM IS the meeting place for the whole School and the Head Master holds an assembly there every Monday morning. But that mundane description obscures the fact that it is a magnificent hall and the focal point of the School. By 1870 the increasing number of boys had created the need for a hall larger than Old Speech Room. The tercentenary of the Lyon charter presented a suitable opportunity for an appeal for funds and on March 30, 1871, a meeting was held, chaired by the Hon Frederick Ponsonby, to launch a fund to be known as the Lyon Memorial Fund. Its object was to "acquire land and erect buildings for School purposes, the first aim being the building of a Speech Room". Enough money was raised not only to build Speech Room but also to add the Gymnasium, Workshop and the Science Schools.

A postcard showing Speech Room before the War Memorial was built in 1926

The site of the Speech Room was purchased from Mrs Russell Gurney, wife of the Recorder of the City of London, but building turned out to be trickier than expected. Money had to be spent on foundations, which entailed sinking large pillars down to forty feet. Fortunately this expense was turned to good advantage as the material removed was used to construct the Chapel Terrace.

Natural obstacles were not the only ones: as with so many projects around this time, the plans were dogged by controversy. William Burges, the architect, was not an easy man and there were other powerful forces at work so, although the foundation stone was laid by the Duke of Abercorn in 1874, the building was not completed until 1877.

The design is masterful: the banked seating of the auditorium allows every boy to see (and be seen) not only from the platform but from almost every other seat. It is extraordinarily versatile: originally built for a school of just over 500, it now accommodates over 800 boys, making use of the choir stalls, without having needed any enlargement. Speech Room can be, and indeed has been, host to the grandest occasions: Kings and Queens, Prime Ministers and dignitaries of every stripe have graced the platform – and not appeared out of place. In November 1940, Winston Churchill (OH), the Prime Minister at the time, attended Songs, and Churchill Songs, as it was later named, became an annual event. Except when prevented by illness, Sir Winston attended each year until his death in 1965 and this tradition has been continued by his widow, his daughter and his descendants ever since. (The names of the principal guests at Churchill Songs may be found in the Timeline). Unfortunately the acoustics of Speech Room are no better than adequate and nowadays a sound system is used.

Speech Room is perhaps at its best when the whole School is present – occasions such as Songs concerts, Glees & Twelves and Leavers' Ceremonies – but it is also

a superb concert hall. It is used as a theatre and before the creation of the Ryan Theatre, most House and School productions took place there. Frankly, it is not ideal for this purpose because of the lack of backstage facilities, but each year the platform is extended over the 'well' and the 'apron' stage is used for the Choral Concert and two Shakespeare plays, performed by the School and the Old Harrovian Players (see *The Shakespeare Play*, page 151). In the past, debates, film shows and even the teaching of Sixth Form Divinity were among the activities that took place in Speech Room.

To commemorate the tercentenary of the Lyon Charter in 1971, Mr Mark Warman and Mr Jeremy Lemmon wrote a Song, *The Centenarian*. It was topical – "My pride it was to meet the Queen/With speech and song and peopled scene", witty – "Here on the hardest seats they've sat in/Grave governors give ear to Latin" – and set to a delightful tune by Mr Richard Drakeford. Sadly it is sung infrequently nowadays.

The design of Speech Room provided for an organ with console in the well: the original was purchased by friends of the School. This instrument was repaired and enlarged in 1924, but extensive damage from an incendiary bomb in 1940 – or more precisely the water used to extinguish it – rendered it unusable. A new organ, the gift of Lieutenant-Colonel J R Warren (OH), in memory of the late Sir Percy Buck, was completed in 1955. The specification was drawn up by Harrison & Harrison, in consultation with the Director of Music, Hector McCurrach. The organ stands in two chambers at either side of the stage: the swell, great and part of the pedal organ on the right, and the choir, solo and other pedal stops on the left. The 32 foot pedal bombardon is behind the panelling at the back of the stage. The console is in the centre of the well, and is movable. Selective restoration work was carried out in 1981–1982, in 2002 and in 2009–10.

Originally the room was furnished with ordinary cane-seated chairs, but in 1901 they were replaced with

The interior of Speech Room, c1910

Songs in Speech Room

plain oak rush-seated chairs. To carry out this plan, each boy was invited to present a chair on leaving, the donor having his name carved on the back of the top rail. After the room had its full provision of chairs, the carving of boys' names continued for a while on the backs of the seats of the choir stalls. The chairs cannot be described as comfortable but when a row of upholstered soft plush seating was introduced as an experiment in 2002, it was greeted with derision and removed.

The back panels of the choir stalls are ornamented with the illuminated coats of arms of deceased distinguished Harrovians. Portraits of many of them also appear in the Giants of Old panels in the War Memorial Building. The first thirteen, designed by George Krueger-Gray FSA and carved under the direction of LA Turner FSA, were completed in 1931. The central section of the panelling contains the names of winners of the Victoria Cross; brass plates near the foot of the pillars in the auditorium give a brief record of each award, as it was here that the banners, later re-sited in the War Memorial Building, first hung. The arms of the seven Harrovian Prime Ministers are on panels in this section.

The wooden boards below the windows around the semi-circular circumference of Speech Room bear the names of the winners of various prizes. These records ceased in the late 1930s and were not continued after the war. In 2010 they were covered with new panels bearing the names of benefactors of the Harrow Development Trust.

The five stained windows behind the platform contain academic subjects designed by JC Bell and executed by Messrs Clayton and Bell. Following the practice begun in Old Speech Room, the windows

around the circumference of the semi-circle contain shields of stained glass bearing the arms of Governors of the School. Behind the central bay is a cinematic projection room.

It is possible, although not recommended, to climb into the north tower through a small door in the inner porch and a stone spiral staircase. Inside there are two rooms, one above the other, the higher of which is reached by an iron ladder and a trap door in the floor. The upper room was used for mathematical teaching at the end of the nineteenth century. Mr CHP Mayo, an Assistant Master (1893–1919), wrote in *Reminiscences of a Harrow Master*, that he had taught Winston Churchill in this unheated room. A dramatic skit by Churchill on the inconvenience of the room was published in *The Harrovian* of December 17, 1892, and was probably his first published attempt at literature. During World War II the room was used for fire-watching.

Before the erection of the War Memorial Building the main entrance to Speech Room was through the gate opening on to the High Street on the south side. It was here that 'cheering on the steps' took place. The Head of the School stood on the raised forecourt and called on the School assembled in the street below to give three cheers as each notability walked down the steps. When the War Memorial was built the cheering was transferred to the forecourt of that building; the practice ceased in about 1950. Nowadays visitors emerging from Speeches are greeted by a pipe band playing on the forecourt, an altogether more uplifting experience.

Churchill Songs 2003

THE VAUGHAN LIBRARY

PRIOR TO 1863 THE ONLY school library was the small Monitors' Library, founded by Head Master Sumner in the 1760s and housed in the Old Schools. This had been exclusively for the use of the Monitors, each of whom was given a personal key. (This explains the origins of the ceremony at which each Monitor, on his appointment, receives a key to the Vaughan as a symbol of his office).

The Head Master, Dr Henry Montagu Butler, can be credited with the idea of building a new library as a tribute to his predecessor, Dr Charles Vaughan (1845–59) and for seeing the project through to a happy conclusion. Having chosen the site, he experienced some difficulty in purchasing it from the owners, one of whom was Mr John Bliss, landlord of the Crown and Anchor inn. Furthermore the Charity Commissioners insisted on an undertaking from the Head Master that he would be able to maintain the building out of fee income. Having satisfied all conditions, the Governors appointed the architect George Gilbert Scott, RA, a pupil of Pugin, whose designs can still be seen in the tiled pavement that leads from the street to the main entrance of the Vaughan.

Dr Charles Vaughan, after whom the library was named

Facing page: The interior of the Vaughan Library, c1900; the book collection appears rather meagre

On Speech Day, Thursday, 4 July, 1861, the Old Harrovian Prime Minister Lord Palmerston, then aged seventy-nine, rode out from London on his grey horse and, under an umbrella held over his head by the Head Master, laid the foundation stone just opposite the south door of the Chapel, riding back straight away to take part in a parliamentary debate.

Dr Butler's vision was that 'the Vaughan' should not just be a place to house a book collection, but also as "a temple in which all memorials of deep interest to Harrow would eventually be deposited". He looked forward to its holding portraits and busts of famous Harrow men; the first treasure was a portrait of the Prime Minister, painted by Francis Grant (OH) who was later knighted and elected President of the Royal Academy. George Richmond's portrait of Vaughan was hung prominently at the north end. Also in the library at this time was the portrait of Lord Byron by WE West. A massive clock, mounted on the south wall, was given by Sir Matthew Ridley and the marble table which had come from the Temple of Peace in Rome and was presented to the Monitors' Library by Captain LR Keane (OH), was placed in the bow window.

The seat by the bow window, looking out over the terrace, is a delightful place to sit and read, and generations of Harrovians have enthused about its charm.

For a century the Vaughan was the School's principal repository for its various treasures and collections. While the Butler Museum came to hold Harrow's ethnographical and natural history items, it was the Vaughan that displayed Marie Antoinette's

The Head Master, Dr Henry Montagu Butler, can be credited with the idea of building a new library as a tribute to his predecessor, Dr Charles Vaughan (1845–59) and for seeing the project through to a happy conclusion.

work box, the Silver Arrow archery costume, the Sheridan manuscripts and the 'Doria throne'.

During the second half of the twentieth century the library's multiple role as book collection, art gallery and study hall put increasing pressure on the limited space available; additionally, the Vaughan was being used as a meeting room for Governors' and Masters' meetings and various School societies. In 1967, following comments made in a School inspection, the Governors made some alterations to the interior: a large cabinet was installed to display the artefacts, and the northern half of the room was subdivided into study booths. Though functional, these were poorly lit and somewhat claustrophobic and had the unfortunate effect of breaking up the openness of Scott's original conception. It was a priority of the 1998 refurbishment that these should be dismantled.

When the Old Speech Room Gallery was opened in 1976, the creation of an environmentally controlled store room meant that the Vaughan's best literary treasures could be better looked after and displayed more appropriately in the Gallery's library showcases. Many of the treasures were removed from the library; the Head Masters' portraits were re-hung in the Old Harrovian Room, and those of distinguished Old Harrovians transferred to Speech Room.

Early in the 1990s the Governors decided that the library should be completely refurbished. The work started in the summer of 1998, but the planning and preparation had begun some years earlier, the first major project being to transfer the card catalogue, then housed in large wooden cabinets, to computer. Prior to this, 25,000 books had to be reclassified and bar-coded. This monumental task was undertaken by Vaughan and voluntary staff. The equally Herculean job of computerising the catalogue was farmed out to a professional firm who completed the work quickly, but with many inaccuracies.

As with the original construction of the building, the refurbishment also had its difficulties. There

The Vaughan Library from the Chapel terrace (above); the interior of the Vaughan Library, c1900 (below left and right)

The new library is now effectively on four floors: at terrace level…a new mezzanine level and the galleries reached by stairways. A single spiral staircase connects the three lower levels.

were objections to the architect's original ideas from the local planners. The second serious setback was the initial shortage of funds: the project had therefore to be undertaken in two stages. The library service continued upstairs whilst the workmen moved in below; then librarians and contractors swapped over.

The 'new' library is now effectively on four levels: at terrace level the Sixth Form Room and another form room known as Vaughan 10 were incorporated into the library, the lower floor was given a new mezzanine level and the galleries reached by stairways added valuable shelf space upstairs on the ground floor. A single spiral staircase in the centre of the building connects the lower three levels. New lighting was installed; Scott's heating system, which had run below the bottom shelf of the wall cases, was removed and replaced with under-floor pipes beneath a reproduction Victorian grille.

Finally the book collection itself required attention: departmental libraries were married with Vaughan stock and approximately 15,000 volumes were moved out to a reserve collection store. The book purchase budget was increased and expanded to include CDs, videos and DVDs. Opening hours were extended and, inevitably but gratifyingly, the number of users rose significantly. Before refurbishment, fewer than 4,000 user visits would be recorded in a term; in the academic year 2001–02 (just after refurbishment) there were 73,000 visits counted.

At the start of the 21st century this much loved landmark found a new lease of life. It had been built with the generous support of OHs and friends of the School; and it was refurbished and brought to its present splendid condition with the equally generous support of a new generation of OHs and friends.

The Vaughan Library frontage from Church Hill

THE WAR MEMORIAL BUILDING

IN THE GREAT WAR of 1914–18 no fewer than 2,917 Harrovians served in the armed forces; 690 were wounded and 644 killed. Although by no means unique among schools, the scale of these losses was traumatic. At first, the fallen were commemorated on panels in the Crypt Chapel but as the war dragged on and the toll continued to rise, a more substantial memorial was envisaged. Early in 1917 a meeting of Old Harrovians was held in the Merchant Taylors' Hall at which it was decided to set up a fund to build a memorial to the fallen and to assist in the Harrow education of their sons. WF (later Sir Francis) Fladgate (OH) was charged with the task of implementing the plan. A year later the Harrow Association Committee made a dramatic decision: they decided to purchase and demolish two major buildings at the very centre of the School, Church Hill House and Dame Armstrong's, and to create a memorial in the triangular space between the Old Schools, Speech Room and the Chapel. The architect, Sir Herbert Baker, was commissioned to design the building and the foundation stone was laid by the Archbishop of Canterbury, The Rt Rev Randall Davidson (OH) on 6 October, 1921.

War Memorial Building

The south wing of the War Memorial building including the Alex Fitch Room was quickly erected but shortage of funds and disagreement over the design delayed completion until 1926. It was finally opened by Archbishop Davidson on 3 June. After the ceremony, the Prime Minister, Stanley Baldwin (OH), addressed the School in Speech Room. "There is one question that will hammer at all our hearts for many years to come," he said. "We have heard it often, the question that the dead themselves might ask: "Have we died in vain?" and the question you hear asked by mothers and widows and orphan children all over the world. I have got to give an answer and you have got to give an answer..."

The Shrine is entered from the forecourt through wrought iron gates in a triple-arched facade. On the left is the Cenotaph. Behind this the wall is apsidal and bears, on a gilt frieze, the first lines of JS Arkwright's hymn, *O Valiant Hearts*. On the other two walls are inscribed the names of 641 of the Harrovians to whom the memorial was built (for no known reason the names of AS Agelasto, FEJ Armstrong and Baron HJ Reuter have been omitted). The ceiling is formed of three domed vaults, each with a coloured shield-shaped boss: the arms of St George, the School arms and the fleur de lys. These symbolise soldiers from England educated at Harrow, who fell in France. A heavy oak door leads to the central chamber.

The wide central chamber is built of stone and has sometimes been known as the Glyptotheca, as it contains busts of some distinguished Old Harrovians. It rises gently by three levels to the Speech Room forecourt at the north end. On the west side of this ceremonial passage, a branching stone staircase leads to the upper floor. On the east side is a second memorial, enclosed by low stone balustrades under outer arches. This is dedicated to the 344 Harrovians who lost their lives in the Second World War 1939–45 and others more recent. Further on are two rooms, one on each side of the passage: the Monitors' Room and the Philathletic Club Room.

The Second World War shrine bears the inscription, "To the sons of Harrow who fell in the war MCMXXXIX–MCMXLV". At each of the apsidal ends, the names of the fallen are engraved on bronze panels. Banners of the nineteen Old Harrovian winners of the Victoria Cross hang from horizontal staffs, each bearing the personal coat of arms or crest on one side and the crest of his regiment or corps on the other. A glass-topped cabinet in the Shrine contains replicas with citations of these VCs. A twentieth medal was awarded to a Master, Captain Godfrey Woolley, later Vicar of St Mary's Church.

Just inside the south door on the left of the central chamber is a small room for the use of The Guild. In the bay next to it, a display of three panels gives a brief illustrated *History of the School.* In a second bay, beyond the staircase, a display entitled *Harrow and War*, gives an illustrated account of the part Harrovians have played in the military history of the nation. On the third level, panels on the walls on either side carry the display: *Harrow School and Churchill.*

In a recess on the first landing of the staircase stands a marble bust of Robert Peel. Above the bust hangs a clock presented in memory of George A Crawley (OH). Surrounding the bust and at the turns in the stairs on both sides are photographic portraits of *Giants of Old,* distinguished former members of the School.

At the top of the staircase, double doors open into the Old Harrovian Room, a fine central hall, the walls of which are hung with portraits of former Head Masters. (Details may be found in the Appendix). A large oriel window looks out over the High Street, giving light to the room, but, alas, the noise from passing traffic keeps it firmly closed. In front of the fireplace at the south end stands the 'Doria Chair', a handsome oak chair, richly carved and upholstered, and supposed to have been

The Old Harrovian Room, on the upper floor of the War Memorial building. Portraits of former Head Masters adorn the walls

used by the Emperor Charles V when visiting the Doria Palace in Genoa. It was presented by John Benjamin Heath (OH) in 1871. The Old Harrovian Room is used for meetings, lectures, concerts and receptions; it also serves as an overflow area for Masters in the morning break. Leading off the Old Harrovian Room on the north side is the Masters' Room, on the south side the Alex Fitch Room.

The Alex Fitch Room is dedicated to the memory of Second Lieutenant Alex Fitch, Royal Garrison Artillery, who was killed in action at Jeancourt in France on September 18, 1918, aged nineteen. On the outside of the door are inscribed in gilt letters the words: "Pass, Friend." These words are taken from the School Song *You!*, which was written by Alex Fitch's House Master at Bradbys, George Townsend Warner.

The Memorial to Old Harrovians who fell in World War II (above); the Alex Fitch Room, given to the School in his memory (below)

Facing page:: The Shrine commemorating those who died in World War II and more recent conflicts; (above); the Cenotaph (below)

The room and its fittings and furniture were the gift of Lady Fitch, his mother. The richly carved and fluted oak panelling was originally at Brooke House, Hackney, which was built in about 1580 by Lord Hunsdon, a cousin of Queen Elizabeth I. The Queen stayed at Brooke House when she held her court at Hackney in 1587. The fireplace dates at the latest from the reign of Henry VII. The floor is made of teak timbers from the *St Vincent,* the famous ship of the line, which saw service in the reign of George III. As Sir Cecil Fitch said at the opening ceremony, "the room itself is history".

The furniture is mostly of Tudor, Stuart, or Cromwellian design. The finest pieces in the collection are the Cromwellian refectory table that occupies the centre of the room, the Jacobean table near the east window, and the carved oak chest. Over the fireplace hangs a portrait of Alex Fitch painted from a photograph; at the wish of Lady Fitch, the portrait is kept lit by day and night. The windows are of modern glass.

Lady Fitch wished the room to be used exclusively as "a place in which parents could meet their boys conveniently". The world has moved on since then and the room is only occasionally used for social or business purposes.

Each November, after the Remembrance Day service in Chapel, the Chaplains, accompanied by a Guard of Honour and many members of the congregation, process across the road to the War Memorial. A piper at the top of the steps plays a lament. In a brief ceremony a wreath is laid at each shrine. The impact of the losses in the two World Wars may have diminished in the twenty-first century, but at Harrow a reminder of those sacrifices remains right at the centre of the School. Stanley Baldwin ended his speech with the hope that future generations would be able to look back and say, "At that time a generation indeed was wiped out, but from their graves sprang a rebirth and a new kindling of the spirit that raised our country to heights that surpassed the dreams of those of her sons who in past ages had sacrificed most and loved her best." Somehow, life seems a bit more complicated nowadays but on occasions when there are events in Speech Room, there is something appropriately symbolic about walking through the War Memorial building, with its echoes of the School's past, up to Speech Room where the whole School – the future – is assembled.

IN MEMORY OF THE
SONS OF HARROW
WHO DIED IN
THE GREAT WAR
MCMXIV·MCMXIX

THE HOUSE

THE BOARDING HOUSE SYSTEM took many years to evolve from its birth as accommodation for the 'foreigners' permitted in John Lyon's statutes to the creature it is today. At first it was entirely a commercial arrangement whereby residents of the Hill let out rooms. The fact that some of the landlords were Masters at the School seems to have been of little relevance; they had no wish to become involved with either the care or the discipline of their tenants. In the first half of the nineteenth century, a few Houses run by Masters began to dominate the market. Organised games began to take hold, soon becoming compulsory, and this helped each House to gain a sense of identity. But the owners, or in some cases tenants, were still running private businesses, although they did have to have the permission of the Head Master. As Tyerman writes, "By the end of the nineteenth century Harrow had become almost a federal school – admissions, sport, social life and finance revolving around established houses, proudly distinct in nature and history…"

By 1930 the School had purchased all the Houses, but House Masters ran their Houses as tenant hoteliers for another eighteen years before they all became salaried.

With this background one can only hesitantly build up a picture of House life from reminiscences (often unreliable), letters to parents (usually highly selective of information and emotions) and contemporary records. The fact is that the experiences of different boys in different Houses at different times is hopelessly… well, different.

The facts available suggest that a 'boy culture' evolved in each House with minimal adult interference. Not surprisingly a hierarchy developed with the oldest and biggest boys at the top, bolstered by fagging, bullying and privileges. These privileges were often absurd, such as being able to walk down a certain passage or wear certain clothes; the use of special names and customs created a sort of mystique. The new boy was frequently exposed to an initiation test, some harmless like being required to know the most intricate details of the rules of Harrow football; some less so like being dangled out of a window by the ankles or having the head doused by the flush of a lavatory. Although some House Masters were more sensitive, many were happy if the system 'worked' and left it to the boys to run the House. There was trust and, by the nature of trust, it was only rarely tested.

Living conditions, originally primitive, nowadays do not lag far behind what the average boy might expect at home. Indeed it could be said that these have been exceeded in the recently built Lyon's House. The combination of the increased influence of mothers, the Children's Act and Health & Safety regulations have ensured that lavatories have doors on them and that a visit to them does not require a descent of four floors.

The wisdom of previous generations has left Harrow with an important legacy of accommodation that for many years was shared only with Eton: the individual room. Although the situation varies from House to House and period to period, most boys will spend one or two years in a 'double' and thereafter enjoy the privacy of a single room. This independence has a much greater impact than many realise.

There is no doubt that the single most important influence on a boy's life at Harrow is his House, and, although the House Master has an important role in creating a good atmosphere in it, the most determining factor is the other boys in the House, with whom he lives for five years. Boys spend a lot of their time in the House, sleeping, working, socialising. And they eat and play games together too. The hierarchy still exists but has been transmuted into a modern, humane form, driven by a whole team of tutors, health advisers, psychologists and psychiatrists, all overseen by a Director of Boarding and backed by a pastoral support committee.

Harrow Houses are all distinct. In spite of efforts by successive Head Masters to reduce the differences, the fact remains that the position, structure of the building, number of boys, personality of the House Master, House Matron and Tutors are all factors that contribute to the unique character of a House. Druries, The Head Master's and Moretons are conveniently central; Elmfield and West Acre occupy the north and south extremities of the School respectively. This might be perceived as a disadvantage but West Acre is probably the most light and spacious building of all, while Elmfield has strong traditions and enjoys a loyalty from its former members that is the envy of many others. The Head Master's is a much bigger House than all the others and is inconveniently arranged, having the Head Master's and Registrar's offices in its midst. But its very size brings other advantages: it has a bigger bank of resources from which to draw in House competitions and can afford to spread its talents around every area of School life.

On top of that there are the House Master's predilections: he may have a penchant for scholars, or games players or musicians or the sons of the landed gentry.

When boys are living together in a boarding school, the influence of fellows is complex and subtle. Relationships can be both creative and destructive. Many an Old Harrovian can look back and recall how he was inspired to explore an area of interest, not by a Master or an external speaker, but by another boy. Underlying School life there may be personal and family complications: the boy whose parents are going through an acrimonious divorce; the boy who feels that he is socially inferior to other boys and who is embarrassed by his parents; the boy whose parents replace parental love by throwing money at him; the clever boy who would really like to be a rugby player; the not-so-clever boy who can't keep up academically; the son who knows he can never match up to the expectations of his successful and demanding father; the boy who realises that he is 'gay' … the list is endless. In this maelstrom the House Master's role, while addressing individual problems, is to keep the ship on course. He tries to create an atmosphere of friendly interaction, an awareness of the values of decency, mutual respect for the interests and qualities of other people especially where they differ from one's own, but also to encourage healthy competition, development of talent and the pursuit of excellence. He has to set clear guidelines and intercept breaches when they occur – but even now, when education about how to behave and treat other people is both specific and pre-emptive, trust still plays its part. Often the helpful, encouraging and sympathetic senior boy can be a greater influence than a well-meaning adult.

For teenage boys the House is the vehicle for this part of the educational journey. It is the opportunity for the pleasure of friendship and shared experiences, good and bad, the excitement of team achievements and successes. Most boys retain a loyalty for their House – often in contradiction to their descriptions of their treatment. It used to be summed up in a phrase since discredited by generations of lampoons: House spirit. It is therefore not surprising that one cannot generalise about individual experiences: where one boy may be blissfully happy in his House, another may be utterly miserable. Is it all a matter of luck? Probably.

A boy's room in The Grove (left); 'House Bill' in The Grove (right)

FOOD

ADOLESCENT BOYS' STOMACHS HAVE always been close to their hearts and Harrovians' have been no different. Food is a key part of our lives, affecting our health, our sense of security, our morale – and our pockets. In the earliest days of the School's existence, lessons ran from 6 a.m. to 11 a.m. and from 1 p.m. to 6 p.m. Christopher Tyerman has suggested that this long midday break was to enable the 'scholars' to make their way home across the fields for lunch. But it was the influx of 'foreigners', permitted under John Lyon's statutes, that changed the character and habits of the pupils. By the 1680s, the 'foreigners' had become an entrenched majority of pupils, and they were boarded out around the town. It seems likely that they would have been provided with at least a main meal by their landlady, but equally that they supplemented this with purchases from the growing number of retail outlets on the Hill. Tyerman again: "Much free time, of which there was no shortage, was occupied in eating and drinking, sometimes being taken to the King's Head for a 'fowl' by a visiting adult, more often supplementing diet and dispelling daily tedium with purchases from the local grocer and confectioner". Daniell Griffiths, a pupil in 1785, "enjoyed quantities of jam, cake, bread, ham, sugar, coffee, fruits, sweets, ices, biscuits, tarts, custard, stews, pies, cordials, tea and beer".

Breakfast in the Shepherd Churchill Hall

As the boarding house system became established, boys were fed 'in house'. This presented House Masters with a difficult balance to strike: they wanted to maximise their income but ran the danger of a reputation that would make their House less attractive. The food in the Dames' houses, which were cheaper, was notoriously bad.

Head Master Longley (1829–36) on election was "instructed by the Governors to investigate the practice of charging the large breakfasts they consumed after First School by buying food and drink from the local shops on credit". These meals came to be called 'finds' because the boys had to find them – or more likely send a fag to purchase the food – rather than have them supplied by Dames or House Masters. The outcome of Longley's investigation is not known but these breakfasts on Sunday mornings and dinners on Saturday evenings were to become an established practice well into the 1960s, the name being retained long after the fagging had ceased. Fagging duties in most Houses comprised 'day boys' (who answered 'boy calls' for running of errands) and 'finds boys' who served House Monitors' breakfasts, made toast and so on.

Longley also asked that parents should desist from sending game to their sons as this involved unsupervised costs for dressing etc.

Throughout the first half of the twentieth century, basic meals were provided in Houses, with wide variations according to the House Master's budget and the skill or otherwise of the House cook. In most cases the standard was pretty poor, with devices such as 'food committees' convened to defray the discontent of the young consumers. Even when full board was provided, the local suppliers did a roaring trade: there were numerous grocers, greengrocers, confectioners and 'newsagents', all selling 'boy food', such as biscuits, crisps, ice creams and fizzy drinks. Most were in the High Street although 'Ma Sullivan's' and the Hill Newstore in West Street picked up a lot of cricketing traffic.

The cafés were also well patronised: The Hill, run by a succession of lessees from the School, notably Fuller's – operating at a loss until the arrival of the legendary and rotund Jim Crook and his wife – occupied the lower part of the premises below the School Outfitters, formerly Gieves. The Corner Shop was between the King's Head and the Post Office; Ann's Pantry was the original 'greasy spoon' café, offering during the days of food shortages the advantage of frying a customer's own egg. "One sausage and chips, own egg" was a familiar cry as another plate of soggy chips found its way from the kitchen. The Tea Shop in West Street was more refined, serving 'crinkle-cut' chips and tea in a teapot – the sort of place a boy could take his parents to. Food was 'on the ration' until 1954.

The King's Head was an altogether different scene and strictly out of bounds as these were licensed premises. Waiters in tailcoats and roasts from the trolley presented some very attractive possibilities to the 1950s Harrovian, but sadly they were out of the question as the entrance was heavily guarded by the occupants of the 'Men's Bar': beaks. Although beer was allowed for House Monitors in Houses, visits to licensed premises were forbidden – except with parents.

The building of the Shepherd Churchill Hall in 1976 brought a big change – although it did not come without a battle. Heavy opposition from House Masters, boys and Old Harrovians of the "over my dead body" variety, led to the design of a Hall, separated into eleven House areas, each resembling its old home. In fact the House Master of West Acre refused to move and continued to operate independently until his retirement – an echo of Cocky Pope and the introduction of 'bluers' in the 1920s.

The advantages were immediately seen: the quality of food improved and there were choices for some meals, although the formal style of House lunch was preserved – at least for a while. The new regime also enabled home teams to entertain visitors for home matches, which had previously been the privilege of a select few.

A further upgrade of the kitchens and service area of the Shepherd Churchill Hall in 1993 – also bitterly opposed by House Masters, as it was another nail in the coffin of 'family service' – moved further towards 'cafeteria service', improved efficiency and made for shorter queues.

The last thirty years have seen huge changes in British eating habits and these have been reflected at Harrow. While boys have not entirely eradicated from their diet the fry-up of yesteryear, fashions have changed: boys have travelled more, have eaten out more regularly, foreign dishes have arrived and tastes have become more sophisticated. They have also become more health conscious. At the centre of this culinary and gastronomic revolution at Harrow has been the School Domestic Bursar since 1990, Mrs Julia Tyler (formerly Palmer-Brown). She has fought miserly bursars, Luddite House Masters, recalcitrant staff, and ungrateful boys, weathered the occasional food fight, and emerged victorious.

But institutional food, however good, can never quite match up either to home-cooking or to the take-away. The refurbished Houses of the 1980s were equipped with 'butteries' on each landing and small kitchens. For senior boys not in school for period 2a, the temptation to knock up a snack in the House is irresistible – although grilling bacon tends to alert the House Master's olfactory senses.

Various restaurants on the Hill have catered for boys' trade: Mr Lam's, a Chinese restaurant, was popular while it existed. The cafés have gone out of business and the new generation comprises a whole range of dining and snacking experiences. The four restaurants are The Old Etonian (joke intended) opposite Moretons, providing traditional if unenterprising food under friendly Spanish ownership and staff; the Connoisseur is Northern Indian, Café Café international and Incanto, Italian with a very popular delicatessen for counter sales and light meals. There is a wine bar, Blues and a pizza restaurant, La Collina. In addition there are two tea shops also serving light meals, The Dolls House and Tea at Three (temporarily closed in 2010).

Nothing, however, has achieved the popularity of the pizza, delivered to the House by Vesper scooter.

Supper in the Shepherd Churchill Hall

SCHOOL DRESS

UNTIL THE MIDDLE OF the nineteenth century, members of the School wore the ordinary costume of the time. Portraits of some of Dr George Butler's pupils (1805–28) show them to be wearing Regency coats and stocks and there was no uniformity of style or colour until about 1850. Around this time, a soberness and uniformity of gentlemen's dress became the norm across the country and a sense of fashion grew up in the School.

ED Laborde describes this as "tyrannical… the slightest departure from normal costume was stigmatised as 'swagger' and fear of being accused of this crime inspired in the boys a conservatism which resisted most of the changes that occurred in London society and preserved in the School the dress that had been in vogue in the middle of the nineteenth century".

School dress comprised a black tailcoat and waistcoat, striped trousers and a top hat of the style known as a 'beaver'. Younger boys wore short jackets without tails. All these conventions were made and enforced by the boys except for Dr Vaughan's ruling that neckties should be black or white. A letter to *The Harrovian* in 1879 stated that the shape of hat worn depended entirely on fashion. Minor modifications were made as fashions and materials for shirts, collars, ties and socks evolved, but there were no major changes until the substitution of the straw hat for the beaver on weekdays in 1915.

The pink silk shirt which the early cricket XIs wore is thought to have been based on the former archery dress as seen here

Facing page: Lord's 1923: Although not in colour, the button hole suggests that this young man may have been an Etonian... note the gloves

The straw hat came from cricket dress; Charles Wordsworth had his broken by a cricket ball while fielding in 1825. In the 1830s they began to be common in the Summer term; Mrs Chatham, whose shop in the High Street was described as "Hatters to Harrow School", is said to have made the early versions to order. The low two-inch crown dates from the 1860s but the brim was narrow up to 1873. Between 1873 and 1877 the brim was gradually widened to its present width of three inches. At some stage during this period the straw hat became an acceptable alternative to the beaver in school dress.

The 'blue' jacket or 'bluer' also came from cricket. In 1881 tail coats were still being worn for cricket, but by 1888 bluers and grey flannel trousers ('greyers') were being worn for games and half-holiday afternoons. By 1900, there were two distinct forms of dress: formal, known as 'school dress' and informal, known as 'half-change'.

During the First World War, as a measure of economy, bluers with a grey waistcoat and greyers were adopted for school dress,

Boys of diminutive stature no longer have to endure the ignominy of the 'bum freezer' ... in the Second World War, the rationing of clothes led to a further relaxation of regulations; top hats were restricted to Monitors.

Mr Trundle, for many years the manager of Gieves, the School outfitters.

Facing page: (top left) This picture of boys on the Old Schools' steps in about 1865 shows that the straw hats at one time had a much deeper crown; (top right) Sunday dress 1930s: The boy on the left is obliged to wear an 'Eton' collar and jacket as he has not yet reached the critical height for 'tails'; (below, from the left) illustrations from Harrow Yesterday and Today, *1948: School Monitor; Monitor in the Philathletic Club: School dress: football flannel; cricket flannel; rugby lion*

although the formal costume was retained as 'Sunday Dress'. After the war these changes were retained although, in 1936, the waistcoat was replaced by a blue pullover.

In the Second World War, the rationing of clothes led to further relaxation of the regulations: top hats were restricted to Monitors – and macintoshes were permitted for the first time!

By the 1950s a complicated (and now seemingly ludicrous) set of dress privileges had evolved. For example, a new boy had to have three buttons of his bluer fastened; a button could be unfastened after one year and another after his first Lord's (cricket match v Eton); after two years the bluer could be worn open, by which time a white silk handkerchief could be sported in the top pocket, this privilege being extended to a coloured handkerchief for 'three-yearers' and so on. Some of these 'rules' were boy-driven, others became part of the School rules: three-yearers could wear starched 'turned down' collars with Sunday dress, the rest 'winged collars'.

An elaborate mosaic of privileges had become firmly embedded, with good sportsmen the particular beneficiaries: cricket 'flannels' wore speckled straw hats, 'bloods' (first team players of major games) wore grey waistcoats with Sunday dress and distinctive woollen scarves in the winter, coloured cravats were awarded for all games and could be worn with half-change.

For the going to and from games even more glamorous and colourful regalia was worn: caps, fezzes and socks in School or House colours, trimmed bluers (or striped for football flannels), blue shorts for rugby 'lions' and football flannels. All these helped to inflate the status of the games player and kept the tills of the outfitters ringing. The practicalities of returning from the football field coated in mud seem to have been ignored – there were always fags to brush the mud off the velvet when it had dried.

In Dr Wordsworth's time, the School cricket XI wore a pink silk jersey, a survival no doubt of the old

archery dress, and a high top hat. Changes followed the practices of adult players, and by the 1860s the XI were wearing white flannel trousers shirts and white boots but others played in half-change. Up to the 1950s a cricketer would play in brown shoes or boots until such time as he was awarded his white boots, and even in 1st XI matches only those already awarded their flannels would be entitled to play in white trousers; the rest wore 'greyers'.

The origin of the blue and white School colours is a mystery: certainly footballers were playing in magenta and black shirts – and knickerbockers buckled below the knee – around 1890.

Headgear of some form seems to have been worn for most games. Eighteenth century cricket prints show the players in top hats and in EM Hemy's painting of Harrow football in 1887 the players appear to be wearing a sort of smoking cap (without tassle) – while the umpire looks all set to join a shooting party in 'plus twos' and a 'fore and aft'. Presumably the smoking cap was the forerunner of the 'fez', the tassle being added later, after players had ceased to wear them while actually playing. The football fez is more of a pillbox, being shallower in the crown than the Turkish version, and secured by elastic at the back. By the 1930s, even House footballers had three different forms of headgear: the standard fez striped in House colours worn to House games, the 'match fez' in single coloured velvet with tassle in the second colour and a 'running cap' for wear to practices and while umpiring.

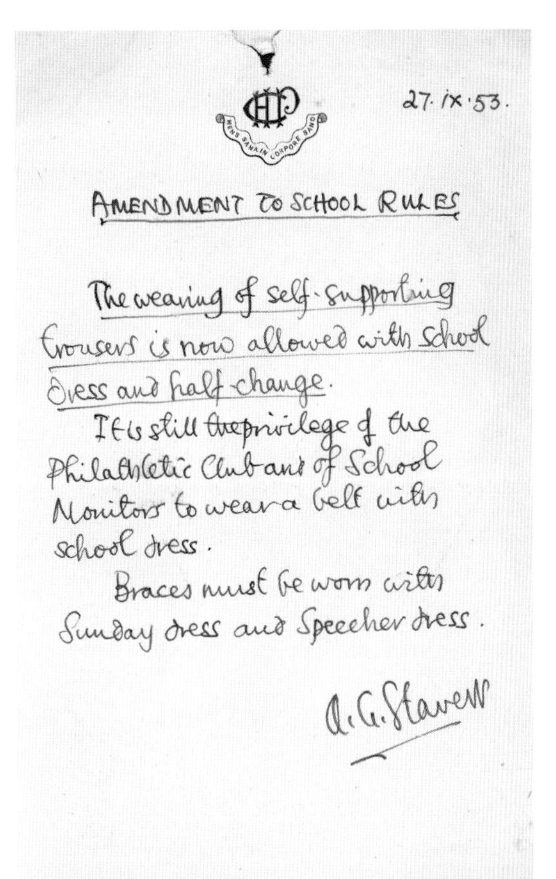

27.ix.53.

AMENDMENT TO SCHOOL RULES

The wearing of self-supporting trousers is now allowed with School dress and half-change.

It is still the privilege of the Philathletic Club and of School Monitors to wear a belt with school dress.

Braces must be worn with Sunday dress and Speecher dress.

A.G. Stavell

The distinctive 'box-shaped' cricket cap is unique to Harrow, although the size of peak has increased over the years. If the purpose of the peak is to protect the eyes from the glare of the sun, the early versions must have been very ineffective. The white cotton sunhat made a brief appearance in the 1990s but the 'forty cap' (blue with thin white stripes) has been re-invented in hoops after complaints that the traditional cap "was difficult to keep on" – odd, as it had "stayed on" for a hundred and fifty years.

Perhaps surprisingly, most of these sportsmen's adornments and other idiosyncracies of the Harrow uniform have changed little since the last war, surviving even the 'slovenly seventies'. Boys of diminutive stature have no longer had to endure the ignominy of the 'bumfreezer' (the short tail-less Sunday coat) since the 1970s; the starched winged collar and turned down collar worn by three-yearers gave way to laundry pressures around 1980 and the last of the speckled 1st XI cricket hats was sold in 2005, no supplier being found, even in the Far East, to maintain this tradition.

Members of The Guild, a club founded by Head Master Ian Beer in the 1980s to recognise artistic or cultural excellence, soon complained that they lacked the distinctive dress privileges of the sportsmen of the Philathletic Club. After twenty years of lobbying, they now have the right to wear a maroon waistcoat with Sunday Dress and a striped bow tie on week days. The rarely seen Triple School Blood (cricket, rugby, soccer) claims the privilege of wearing a burgundy bow tie.

Sportswear for all boys has evolved during the 2000s, influenced by national trends, as well as a demand for 'leisurewear' now worn by most boys in the afternoons after 'eccer'. The Harrow tracksuit, sweatshirt, reversible rugby/soccer shirt and 'beanie' have become standard items, whilst most Houses boast a range of optional extras, including even the 'hoody', beloved of all teenagers in this decade. And yet, in spite of *Existing Customs* permitting a more relaxed style of dress for many more hours of the week, today's Harrovian still seems to enjoy dressing up. The outfitters continue to do a brisk trade in Palmerston Society ties and footer fezzes and, anomalous though the Harrow hat and the tailcoat may sometimes seem, a straw poll (no pun intended) always reveals that the boys would be the last to vote for their abolition.

Facing page: (clockwise from top left) A Monitor and member of the 'Phil' in Sunday dress; School dress – the Monitor on the left wears a crest on his hatband and a crested tie; a cricket 'flannel' (centre) – fancy waistcoats are allowed on Speech Day; A rugby lion (on the left) and Monitor's scarves worn with School dress.

RELIGION

ALTHOUGH HARROW IS NOT a religious foundation, the Founder, John Lyon, was born an orthodox Catholic; he was a young man at the time of the Reformation in the 1530s. By the time of the foundation of the School, he was probably a Protestant Anglican, but he made no attempt to impose religious restrictions on his school and he is known to have had associations on both sides of the divide. In his statutes he prescribed use of the Calvin catechism. In 1591 he provided for the preaching of thirty "good learned and godly sermons" in the parish church, sponsoring preachers being a characteristic of enthusiastic educational reformers at the time; he also urged 'the Master' to lecture the scholars on Scripture. In practice there was little religious instruction or worship for the first two hundred years of the School's existence, which was surprising considering that all the staff were clergymen – and that one of the Head Masters was to later become Archbishop of Canterbury. There was the translation of the Greek New Testament on Sunday afternoons, but that was more an academic than religious activity. In fact it was the "virtual guarantee of a certain educational standard as much as religious orthodoxy" that was behind such appointments.

The Head Master can have a profound effect on the religion of the School – or none at all, as we shall see. Dr Wordsworth (1836-44) was the first Head Master to be religious in any effective sense and he adopted the role of Chaplain. He believed that the School should be led from the pulpit and built the first School Chapel in 1839, partly to free himself from the constraints of the parish church and partly to negate the meddling of the Vicar.

His successor, Dr Vaughan (1845-59), a disciple of Thomas Arnold of Rugby, insisted that Harrow was a 'Reformation School' – predominantly evangelical – and promised to devote himself "earnestly to the furtherance of the great work of Christian education". He therefore re-emphasised the importance of Chapel and preached to the School every Sunday. The Oxford Movement (1833-41), which promoted the revival of Catholic beliefs and practices in the Church of England had few supporters on the Hill until the arrival of Lionel Ford in 1910.

Dr Montagu Butler (1860-85) continued Vaughan's emphasis on Chapel and preached every Sunday at Evensong. By the mid-1870s he was established as a preacher and became Honorary Chaplain to the Queen.

After the Clarendon Commission and the Public Schools Act of 1868 came the first crack in the all-embracing Chapel-centred School religion: in 1874 a 'conscience clause' allowed home boarders by right, and boarders by permission of the Governors, to be excused Chapel, prayers and religious instruction. The first declared Roman Catholic pupil was admitted in 1871 and the following year the notion of a Jewish House was proposed. A building at the top of Waldron Road was opened in 1880 with Dr Joseph Chotzner as House Master; the following year a visiting Rabbi from Cambridge was appointed to provide instruction. However there was pressure to integrate the Jewish boys with the rest of the School and the House was closed in 1903. Thereafter Jewish boys were admitted to all Houses, initially with a quota of two per House.

Dr Welldon (1885-98) re-asserted that nineteenth century Harrow was an evangelical Christian school and that the sermon rather than the sacraments lay at the heart of School worship. A little surprisingly, in 1890 he proposed a scheme for a Muslim House with a Muslim House Master: this was out of character as he was bitterly opposed to Roman Catholics and Jews – and Chinese! Anyhow, nothing came of the idea.

Dr Wood seems to have made little impact on the religious aspect of School life but the appointment

Facing page: The Chapel choir at the Christmas Carol service

of his successor, Lionel Ford (1910-25), broke the mould. Dr Ford had trained as a priest at Cuddesdon Theological College, where the emphasis lay with the sacraments, and on arrival at Harrow he introduced Holy Communion on Sundays and during the week, and said Matins daily in the Crypt after early morning school. Ford declared his priorities to be "first Christian faith, then character based on it, then intellectual achievement". His later introduction of a Sung Eucharist offended some evangelical Masters.

The period between the wars was notable for theological, liturgical and ecclesiological squabbling. Cyril Norwood (1926-34) was the first lay Head Master of Harrow. However he held strong views on school religion and declared, "I do not know of any surer foundation for spiritual values other than the foundation of the Christian faith" i.e. in his case Protestant Anglicanism. He abolished all sacramental innovations, but ironically the Master he appointed as Chaplain was an Anglo-Catholic, The Rev EM Venables. Paul Vellacott (1934-39) also held anti-Roman Catholic views but, for the most part, School religion reflected the view of parents: it was an integral part of education but also conformist and conventional – a social as much as religious ritual. As before and after, many Masters were opposed or indifferent to religion; not many attended Chapel unless they were on duty, to mark in, for example.

Dr Ralph Moore (1942-53), known as 'Holy Joe', was a devout Christian and published books on devotional topics. Rather than bickering about liturgical practice, the main discussion shifted to the teaching of Divinity, Confirmation instruction and compulsory Chapel. After 1945, the role of Chaplain changed from that of a schoolmaster in a dog collar to that of the School's parish priest.

The Chaplain conducting a School service in Chapel

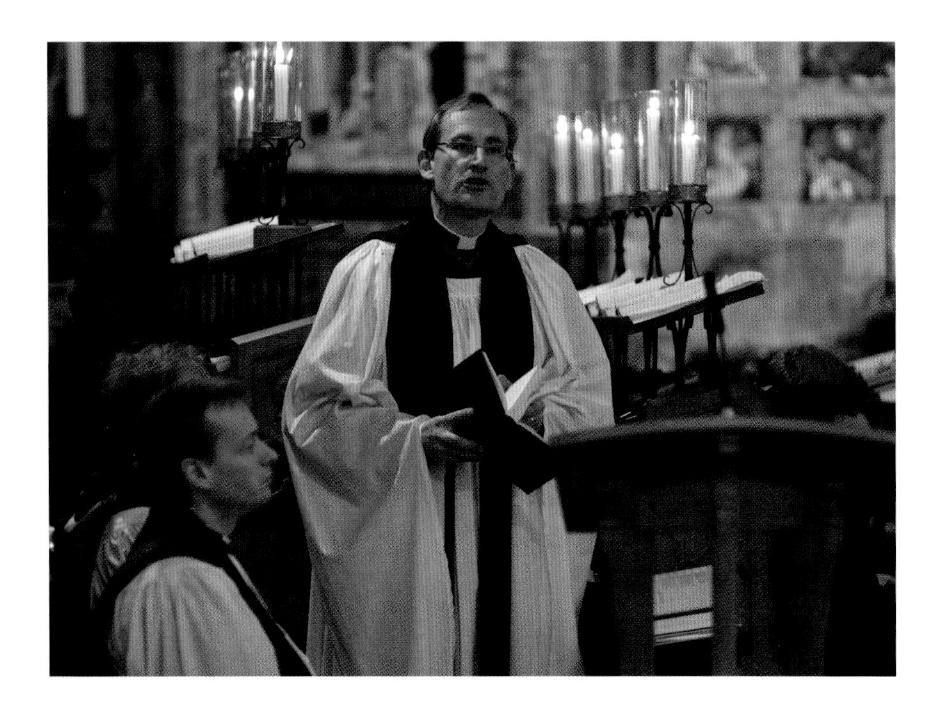

Dr Robert James (1953-71) considered Chapel, Divinity lessons and House prayers to be unquestioned parts of public school education, as much for social as for religious reasons. He disliked outward show and was happy to tolerate the worthy but uninspiring Chaplain, Philip Bryant. Daily Chapel, voluntary Holy Communion at eight in the morning, Matins and 'Whole School' Evensong on Sundays were the norm.

For the spiritually curious boy, for whom Chapel provided little of interest, an alternative popped up at Iwerne Minster. The Varsity and Public Schools Camps provided sports-related holidays centred on evangelical Bible study. These began to make serious inroads at Harrow. Off-shoot groups were formed in the Houses, stimulated by visits from the 'officers'. This led to the formation of a School-based society, named 'Flambards' after the house in which meetings first took place. It is a style that has held its appeal for over fifty years. Meanwhile the Roman Catholic boys made their way through St Mary's churchyard to the Catholic Church of St Thomas of Canterbury in Roxborough Park, led by a Catholic Master, Mr CL Walton.

Head Master Michael Hoban (1971-81) relaxed Chapel attendance, while retaining compulsion for professed Anglicans, and introduced a more accessible form of religion. This was the way school religion was developing at this time, but Hoban encouraged the challenging, liberal ideas of his Chaplain, The Rev Martyn Hughes. Moreover the backgrounds of the boys in the School had begun to change: with international travel becoming easier and financial pressure at home, the issue of race (and thereby the admission of non-Christians) was becoming more important. Harrow had long been an Imperial school, educating countless Maharajas as well as a few Middle Eastern monarchs, but the exclusion from what every Head Master from 1914-1991 had considered to be the centre of the School, Chapel, was insensitive to the point of offensiveness.

Ian Beer (1981-91) encouraged a new flavour to religious life, bringing with him from Lancing (the Anglo-Catholic Woodard school) a second Chaplain and licensing a lay reader. The appointment to the staff of The Rev Peter Jackson, the name of a Master already in the School, gave Mr Beer the chance to announce that the former would be known as "Father Peter" – "to avoid confusion" – thereby raising a significant Anglo-Catholic flag. He reintroduced the concept of Christian manliness, the concept of holistic education: academic learning for the mind, sport for the character and religion as the basis for social behaviour. He also recognised the need to provide opportunities for instruction and worship for non-Anglicans and appointed Fr Lawrence Soper, a Benedictine priest from Ealing Abbey, and a Rabbi. However his good intentions were frustrated when faced with Islamic provision, perhaps not then realising the animosity between different Muslim sects. The Hindus and Buddhists were altogether too daunting a prospect.

The Roman Catholic initiative was nearly sunk by its very success: Catholic parents soon saw that they could give their sons a Harrow education and at the same time be assured that they would receive the pastoral care that up to then had only been available at a Catholic school. It was a win-win situation: confidence soared. Catholic confirmations took place in Westminster Cathedral as well as Ealing Abbey. On one occasion even Cardinal Hume presided. As other Anglican or non-aligned schools followed suit, the result was a serious drop in numbers at the Catholic schools: Douai closed and attempts were made by the Roman hierarchy to reverse the situation, but it was too late.

Head Master Nick Bomford's (1991-99) role had been defined by the Governors as that of a consolidator and he was certainly not one to rock the religious boat. His interference was minimal and he even chose not to give the traditional Head Master's beginning and end of term sermons. For the first time for many years Chapel ceased to be the focal point of the School, but the formation of the Religious Studies department in 1989 and the introduction of the study of comparative religions together with 'Thought for the Day' for non-Christians led to a greater understanding and tolerance of religious traditions and practices – at least among the boys.

The appointment of Father Andrew Wadsworth to the teaching staff in 1998 underlined the trend. It was not long before Roman Catholic Masses were held in Chapel after the Anglican Eucharist. By 2008, 18% of the School was Catholic (66% Anglican).

For the most part, school religion reflects the practices of the parents and, to a lesser extent, that of the Anglican church at large, with the Head Master keeping a hand on the tiller. The arrival of Barnaby Lenon (1999), the son of a clergyman and educated at a school for such, might have been expected to have had a greater impact on school religion than it did. His objective was to create a successful school with a high national and international profile. To do that, he raised the academic standard, the position in the league tables and sought excellence in every aspect of school activity. This was not a time to interfere with an aspect of the School that appeared to be meeting everyone's expectations. His occasional forays to the pulpit were directed towards intellectual analysis of scripture: there were no uncomfortable questions about faith and beliefs.

However school religion in the first decade of the twenty-first century has never been stronger in the sense that it operates on several distinct levels. For the committed Christian, the regular Anglican worship, with special services such as 'whole school' services at the beginning of term, Remembrance Day, Founder's Day, Association Day, Confirmations, Sunday Eucharist and mid-week celebrations in the Crypt, led and directed by the Chaplain, The Rev James Power, is complemented by the provision of Roman Catholic worship and the pastoral care of a Catholic chaplain. For the more intellectually inclined, the Gore Society meets to discuss theological matters. At the other end of the ecclesiastical scale there is 'Flambards', providing the opportunity for regular Bible study and evangelical worship, while 'Thought for the Day' led to an opportunity for thought and reflection in a non-sectarian context, led and supported by several Masters.

Statistics 2008

Anglican and "Protestant" Christians: 528; Roman Catholics: 140; Russian and Greek Orthodox Christians: 5; Jews: 16; Muslims: 1; Hindus: 23; Buddhists: 6; Sikhs: 4; Zoroastrians: 1; Non-aligned: 59.

The Roman Catholic Chaplain at Mass in Chapel

DISCIPLINE AND PUNISHMENT

THE FOUNDER JOHN LYON'S Rules to be Observed for the Ordering of the School stated: [The schoolmaster] "shall have regard to the manners of the scholars and see that they come not uncombed, unwashed, ragged or slovenly, but before all things he shall punish severely swearing, lying, picking, stealing, fighting, filthiness or wantonness of speech, and such like". He went on to be specific about punishments:

"The Schoolmaster shall use no kind of correction save only with a rod moderately, except it be a very thin ferule upon the hand for a slight negligence; so like wise the Usher. If they do, by discretion of the Governors after admonition they shall be displaced."

So what happened at Harrow (and at other schools) that allowed the bullying and terrorising of young boys by their elders and by teachers, that continued well into the twentieth century? The belief that 'flogging' was a normal way to discipline a child seems to have been accepted since biblical times and Samuel Butler's recommendation that "to spare the rod is to spoil the child" dates from 1662.

In the early years of the School's history, the Head Master's only concern in matters of discipline was in the form room. Punishments in the form of lines of Latin to be learned or written out seem to have been established at an early stage, although physical punishment was normal too. The Head Master took little notice of what happened outside the form room unless it was brought to his notice, for example when a boy was flogged by Dr Sumner (1760–71) for trespassing on a field next to the School. It was only when the 'foreigners' arrived in sufficient numbers to dominate the School and when it became a boarding school for the wealthy and aristocratic, that institutionalised violence in the name of discipline and good order took hold.

Head Master Thackeray (1746–60) was said to be reluctant to beat, although the same could not be said of his Under Master, William Prior, who had a reputation as a brutal sadist.

Benjamin Heath (Head Master 1771–85) was an enthusiastic flogger. Joseph Drury (Head Master 1785–1805), on the other hand, declined to beat senior boys and was even reluctant to set them lines. He did however allow Monitors to beat – with canes rather than birches – and this was perhaps the beginning of the culture of approved barbarity. Boys were used to settling differences with physical violence and Drury's decision merely gave it official approval.

Under Head Master George Butler (1805–29), Harrow gained the reputation for being a lazy school, with an endless succession of whole holidays. It was also a disorderly school – even by the standards of the

The birch was the favoured instrument for Head Masters' floggings

962 361

his admitted offence was deserving of a Monitor's whopping which was to take place in the 4th Form Room next morning at 8.45. However, late at night the Head-master sent to inform the Head of the School that he could not permit it to take place at that time, as there would be too many boys about. The head of the offender's house, a Monitor, also wrote demanding a reconsideration of the case. Consequently it was found necessary to abandon the plan adopted, and another meeting was hastily summoned at 9.30. It was then decided that unless the 'actual ring-leader', whom the accused boy declared to exist, would come forward, the Monitors held to their former decision, to inflict a whopping of five strokes, upon the accused, as the worst known offender. He then, informed the Head of the School that he appealed to Mr. Welldon. Of course he had a perfect right to do so, but he was by no means successful, as the Head-master not only flogged and degraded him, but also requested him to leave at the end of the term.

A report written by the Head of School in 1896, describing the complicated protocols leading to the administration of punishment. The offence? Organising cheering at Bill for a discredited captain of cricket.

Head Master Welldon (1885-98) was said to consider Harrow 'overdisciplined' and claimed to have relaxed it. However his record in the Punishment Book of around a hundred floggings a year suggests otherwise.

time: there were a number of well publicised scandals. Sadistic flogging seems to have reached new heights – without having any noticeable effect on boys' behaviour. Throughout his time there are accounts of fighting, drinking, stealing and bullying. By this time boarding was well established and descriptions of Butler's House suggest complete mayhem, which he made no attempt to control. The 'Lord of the Flies' scenario of bullying and unsupervised fagging culminated when Monitors were found to be carrying out their own floggings in the Fourth Form Room. The ensuing expulsions led to a riot. A further bullying scandal in 1826 nearly brought the School to its knees. This was probably the nadir of barbarism in Harrow's history.

After Butler, flogging by the Head Master was reduced, although that by other Masters and Monitors was unabated in its savagery. Dr Longley (Head Master, 1829–36) was uneasy about it: he took advice from Dr Arnold of Rugby fame, whose advice was to reserve the punishment for serious or repeated offences but, if used, it should be "administered in earnest". Dr Vaughan (Head Master 1845–59), a disciple of Arnold, increased the number of Monitors from ten to fifteen but tried to inject an element of responsibility into their position. He took a high-minded and rather unrealistic view of the role of the Monitor as being an instrument of his own authority. He also saw the monitorial system as a means of releasing Masters from the responsibility of spying on boys – a bit of a cop-out. Vaughan himself was not averse to beating: this was conducted with a birch on bare backsides in the Fourth Form Room, with Custos as a witness. Monitors' beatings (or 'whoppings') were administered with canes across the clothed backs and shoulder blades.

Throughout the nineteenth century attempts at discipline were dominated by a culture of mundane written punishments, punctuated by ritualised violence. By 1870 flogging had taken on a life of its own and had become a "sacred initiatory rite". Given the exhaustive catalogue of petty crimes punished by caning, for example, leaning out of the window or eating in the street, the vast majority of boys must have suffered such punishment at some time. Spencer Gore's song, *Jerry*, written in 1885, although light-hearted in tone, no doubt gives a real example: "Jerry a poor little fag/Carrying kettle and tray/ finding his energy flag/ let them all drop on the way./On him his monitor dropped/"Pick up the pieces at once!/Off to my room to be whopp'd,/Jerry, you duffer and dunce."

Head Master Welldon (1885–98) was said to consider Harrow "overdisciplined" and claimed to have relaxed it. However his record in the Punishment Book of around a hundred floggings a year suggests otherwise. Head Master Wood (1898–1910) did indeed reduce this statistic to an average of forty-four a year but by then the tyrannical rule of the 'bloods' was a much more terrifying proposition. Ford (1910–25) reduced the frequency further to about seventeen a year and abandoned the Fourth Form Room birching in favour of caning in his study. Norwood (1926–34), a keen disciplinarian, lowered the average to four a year and Vellacott (1934–39) decided to call a halt to what he described as a "tale of degradation, ugliness and tears". However that was by no means the end of Head Masters' beatings; indeed the Victorian tradition of Head Masters, House Masters and Heads of House beating continued right up to the 1970s. Dr Moore (1942–53) reinstated the Punishment Book on the grounds that records should be kept. Here he was ahead

AME Carruthers FOR ABC AMOUNT 100x DUE BY 7.15pm ON Tues 4th
(date)

Letters must touch both lines. Hand to House Master. (41 letters)

O what a rogue and peasant slave am I! Is it not monstrous
that this player here, But in a fiction, in a dream of
passion, Could force his soul so to his own conceit That
from her working all his visage wann'd, Tears in his eyes,
distraction in's aspect A broken voice, and his whole
function suiting With forms to his conceit? and all for
nothing! For Hecuba! What's Hecuba to him, or he
Hecuba, That he should weep for her?

A more modern punishment: "double"

of his time, although why corporal punishment should be singled out for such scruples is unclear.

Up to the 1980s it was normal practice for House Masters to allow the boys 'to run the House'. This could be educational, with layers of responsibility (and privilege) at each stage. It could also be abused and if the 'wrong' boy was at the top of the pile, bullying and rule-breaking thrived.

A particularly unpleasant form of official bullying, condoned and indeed encouraged by House Masters, was the ritual House beating. This took the form of the victim being informed by the Head of House that he would be beaten for a certain offence. After 'flicks' (lights out) the Head of House would give a 'boy call' (shout for a fag) thereby informing the House that a beating would take place. The victim was summoned to the House Library in his pyjamas, where the Monitors would be in attendance. The punishment would then be inflicted by the Head of House with a bamboo cane, the severity being largely at his discretion. Readers old enough to have seen Lindsay Anderson's film *If* will have witnessed only a slight exaggeration. Fear, sadism, schadenfreude, self-righteousness – and in rare cases disgust – all jostled for position under the emotional canopy.

In most prep schools in the first sixty years of the twentieth century, beating by the headmaster was *de rigueur*. One pupil at a traditional prep school in the 1950s described his shock, coming from an affectionate, non-violent family, to find that corporal punishment was virtually part of the curriculum. So it was no surprise to him to find it continuing at his public school. Tradition and respect for the past is a feature of human behaviour that is particularly prevalent in schools with a long history and it is right not to dispose of established practices lightly. However, in a more permissive age, we look back on such customs with profound disapproval; many of the most objectionable were allowed to continue because boys were not properly supervised.

Beating died out slowly at Harrow: Michael Hoban (1971–81) was the last Head Master to beat. By the mid-1970s it was very rare indeed. Corporal punishment was outlawed in all state schools in 1986, in private schools in 1998.

All through Harrow's history, there have been other punishments, short of caning, for minor offences: usually some form of academic imposition. Dr Wordsworth once set two boys caught in a pub the task of translating Psalm 119 (renowned for its length) into Greek. For those imposed by Masters – usually for work not, or badly done – an academic punishment would be appropriate: this was formalised in the 'skew' to be signed by the House Master, re-done and delivered by 'lock-up' the following day. In recent years 'detention' has been used as an extension of this. For bad behaviour, 'double' – the writing of a passage of English blank verse on ruled copy-writing paper i.e. letters to touch the top and bottom lines – is also still in use. Again the House Master's signature and correct delivery is required. A 'georgic' – five hundred lines, originally to be written in Latin – is rarely, if ever, imposed nowadays.

Attempts to ensure that boys "come not unwashed, ragged or slovenly" persist. 'Custos's report' is a sanction for dress offences, the modern boy's favourites being 'top button undone' and 'tie at half mast'; 'shirt hanging outside trousers'; 'trousers worn at a dangerously low level' and 'broken hat'.

House 'skews' – those imposed by House Master or Monitor – have also been modified in recent years. 'Gating' and 'rooming' have fallen foul of modern legislation; extra household chores are sometimes imposed but, generally, removal of privilege is the most generally accepted form of punishment.

Schools reflect the attitudes of the world outside and independent schools, which depend on parents' fees, especially so. The Victorian upper and middle classes had distant relationships with their children: nannies, governesses and servants often had much closer contact. Physical punishment at home was not unusual. As social and family life has changed, the servants have largely disappeared and parents have become closer to their children. As a result, some parents are unwilling or unable to apply the level of discipline to which they aspire: they look to the School to impose standards of behaviour they are not prepared to impose themselves. The over-indulged child is not an unknown phenomenon among affluent middle class families.

The modern parent expects the School to apply a code of discipline that is fair, structured, acceptable to boys and seen to be constructive. It should inculcate in a boy a self-discipline that will enable him to go out into a world where there are no rules with confidence. Fagging and beating have gone and bullying is but a shadow of its former self, but a boarding school can provide a structure and discipline to teenagers' lives that they might not get at home. Having a private room gives a sense of independence and is one of the most valuable parts of a Harrow education. Having to get up in the morning, wear a jacket and tie, organise a personal work schedule, act in plays, play games, and practise a musical instrument all help to structure a young person's life. For many of them the route has already been mapped out at prep school.

"HARROW-SPEAK"

IT IS A WELL-KNOWN human phenomenon that groups – particularly teenage male groups (or gangs) – need to define their identity in distinctive ways. Special clothing, territorial boundaries, weird customs and a language incomprehensible to outsiders are common features. Harrovians have been no exception.

Most English public schools of the nineteenth century developed an 'in-speak' – Winchester's was reputed to be particularly extensive – and its purpose was to distinguish 'us' from 'them'. In May 1940, *Time Magazine* reported, "Last week Britons able to take their minds off death in Flanders could amuse themselves with an authoritative new dictionary of schoolboys' slang (*Public School Slang*, by Morris Marples – Constable & Co)". Terms were devised to describe everyday objects, people or events; many were just abbreviations (a 'pun'); some were witty (the House 'beak' 'slimed' into 'sicker'), others are of unknown origin ('groise' and 'froust'). The most common form was and is the '–er' ending to almost anything: 'bluer', 'speecher', 'footer', 'eccer' and so on.

Naturally as the object went out of use or the custom ceased, the word disappeared from the lexicon, but also the reluctance of new Masters to adopt Harrow terminology ('division' rather than 'set') has led to an erosion of some traditional words. No longer will a 'chaw be whopped in reader' but a 'footer flannel' will still take 'a tosh after eccer'. The list that follows is almost certainly not comprehensive.

"HARROW-SPEAK"

Base – a goal in football
Beak – teacher, also known as a "master" (both male and female)
Bill – a roll call held in each House that boys from the House must attend. School Bill, held in the School Yard, which used to occur every half holiday, is now held only on Speech Day
Bill Book – a small blue book published each term providing essential information about all aspects of the School and a calendar of main events, fixtures etc.
Bluer – the 'blue' uniform jacket.
Blood – a boy who has won 'flannels' for cricket, soccer, football or a 'minor sport' or a 'Lion'. In particular a "triple blood" has won three such distinctions.
Bum – a Monitor (not derogatory)
Bumpf – paper
Call-over – alternative word for Bill (see above) in some Houses
To cap – a salute to a beak raising index finger to hat rim (obsolescent)
Chit – a note, probably from a Master giving permission or excusing lateness.
Copy – an award for twelve 'send ups' (see below), or to the top boy in each division in a subject each term; eight copies win a prize
Cut – not to turn up for something; in earlier days, if a Master was more than ten minutes late for a lesson, the division could 'take a cut'
Division or Div – an academic 'set' or group.
Double – lines on special paper, set as a punishment
Ducker – the swimming pool formerly on the other side of the Watford Road, now in the Sports Centre
Eccer – exercise: any form of games
Fez – tassled cap awarded for Harrow football; also used to describe the winner of such
Fifth Form – third year group of boys, taking GCSE

MORE "HARROW-SPEAK"

Flannels – School colours for cricket, football, soccer or in exceptional circumstances for a minor sport
Flicks – a signal for lights out at night (discontinued in most Houses)
Footer – Harrow football
Form room – classroom
Gating – a punishment forbidding going off the Hill
Georgic – punishment for a particularly serious offence: copying 500 lines in Latin.
Greyers – grey School trousers
The Guild – an elected group of senior boys who have shown artistic or cultural excellence; they have a distinctive maroon tie and can wear a maroon waistcoat with their tails
The Hill – School tuck shop
Lion – a member of the First XV rugby team
Locking Up – the time after which pupils may not leave their House without permission
Mill – a fight. The Milling Ground was formerly the place assigned for settling personal differences
Monitor (School) – School 'prefect', a senior boy in the School
Monitor (House) – House 'prefect' (also called a Sixth Former or 'priv' in some Houses)
Philathletic Club – the School's top athletes. They can wear a black bow-tie. Commonly called 'The Phil'
Prep – preparation of work for the next day: 'home work'
Priv – House Monitor in some Houses
Queue – times each day when the House Master is available for withdrawing money, to report send ups and skews, and for other matters of business or concern
Reader – House library
Rears – a lavatory
Remove – the second year group of boys
Rooming – a punishment forbidding a boy to leave his room (and others to visit) except on approved business
Send Up – a piece of good work sent up to be signed by the House Master.
Shell – the youngest year group of boys
Shepherd – a boy in the year above whose job it is to look after new Shell boys for their first two weeks
Sicker – House sick room
Sixth formers – members of the fourth and fifth years in the School. In some Houses, House monitors or privs are known as 'sixth formers'
Skew – punishment from a beak for poor or incomplete work; a House skew is for bad behaviour
Speecher – Speech Room
Sunday dress – tail coat, waistcoat and striped trousers worn on Sundays and other major occasions
Tails – Sunday dress
Tolley Up – permission to work after lights out (only used in a few Houses).
Torpids – House sports team, aged under sixteen
Tosh – a bath or shower
Trials – internal School examinations
Up – being 'up to a beak' means being in his division. Also 'up to School'
Yarder – game played in a House yard (also used to describe this area)
Yards – a fair catch in football. Hence 'give Yards' and 'take Yards'
Yearlings – first year teams or groups

"HARROW-SPEAK" FROM AN EARLIER ERA

To bag – to confiscate
Boy – 'On boy' – on fagging duty; see also 'on finds' (below)
Brew – cooking in the House
Brisser – a bowl for discarded bones at a meal
To buck up – to play hard
Bum-freezer – an Eton jacket (without tails)
Chaw – a cad
To be chawed up – to be prevented from doing something
Con – a piece of Latin to construe (analyse the syntax)
Dab – a skillful person
To be degerd (pronounced 'daygerd') – to be demoted
To be de-privved – to have privileges removed
Finds – Monitors' breakfast or dinner
To froust – to lie in bed after the rising bell
Frouster – an armchair
Fug – yard football
Harder – rackets, to distinguish it from squash (softer)
Hotter – toast or crumpets
Groise – a swot or hard worker (derogatory)
Jaw – a reprimand
Lecker – electric light
Ma – a female shopkeeper e.g. Ma Sullivan's (not disrespectful)
To mow – to move silently. See also 'slime'
Mucker – a heavy fall (rather than the usual meaning of 'a friend')
Poler – a kick at base in football that passes over the upright
Poop – a kick in the groin at football
Pun – punishment
Pupe – pupil room; a room in the House where private tuition took place
Rep – repetition (a piece of work to be learned by heart)
Saturday Nighter – an essay to be written over the weekend
Seconders – a non-representative House sports team
Shifty – scared (rather than the usual meaning of 'devious')
To slime – to go round quietly; see also 'mow'
Softer – squash rackets
Special – a private lesson OR a Monitor's personal fag
Speck – to expect to achieve some distinction
Stinks – Chemistry
Swagger – taking privileges to which a person is not entitled
Swell – a boy who is successful in the eyes of his fellows
Tique – Mathematics (after the pronunciation of Mr Marillier, a French Maths beak)
Tizzy tick – a card permitting credit at shops
Twenty-liner – lined paper, now replaced by A4
To twig (past tense 'twug') – to catch someone doing something
Wagger – waste paper basket
Whopping – caning
Worker – former School engineering workshop.

HEALTH

FOR MANY YEARS AFTER the establishment of the boarding system, all arrangements for the care of sick boys were part of the duty of House Masters. In 1862 Lord Clarendon, President of the Public Schools Commission, wrote to the Head Master suggesting the institution of a sanatorium. This together with a severe epidemic of scarlatina in the Spring term of 1861, led Dr Butler to raise subscriptions from Masters, Old Harrovians and parents and on 1 October 1864, he began the equipment of a sanatorium on the south side of the Hill. The architect was CF Hayward. The new establishment was opened in 1867 as a 'private concern' under the general management of trustees, but was handed over to the Governors by the surviving trustee, Dr HM Butler, in 1877.

At the beginning of the twentieth century, the Sanatorium was becoming too small for the increased needs of the School; indeed during the winter of 1903–4 the Copse was used as an overflow. In 1919 a new Sanatorium Fund was opened to raise subscriptions from parents and others. No progress was made, however, until 1929 when Bowden House – formerly Sudbury Hill House – off Sudbury Hill, on the site of the present Harrow Fields Gardens, was bought and converted into a sanatorium. The building had previously been used as a nursing home. The Sanatorium, under a nursing Sister and staffed with qualified nurses, was fitted out to accommodate sixty-five boys. In 1930 a fully equipped operating theatre was added.

Nurse McCotter (date unknown: probably 1890s)

The Sanatorium had spacious grounds, nearly thirty acres in extent, about twelve of which were leased to the (then named) Lower School of John Lyon and to the Old Gaytonians (the former pupils of Harrow County School for Boys). Later these became the playing fields of The John Lyon School.

With the creation of the National Health Service 1948, the needs of the School began to change. For boys who were seriously ill or injured, Harrow Hospital in Roxeth Hill provided a safer (and free) medical service, and the fact that it was actually nearer the School than the San made it easier for boys and Masters to visit patients. At this time the School Doctor had a surgery off the High Street just below the Bursar's Office.

Improved preventative medicine and the quality of the NHS treatment was making the School San redundant. By 1970, when Northwick Park Hospital was opened on the Watford Road opposite the football fields, the San's operating theatre had not been used for years. It was beginning to look increasingly like a white elephant. Within two years it was sold and replaced by a medical centre with six beds, situated over Gieves, the Outfitters, on the High Street. Sadly the Old San, a handsome building, was demolished except for its façade in a redevelopment programme.

The transfer had the great advantage of drawing together the School Doctor's surgery and the Sister's medical centre under one roof in the centre of the School; the disadvantage was that access was up an external metal staircase – a tricky

manoeuvre for patients unable to walk – until a lift was built, twenty years later.

Weekday morning surgeries and emergency Saturday morning surgeries continued to be held, and the doctor or one of the practice partners provided out of hours cover. Currently a partnership of five doctors performs the School Doctor's role. In line with national arrangements, out of hours cover is provided by the local GP consortium based at Northwick Park Hospital.

The Medical Centre is staffed by a team of registered nurses on a twenty-four-hour roster. These are highly qualified nurse practitioners, who can run their own surgeries and can prescribe under patient group directives. During the Autumn and Spring terms St John Ambulance provides First Aid cover at rugby and football matches; the Doctor is also available, with support from one of the senior Sisters.

The nature of medical care has changed in emphasis in a number of ways in the last twenty years. First, the Medical Centre has extended its range of services so that it is now more like a minor accident unit or GP unit, and provides a significant number of services on-site, such as Asthma Clinics.

Second, there has been a steadily increasing pressure on boys to recover from sporting injuries more quickly in order to resume playing: this has come from Masters, parents and the boys themselves. To meet this need, a private physiotherapy service was introduced and treatment was made available in the Medical Centre twice weekly.

Third, the trend for boys to be sent home for parental care when ill has become well established and has increased.

Fourth, in keeping with the vast strides in the development of pastoral care in the School, an adolescent psychiatrist visits the School weekly, both to consult with the Doctor and to see individual boys.

The opening of the Clementine Churchill Hospital, a private hospital in Sudbury Hill, in 1981 was a significant event. Most boys have some sort of private medical insurance and much use has been made of the 'Clem' for treatment of sports injuries and physiotherapy, as well as for more serious conditions.

When Dr Kaye was School Doctor he played an active role in the School's Physical Health & Safety programme. This no longer happens and these days the doctors largely confine themselves to attendance at surgeries. The School Doctor is a member of the Medical Officers of Schools Association, an association of nearly 400 GPs with independent schools in their practices.

Plan for the original Sanatorium (The Builder *1869)*

FAGGING

WITH THE ESTABLISHMENT OF boarding in the eighteenth century came a number of practices that later became an accepted part of the School's way of life. The original boarding houses were numerous, some run by Masters, others by local house owners known as Dames. These varied in size, from just one or two boys in many cases to the Head Master's, which accommodated up to ninety boys in 1774. The occupants were largely unsupervised, neither of the categories of landlord above considering it their responsibility to regulate the behaviour of their tenants.

At this time boys in the School were spread across a wide age range (from six to eighteen in 1801) and the power base was concentrated where it is in any gang: with the biggest and strongest. It was natural that the older boys should get the young ones to work for them. Drinking and hooliganism were rife and bullying commonplace; it is not an attractive picture.

By the middle of the eighteenth century, fagging (as this forced labour came to be known) was compulsory for those below the IV Form. As promotion through forms was based on academic progress the less intellectually gifted could spend years as a fag. Head Master Butler banned 'night fagging' in 1827.

Apart from 'personal' duties, shopping and so on, cricket and rackets were particularly dependent on small boys' help. Because there were no nets, cricket practice required any number of 'fielders' to fetch and return, and the rackets 'courts' in the School Yard, each with one wall only, had a similar need.

Although fagging was officially condoned – even approved – this did not mean that there was no longer abuse; indeed one Head of House was expelled from the School for beating up his fag in 1837. The following year, Head Master Wordsworth had the rules for fagging put in writing, restricting the duties in boarding houses to serving breakfast, running errands for Monitors and the like, and, out of Houses, to cricket fagging. It must have been around this time that the term 'Finds' came into usage for breakfast fagging. As this was not a meal provided in the House, fags would be sent out to 'find' or shop for the food and then serve it. 'Finds breakfast' and later 'finds dinner' were the names given to meals at which the Monitors were the hosts and they and the guests were waited upon by fags. This practice continued until the 1970s.

As Victorian attitudes began to take hold, fagging was seen to be a 'character-building' exercise and indeed there was a certain, if by no means universal, honour attached to responsible use of the system. Although fagging was by then regulated, as before the practicality depended on the nature of the ruling regime. Edmund Howson's song, *Boy!*, glorifies the role of the fag who falls asleep in front of the fire and dreams of the day when he will be a Monitor and a cricketer "arrayed in flannels batting for the school at Lord's". The treble solo is backed by a 'boy call' which wakens him to reality.

Christopher Tyerman describes fagging as "time consuming drudgery". At best it was a harmless system. Personal fags (specials) performed domestic duties: bed-making, room-tidying, shoe-cleaning, fire-lighting and in return, if they were lucky, they received the patronage of the Monitor: help with prep, encouragement in games or other activities of mutual interest, sometimes even payment. Other fags would have a duty day each week on 'boy' or on 'finds'. 'Day boys' answered 'boy calls'(last one there got the job) usually for some errand, shopping or taking notes to other Houses; 'finds boys' served Monitors' breakfast – including the special Sunday

Head Master Wordsworth had the rules for fagging put in writing, restricting the duties in boarding houses to serving breakfast, running errands for monitors and the like, and out of Houses to cricket fagging.

'finds breakfast' when Masters and their wives, and Monitors from other Houses, might be guests. At worst a vicious, sadistic or vindictive Monitor could make life miserable for a fag – and there is no doubt that sexual malpractices took place too.

As with so many practices handed down from generation to generation in a school, boys tend to treat others as they were treated themselves – or, occasionally, to react violently against that treatment. It requires adult intervention to change the culture. Fagging was gradually phased out in the 1980s, first being reduced to 'community fagging', 'personal fagging' becoming outlawed. This was really because it was seen as an archaic practice with no place in the modern world. It should also be noted that many of the duties performed by fags had been overtaken by modern technology: central heating for coal fires; duvets for bed-making; microwave ovens for cooking; mobile phones for communication and so on. It took longer to die out in some Houses than others… And Tyerman also observes, "It may be pure chance that the eradication of the acceptance of homosexuality as part of Harrow boarding life coincided with the demise of fagging. There again it may not."

The fagging system was not all bad but it has no place in the School of the twenty-first century.

A replica 1870s boy's room in the Museum of Harrow Life; the fag is seen to be returning the Monitor's bed to its daytime position

ACADEMIC CURRICULUM

THE FOUNDER, JOHN LYON, laid down in his Statutes a plan of education for his school, based entirely on the classical subjects Latin and Greek. Although the younger pupils had to learn to read and write in English in a form known as the "Petties", the curriculum followed this plan for 150 years. There were five forms: in the First Form a beginning was made in Latin grammar. The Second Form continued with grammar and began to translate Aesop, Cato and Erasmus; they also learned to write Latin sentences and to translate *into* Latin. The Third Form concluded the study of grammar and translated some authors such as Cicero and Ovid; they were also taught to write connected prose. The Fourth Form's texts were Cicero, Virgil, Horace and Erasmus; they also began verse composition and embarked on Greek. In the Fifth Form the Latin authors studied were Virgil, Caesar, Cicero and Livy while the Greek syllabus comprised the works of Demosthenes, Isocrates, Hesiod, Heliodorus and Dionysius.

The procedure was for the Master to go through a passage in the text book, translating each word literally; then the boys would 'construe' the passage to the Master, each boy taking a few lines. The Third, Fourth and Fifth forms spent an hour each day in the medieval practice of 'disputation', that is, asking each other questions on grammar or vocabulary.

All this was done in conditions of considerable discomfort: as there were no desks, all writing had to be done on the knee, while the inkhorn was stuck in the belt or precariously held in the other hand. As the whole School worked in the same room, the atmosphere is unlikely to have been one of quiet study – although the rule that Latin only could be spoken would have reduced the noise considerably. When it was dark in winter, each boy had to light his own candle, although where he put it is unclear. Heating was rudimentary to say the least, a small wood fire being lit in the grate at the start of the day and allowed to burn out.

Facing page: A Physics lesson

Morning school began at six and ended at eleven. Afternoon school ran from one to six. There were no half or whole holidays and on Sundays pupils attended morning service at St Mary's after which there was some religious instruction. This seems to have been conducted in the same formal way, with boys learning the Lord's Prayer, Ten Commandments, Thirty-nine Articles and so on, in English then in Latin. Most of the actual teaching occurred in 'pupil room', a private arrangement between teacher and pupil.

Under Head Master Bryan (1691–1730) extras were beginning to be added on to the school day – Handwriting, Mathematics, probably some modern language, Dancing and Fencing – although these were taught outside the form room and had to be paid for by the participants. French and drawing were added a little later. By the middle of the eighteenth century, Latin had ceased to be an international tongue in Europe outside the Roman Catholic Church, and French had become the language of diplomacy. With foreign travel increasing too, the mood in education was to spread to a wider field of study. Private academies had already begun to include Mathematics, French and Modern History in their curricula but unfortunately these subjects lay outside the Lyonian prescription. At Harrow the local farming community, for whose sons the School had been founded, was becoming increasingly disillusioned with the purely classical education provided and gradually ceased sending their sons to the School.

Two ways were found to get round this problem: the first was to allow non-classical studies to be taught by 'Extra Masters' outside School hours, the lessons

UMBRO

Sixth Form.

Monday.	½ past VII.	Repetn. Friday's Horace. Look over Lyrics.
	XI.	Horace, Odes. 60 lines.
	III.	Homer, 50 lines. Modern History.
	V.	Historia Romana, 50 lines. Set Theme.
Tuesday.		Bills at IX. XI. II. IV. & VI.
Wednesday,	½ past VII.	Repetn. Monday's Homer. Look over Verses.
	XI.	Virgil's Aen., 50 lines. Extracts fm Roman Histy.
	III.	Euclid & Vulgar Fractions.
	V.	Poesis Graeca 50 lines. 4 pages of Melkin's Greece. Set Translation or Essay.
Thursday,	½ past VII.	Repn. Wednesday's Virgil. Look over Theme.
	XI.	Thucydides. Set Lyrics. Græcian Antiqus & Chronology, etc.
	¾ past XII.	Modern History Lecture.
Friday.	½ past VII.	Repetn Monday's Horace. Look over essay.
	XI.	Demos. de Coronâ etc. 50 lines. Græcian Antiqs & Chronology, etc.
	III.	Greek Play.
	V.	Horace, Sat. or Ep. 4 pages of Melkin's Greece. Set Verses.
Saturday.	½ past VII.	Scholarship Gk Testament. Beausobre (?) etc.
	XI.	Thucydides and Hist. Romana alternately.
Sunday.	VIII.	Epistles to Romans & Hebrews. Newton on Prophecies. Articles of Church of England.

Fifth Form.

Classics and Exercises nearly the same as 6th Form. The Divinity—The Acts of the Ap[illegible]es, Paley's Evidences and Well's G[illegible]y of N T

being paid for directly by the pupils. The second was the 'pupil room' system, whereby Assistant Masters taught private lessons, also out of School hours, and received payment. By 1770 French, Maths, Dancing, Drawing and Fencing were standard additions to formal school work. However the solution to one problem created another, in that these extra lessons were not affordable by the foundation scholars and became a benefit for the 'foreigners'.

By the end of Dr Sumner's Head Mastership in 1771, the School hours had changed considerably: 1st School: 7–9; 2nd School: 11–12; 3rd School 3–4; 4th School; 5–6. There were no lessons on Tuesdays and numerous whole holidays, allowing plenty of time for the 'extra', and for Masters more profitable, activity of private tuition. By 1773 some of the swarm of unofficial academic hangers-on had become regularised. In 1775 a Sixth Form was introduced for the academically most able. In 1780 a Shell form was created between forms IV and V.

Under Dr Butler (1805–29) the amount of time spent in school was reduced even further: 1st School: 7 a.m. – 8 a.m.; 2nd School: 11 a.m.–12 noon; 3rd School: 2 p.m.–2.30 p.m.; 4th School; 4.30 p.m. – 5.30 p.m. Thursdays and Saturday were half holidays and Tuesday a whole holiday. By then the teaching staff consisted of the Under Master, two Master's Assistants, the Under Master's Assistant and two Writing Masters. There were also two Extra Masters who taught French and Dancing. In 1837 Dr Wordsworth appointed an Assistant Master in Mathematics and the subject gained a regular place in the teaching timetable.

In the 1850s the armed services were the most popular single career for Harrovians and Dr Vaughan (1845–59) set up the Army Class in 1851. Members received extra Mathematics and studied a course in Military Science. By 1854, with 400 boys in the School, the forms were the Monitors: the Upper and Lower VIs, four divisions of the V, a Remove, four Shells, three IVs, and a very small III. There were fourteen Classical Masters, four Mathematical Masters and two Modern Language Extra Masters. Vaughan introduced further compulsory modern languages, French for all and German for those good at French.

Reforms were well under way by the time Dr Butler became Head Master in 1860: a Natural Science Master was appointed in 1867. In 1868 a major change occurred with the Public Schools Act that followed the Clarendon Commission. Academically the School was freed from the restrictions of the Lyonian Statutes. In practice Classics still remained the lynchpin of the curriculum, but in 1869 the Modern Side was instituted under Mr Edward Bowen. In this new department, History, Modern Languages, Mathematics and Natural Science were the main subjects, although Latin was also retained. Initially admission was restricted to those who had made a year's good progress on the Classical Side, so that in 1883 there were just seventy-one boys out of a total of 553 in the School. One of the drawbacks was that the universities still required Greek for entrance.

Butler was also anxious to improve the academic standards of the School, and introduced three measures to achieve this: in 1865 he introduced some entrance scholarships; he also substantially increased the number of prizes and in 1868 – rather more contentiously – a superannuation rule whereby boys who had not reached a certain form by a certain age would be required to leave.

Extract from Dr Longley's Notebook showing the Table of Work in 1829. Note that Tuesday is a whole holiday (with five 'bills'!)

In 1875 annual examinations for higher and lower certificates were introduced by the Oxford & Cambridge Examinations Board. These together with the entrance examinations to RMA Woolwich, RM College, Sandhurst, and Civil Service, India, meant that, for the first time, boys were being assessed by external bodies. Reacting to external pressures and with examinations in an ever widening range of subjects, Dr Welldon (1885–98) reorganised the School into three blocks: A: VI and V Forms; B: Removes and Shells; C: the IVs. The Clarendon Commission had recommended that Public Schools should not accept entries below the age of twelve and this, combined with the rapid expansion of preparatory schools, had sealed the lowest Form at the IV Form. The purpose of creating blocks was to allow 'streaming', that is for boys to be placed in 'divisions' according to their ability in a particular subject. In Butler's time Mathematics had been divisionalised; Welldon now extended the system to French and Science in the Upper School.

Welldon also reformed the curriculum: Latin, English, French, Mathematics, Science and Religion were to be taught at some stage to all boys below the VI Form; Gymnastics and Drawing or Singing were added in the IV Forms and Greek became optional. These reforms required more teaching periods, thus cutting into spare time and pupil room, causing predictable displeasure among both Masters and boys.

In 1905 the Oxford and Cambridge Examination Board introduced the School Certificate Examinations. It soon became almost universal practice for boys to take these examinations when they reached the required standard.

Lionel Ford (1910–25) continued the reforms begun by Welldon: he abolished 'pupil room' and introduced a new timetable, providing more time for teaching and clearing the mornings for academic work. He introduced into the VI Form a system of optional studies which included advanced Classics, Mathematics, Modern Languages, Special History, Natural Science,

On the High Street

English Literature, Music and Art; German and Spanish were added for the first time. He followed this in 1917 by abolishing the distinction between the Classical and Modern Sides. Between 1920 and 1925 he separated the VI Forms into specialist groups, each having a main subject of study and a number of subsidiary subjects. The main subject could be chosen from Classics, Mathematics, Modern Languages, History and Natural Science. Ford's successor Norwood added Geography to the list of main subjects and Economics to the subsidiaries. By the 1930s Harrow was well integrated into the national educational system.

Early morning school was abolished in 1940 and in 1952 an extra period of morning school (2e) added on Tuesdays and Thursdays. This was later extended to Monday, Wednesday and Friday.

In 1951 the General Certificate of Education Examination replaced School Certificate and Higher Certificate. GCE had no age boundaries and it was not uncommon to find boys from three different year groups in the same division. Boys were placed on entry according to their level of ability, these being IV Form, Shell, Remove, Lower Fifth (V.2: O-level form), Upper Fifth (V.1), Lower Sixth (VI.2: A-level form) and Upper Sixth (VI.1: University entrance and Scholarship form). For scholars arriving in Lower Fifth and taking GCE a year later, specialisation was seen at its most extreme. The forms from the V.2s upwards were designated by subject, for example V2 Class, V2 Hist, V2 Maths, V2 ML and V2 Sc, thus pre-determining the course of study: VI 2 M would do A-level in 'Double Mathematics' and Physics; VI2 ML would take French, German and a third language. Some boys would take A-level after three years and then leave the School; others would stay in the Upper Sixth Form for three years doing more advanced but necessarily narrow studies.

The problem of over-specialisation was conveniently solved in the 1980s when Oxford and Cambridge Universities ended 'seventh term entry' (i.e. a competitive examination in the term after A-level). Entrance scholarships to the universities were abolished and places awarded on A-levels and interview or short tests. With boys leaving now almost exclusively in July, Head Master Ian Beer (1981–91) seized the opportunity to move to a single term entry in the September of each year and to deliver a five-year course. All boys now entered the Shell (the demise of the IV Form causing dismay among some distinguished Old Harrovians who had begun their school careers there) and progressed through three years to GCE and a further two to A-level. A further assault on specialisation abolished the subject-based forms in the Upper and Lower VI and enabled boys to choose subjects from four groups. While not allowing every possible combination, it meant that boys were freed from some of the former constraints. Each boy was assigned to a tutor group, the tutor being a teacher of one of his chosen subjects.

In 1988 the National Curriculum was introduced. At the same time GCSE replaced O-level and CSE. Ostensibly it was to remove the two-tier nature of the examinations but it also provided an opportunity to review their nature and style, subject by subject. This is not the place for a detailed critique of the changes: let it suffice to say that some welcomed the relevance of the new courses while others deplored the loss of rigour. Since then, increasingly, perceived "dumbing down" has seen both Mathematics and History flee to International GCSE. Similar "grade inflation" at A-level led to the introduction of the A* grade in 2010.

League tables were introduced in 1992. Although greeted with apparent disdain, these soon had an effect on the number of lessons taught and preps set. An extra afternoon lesson was introduced on whole school day afternoons. Currently the teaching week is divided into thirty-eight teaching periods, each forty minutes long.

A curriculum review was carried out in 1999 and mainly affected the balance of periods between subjects in the Lower School: English, Maths and French were given the most teaching time and optional GCSE subjects were given the same amount of time. PE was dropped from the timetable and Information Technology introduced on a single period a week in the Shell only. The former practice of boys making final GCSE choices at the end of the Remove was stopped after 2000 and instead boys in the Shell made their GCSE choices for the following two years.

At various stages over the years, the blocks have been re-named to comply with general practice. They are now: Shells (Year 9), Remove (Year 10), Fifth Form (Year 11), Lower Sixth (Year 12) and Upper Sixth (Year 13).

In recent years the main preoccupation has been with Government initiatives, which have rained down like hailstones. Coursework has arrived and in some cases departed; 'modular' A-level examinations have survived in a modified form. The problem for schools has been that few initiatives have been allowed to bed in for long enough to test their worth.

Boys in school

CLASSICS

IN THE WELL KNOWN Harrow Song, *Five Hundred Faces*, a treble soloist sings of the experiences that confront him as a new boy. One of the experiences of which he sings is that of enduring the academic fare on offer in Victorian times:

Nothing but proses and reps and con!
O for the future when I'm a man
With no more Virgil to learn and scan
And no one to say to me, 'Please go on.'

As Christopher Tyerman has pointed out, though quite a lot of Greek and Latin was read in Harrow in the nineteenth century, the pupils were subjected to the "unrelenting monotony of construe and composition, recitation, exercises, and themes". Until 1874 the School's statutes laid down that Latin must be spoken even at play, though common sense would suggest that the rule must have been frequently broken. This is not as mad as it sounds. At the time of Harrow's foundation, Latin was the language of communication in diplomacy and scholarship (including science). For centuries some acquaintance with it was a social marker, part of what defined a gentleman. Hence the symbolic importance of the Head of School's annual Latin report to the Governors, the Contio, a tradition launched in 1674 which has continued, with only a few gaps and one foray into English, until the present.

Mr EVC Plumtre's Classical Sixth Form of 1956, all of whom went on to Oxford or Cambridge, eleven of them with awards. On EVCP's right is Robin Butler, now Lord Butler of Brockwell

Yet it is profoundly depressing to reflect that Mr EW Howson, the writer of the words of *Five Hundred Faces* and a Classics Master at the School, should convey so grim a picture of the Latin lessons. Reading Virgil is potentially one of the most rewarding and life-enhancing experiences offered by European literature. The last line of the quotation, at first sight so lame, in fact gives an only too credible impression of the grisly monotony of studying the poet at Harrow in 1883, the year of the song's composition.

The main problem was that, while exposure to the Classics was no doubt rewarding for some, compulsory Latin for all throughout their time at the School proved ill-suited to the vast majority. Harrow clearly had some Masters of genuine academic distinction. Mr Henry Nettleship, who launched the School's Essay Club, its most prestigious and still thriving society, with a paper on 'The Religion of the Romans in the time of Cicero' in 1872, went on to be Professor of Latin Literature at Oxford. And clearly there was the occasional inspiring teacher who breathed life into the sclerotic methodology. One of these was Mr EVC Plumptre, Head of Classics in the middle years of the twentieth century. As Tyerman remarks, he "managed the trick of inspiring enthusiasm and belief in the subject as well as expertise; postcards to pupils could as easily be in elegant Greek as in his limpid English prose". He also brought light into his pupils' lives in a broader educational sense. They might, for example, find themselves whisked off to Covent Garden, Glyndebourne or the National Gallery. It is no less than just that the School has set up its most distinguished Sixth Form scholarship prize in his honour.

But the time was to come when the occasional presence of such remarkable figures proved insufficient to preserve the *ancien régime*. The decision of Oxford and Cambridge in 1960 to stop demanding a qualification in Latin as a requirement for entry quickly put paid to the unquestioned place of Classics in the School timetable. The response from the Harrow Classics department was speedy. In 1965, Mr Maurice Balme and Mr Mark Warman, who alternated as Heads of Classics between 1966 and 1979, produced a book called *Aestimanda*. It was a collection of Greek and Latin passages which were presented as material for literary discussion. The responses to classical literature, notably absent in the experience encapsulated in *Five Hundred Faces*, began to be elicited as a conscious part of the educational process. The importance of *Aestimanda* can scarcely be over-emphasized. Suddenly throughout the English-speaking world students and teachers alike were not just paying lip service to the idea that the overriding aim of learning the Latin and Greek languages was the understanding and enjoyment of the works written in them; they were actually experiencing that understanding and enjoyment for themselves.

Aestimanda was the first of a stream of classical books from Harrow, the most massive of these publishing enterprises being Balme and Mr James Morwood's *Oxford Latin Course*. Mr Mark Greenstock was a leading figure in the development of Ancient History as a modern A-level subject. Miss Judith Affleck more recently kept the publishing tradition on the road as an editor of a lively series of translations of Greek drama for the Cambridge University Press, to which her successor, Mr Ben Shaw, has also contributed. In so far as publications can come to the aid of Classics in its beleaguered years, Harrow has led the way.

The School's proximity to central London has led to the sharing of Harrow's superb resources with a wider world. At their zenith, a series of Sixth Form Conferences brought hundreds of students to Harrow, many of them from maintained schools, all over the South East of England. Miss Affleck started collaborating with state schools in the Harrow area to ensure that Latin and Greek A-level are open to all. A significant and moving moment occurred in 2000 when a student from a local school stepped up onto the Speech Room stage on Speech Day to accept her Harrow prize from the Head Master.

So what actually happened to Classics while all this labour was being expended? The story goes something like this. In a little-known essay called *The Parthenon and the Optative*, CS Lewis quotes, with evident approval "a grim old classical scholar" looking up from some entrance papers and saying, "The trouble with these boys (sic) is that the masters have being talking to them about the Parthenon when they should have been talking to them about the Optative." (The optative, a word that nobody knows quite how to pronounce, is a part of the Greek verb even more remote than the subjunctive!) The idea is that the optative stands for hard learning, the Parthenon for wishy-washy art appreciation. So Lewis agrees with the scholar that study of the optative is a 'good thing' while study of the Parthenon is a bad one. Lewis's view was pre-echoed by Joseph Wood (Head Master 1898–1910) when in 1899 he responded to an offer of slides of Greek and Roman sites and buildings with the comment that "getting the optative right was much more important", adding that he would be glad to borrow a slide which would help in teaching it! Though there are doubtless classical backwoodsmen still around who agree with this Philistine nonsense, they will not be found at the Harrow of today. Classical civilization is far more than two languages. It is two whole worlds in microcosm. And now, at last, classicists, both at Harrow and in the world outside, have fully realised what that means.

And the modern methodology actually works. The top performer in 'Greats' (the final exam) at Oxford in 2009 was an Old Harrovian. He claimed that he owed his First in 'Mods' (the preceding exam) to the current Head of Classics at Harrow School.

A Classics lesson in the New Schools, taught by Mr Ben Shaw

STORES

DESIGN AND TECHNOLOGY

ONE OF THE BENEFACTIONS of the Lyon Memorial Fund, launched to celebrate the School Tercentenary in 1871, was a new School workshop. This was the lower part of a building, on a site just below the rackets court, shared with a new gymnasium; it was designed by Mr CF Hayward and completed in 1874.

The workshop was left unequipped for some time, but in 1876 William Halliday, who had come from Somerset to teach wood-carving in a small shop in the High Street, supplied the sum required for the purchase of lathes and tools. He assumed management of the workshop under the supervision of a Master, Mr FE Marshall, and started with fifty pupils. At first gas lighting was used but electric power was installed in 1907.

In 1883 *The Harrovian* described the Workshop as "well attended... Boats, steam engines, bicycles, tables, cabinets, a Roman Villa and a ferret box" were among the items created. The success of the Workshop was such that in 1892 a large extension for the building of boats, later to become a machine shop, was added. In 1920 a metal lathe was installed and in 1921 the Onslow Library, the engine-room, the battery-room and the Willans Room were built. The Willans Room was extended in 1928 for use as a drawing office and a lecture room, and a foundry was added. First under Eng-Lieut WC Oliver RN (1919–21) then Lieut RJ Conway (1921–57) 'Worker' became a popular institution with boats, bicycles, engines of various sorts, and domestic furniture all coming off the construction line. Several prizes for 'general proficiency', handicraft and engineering were endowed by parents and Old Harrovians.

For more than forty years all attendance at Workshop was voluntary and outside the curriculum, but Mr CL Bryant who became master-in-charge in 1917, persuaded the Head Master, Lionel Ford, to allow certain boys to do Engineering instead of Latin and to make Handicraft a compulsory subject taught in the IV Form. It later became possible for all boys to choose Workshop as a subject: in 1924, 252 boys took advantage of that option. A further boost to Worker came when the Oxford & Cambridge Board included Handicraft in the School Certificate Examination.

In 1924 the Engineering Society was formed and soon began to thrive. Exhibitions were held each year with new achievements proudly displayed: mass production of steel eye-bolts, cast bronze ashtrays (1937), a model electric locomotive, a refrigerator with a time-switch (1939), and so on.

In the 1940s attention was diverted to the war effort and 'sub-contracts' demanded work of a less creative nature: in 1941 it was claimed that three-quarters of a mile of holes had been bored. All this was top secret at the time and only later was the full extent of Worker's involvement revealed. It began when the Army decided that six-pounder guns were to replace two-pounders on a certain tank, requiring large 'holding bolts'. The firm given the contract experienced serious difficulties when their screwing machines broke down and Worker was called in to help. Late in 1941 Worker agreed a contract for five different sorts of tank parts with the Acton Bolt Company; an order from Morris Motors of Birmingham had to be sub-contracted to local firms with Worker responsible for the quality of the final articles. A shortage of raw materials and threading equipment from the USA caused delays but by October 1943 over 42,000 parts had been manufactured. In March 1943 the Ministry of Supply requested another 24,000 parts and 84,000 army lorry parts were produced for Vauxhall Motors. In addition various sample and experimental parts were made for the Ministry of Aircraft Production. All this represented a remarkable effort, not least by members

Design Technology in the Churchill Schools

of the School unconnected with Worker, who helped in various ways: moving raw material from the foundry to the machine shop, counting and bagging finished articles for despatch, and in rough machining.

After the war, the activities of the Engineering Society branched out to embrace trips off the Hill: Messrs Arnott & Harrison, machine tool manufacturers, McCorquodale's Printing Works and Osram Lamps works were all hosts. The Motor Show was particularly popular. In 1950 the highlight was a visit to the Festival of Britain, courtesy of the London Master Builders Association, and in 1951, the Master Builders arranged for a party to see the Old Bailey about to be restored after being bombed in the war. The master-in-charge of School Workshop from 1946–62 was Mr Eric Hudson-Davies, although the technical side and teaching were in the hands of Messrs Conway and Pitcher.

Mr Hudson-Davies was succeeded by Mr Philip Francis, a Mathematics Master, and two instructors Fred Martin (woodwork) and Len O'Dell (metalwork). Throughout the 1960s and 1970s the popularity of the Workshops continued but little if any technology theory was taught. In 1977 Head Master Michael Hoban appointed Mr Alan Jaggs to teach metalwork. Mr Jaggs came from industry where he had been working on the Concord project and he was the first Master specifically to be appointed to teach a workshop subject.

When Mr Beer arrived as Head Master in 1980, he introduced 'Head Master's Projects' in which each new boy had to produce something creative in his first year.

Design Technology in the Churchill Schools

Many looked to Worker for inspiration. *The Harrovian* correspondent saw the broader picture: "...the Spring term has brought about various seasonal necessities: toboggans and skis were prominent at first, but the merest hint of warmer weather of late has generated electric fans and a crop of bird tables...Boys also continue to furnish their rooms with wardrobes, tables, bedside lockers and chairs. Their eyes are constantly open and some unusual items such as hairpiece stands, grappling hooks and photographic filters have been made." He ends by saying, "The roof still leaks, the machines break down but the work goes on and on." He did not know then that the brave new world was just round the corner,

In the mid-1980s there was a generally held belief that Craft Design Technology would become a compulsory part of the National Curriculum; Harrow's workshops were clearly inadequate for such a purpose. Accordingly a designated building (the lower floor housing the Geography department) was created on a site between The Grove and The Copse. The layout for the Churchill Schools (as it was named) was strongly influenced by Mr Jaggs's experience in industry: it is open plan and has all round visibility to enable maximum supervision. There are double-glazed windows for sound-proofing and a suspended floor for cabling computer networks. The Churchill Schools was opened by Sir Herman Bondi, Master of Churchill College Cambridge, in 1988 and is one of the best equipped in the country.

The new workshop raised Design Technology in the School to a new level. Mr Jaggs became Director and the first workshop technician was appointed: Mr Tom Macmillan. A Master was appointed to teach electronics, robotics and computer numerically controlled (CNC) application. Computers were introduced and new lathes, mills and plastics and woodworking equipment were acquired; later internet facilities. The Head Master's Projects, re-named 'new boy projects', continued with over 90% of projects being undertaken in the workshops in some years. An inter-House technology competition was started and became very successful. 'Technology week' started with guest speakers and competitions. A variety of motor vehicles were restored. Large displays for Speech Day took up the whole of the department and very often had themes and games to play. One large project was the construction of a hovercraft, which was flown on Park Lake on Speech Day, reaching a speed of thirty-seven knots.

Excitement over all this activity was not confined to the Hill: thousands of visitors – among them Mrs

Margaret Thatcher – visited the department, and several coach loads of MPs came in search of inspiration for the new city technology colleges.

Design Technology (as it is now known) is now a mainstream subject with four Masters and two technicians. There is a collection of traditional wood and metal-working machines along with purpose-built areas for plastics technology, electronic product production and foundry work. Extensive computer technology includes CNC routers, two lasers, lathes and a heat image transfer machine for producing textile and ceramics. There is an electronics laboratory, two computer suites, a CNC room, plastics area, two exhibition areas and a Sixth Form upper level glass graphics room, for natural light and space.

All boys do two periods a week in their first year, making ipod holders, clocks, stools and electronic toys. In the next two years, about thirty-five boys choose DT as a GCSE subject, attending four periods a week. They have two options: 'Resistant Materials' and 'Electronic Products'. In the GCSE year they make speakers, amplifiers, fans, sensors, lights and mechanical toys. In the Sixth Form about a dozen boys take AS-level and about half of them go on to A2. They can make anything from a coffee table to a catamaran.

DT is open seven days a week for boys to come in for projects of their own choice: often furniture for home, Christmas presents, T-shirts, wooden bowls, candles, castings, even radio control cars and planes.

The House DT competition

ECONOMICS

DR NORWOOD WAS THE educational pioneer who introduced Economics into the curriculum in the 1930s. He may well have been influenced by his exact contemporary, the renowned economist and Old Harrovian, AC Pigou, Professor of Political Economy at Cambridge. For many years Economics was paired with Geography; indeed the first appointed Head of Subject, Mr JM McSwiney, was appointed Head of Geography & Economics in 1957. It received full subject status in 1965. However for some years it was the Cinderella of A-level choices, with few House Masters and academic advisors guiding clever boys in its direction. Other academic subjects have the advantage of familiarity to boys selecting subjects for A-level, and Masters can do much to attract the clever ones in the years leading to GCSE. Economics does not have that advantage. Thomas Carlyle's condemnation of Economics as the 'dismal science' was a cloud that hovered over it for many years at Harrow.

AC Pigou, Head of School in 1895 and later Professor of Political Economy at Cambridge, after whom the School economics society is named

The vicious circle was perpetuated by the fact that Economics was unwisely chosen by boys with weak mathematical ability resulting in poor grades and gaining for the subject the reputation that it was difficult as well as dismal. Economics is not a subject for the innumerate. In 1925 when Winston Churchill was Chancellor of the Exchequer, he felt intuitively that to return sterling to the gold standard would be an error but he lacked the background knowledge to stand up to the wrong-headed experts. Economics is an integral part of the PPE course at Oxford, one favoured by many successful politicians nowadays.

Economics at Harrow took off in the 1980s through the combined influences of Head Master, Ian Beer, and Prime Minister, Mrs Margaret Thatcher. Mr Beer, when he arrived in 1981, put Economics at the top of his list in the big expenditure programme that he had agreed with the Governors. Mrs Thatcher's contribution was less direct but equally critical. Economics dominated the headlines: 'privatisation' and 'monetarism' became buzz words and people wanted to know what they meant. At a Governors' dinner once, the Head of Economics was asked by Churchill's daughter, Lady Soames, what the difference is between a monetarist and a Keynesian. [His answer: "A monetarist believes that the rate of growth of the money supply is critical, but a Keynesian does not".]

Since the turn of the century, the number of able boys choosing Economics has climbed steadily, as have the A-level grades. Nowadays there are around eighty boys opting for economics at AS, which makes it the second-largest A-level subject after Maths. A year group of around forty to forty-five is common in the Upper Sixth. Intellectually they cover the whole range: some are the cleverest boys in the School but there is also a significant number from the tail of the intelligence distribution.

The AQA Economics course, like all A-levels, is modular. There are four modules in total: two at AS and two at A2. The AS-course gives a good basic overview of Economic concepts and issues, and boys sit one paper in Microeconomics and one in Macroeconomics. In the Upper Sixth, boys build on the knowledge and concepts they have acquired and study another microeconomics paper, *Business Economics and the Distribution of Income*, and another macroeconomics paper, *The National and International Economy*. Very

Since the turn of the century the number of able boys choosing Economics has climbed steadily, as have the A-level grades… Intellectually they cover the whole range…

little has changed in the Economics course over recent years: basic principles are always the same, and there is little need to be radical in terms of course content. The only real change is that coursework has now been dropped, denying boys a built-in opportunity to pursue independently areas of personal interest. Many boys apply to read Economics and Economics-related subjects at university, particularly PPE at Oxford.

The department organises occasional study trips: a visit to the Bank of England perhaps, or to a lecture in London. A team enters for the Bank of England "Target 2.0 competition" for schools, which involves a team of four boys making a presentation to representatives from the Bank of England about what they think ought to be done with the base rate of interest and why. The Pigou Society attracts high-calibre speakers to broaden the boys' exposure to modern ideas.

The rooms in the Science Schools, formerly occupied by the Physics department, were converted into Economics form rooms in 1973, although it was some time before they achieved the vibrant welcome with what AC Pigou would have called 'intellectual gymnastic'.

The western section of the Science Schools is now occupied by the Economics department

ENGLISH

UP UNTIL COMPARATIVELY RECENT times English was considered by some to be a subject for dunces. The greatest Old Harrovian, Winston Churchill, wrote in *My Early Life* of his indebtedness to his English teacher: "We were considered such dunces that we could only learn English. Mr Somervell – a most delightful man, to whom my debt is great – was charged with the duty of teaching the stupidest boys the most disregarded thing – namely to write mere English….As I remained in the Third Fourth three times as long as anyone else, I had three times as much of it. I learned it thoroughly. Thus I got into my bones the essential structure of the ordinary British sentence – which is a noble thing. And when in after years my schoolfellows who had won prizes and distinction for writing such beautiful Latin poetry and pithy Greek epigrams had to come down again to common English, to earn their living or make their way, I did not feel myself at any disadvantage. Naturally I am biased in favour of boys learning English. I would make them all learn English: and then I would let the clever ones learn Latin as an honour, and Greek as a treat. But the only thing I would whip them for is not knowing English. I would whip them hard for that."

As recently as 1951 the school inspectors noted the lack of an effective English Sixth Form at Harrow and Mr MW Vallance (1961–72) was the first English Master to hold a degree in the subject. The English department moved into its first and present permanent home, The Copse, in 1976. This was the house that Edward Bowen, founder of the Modern Side, had built for his retirement but did not live long enough to occupy; he bequeathed it to the School. The building retains its delightful informality and woodland setting but maybe the time for a move to more spacious accommodation is fast approaching.

In a sense, English as a subject began in 1661 at the instigation of the Head Master, William Hide, who established the role of the Writing Master, a system of teaching local children to read. He secured an annual stipend of £6 13s. 4d for teaching the 'free scholars' to write, a task devolved on the 'writing master'. In the same year, Hide organised the teaching of poor children to read in Harrow and the surrounding villages.

It would be wrong, however, to think that the teaching of English at Harrow was purely functional: in the 1760s, in spite, or perhaps in defiance of the narrow curriculum, clever boys were encouraged to study modern English writing and authors like Swift, Addison, Johnson, the imitation bard, Ossian, and Shakespeare were being read.

Harrow's great tradition of the public reading and reciting of verse and prose was established under Robert Sumner, Head Master in the 1760s. The great Restoration playwright, Richard Sheridan, mourned him "as a father". A favourite exercise of Sumner's successor, Joseph Drury, was the English essay, which, if good enough, was rehearsed by the author for declaiming aloud to the rest of the School. This provided Byron with his first taste of public oratory.

English literature first became part of the syllabus in 1869 with the creation of a Modern Side which broke the monopoly of Classics. Boys who were unable to learn Latin verse were set the next best thing, Milton. One Master, Mr FW Farrar, taught Coleridge to his Removes. Both these poets still feature in the curriculum.

It took a long time for Harrow School to come fully to believe in English as a separate subject requiring specialists and its own space. English was taught by 'form masters' who covered several other subjects and whose form rooms were scattered all over the Hill. The status of English was perhaps sustained by the 'Saturday Nighter', a prep set by the Head Master and marked by Form Masters for several decades until the 1970s, effectively meaning that every boy in the School had to write a weekly essay. This was supported by The Winston Churchill Essay Prize for which every boy from the Removes upwards wrote an entry. Even as recently as 1990, well after the move to The Copse, there were seventeen Masters teaching one or more English divisions in several different buildings.

During the period from 1966–90, Mr Jeremy Lemmon was Head of English. A formidably scholarly English teacher, actor and director of Shakespeare plays, Mr Lemmon was a dominant intellectual force in the School for over forty years. A significant boost to the literary life of the School came in 2000 with the refurbishment of the Vaughan Library. This gloomy and forbidding building was transformed into a bright, airy and welcoming space, and has done much to encourage boys to read.

The present English department is still based in The Copse where rooms are named after some of Harrow's great writers – Trollope, Galsworthy, LP Hartley, Byron, Mortimer and Sheridan. The department has weathered the storm of changes in syllabi since the late 1990s and is populated by an eclectic range of younger and experienced teachers. Results at GCSE and A-level have been outstanding but the department has maintained its role as a cultural force in the School. A-level numbers remain high and the department is about to embark on a new adventure in introducing International GCSE, offering boys a wider and more interesting experience of reading and writing. Shakespeare is still the most frequently studied writer but in their coursework boys write with enthusiasm about a huge range of modern playwrights, poets and novelists. There is a thriving creative writing society, and the Sheridan Society hosts writers-in-residence, most recently the performance poet Patience Agbabi and the novelist Tobias Hill. Every year groups of enthusiastic boys go for a weekend at the Cheltenham Literature Festival where they attend a stream of lectures, readings and discussions. Some have hunted the ghost of Thomas Hardy in North Cornwall. In the busy life of modern Harrow one hopes that the aptly named Copse can become a place of serious thought and refuge. In his memoir, *Clinging to the Wreckage*, OH Sir John Mortimer affectionately remembers reading Wordsworth with his English Master:

> "I think the Reverend Arthur Chalfont and I were the only people in the class who got any pleasure out of the old Sheep of the Lake District and we used to read each other long passages from *The Prelude* and *Tintern Abbey* to the fury of Tainton who said we sounded like a couple of expiring goats. He was clearly short on humour and capable of writing some of the silliest lines in the English language. I also knew that my great friend and ally, Lord Byron, couldn't stand Wordsworth for many years…All the same in those endless afternoons when the Reverend Arthur Chalfont and I read to each other I came, slowly and reluctantly, to the conclusion that between Wordsworth and Lord B, the old fumbler from the Lake District was by far the better poet."

Harrow afternoons may not now seem so endless but one hopes that in different ways Harrovians' experiences in The Copse will do something more than provide them with examination success. Mortimer wrote of his sense of wonder on listening to Wordsworth: it may not be quite like this in today's fast and furious world but the love of literature and self-expression are qualities that more than ever need to be fostered.

An English division up to Mr John James

GEOGRAPHY

WHEN DESCRIBING THE RANGE of literature read by Philip Yorke, a pupil at Harrow in 1771, Christopher Tyerman lists a number of Latin and Greek authors, the Greek New Testament "as well as a catechism and some geography and history". Thus it seems that Geography was being taught informally a long time before the curriculum was broadened to include non-classical subjects. When the Modern Side was created in 1869 a number of Masters, notably Mr FW Farrar and Mr R Bosworth-Smith, jumped at the opportunity to stimulate boys' interest by varying the indigestible diet of Latin verses with some English Literature, Geography and History.

When the real reform arrived, led by Head Master Dr Welldon, specialisation was introduced into the VIth and Vth Forms for a few hours a week, and Geography was included. The Army Class also included Geography among those subjects taught "for their particular relevance to the Army entrance exams".

Between 1920 and 1925, under the direction of Dr Ford, the VIth Form was progressively separated into specialist groups, each of which made a particular study of the main subject. It was his successor, Dr Norwood, already a leading educational reformer, who took this a stage further by placing Geography on an equal footing with the other modern subjects. Geography had arrived.

The status of the subject owes much to Mr ED Laborde, who wrote (and translated) a number of Geography textbooks. He donated a huge collection of geographical glass slides to the School; these are now stored in the Royal Geography Society's archive.

Originally Geography was taught in form rooms scattered throughout the School and shared with other subjects; some rooms were even equipped with science laboratory apparatus, which came in useful for such studies as soil sampling. Geography Masters were also expected to teach other subjects: many taught a wide range, varying from related topics such as Geology to Modern Languages and English. Geography only moved to its present location in the lower ground floor of the Churchill Schools in 1987; it is now housed in purpose-built rooms with its own excellent IT, library and office facilities.

For some reason – maybe accidental, maybe not – the department has attracted some influential members of the teaching staff in recent years: in 2007–2008 the nine Masters teaching geography included the Head Master, the Deputy Head, the Director of Boarding and a House Master. As all these Masters teach reduced time-tables, the size of the department may be misleading but the number of boys studying Geography has remained consistently high, showing the enduring interest that there is in the subject, as well as the success it achieves for its students.

Fieldwork has always been a strength of the department, beginning with Mr Laborde's pioneering 'look & see' field trips to the Rhineland and continued through countless further expeditions. Before the recent introduction of stricter syllabuses and school league tables (which call for more focussed form room teaching) there was more time and energy to spend on exploring geography at work in the world around, and past records show detailed mapping surveys of the streams and swallow holes of the North Mimms area, Hertfordshire. Two articles from the *Geographical Magazine* in 1970s record the results of Harrovian mapping surveys of moraine and lake deposits in Cwm Idwal, north Wales. The annual trips to Lulworth and Slapton still continue but the most long running and successful of the overseas trips has been to Jordan, first set up and run by Mr Tony Escritt. This expedition was suspended in 2001 with the outbreak of the Gulf War but is planned to restart in 2010.

At one time the School owned Nanoose, a field centre near Wool in Dorset, which the geographers used for regular residential field trips – although it was also used by other departments such as English and Maths and the Marmots (the School's rock climbing and mountaineering club). This was sold around 1978 and is now home to 'Monkey World'.

Ever since Geography became established as a School subject (and informally before that) there has been a Geography Society; this has fluctuated in size and strength as well as adapting to the times. It was probably at its most popular in the 1960s – before the days of House televisions and alternative weekend entertainment – when several hundred paid-up members came to watch lectures and films on Saturday nights. Today there is a smaller, but still active society, which enjoys regular meetings, trips and lectures throughout the year.

The Geography department can also boast of several Old Harrovians who have gone on to further achievement in geographically related areas. In the world of academics, Professor Richard Lampitt is Professor of National Oceanography Centre at Southampton University, Professor Mark Shucksmith is Professor of Planning at University of Newcastle and Dr Charles Warren is a senior lecturer in Geography at the University of St Andrews and author of *Managing Scotland's Environment.*

The list of explorers, pioneers and adventurers is too long to list here (but may be found in the Appendix). Recent explorers and adventurers include: Rupert (Pen) Hadow, Arctic explorer who became the first person to walk the 478 miles, solo and unsupported, from the northern coast of Canada to the North Pole in 2003; Tom Avery, explorer and mountaineer, who has led a number of mountaineering expeditions to explore previously uncharted mountain ranges, and in 2002 set the record of becoming the youngest Briton ever to ski to the South Pole; and Henry Cookson, who was part of the Team N2i who kite-skied to the Pole of Inaccessibility in 2006.

Geography fieldwork at Slapton

HISTORY

THE HISTORY DEPARTMENT AT Harrow occupies the upper floors of the Old Schools building, above the Fourth Form Room, the original school room. Teaching has been carried out here for nearly four hundred years; it is a building that breathes history and is an entirely appropriate place for the teaching of the subject.

For the first 250 years of the School's existence, Harrovians' only formal exposure to History was through classical literature, as part of the curriculum, and the Bible on their Sunday visits to St Mary's Church. At least their studies of the ancient world and of the Judaeo-Christian tradition gave them some idea of the foundations of western civilization. Outside the formal curriculum, the more intellectually curious would have read some history on their own initiative and no doubt some of the Masters and others who taught private lessons would have strayed into their favourite topics from time to time: Dr Montagu Butler is reputed to have had an enthusiasm for Napoleon's 1796 Italian campaign.

Mr Edward Bowen, the first head of the 'Modern Side'

Facing page: The Rev FW Farrar, 1855-70 and Mr Charles Colbeck, 1871-1903 (top left, right); Mr George Townsend Warner (OH), 1891-1916 and Mr LW Henry, 1919-44 (below left, right)

In 1869, freed from the fetters of the founder's curriculum, Dr Montagu Butler began the Modern Side as an alternative to Classics, introducing the teaching of History in its own right, alongside English Literature, Modern Languages, Geography and Science. Masters FW Farrar (1855-70) and Edward Bowen (1859-1901) had been agitating for some time for boys to be released from the drudgery of rote learning of Classics, seeing teaching as essentially helping pupils to learn. One of Bowen's enlightened ventures was to take parties of boys to follow the path of Garibaldi in Sicily. Farrar left Harrow to become Master of Marlborough but Butler appointed Bowen to establish the Modern Side.

It was Butler's successor Dr Welldon (1885-1998) whose new timetable in 1888 further broadened the curriculum and made History a form subject for those on the classical side, and compulsory for all in the Shells and Removes. Then, in 1891, Welldon appointed Mr George Townsend Warner to the teaching staff and, in 1903, to be Head of the Modern Side. Townsend Warner was described by Christopher Tyerman as "the most brilliant teacher of his time"; his impact on History teaching at Harrow was huge. GM Trevelyan, later to become Regius Professor at Cambridge and Master of Trinity, referring to Townsend Warner, said, "I was better taught in history than any other schoolboy then in England". He further added "the adaptation to school teaching of modern methods of studying history owes much to Harrow's experiment at that period."

In 1887 Mr Bowen wrote to the Headmaster of Elstree School, Mr Lance Sanderson, who had been a Master at Harrow from 1864-69, suggesting a Harrow History Prize. Elstree was a preparatory school, then at its original site at nearby Elstree, that sent (and still sends) a number of pupils to Harrow and Bowen's aim was to stimulate the study of History there. The proposal was accepted and in 1895 Elstree was joined by The Dragon School, Oxford. Gradually the competition spread to include other schools. Indeed, the prize was one of the first matters on which preparatory schools had any communication, coming probably just after a lengthy correspondence on the most desirable size of a cricket ball for inter-school matches.

Mr Charles Colbeck administered the prize competition until 1905, followed by Mr Townsend Warner. In 1912, the later popular historian, Arthur

Head Master Dr Montagu Butler is reputed to have had an enthusiasm for Napoleon's 1796 Italian campaign ... in 1934 Dr Paul Vellacott, a Fellow of Peterhouse, and a distinguished historian of the Glorious Revolution, was appointed Head Master, the first historian in that position.

Bryant, was awarded, not a prize, but a card of commendation. Mr LW Henry from Harrow and Mr C Henry K Marten from Eton then agreed to take it in turns to set and mark the papers, and award the prizes. In 1922, they decided to change the name from The Harrow History Prize to The Townsend Warner History Prize. Since 1956 the prize has been under the auspices of the Incorporated Association of Preparatory Schools, but the strong link with Harrow has been maintained: Mr Roger Ellis, later Master of Marlborough College, was followed by Mr Howard Shaw and Mr Tony Beadles, both Heads of History, and by Mr Hugh Thompson. The number of competitors and schools involved has risen dramatically: in 1905 it was thirty-nine from fifteen schools; in 1989 the total peaked at 888 from 130 schools. The 1966 winner was JP Simpson and the runner-up CJ Tyerman, both of whom entered Harrow.

In 1917 a fully integrated timetable replaced the distinct Classical Side, Modern Side and Army Class, but some of the old customs remained, one of which was the belief that a 'modernist' could and should be able to turn his hand to teaching almost anything. Bowen had had to learn German from scratch in order to teach it and the Balliol historian, RM Baldwin, (1922–1957) was also expected to teach French and Latin.

In 1934 Dr Paul Vellacott, formerly a Fellow of Peterhouse and a distinguished historian of the Glorious Revolution, was appointed Head Master, the first historian in that position. He appointed Mr LW Henry as Head of History (and, after the war, whisked him off to Peterhouse, where Vellacott had become Master). Henry was, in Dr Tyerman's words, "class, when health permitted". He was House Master of The Grove from 1935–44 and a powerful figure in the internal politics of the School

Charles Lillingston was Head of History from 1944–68 – rather too long to maintain vibrant enthusiasm, perhaps. It is said that he taught from the Edward's notes he had used at Cambridge in the 1920s, a fact that did not escape the attention of the Inspectors in 1965. From 1956 he was also House Master of Druries, which absorbed most of his interest, and his department was in effect run by Mr Ellis. The History department at this time formed a distinguished team, many of whom went

From left to right: Mr Geoffrey Treasure, 1955-92; Mr Howard Shaw, 1961-97; Mr Hugh Thompson, 1975-; Dr Christopher Tyerman (OH), 1987-2002

on to become headmasters: RW Ellis (1952–1967) and JW Rae (1955–1966) both of whom became Chairmen of HMC; CJ Swallow (1961–73) and AH Beadles (1967–1985). GRR Treasure (1955–1989), a prolific historian of seventeenth-century France, DJ Parry (1961–1993), CH Shaw (1961–1997), JR Beckett (1966–2005) and JFEC Gates (1969–2000) all remained at Harrow to become House Masters.

It is a reflection of the quality of the history teaching that emerged through the 1960s that in 1974 the Oxford and Cambridge A-level examiners report remarked that Harrow's entry was the largest that they had encountered. Furthermore, between 1964 and 1975 there were regularly two divisions studying for entrance to Oxford and Cambridge, yielding an average of more than three awards each year, and six in 1971.

In 1925 Sir Edward Hulton, owner of the publishing company that produced among other titles the *Picture Post*, presented the School with a collection of books "for history specialists" and an endowment to expand the collection each year. With the History department established in the Old Schools in the late 1970s, an opportunity arose to give the collection a permanent home. The Hulton Library, as it became known, now occupies a room in the 'cock loft'.

Dr Tyerman left to become a don at Hertford College, Oxford in 2002 and his successor, Dr Dominic Luckett became Headmaster of Mill Hill in 2007, so the History department's tradition of influence beyond the Old Schools continues.

For boys who wish to extend their exposure to historical information and discussion there are a number of societies: the Trevelyan Society is the School's historical society; its political cousin is the Palmerston Society. Commemorating the Old Harrovian Field Marshal, the Alexander Society was founded in the 1990s for those with a special interest in military history. Finally, there is the Mediaeval Society. Harrow's historians have the chance to hear distinguished speakers most weeks.

A History division taught by Dr Nick Kemp

MATHEMATICS

MATHEMATICS TEACHING BEGAN AT Harrow in 1819. Before that date, boys in the VIth Form 'read' Euclid for one period each week with the Head Master. The subject became compulsory in 1837. It seems that the syllabus for most boys in the School consisted mainly of arithmetic with some algebra and a careful reading of Euclid.

Two early Mathematics teachers deserve mention. The first was Mr Colenso (1838–42) who subsequently became the Bishop of Natal: an unlikely promotion for a modern Maths beak. The second was Mr JF Marillier (1819–69), who lived in a house on the High Street, now part of Bradbys and still called 'Marilliers'. M. Marillier was French and spoke of 'arithmétique' and 'mathématique'. Imitating his pronunciation, for many years Mathematics at Harrow was known as 'tique' and a Mathematics Master as a 'tique beak'. It is possible that the mathematical knowledge of some of the early 'tique beaks' would not rival that of current Masters, but another from the nineteenth century, Mr RB Hayward (1859–93) held unusual distinction. He was a Fellow of the Royal Society and a former examiner for the mathematical tripos at Cambridge: this too is a feat unmatched by any of his successors.

In the early days, teaching for most boys in the School was described as "very mechanical", but it began to change with the arrival of Mr AW Siddons (1899–1936). Arthur Siddons published many text books and saw through a revision of the mathematical syllabus. Problems in geometry (and not just an appreciation of the propositions of Euclid) were introduced, as was graphical work and trigonometry. The introduction of trigonometry caused a controversy in an unexpected way: when Mr Siddons included for the first time some questions on trigonometry in a 'trial', he told the boys to bring up their books of 'four figure tables'. This created the sort of controversy that calculators were to invoke some seventy years later. Mr Siddons was told that computing aids were not permitted in examinations and that books of tables were tantamount to cheating. He explained that boys could not answer questions on trigonometry without tables and the point was reluctantly conceded. From then on, four figure tables became a memorable part of every boy's life until the arrival of the slide rule, which was swiftly overtaken by the calculator. It was during Mr Siddons's time – in 1904 – that The Copse became the home of the Mathematics department.

In 1969, in the pioneering days of computing, the School set up a terminal in the Copse, linked to the BP computer. The idea was that, at a considerably reduced cost, the BP computer would process programs and return the results during 'quiet times'. It was a good idea. The downside was that the terminal would splutter into life at unexpected and unpredictable times – usually in the middle of a lesson – spewing out paper in all directions and destroying reflective moments with its insane, mechanical clatter. It may have been a rather arcane device but there was pride that Harrow had become – even at the length of a telephone line – a part of the white hot technological revolution.

Harrovian mathematicians have been fortunate to have been taught by some distinguished Masters over the years. Arthur Siddons was followed by Messrs KS Snell (1930–61), JB Morgan (1946–71) SL Parsonson (1960–1993) and Dr FW Dalton (1973–2006). The names of Siddons, Snell and Morgan roll off the tongues of those who used Mathematics text books around that time. Both Mr Snell and Mr Morgan became, during their time at Harrow, Presidents of the Mathematical Association.

In the revolutionary 1960s, Mathematics teaching also underwent huge changes. 'New' Mathematics arrived with such topics as set theory, transformation geometry, linear programming, Boolean algebra and probability theory. Some believed that Mathematics had become too abstract and perhaps a little distant

from 'the real world'. Stuart Parsonson, with others, set up the Mathematics in Education & Industry (MEI) syllabus, a course that combined new topics with, whenever possible, their application in real situations. This syllabus was introduced to Harrow, very successfully, in the early 1970s.

In 1976, the Mathematics department moved into its present home, the purpose-built Mathematics Schools.

Personal computers arrived at Harrow in 1982 and, for each Shell division, one of their five Mathematics periods was to be devoted to computing. The only software available was BASIC and so the Shells were to be taught computer programming. Some of the beaks found this quite a challenge and it soon became clear that many of the boys knew very much more about computing than their teachers: for four periods each week, the beak held court, dispensing mathematical (and other types of) wisdom while for the fifth, roles were reversed. But such was the growth in computer technology that it soon became necessary for there to be a separate computer department and the PCs left for the Churchill Schools. It would be nice to record that Euclid came home and order was restored, but life is never that simple.

Under Dr Philippa Davies and, currently, Mr I Hammond, the Mathematics department at Harrow has continued to expand: Mathematics is now the most popular AS-level subject in the School, being chosen by upward of 120 boys, a situation that would have been impossible a generation ago, simply because of the difficulty of the course. The Mathematics Schools, deliberately built to be larger than was needed at the time, is now too small. There are, however, smart boards in all ten teaching rooms. In the present GCSE, there is not much basic arithmetic. However, calculations involving (for example) percentages, areas and volumes, direct and inverse proportion are still with us. Euclid does not get a mention, but there is a small amount of geometry, mainly centered around circle theorems. Trigonometry is a significant topic: four figure tables are no more, but anxieties about computational aides – calculators – remain with invigilators being required to check before an examination that the calculators being used lie within the permissible set. Also currently in the syllabus are: probability with some statistical methods, calculus (differentiation and integration with some max/min questions) and hefty chunks of algebra. Boys in 1819 would not have made much sense of today's mathematics examination papers; it is equally likely that current boys would find the repetitive, mechanical processes of that earlier period insufferably boring.

A Mathematics division up to Mr Ian Hammond

MODERN LANGUAGES

IN THE ALL-CLASSICAL SCHOOL that persisted until the educational reforms of the 1870s, additions to the subjects taught had begun to creep in outside the timetable over a century earlier. By 1750, French, Mathematics, Dancing, Drawing and Fencing had become standard additions to the formal School work. These were taught by Extra Masters as distinct from the Assistant Masters who taught the Classics. But this was not enough for reformers whose central demand was the introduction of French to the School timetable. In 1835 Head Master Dr Longley made an attempt to include French in the curriculum but he met a number of obstacles, beyond those of reactionaries who wished to maintain the status quo. Clever boys resented the time spent away from their classical studies (which were the route to scholarships and further academic advancement); the less talented disliked the extra work involved; Masters saw it as a threat to the financial monopoly of private lessons in 'pupil room' and parents disliked the extra cost. Longley's introduction of French, with Italian as an alternative, and an additional guinea on the school fee was quickly abandoned. Christopher Tyerman suggests that a further reason may have been the lack of cooperation of the French Master, Mr Jacques Marilliers, who preferred teaching private pupils at less effort for more money; he left the School in 1839. It seems also that French was very unimaginatively taught. As Tyerman observes, "Serious teaching of modern languages had to wait until the establishment of the Modern Side in 1869."

M. Gustave Masson taught French from 1855–88, but he had to assume an English accent

M. Gustave Masson, a French historian and writer, was appointed by Dr Vaughan in 1855, although he was "forced by custom and prescript to teach his pupils to speak French with an English accent" but it was the arrival of two Frenchmen from the Sorbonne, M. Antoine Duhamel (1888) and M. Bernard Minssen (1891), who pioneered a revolution in language teaching by introducing colloquial French.

With the Modern Side well established, Modern Languages had achieved almost equal status with the Classical Side by the time of the arrival of Dr Ford in 1910. He increased the teaching time, added Spanish to French and German as the modern languages taught and introduced some divisionalisation (now known as streaming) in the Vth and VIth forms. Modern languages and some science were also taught on the Classical Side.

The second half of the twentieth century was dominated by Mr CL Walton, a colossus who was Head of Modern Languages from 1953–72, although in his later years he became increasingly detached from his department and most of the work was done by his

successor, Mr John Jeremy. Described by Mr Jeremy as "magnificently erudite", Mr Walton had spent the latter days of the war "on business with the Russians" based in Tehran, and Russian was soon added to the languages on offer. He was however a traditionalist, and languages continued to be taught in a formal way with emphasis on vocabulary learning, proses and translations, punctuated by the occasional dictation. By the 1960s tape recorders were being used, enabling boys to hear speakers other than their teachers, and in particular native speakers. A decade later the arrival of the video enabled foreign programmes to be recorded and replayed in the form room.

Under Mr Jeremy's sensitive guidance the Modern Languages department became a cohesive unit rather than a collection of linguists doing their own thing. He made sure that all members had the regular opportunity to teach the top divisions at each level and that meetings were held regularly. Nor was he afraid to experiment: one Master was sent on a four-week course, run by the French government, training foreign teachers to teach French by audio-visual methods. Some of the techniques were incorporated into the traditional O-level syllabus.

The arrival of GCSE placed greater emphasis on the spoken language, with role plays and practical usage: language assistants were employed to inject a further element of realism into form room teaching. In response to world events, Arabic and Japanese were added to the language options.

Since the concentration of departments in their own buildings in 1980s, Modern Languages has occupied the Leaf Schools. These small, poorly soundproofed, low-ceilinged rooms became increasingly unsuitable and developments in modern technology made the need for purpose-built facilities urgent. In 2007 the Modern Languages Schools were opened on the site of the former Spinney Cottages, next to the Music Schools. This state-of-the-art building provides vastly superior accommodation for the ever-widening range of languages on offer at Harrow and, for the first time, allows all members of the department to be housed within the same building. Every form room is equipped with built-in digital projection and sound facilities as well as networked computer access and a digital TV system, with the ability to broadcast, record and edit a whole range of foreign programmes. In addition to this, the building boasts a virtual language laboratory and a dedicated staff room. The Modern Languages Schools also incorporate a range of smaller seminar and interview rooms, which are used by the now large numbers of visiting language teachers, the language assistants and by Masters conducting oral examinations.

However, the passage of language teaching has not been free of obstacles. One of the problems has

Mr Leonard Walton (1947–82), Mr George Attenborough (1963–2001), Mr John Jeremy (1957–1994), Mr Derek Swift (1994–2007) (above, from left to right); the Modern Languages Schools opened in 2003 (below)

This and facing page: A Modern Languages division up to Mr Nick Page

been that, since the 1980s, Government quango interference in examinations has deprived examination boards of their autonomy, imposing syllabus changes every five years; syllabuses have now even to be called "specifications". By the year 2000, Harrow had been obliged to do four different A-level syllabuses in six years. A language teacher at that time comments, "At GCSE level one set of government advisors would impose completely different criteria from those of their predecessors: examinations permitted the use of dictionaries, then a few years later dictionaries were banned; questions were asked and answers required in the target language, then this was changed to English. Grammar had become a dirty word. Translation, which is the only task a linguist is ever asked to perform, was almost entirely removed from examinations. Literature questions had to be answered in the target language. Against this background of national administrative chaos, the Modern Languages department at Harrow maintained its remarkably high record in public examinations, resolutely refusing to participate in the farce of coursework, which is so open to abuse. Much of Harrow's success in these troubled years was down to a maintenance of academic rigour and a resistance to transient philosophies."

In its new building, the study of modern languages at Harrow continues to thrive and to achieve good examination results whatever the board or latest change

in specification. The languages currently on offer are: French, Spanish, German, Russian, Italian, Mandarin, Cantonese, Japanese, Arabic, Polish and Modern Greek. This very wide range is thanks to a flexible timetable and a band of excellent peripatetic teachers who visit Harrow on a part-time basis to teach languages that either cannot be offered in the regular curriculum or are being studied in addition to those timetabled.

Boys arriving at the School in the Shell year are offered a choice of French or Spanish and those in the upper two thirds of the year group select a second language from French, Spanish, German and Classical Greek; the majority of Shell boys are also offered the choice of Latin or Mandarin. When making their GCSE choices, boys must continue with at least one modern language, although many choose to take two or more. Some forty boys are offered the chance to take GCSE French a year early; these boys then go on to complete a one-year crash course to GCSE in either Russian or Italian in the Fifth Form. Between fifty and sixty boys annually choose to continue at least one modern language into the Lower Sixth.

In addition to all that is on offer on the timetable, all of the languages mentioned above are available outside the normal timetable and boys regularly take up this opportunity for extra study with gusto; some 200 pupils currently study one or more languages on this basis.

SCIENCE

ALTHOUGH SIR JOSEPH BANKS was a pupil at Harrow in the 1750s there is no evidence that the seeds of his interest in botany were sown at Harrow. He left at the age of nine to go to Eton. The first signs of awareness of Science as a school subject appeared in prizes to encourage the study of science established by Dr Vaughan (1845–59). The Scientific Society was founded by The Rev FW Farrer in November 1865. This began with meetings once a fortnight on Thursday afternoons, each member reading a paper. By 1871 there were thirty-nine members. It reached zenith in 1872 but then declined when Science began to be properly taught in School.

The modernist movement inside the School to broaden the curriculum beyond its traditional classical monopoly came from Messrs Bowen, Farrar and Bosworth-Smith. Farrar's *Essays on a Liberal Education* in 1867 and the foundation of a Natural History Society attracting lecturers such as Tyndall, Ruskin and Huxley added to the pressure to include Science in the curriculum. Montagu Butler agreed to its introduction and appointed Mr George Griffith, the first Science Master. Mr Griffith provided a basic grounding at least in Physics and Botany, teaching such topics as magnetism, light, induction, telegraphy and the classification of species in biology. It was a modest attempt at modernity and was the precursor of the establishment of Modern Side two years later.

A Physics lesson

Facing page: Mr Chris Bates teaching Biology

Science entered the curriculum as a taught subject when the Modern Side was created in 1869. The Science Schools were built using funds from the John Lyon Memorial Fund. They were opened in 1874 but were not equipped and ready for use until 1876. For some years the building was too large for the needs of the teaching of Natural Science in the School and the ground floor was used to teach other subjects.

A revival of the Scientific Society in 1884 allowed that "once a term a paper of literary or other not purely scientific paper may be read." Topics were: "Musical Intervals; a new method of representation"; "Harrow Water"; "Photography", "Deeside of Scotland", "Danish & Norwegian Names in the British Isles", "Ornithology" and "Barry, Pomeroy Castle"; the following year it was "Gems, "New Zealand", "The Geology of Yorkshire"and "Fauna of the Deep Sea". There were also expeditions: to the Zoo, and to SS Austral in Victoria Dock.

The Museum Schools with the Butler Museum on the top floor were built in 1886. Originally the exhibits were mainly connected with Classics but when the Gardner Wilkinson collection was moved to the Vaughan Library, the emphasis moved to Science. Exhibits then centred around 'British animals of local origin' collected by GEH Barrett-Hamilton who produced papers on the subject while still at school and whose later work became well known. There was a large bird collection;

fish and invertebrates were also represented; there was also a geological section. In later years the Museum became home to the Natural History Society and housed members' aquaria and private collections.

The reorganisation of the curriculum in 1888 retained the distinction between Classical and Modern Sides but enabled some Science to be taught on the Classical Side. In both Sides teaching by divisions was introduced in the VIth Form. The Science course embraced mainly Botany and Chemistry with a little Physics, but Dr Welldon added Biology before his departure in 1898. Following the appointments of Mr BP Lascelles in 1885, Mr CE Ashford in 1893 and Mr Archer Vassall in 1896, Science became an established part of the curriculum. The School was well served by some good teachers in these early days: Vassall was excellent; Bushell introduced some Astronomy and Lascelles taught some Chemistry off timetable. Vassall went on to become House Master of Elmfield and a powerful influence in the scientific lobby.

Dr Ford further advanced the march of science. In 1914 an upper floor was added to the Science Schools to give better accommodation for Chemistry teaching and the old Chemistry department was converted into Biology laboratories and lecture rooms. In 1922 a new Physics laboratory and a lecture room were added at the west end of the building; the lecture room was dedicated to the memory of ET Busk (OH) who had invented and built the first stable aircraft. In 1934 a larger lecture room was built over the new Physics wing. The Science Schools then comprised three lecture rooms, nine laboratories, balance rooms, a large tank room for experimental work in hydrostatics and a number of prep and store rooms. At the time the Science Schools

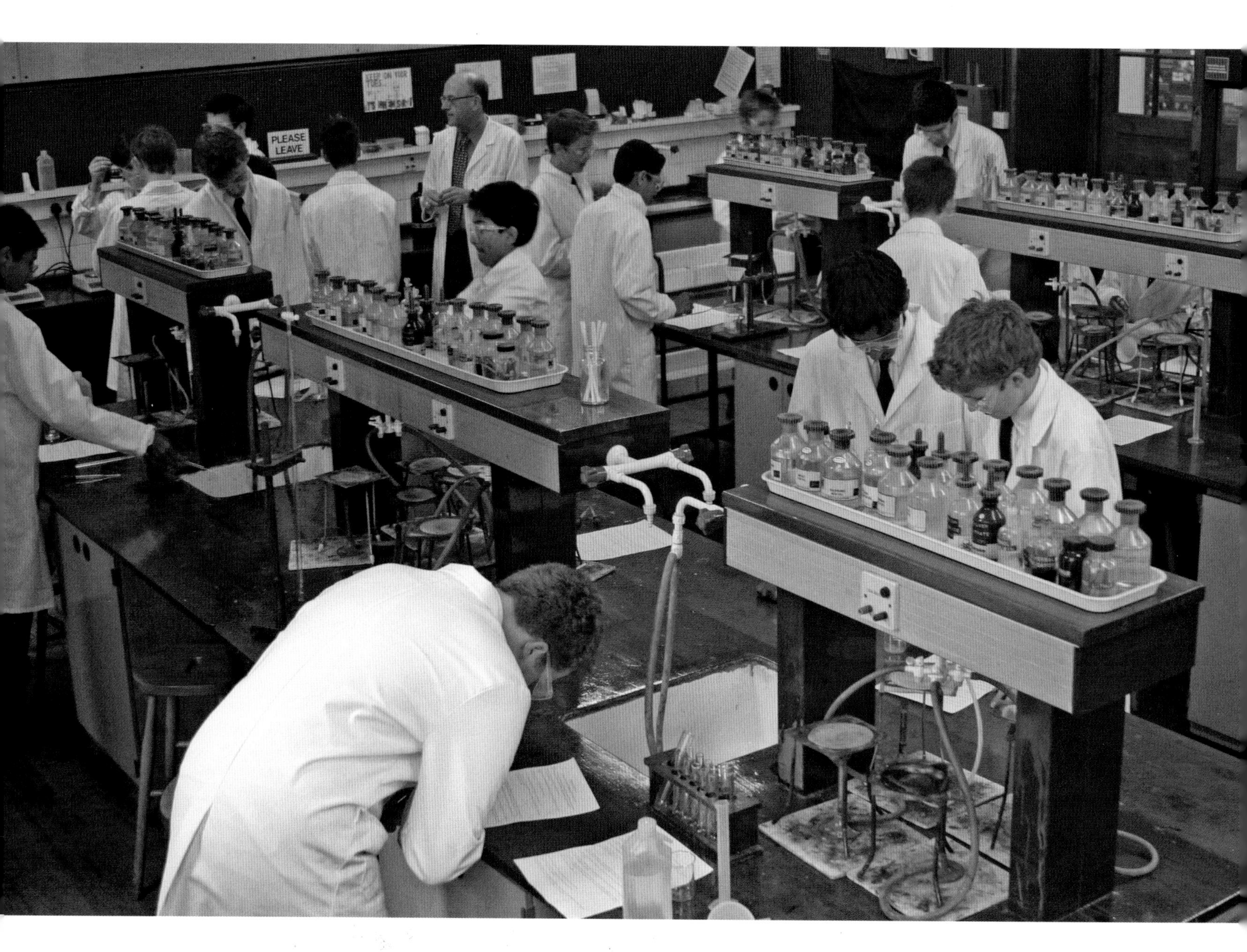

A Chemistry division being taught by Mr Tim Hersey

were described as "generously equipped", "in particular the lecture apparatus for experiments in sound are probably unique in a school." The Scientific Society also continued to be very active: in 1932, for example there were lectures on Liquid Air, Aluminium, Moths & Butterflies and Aero Engines among other topics.

In the 1960s the Nuffield science projects did much to modernise teaching but this was a period of high specialisation and it was still possible for a boy to pass through the School without learning any science at all.

In 1972 the Physics department moved to a purpose-built new building between the Museum and Music Schools. At the same time the Biology department took over the Museum Schools.

In 1977 Shell boys had two lessons per week of Science: one term for each of the three subjects. In the Remove this became two lessons per week for each subject. Remove boys then chose to do one, two or three science subjects to O-level, or Environmental Science – a course developed by Mr Andrew Bishop, who was to become an influential figure in the science teaching world as editor of *The Science Review*.

Head Master Ian Beer (1981–91) was a biologist. Although there is no suggestion that he favoured the sciences unfairly, in his time the allocation of periods for Shells was increased to six periods per week of Science: two of each subject, later three, which continued to the Remove year when they chose their O-level options.

Head Master Barnaby Lenon carried out a review in his first term and produced the curriculum currently in place, with eight periods per week of science in the Shells; boys can then choose which, if any, of these subjects they wish to pursue to GCSE; each option is then allotted four periods per week in the Removes and Fifth Form. A-level Science continues to be popular, with an increasing number of boys choosing each subject: the three Science departments are among the biggest in the School.

Perhaps surprisingly for an evolving subject, the content of the courses has changed little in the last forty years, although there has been a shift of emphasis. In Chemistry there is less theory; there are more applications, and environmental issues have featured increasingly. Coursework is an important part of the Chemistry A-level course in spite of the restraints imposed by Health & Safety regulations. The core syllabus of Physics remains: heat, light and sound, electricity and magnetism, but at A-level modern topics include particle physics and cosmology. The greatest changes have occurred in Biology, driven by the 'green revolution' which began in the 1980s. This led to such topics as productivity of crops, which in turn led to molecular biology, genetics, and the study of stem cells and DNA. Dissection is no longer a compulsory part of the syllabus, but is considered an important part of Harrow's Biology course.

The Scientific Society has established an annual lecture named after Lord Rayleigh (OH), Harrow's only science Nobel Laureate. Past speakers have included Nobel Laureates and the President of the Royal Society. Each Science department also organises up to five lectures per year: two in each of the Autumn and Spring terms and one in the Summer term. A recent trend is to invite the speaker during lesson times to speak to a whole block of boys. Boys are sometimes escorted to lectures at London University, especially Imperial College and UCL and to institutions such as the Royal Institution and the Royal Society. Other activities include visits to places of scientific interest such as a brewery, Kew Gardens, the Natural History Museum, the Thames Barrier, a metal processing plant, Kodak (before it closed down) and ICI Paints in Slough.

Boys are encouraged to take part in competitions such as the Physics, Chemistry and Biology Olympiads, essay competitions organised by universities and scientific institutions, and engage in project work such as the Engineering Education Scheme – in all of which boys have been very successful. The Medical Society is also very active with speakers, meetings and visits to hospitals, especially Northwick Park.

The Butler Museum began to be dismantled in 1980, largely because of the difficulty in properly caring for the exhibits. The best specimens can still be seen in the Old Speech Room Gallery and the Biology Library, but recently the collection of butterflies and moths was sold at Sotheby's and the herbarium was sent to the Natural History Museum of Wales. Both these collections are of considerable specialist interest and value.

Perhaps the best salute to science at Harrow is the impressive list of distinguished scientists the School has produced. There are too many to list here but they may be found among the register of distinguished Old Harrovians in the Appendix. To give just a handful of examples from different disciplines and eras: Dr Edward Munro (1803), physician to King George III; William Fox Talbot (1811), photographic pioneer; Professor Gavin de Beer (1913), embryologist; Thomas Manning (1926), zoologist and explorer; Professor Raymond Harley (1948), professor of botany; Professor Alain Townsend (1967), professor of molecular immunology; and Dr Nicholas Patrick (1978), astronaut.

ART

UNTIL FAIRLY RECENTLY, ART and History of Art, although long offered as A-level subjects, have been considered by academics to be rather soft options. Certainly, for most of the nineteenth century and before, as in all schools, the place of Art in education appears to have been of little importance, but it is worth noting that the early years of the nineteenth century produced Sir Francis Grant (OH), portrait painter and President of the RA, and Hercules Brabazon Brabazon (OH), who was persuaded by Whistler to exhibit for the first time in his seventies.

As so often, it was the influence of just a couple of individuals that inspired a surge of enthusiasm for Art towards the end of the nineteenth century. 'Will' Egerton Hine (son of the famous watercolourist HG Hine) joined the teaching staff in 1892 and by his infectious enthusiasm and force of character persuaded the Head Master and Governors not only that Art should be in the curriculum but that it should be an essential part of education. Art suddenly became the significant feature of School life that it has remained ever since.

Raising funds was, as always, the main hurdle, but Harrow was fortunate to find a significant benefactor, Henry Yates Thompson (OH). Yates Thompson was a publisher, who had devoted much of his energy to acquiring a fine collection of rare books and illuminated manuscripts. He funded nearly the entire building of the Art Schools, as well as the annexe added in 1913, and he made provision for lecture fees as well as donating valuable pictures and books. The purpose-built Art Schools, which transformed the teaching of the subject at the School, was way ahead of its time and had a profound influence. The annual Yates Thompson prizes were also his endowment and an impressive array of early winners included Spencer Gore (1897), RO Bell (1903), NA Walton (1907), Harold Alexander (later Field Marshal Earl Alexander of Tunis) (1909), Cecil Beaton (1920), Edward Le Bas (1921) and Victor Pasmore (1924).

Hine retired in 1922 and was said to have done "more than any man to further the interests of Art in the public schools and to place the teaching of it on a firm foundation". His legacy is still evident at Harrow today. His philosophy was not so much to produce artists or even art, but to foster an understanding and appreciation of what is fine and beautiful. To this end, the lectures begun in his time were established on a regular basis by his successor, Mr Maurice Clarke (1922–36 and 1940–45). And it was in the same spirit that the Hegan watercolours and Gardiner Wilkinson antiquities were donated to the School: they were never intended as precious museum objects but rather as educational aids. For many years the watercolours hung on the staircase of the War Memorial. It was only when some valuable exhibits 'disappeared' one day, only to be miraculously 'found' by some boys under a bridge in Pinner, that the School authorities realised how irresponsible their custody of these valuable objects had been. Some of the Gardiner Wilkinson pieces had made their way to the Art Schools: a fine, large Greek Cypriot vase was found in the role of a brush pot. Today they form the nucleus of the School's 'Treasures',

The happy outcome of all this chaos was the creation of Old Speech Room Gallery. With its permanent and temporary displays, active boys' committee and frequent excursions to London's museums and

Mr Will Egerton Hine, a pioneering teacher of Art, who joined the staff in 1892

Facing page: The Art Schools in c1900

Hine retired in 1922 and was said to have done "more than any man to further the interests of Art in the public schools and to place the teaching of it on a firm foundation"... . His legacy is still in evidence today

galleries, the OSRG has probably done as much as anything to develop the aesthetic sensibilities of Harrovians over the last thirty years.

Since the war, the story of the Art Schools has been one of gradual but continuous expansion. First under Mr Maurice Percival (1945–54) and then Mr Robin Treffgarne (1954–76), a fertile collaboration on the Shakespeare play forged a bond with Harrow drama that is as strong today as it is demanding, now that the Ryan Theatre has been built. Under Mr Jonathan Turner (1976–82) and Mr Jason Braham (1983–2007), the pottery, a full range of traditional and modern printmaking facilities and a sculpture studio have been added. The building of the Modern Languages Schools has allowed the creation of the Pasmore gallery, and enabled the Art department to spread into the Leaf Schools. Anyone unacquainted with the Art Schools since the 1960s would be astonished by the variety and sheer ambition of much of the work produced by current pupils. Past and present generations of Harrovians then have every reason to be grateful to a handful of individuals whose inspiration and dedication have combined to make Harrow Art amongst the very best in the country.

The Art Schools in the 1940s

Facing page: The interior of the Art Schools seen from the mezzanine gallery, 2010

Art
Art

DRAMA

WHEN THE RYAN THEATRE opened in 1994, the School's historian Dr Christopher Tyerman wrote some fascinating 'Historical Notes' for the Gala Opening Programme. From them, we learnt that the first recorded School plays were the regular theatrical evenings held on the three nights at the end of the Christmas term for some years up to the early 1750s. These 'fêtes' were sponsored by the Head Master himself, Dr Thomas Thackeray, who wrote prologues for them and borrowed costumes from John Rich, the celebrated manager of Covent Garden.

'Buttons' in the Rattigan Society production of Cinderella Charleston, *2006*

The 'fêtes' were terminated when a 1752 performance of scenes from *Romeo and Juliet* with Tate Wilkinson (later a notable actor-manager) as Romeo, and John Rushout (later Baron Northwick) as a sensational Juliet, led, says Tyerman, to public conversation, a hastily-convened Masters' Meeting and a decision by Thackeray to stop future plays lest Harrow gain a reputation "for breeding up actors in lieu of scholars".

So opportunities for acting at Harrow were subsequently restricted to occasional public orations – polymath William Jones gave Mark Antony's Forum speech in 1760, and RB Sheridan, sporting an officer's uniform, gave a Greek speech – and to the long tradition of 'Speeches' on official Speech Days (three a year until reduced to one in 1844) which began in 1772. Dr Joseph Drury, Head Master from 1785 to 1805, was a theatre enthusiast, and encouraged declaiming in English as well as acted scenes. In 1804 and 1805, Byron acted in a scene from the *Aeneid* and gave passionate declamations from Young's *Zanga* and Shakespeare's *Lear*: "I regarded myself as a Garrick revived," he later recalled.

The Victorian Age favoured music over drama. The new Speech Room (1887) was used for Songs rather than plays; nonetheless, the play-scenes in Speeches were very popular and John Galsworthy recorded that parts in "Greek and English plays" were much coveted.

After the Great War, a 'Golden Age' for Harrow Drama developed. AP Boissier, a Master from 1919–42, and wartime Head Master, introduced a period when costumes and make-up were added to the increasingly elaborate play-scenes in Speeches. Terence Rattigan, a boy in The Park from the mid-1920s, played Olivia in three scenes from *Twelfth Night* and Caesar in *Julius Caesar* opposite Dorian Williams as Calpurnia.

At the same time, plays were welcomed at Harrow. Visiting companies from the West End and the universities performed: Nigel Playfair (OH) brought a reading of *Hamlet* with Sybil Thorndyke; in 1930,

The Trial *by Steven Berkoff, 2009*

the Schools Theatre company performed *The Tempest* with Donald Wolfit as Caliban; Old Rendallian George Howe brought a company in 1931 to read *Hamlet* again: Harrow Master and superb actor and director, TF Coade, later an inspiring Head Master of Bryanston, was recruited to play Claudius; John Gielgud read *Hamlet*.

In 1938, Mr Boissier staged a magnificent production of *The Tempest* in the gardens of a School residence, Deynecourt. Mr ARD Watkins played Prospero. This spectacle led directly to the establishing of Harrow's greatest dramatic tradition: the Shakespeare Play. This, in turn led to the foundation in 1952 of the Old Harrovian Players, who still perform their own annual Shakespeare Play in Speech Room early in the Summer term. The continued existence of the Society is a great testimony to the powerful hold that Harrow Shakespeare has exerted over its youthful performers.

For many years, Speech Room, with occasional forays to the Music Schools and open air spaces such as the Deynecourt garden described above, was the School's only theatre. In 1983, Head Master Ian Beer appointed Mr Martin Tyrrell as Harrow's first Head of Drama. He built on the already burgeoning House Play tradition, and today every House stages its own full-length and often large-cast play every two years. These are almost always directed by Masters; many are farces and comedies, although striking dramas are also chosen.

In 1990, Mr Tyrrell introduced a festival of new boys' drama, which is staged each October. The new boys from each House stage twenty-minute pieces directed by senior boys. Shell Drama helps new boys and their elders to create widely-recognised team endeavours: it also reveals new talent in considerable numbers.

With the expansion of dramatic activity at Harrow, it soon became clear that a dedicated rehearsal and performance space should be made available. Messrs Chris Deacon, Roy Murray and Tyrrell were the Working Party charged by Mr Beer to plan and supervise the creation of a Drama Studio in the bowels of the Economics Schools. The Studio opened in 1984, and was a 'black box' seating up to 100 (at a distinct pinch) with a flexible lighting grid and separate areas for lighting and sound operation and non-Shakespearean costume storage. Smaller-scale House Plays, small-cast Rattigan Society productions, Theatre Studies practicals and, most valuably perhaps, occasional boy-written and boy-directed pieces were the staple diet of the Studio. Eventually, the need for Photography to have a dedicated space led to its demise in 2003, but there are currently very welcome plans to open a new one on the site of the present Sculpture Studio.

The Studio notwithstanding, the great increase in productions, ever more professional set-designs, notably of Jason Braham (Director of Art 1983–2007), and the taste for modern, complex lighting designs (valiantly facilitated in Speech Room by Mr Deacon and his boy teams) led perhaps inevitably to calls for a theatre to be built. These ambitions were not new, of course – indeed, in 1944, Ronnie Watkins had proposed the building of a replica Globe in Harrow Park – but late in 1985 Ian Beer found a donor, Sir Peter Green, who was prepared to make a donation large enough to guarantee that the long-cherished dreams of Masters and boys be realised.

An expanded Working Party, now including Messrs Braham, Jeremy Lemmon, Andrew McGregor, James Morwood and Appeal Director, Philip Balcombe, drew up a considered 'wish list', and architects Kenneth Reed & Associates were appointed. The site was to be below the Old Gymnasium, and it was eventually decided to go for a wide proscenium-arch stage, with a thrust recalling the Speech Room staging's ability to go into the heart of the auditorium. A much-expanded Wardrobe and set-building facilities extend backstage under the Old Gymnasium. Seating on two levels caters for 390 and a foyer provides warmth and refreshments on performance days and valuable additional rehearsal space at other times.

Les Misérables, *2008*

The new theatre led to a surge of interest in drama. A-level Theatre Studies was introduced in 1994: boys regularly achieve practical marks in excess of 90%, studying a wider range of world drama than School or House plays can usually cater for. The Modern Languages and Classics departments regularly stage plays, particularly in German, Latin and Ancient Greek. Professional companies visit, notably Opera East with OH conductor Ollie Gooch, and Firewalk Theatre Company, which stages innovative work in Spanish. A peculiarly British tradition has also become part of Harrow drama: a School Pantomime is performed once every five-year generation, featuring over 100 boys, girls, Masters, staff and their families.

The Rattigan Society, founded in 1983, is the School's Dramatic Society, and organises trips to plays and talks by distinguished professional speakers. It stages an annual production, in one year a great play, in the next a spectacular musical in conjunction with the Music department, such as 2008's *Les Misérables (Schools Edition)*. Girls from local girls' schools are welcome guests in Rattigan Society productions. Harrovians have also taken plays to the Edinburgh Fringe Festival and to the East Coast of the USA.

Since the Ryan Theatre opened, the OH Players have branched out into additional non-Shakespearean performances in that different space: regular OH directors have included John D Collins and Tom Noad, both professional actors. Noad directed Rattigan's *The Winslow Boy* in 1998, a production notable for its star turn by then Harrow parent, Peter O'Toole.

For some years now, Drama has been one of the most successful of the School's many successful activities and much of that has depended on teamwork. Mr Curt Peirson, Technical Manager, constructs magnificent sets and has encouraged the many Harrovians who find technical aspects of theatre to be their chosen niche. Mrs Maggie Bishop is the dedicated Wardrobe Mistress. Mr Tyrrell writes, "Drama is a social, collaborative art: we are very fortunate that at Harrow, so many talented boys, Masters, staff and their families have chosen to take part in it." What he modestly fails to add is that it owes almost everything to a remarkable Director, who has raised the standard of Harrow drama to unimagined heights and who has maintained his enthusiasm, energy and flair for inspiring young people for twenty-seven years.

Accidental Death of an Anarchist *by Dario Fo, 2008 (left),* Plunder *by Ben Travers, 2008 (right)*

MUSIC

SOME SCHOOLS HAVE A musical tradition that can be traced back to the establishment of their chapels and their choirs. Musical life in these schools can be heavily dependent upon the elite body of pupils admitted on the strength of their musical talent. At Harrow, things are different.

The Harrow School Musical Society, which had been formed in 1857 by Capel Henry Berger, had met two or three times a week for orchestral practice in the presence of Mrs Vaughan in the upper room of a local club known as the Young Men's Society. The conductor was the organist of St Mary's Church.

This was the beginning of a tradition that owes almost everything to the strength, vision and determination of one remarkable man, John Farmer, and the dedicated colleagues who supported him in his aim to create a musical culture at Harrow that was truly inclusive. As one of the first full-time Music Masters to be appointed in an English school (as opposed to someone just responsible for Music in Chapel), it is hard to imagine what John Farmer must have felt when he arrived at the School in 1862 and found it to be a musical desert. The challenge facing him was formidable. Eager to engage as many boys as possible in musical activity, he saw communal singing in the evening as the way forward. He faced, of course, much opposition, and on one occasion was greeted with a hail of football boots. He remained undeterred and, with the assistance of his fellow songwriters, founded a tradition that has given generations of Harrovians tunes and lyrics that remain in the blood long after their departure from the Hill. (See *Harrow Songs*, page 228)

Mr (later Sir) Percy Buck, Director of Music, 1901–27; he composed the music for You? *and* The Silver Arrow

In 1873 Frederic Rendall undertook to erect a building following the plans of the Musical Society and to rent it to them. This was the Old Music School at the junction of Peterborough Road and Football Lane, now used as a small lecture room and housing the Museum of Harrow Life. It was small, damp and not soundproof. Its successor, the fine building we have today, was built in 1891. This is a wonderful space for music-making, with a beautiful recital room at its centre. One imagines that it must have been a luxurious resource at this time – and probably still was in the 1950s.

Following in Farmer's footsteps, a succession of eminent Directors of Music have sought to promote music, raise its profile and inculcate a love of music amongst their charges. Percy Buck, a composer of renown, was Director from 1901 to 1927 and taught boys the piano and musical appreciation; he also organised concerts of compositions by Harrow boys which were well publicised in the *Musical Times* and which must have been unique at the time. But Sir Percy (as he later became) seems to have managed to combine his duties at Harrow with being Professor of Music at Trinity College, Dublin, then London University, a thought that would raise the eyebrow of a present-day Director. But the music-making at Harrow in the first part of the twentieth century was a peripheral activity, one that was tolerated and gently encouraged, but certainly not something in which a significant proportion of boys engaged – except of course in Songs. This is reflected in the fact that Hector McCurrach, in 1962, was the first Director to become an Assistant (as opposed to an "Extra") Master.

In the middle of the twentieth century, the fashion of large-scale choral works performed by either the entire School or a large choral society, adopted by many public schools, was taken up at Harrow. After morning Chapel the whole School would trudge across to Speech Room to be rehearsed in their 'unison part'. For non-musical boys it was an exposure to choral music that few will have later regretted.

All the time, small steps were being taken to raise the profile of music and musicians: in 1953 Dr James awarded a half-holiday each term to the choir and orchestra. In 1973 entrance scholarships, hitherto purely for academic talent, were awarded to musicians. The creation of The Guild in 1991 gave leading musicians along with actors and other artists recognition by their peer group.

Today the face of Harrow's music is unrecognisable. Mr Richard Walker, Director 1985–2005, deserves much credit for achieving greater time and resources for music, and also for attracting boys to Harrow on music scholarships. The present Director has built on these foundations to create a vibrant department at the very heart of School activity. Nowadays about 40% of boys learn a musical instrument, and with many learning more than one, in excess of 500 music lessons are given every week. The School's proximity to London means that it is able to attract teachers of the highest calibre, who are also often performers of national and international repute.

The Champion House XII, 1905 (above); the Music Society c1853 (below)

Choral Society Concert with the girls of the Francis Holland School, Clarence Gate

Boys frequently attend concerts in London and well-known musicians visit Harrow to give concerts and conduct master classes.

All boys hear live music regularly: there are solo and ensemble performances at Monday morning Speech Room. Many boys attend music competitions. Of these, the Glees and XIIs competition is undoubtedly the one that provokes the keenest interest. The whole School attends and the event has important educational implications. Firstly, the boys run it: the senior boys in a House rehearse and inspire the younger ones. Were it not for Harrow's House system, they would not be able to have had the valuable experience of being a musical director. Secondly, it is important to consider this event not merely as a competition but as a concert, remarkable for sheer variety and diversity of performance. It is an evening of music that encompasses a range of music from pop songs to difficult close harmony renditions, Schubert lieder, and operatic arias.

For the more musical boys, there is a wealth of opportunities for musical performance: more than eighty events in a typical year. These include informal concerts in the Music Schools, weekly recitals by boys at St Mary's Church, House concerts, and large-scale concerts in Speech Room. It is, however, a disappointment to see how few people, adult members of the School community, members of the public and boys attend these concerts. It may be a price to pay for a boarding school where few of the parents live locally, and in a part of the country awash with opportunities for musical entertainment.

Groups of Harrow musicians also go on tour giving concerts both at home and abroad. These groups are not the preserve of any particular musical elite. Although the seventy or so of the music scholars and exhibitioners provide Harrow's musical life with a strong backbone, they have no monopoly over it but share their music-making with a large number of boys. There are two choirs of about sixty boys each that perform regularly in Chapel. There are more than eighty boys in the Concert Band, more than seventy in the Orchestra and more than 200 take part in the Choral Concert. Smaller ensembles, such as the Chamber Choir and Byron Consort, tackle works that stretch the most able. A new contemporary music group, *The Kandinsky Ensemble,* undertakes works that provide a formidable challenge for instrumentalists. Chamber Music is a real strength at Harrow, and String Quartets and Piano Trios have earned an enviable reputation for reaching the finals of the Schools National Chamber Music Competition.

At the lighter end of the musical scale there is a Swing Band, some Jazz ensembles and, of course, that mainstay of teenage culture, Rock Music groups. Five years ago a new Music Schools annexe was completed and this is now a dedicated space for music technology, music-recording, production and rock music. Regular rock concerts provide opportunities for several bands to display their talents, and many boys write their own material. The majority of boys competing for the annual Mortimer Singer prize for solo, self-accompanied singing, now sing their own compositions, and there is a new class for Rock Bands to help young performers prepare for this competition. Whilst the boys enjoy the thrill of the competition, they also derive benefit from having their work and performance adjudicated by a leading musician in this particular field.

From the Gaelic fringe of school music there is the Pipe Band which, in addition to its performances on Speech Day and Remembrance Sunday, now summons the Rifle Corps to parade each week.

There is also collaboration between the Music and Drama departments at Harrow when there is a full-scale musical, or boys compose music for the Shakespeare Play and other productions and perform it themselves.

The 1891 Music Schools has recently undergone a major refurbishment, and though it does not meet all the needs of music-making in the twenty-first century at Harrow, it is, nevertheless, a building of which the School can be proud.

On Speech Day, the Pipe Band greets the crowd emerging from Speeches with a short programme. After lunch the Concert band plays on the War Memorial forecourt, followed by a Chamber Music Concert in Chapel. The day is rounded off by Songs accompanied by the School Orchestra. It all seems a far cry from the days when a regimental band had to be hired to entertain the parents on the Chapel Terrace – and these days nobody throws football boots at the Director of Music.

Elliot Smith playing in the Concerto Concert, 2010

THE SHAKESPEARE PLAY

THE TRADITION OF PRODUCING Shakespeare in Speech Room was in part the result of an unsuccessful German bombing mission. The pilot dumped his bombs on the way home one night in 1940 and an incendiary lodged in Speech Room roof, destroying the mechanism for suspending a proscenium curtain and the wiring for floods and spots. This provided the opportunity for Mr ARD Watkins to put into practice the naturalistic theories he had been developing, aimed at reproducing as closely as possible the conditions that prevailed in the Elizabethan Globe Theatre. In fact *Twelfth Night*, the first production in 1941, was presented, according to *The Harrow Observer,* without benefit of scenery, lights or "stage equipment to speak of", though the stage did contain, according to *The Harrovian*, "a couple of box trees and a beer barrel". Wartime costumes were designed by Mr Maurice Percival and incidental music written by Mr Henry Havergal, the Director of Music, and his successor Mr Hector McCurrach. The subsequent wartime productions were *Henry V* (1942) and *Macbeth* (1943). Fears about the V1 flying bomb prevented a performance in 1944 but the first production of *A Midsummer Night's Dream*, took place in 1945.

Over time the various features of the later stage emerged: the two pillars in 1946 and the 'Chamber' and 'Tarras' in 1949. 1949 was also the first year in which Ronnie Watkins was assisted with the production by Mr Herbert Harris. Mr Watkins's productions quickly attracted wider critical attention with reviews in *The Times* from 1946 onwards and regularly in *The New Statesman* from 1947 by Desmond MacCarthy and others.

The 'Harrow Method', as it became known, was built round the 'Golden Rule' that nothing should be done in performance that Shakespeare's company would not have done, and that words should be the chief instrument of theatrical illusion. In this it was extraordinarily successful. As MacCarthy himself wrote, "Here is a stage fitted to the kind of dramatic illusion at which Shakespeare aimed; a stage which both by its formalism and its naturalism in details – a tree, a bench a table – is the kind most favourable to *the creation of atmosphere through words* – in short to Shakespeare's dramatic technique." Ronnie's ability, without the assistance of any artificial sound or lighting, to make palpable Lorenzo's invitation to Jessica:

How sweet the moonlight sleeps upon this bank!
Here will we sit and let the sounds of music
Creep in our ears: soft stillness and the night
Become the touches of sweet harmony

is for those who experienced it, one of the lasting memories of his genius.

There were two major consequences of Mr Watkins's work. The first was the emergence of a succession of exceptionally gifted schoolboy actors. Mr Jeremy Lemmon (who, had he not been the author on this occasion, would undoubtedly himself have been included) lists some of them in the piece that he wrote for *Harrow: Portrait of an English School* the Hamlets

Mr Ronnie Watkins at The Globe Theatre, Bankside, 1994

Facing page: Henry Ashwell and Will Hamilton in The Tempest, *2008*

of Alexander Schouvaloff and James Dreyfus; the Lears of Costa Carras and Crispin Black; Peregrine Massey as Coriolanus; Alastair Boag as the Duke of Vienna; Michael Stone's Cleopatra, Colin McLean's Leontes, Toby Dantzic's Richard III, Giles Havergal's tragic Constance. In recent years many more talented actors have cut their teeth on the Speech Room stage; foremost amongst them was Benedict Cumberbatch, now a major light of the British theatre scene.

As *The Times* wrote of the 1951 production of *Hamlet,* "By the time the cock crew behind the battlements one had forgotten that the actors were schoolboys, by the time the oath was sworn on Hamlet's sword one was ceasing to judge them as amateurs; and by the arrival of the Players one had forgotten everything except that here were the living creatures of the poet's imagination moving in the midst of a modern audience to show the very age and body of the time his form and pressure."

Guy Boas recalled this same production in his *Shakespeare and the Young Actor*: "I have seen celebrated performances of *Hamlet* all my life, but I can sincerely say that I have never been so moved by the tragedy as a whole as when I saw it performed in its entirety by the boys of Harrow School...in addition to the qualities of Hamlet and Claudius, the player of the Queen was so haunting in gesture, poise, and above all beauty of vocal tone, that in respect of these players alone the production proved the complete capacity of a boy to enact full-length Shakespeare roles both male and female." The player of the Queen on that occasion was Jeremy Lemmon, already an unreclaimed enthusiast.

Benedict Cumberbatch (above) and James Dreyfus (centre below) are both professional actors

The second consequence was the re-emergence of the Elizabethan convention of boys playing women. Desmond MacCarthy again: "Of course it is also interesting to see what Shakespeare took for granted: boys impersonating women. The effect of that convention was by diminishing personal interest to direct the attention of the spectator towards the character impersonated rather than upon the impersonator." He added later, "It may be of some significance that the decline of poetic drama to which that technique was so admirably suited begins when women began to play female parts."

The repertoire tended, of necessity, to reflect the examination curriculum. Nevertheless the list of plays performed by the School from 1941 to the present is impressive and includes, in addition to those more obviously suited to school productions, *King John* (1953), *Coriolanus* (1968), *Cymbeline* (1989) and two productions of *The Tempest* (1978 and 2008). *A Midsummer Night's Dream* has become perhaps the 'signature' Harrow School production with performances in 1945, 1952, 1960, 1974 and 1991. The 1960 production was notable for performances by Julian Holloway (Bottom) and Carey Harrison (Demetrius) at the same time as their respective fathers (Stanley and Rex) were starring in the record-breaking West End production of *My Fair Lady*.

Mr Watkins's last School production, *Julius Caesar*, was in 1964 and WA Darlington in the *Daily Telegraph* summarised what in many ways was his greatest achievement: "He has proved what otherwise we might have found it difficult to believe, that miracles of stage illusion can be achieved by suggestion alone – illusion of darkness, for instance, of a stage uniformly and brightly lit." Mr Watkins was far from retired however, directing the Old Harrovians at Haddo House and appearing shortly afterwards for them as Rumour in *Henry IV pt 1* in Speech Room. He continued to write and lecture on Shakespeare, producing, with Jeremy Lemmon, titles on *Macbeth, Hamlet* and *A Midsummer Night's Dream* in the 'In Shakespeare's Playhouse' series, and lecturing everywhere from St Andrew's to the Rocky Mountains where the University of Colorado awarded him an honorary Doctorate.

Mr Watkins's successor was his former pupil, Jeremy Lemmon. The more than thirty years of his management of the play saw important changes in the Harrow Globe tradition, reflecting developments in the Shakespeare scholarship, and, of course, responding to the changing atmosphere and circumstances of the School itself. In 1971 the production of *The Winter's Tale* included Richard Curtis, the author of *Blackadder* and *Love Actually*, playing a "grave and beautiful" Hermione.

Faced with the daunting task of following a legendary director, Mr Lemmon managed to bring his own style – and a little idiosyncrasy – to the productions without losing their essential character. His method of casting brought an element of mystique and created a deliberate tension at the same time as allowing him to make best use of the available talent. Aspiring actors were invited to audition in Speech Room. No decisions were taken or invitations issued until all had been heard. Some weeks later the lucky ones would receive a small, brown envelope. Inside the envelope would be a slip of paper offering a particular part: Hamlet perhaps or – less demandingly, 'Attendant on Peruchio'. This allowed Mr Lemmon to cast the play over a period of a couple of months.

Mr Lemmon's enthusiasm for the play ensured that rehearsals were fun and his knowledge and passion inspired great energy and confidence in the cast. Former actors have said what a privilege it was to have performed under such a skilful and dedicated director.

In 1994, before the Elizabethan reconstruction of the Globe theatre was fully complete, the School was invited to Southwark to perform that year's play, *The Taming of the Shrew*. Following the play, there was a brief presentation and a few speeches after which Ronnie Watkins, who was by then very frail, cut a cake. The first full-length Shakespeare play presented within the walls of the new Bankside Globe was performed by Harrovians – striking testimony to the high regard in which the School productions were held.

When, in the late 1980s, Shakespeare set texts ceased to feature in the GCSE examinations as a summer focus, the relevance of the play for most boys was diminished. When boys' attendance ceased to be compulsory, a straight choice between a hard seat in Speech Room and lolling in front of a television set in the House led to predictably diminished audiences. Removes and Shells are now each required to attend one or other of the School's and the Old Harrovian Players' productions.

Mr Lemmon retired in 1996 since when responsibility for directing has been shared between a number of Masters. Changes that Harrovians from an earlier era would notice include the stage posts which were truncated, mended and then replaced. The unhistorical perimeter black railings have not been seen since 1996.

The School Shakespeare Play, as produced and performed since that first production of *Twelfth Night*, has been one of the cultural glories of a Harrow education. All those who have been involved in any way have cause to be grateful to the succession of talented Masters who have maintained the tradition that Ronnie Watkins inaugurated in that darkest of wartime springs.

Souvid Datta in Othello, *2009*

THE OLD SPEECH ROOM GALLERY

WHEN THE EXTENSION TO the Old Schools was completed in 1819, the large space mirroring the Fourth Form Room became 'Speech Room'. It was long and narrow, and acoustically appalling – a more unsuitable space for speech-making it is difficult to imagine. Fifty-eight years later it was superseded by the building we now know as Speech Room; 'Old' Speech Room seems to have been used as an examination hall and not much else for a hundred years.

In 1976 Old Speech Room was converted into a museum to preserve and display the School's collection of treasures. It was designed by Alan Irvine and unsurprisingly took the name 'The Old Speech Room Gallery'.

The Gallery contains a number of collections of antiquities and fine art, of which The Gardner Wilkinson Collection forms the core. In 1864 Sir John Gardner Wilkinson (OH), one of the first British Egyptologists, presented the School with a large and celebrated collection of Egyptian, Greek, Etruscan and Roman antiquities. He rightly thought that they would inspire later generations. The display of nearly 300 items is arranged thematically to illustrate Gardner Wilkinson's travels and a variety of aspects of life and death in ancient Egypt.

Black Monday or the Departure for School *by William Redmore Bigg, 1789 (a painting on permanent display in The Old Speech Room Gallery)*

The Hegan watercolours collection was given by CJ Hegan (OH) in 1935. It also is a distinguished collection, comprising works by Turner, Girtin, de Wint, David Roberts and John Sell Cotman among others. For many years these paintings hung on the stairs leading to the Old Harrovian Room in the War Memorial building. This was both bad for the paintings and bad for the viewers. Nowadays paintings on staircases contravene health and safety regulations anyhow! Paintings from the Hegan collection are regularly displayed in the Gallery in thematic exhibitions focussing on individual painters.

Sculptures in the Gallery range from a spirited Roman marble torso to Thomas Woolner's Pre-Raphaelite statuette, *Elaine*. Also on permanent display are busts of Old Harrovians such as Sheridan, Byron and Spencer Perceval by Joseph Nollekens.

There is an early portrait of 'John Sayer' – he of the Sayer Scholarships at Caius, Cambridge – by George Romney. It was painted when Sayer was Head of School in 1770 and he is portrayed in the archery dress of pink satin tunic, white lace collar and blue sash.

Modern British pictures on display include David Jones's numinous *Tree at Harrow* (c1950) and works by Old Harrovians such as Winston Churchill, Spencer Gore, Cecil Beaton, Victor Pasmore and Richard Shirley Smith.

Also in the Gallery can be seen a small collection of medieval manuscripts and incunabula; a French

fifteenth century Book of Hours; a collection of books published by the Aldine Press, mainly in the sixteenth century; a 'Great Bible' of 1539 (the first translation in English), as ordered to be placed in every church by Henry VIII; and a first edition of the 1611 Authorized Version. Also transferred from the Vaughan Library are three Bibles that contain curious translations or misprints: two 'Breeches Bibles' of 1599 and 1607 (where Adam and Eve sew breeches of fig leaves to cover their nakedness) and a sumptuously bound 'Vinegar Bible' of 1717, once in the Blenheim Palace collection, where the running title in St Luke's Gospel reads "The parable of the vinegar" (for 'vineyard').

Some of the treasures have recently been moved to the School Archives: the notable Byron collection, the most interesting items of which were bequeathed by H Panmure Gordon (OH) in 1902, and rare books that used to be kept in the Vaughan Library. More modern treasures, also transferred, include a manuscript of part of Trollope's *Framley Parsonage* and Winston Churchill's essay, written as a schoolboy, about an imagined Russian invasion of Afghanistan. These are, of course, available for exhibition when the occasion arises.

The creation of the mezzanine floor and the introduction of carpeting in 1976 effectively cured the former acoustic problems and the finals of various verse-reading competitions and the Lady Bourchier Reading prize are frequently held in the Gallery.

The School is extremely fortunate to possess such treasures and the Gallery has an active exhibition programme, under the direction of its Curator, Carolyn Leder. There are several major shows each year; these comprise a mixture of works on loan as well as treasures from the School's collections. There is free admission to the public. The Old Speech Room Gallery Arts Society enables boys to take part in the running of the museum and the mounting of exhibitions; it also serves as the fulcrum for a regular programme of external visits to museums and exhibitions in London.

Harrow on the Hill *by John Inigo Richards, 1793 (a painting on permanent display in The Old Speech Room Gallery)*

CRICKET

CRICKET HAS LONG PLAYED a major part in the life of the School. In the period from 1850 to 1939 this was largely due to the social significance of the Eton match at Lord's (see page 162) but much of the credit for the game's high profile must go to to two nineteenth century champions of Harrow cricket, Frederick Ponsonby, Lord Bessborough and The Hon Robert Grimston.

Although Percy Thornton claims that "in Dr Drury's time the eleven played on a field …situated on the brow of that part of Harrow Hill which you ascend when coming from Sudbury, about half a mile from the school centre", a more popular view is that the only School playing field at that time was part of the church fields, later to become the site of the old rackets court and gymnasium. It must have been a curious kind of cricket, played on a steep hillside, on ground mown only by sheep. The 1772 painting *The Masons at Cricket* depicts two brothers playing at Harrow on a suitably mountainous terrain; the landscape may be imaginary, but there are several references to the game being played at the School at this time.

In 1803 the Governors were allotted a parcel of land in lieu of the common rights lost by the enclosure of Roxeth Common. This comprised the present VIth Form ground and the site of the John Lyon School, about eight acres. It was still a very poor provision for the School's cricket but improvements were slowly made between this time and 1850. Between 1849 and 1893 a further six acres of land were leased, later purchased and added to by gift, until it became the playing area we know today as the Philathletic Ground (The Phil). In 1883 the VI Form pavilion was built largely at Grimston's expense and the following year the path of Lower Road was altered to increase the size of the VI Form Ground. This apparently harmless diversion created a dangerous bend at the bottom of West Street, which in later years was to be the cause of several motor accidents. In 1884 the Field House was purchased by William Nicholson and Ponsonby and given to the School for cricket purposes. In 1892 the Nicholson Field (later to be re-named the Bessborough Ground) was purchased and leased to the School; on it stood an old manor house, High Capers, which was demolished and the field levelled in 1894. In 1893 a pavilion was built on the Bessborough Ground in memory of the Rev W Law and in 1894 another on the Phil in memory of CD Buxton. The VI Form Ground, still "rugged and precipitous" in 1863, was at various times and by degrees levelled.

The Hon Robert Grimston (above) and Frederick Ponsonby, Earl of Bessborough (right)

In 1898, fifteen years later, Spencer Gore was able to write: "In the last twenty-five years we have more than trebled the size of the original freehold cricket field. We have diverted a public road, acquired a club for Old Harrovians, built four new cricket pavilions, and excavated and levelled land which former volcanic conditions never intended for cricket purposes. And the whole expense has been borne by voluntary contributions, a record of which any school may be justly proud."

In 1913 Roxeth Farm was purchased and added to the Philathletic Ground. At the same time the Vth Form pavilion was built in memory of John Richardson. Gifts and the bequest of John Apcar enabled a further seven-and-a-half acres to be added to The Phil between 1917 and 1924. After this torrent of activity on the

cricket fields and pavilions, amazingly, little more was done for another seventy years.

The history of cricket coaching at Harrow can be said to have begun with Ponsonby and Grimston, two Old Harrovians who came down to the School every day in the season for that purpose. In an era before Masters took any interest in the coaching of sport, they can be fairly said to have been the moving spirits of Harrow cricket during the period from 1828–1884. Their aim was to teach "sound unselfish cricket with the sacrifice of 'self' to 'side'." These ideas may appear somewhat old fashioned in the twenty-first century: in 1872 Grimston claimed, "for our cricket ground and football field a share, and a very considerable share too, in the formation of the character of the English gentleman. Our games require patience, good temper, perseverance, good pluck and above all, implicit obedience" – just the qualities required to run the Empire. They also employed (at their own expense) professional bowlers: Gilby, the groundsman, was one up to 1871, then 'Pipes' Chadd and W Clarke. Before 1860, when nets were introduced, practice must have been a precarious business for batsmen, who were lined up side by side – presumably some distance apart. One imagines hooking and square cutting was discouraged. It was the job of fags to field the balls and especially to 'long-stop'. Then nets were introduced – initially just side netting for safety.

Grimston and Ponsonby were to be followed by ID 'Donny' Walker and AJ 'Webbie' Webbe, although in a rather lower key, for at this point Masters were beginning to become involved in School cricket. Mr Edward Bowen devised 'cricket bill' whereby players, instead of toiling up the hill to School Bill, could answer their names on the cricket fields. Mr MC Kemp, "The Bishop", an Old Harrovian and Oxford 'blue', was appointed a Master in 1888 and immediately took responsibility for School games.

Up to 1930, the cricket season continued into the Autumn term until Michaelmas (29 September), finishing with the Goose Match between the XI and an Old Harrovian team, so named because the two teams dined together after the match (as they still do) on the traditional Michaelmas fare of roast goose.

Most of the cricket in the nineteenth century was internal and House-based, although for the First XI the climax of the season was the match against Eton at Lord's. Lord's was also host to a match against

The Masons at Cricket, 1772

Winchester from 1825 until 1854. In 1884 the First XI fixture list comprised Harrow Town, I Zingari, The Household Brigade, Oxford Harlequins, Cambridge Quidnuncs, Lord Bessborough's XI, Mr Bowen's XI and Old Harrovians, Eton being the only school opposition. Particularly of note was the XI of 1887 when FS Jackson and AC MacLaren, two future England captains, were in the side. By 1910, the MCC, Free Foresters and Oxford Authentics had replaced the two scratch sides but the only school opponents apart from Eton were an American touring side from Philadelphia, Haverford College.

After the Great War, the Butterflies was added to the list of clubs and Winchester and Charterhouse were new school opposition. This balance of club to school opposition slowly swung as the century progressed. A third school, Marlborough, was added in 1939 (but not retained after the War) and by 1954 Haileybury, Wellington and Malvern (recognising the close wartime relationship) made the ratio six clubs to six schools.

Such was the importance attached to Harrow cricket by Old Harrovians that, after the Great War, a number of them clubbed together to form a 'bowling fund', the purpose of which was to employ professional coaching. The 'pros', which included some famous names – Ernie Bale (Worcestershire), JT Hearne (Middlesex), Wilfred Rhodes (Yorkshire), Patsy Hendren (Middlesex), Lofty Herman (Hampshire), Tom Barling (Surrey), Percy Davis (Northamptonshire) – worked Summer term only. In the 1950s there were four: Barling, Les Fletcher, Joe Skelton and the head groundsman, Stan Haywood and later Peter Ward. Not until the appointment of Ramesh Sethi in 1988 did the School employ a full-time coach/groundsman.

In 1925, the bowling shed, housing two nets (one concrete based, the other marl) was donated by G Hutton-Potts. His sons turned out to have no interest in cricket but became very good swimmers!

Although no victory at Lord's was recorded between 1908 and 1939, there were some fine sides between the wars, and fifteen players from these years went on to win 'blues' at Oxford and Cambridge.

Dr Norwood was the first Harrow Head Master actively to recruit Masters to coach games. Although the conversion to rugby was his main concern, he appointed two cricket 'blues', Mr JW Greenstock and

Sixth Form cricket ground, 1874

Facing page (left to right, and top to bottom): Harrow XIs of 1863, 1870, 1875, 1880, 1896 and 1908

Cricket has always been a very important part of Harrow life – some have even suggested it is the *most* important part. The modern game may be a slimmer and leaner beast than that of earlier years but it is alive and well

Top row (from left to right): Harrow XIs 1917, 1928, 1952 and 1961

The Rev EH Killick in 1930. Norwood's successor, Dr Vellacott, capped this with the appointment of the 1935 Oxford captain, Mr DF Walker, and the outstanding games player from Cambridge, the Wykhamist, Mr RdeWK Winlaw. Tragically, both were killed in 1942.

After the Second World War, in which the fortunes of the School had taken a serious dive in finances, numbers and sporting successes, seven of Head Master Dr Moore's first appointments were Oxbridge 'blues'. The cricketers were Mr Mark Tindall (Cambridge University & Middlesex) and Mr Jack Webster (Cambridge University & Northamptonshire), who were to be masters-in-charge in turn up to 1970. They were succeeded by Mr GM Attenborough, Mr W Snowden, Mr CMB Williams and Mr SJ Halliday. But, however good the coaching, success depends on talent. RG Marlar (Sussex), ARB Neame (Kent), AC Pigott (Sussex & Surrey), MK Fosh (Essex), RM Tindall (Northamptonshire), NRD Compton (Middlesex and Somerset), SA Northeast (Kent) and GS Ballance (Derbyshire and Yorkshire) all represented counties.

The introduction of Outstanding Talent and All Rounder 'scholarships' in 1999, especially the Sir John Beckwith Sports Scholarships, had a dramatic effect on the standard of 1st XI cricket. There were those opposed to the scheme, largely on the grounds that an 'imported' outstanding cricketer denied a well established A team player a place in the team at Lord's; opposing schools did not like it either – until they began to do the same thing. However, there were few dissenting voices when Harrow beat Eton at Lord's for four consecutive years from 2005 to 2008.

In 1999 the Bowling Fund, renamed the Cricket Fund, was amalgamated with the Field House Club and became a charity. Its function is to give financial support to Harrow cricket and, with this aim in mind, resources have been used to supplement the Development Trust's funds in a programme of major refurbishment on the cricket fields.

In 2002, the V.1 (Richardson) pavilion was restored and in 2005 similar modernisation was carried out at the VI Form pavilion, with an extension built to accommodate visiting teams. The following year, the 'flannels' boards were updated by the ingenious device of covering the existing name boards with those of new teams, leaving the old boards accessible underneath.

Meanwhile the Bessborough 'A' square was re-laid as was the VI Form square, strip by strip. But the most dramatic changes have been made on the Philathletic Ground, for many years the scene of up to fifteen overlapping games. The redesign was not entirely for aesthetic reasons; a generation of bigger boys wielding heavier bats had become a danger not only to players on adjacent games but also to the general public using the nearby roads. A redesign was made easier by the demise of House and Torpid leagues so that fewer pitches are now required. There are now six individual grounds, the separating areas having been landscaped with newly planted trees to give each its own character. The grounds have been named to commemorate the giants of Harrow's cricketing heritage: Grimston, Jackson, Hornby, MacLaren and Walker.

The Field House Club has also been refurbished as a museum and club house, with a bar, lounge, television room and balcony. Now that there is no requirement for changing rooms and showers, the Club can be enjoyed as a tangible display of the School's distinguished cricketing past. Cricket has always been a very important part of Harrow life – some have even suggested it is the *most* important part. The modern game may be a slimmer and leaner beast than that of earlier years, but it is alive and well. The School runs sixteen teams at four age levels and there are House competitions at three age levels. The First XI plays about sixteen matches a season and there are overseas tours every three years. Recent destinations have been: South Africa (2001), Sri Lanka (2004) and India (2007). Each season there is a pre-season trip to Malta.

Bottom row (from left to right): Cricket XIs of 1975, 2000, 2005 and 2009

THE ETON v HARROW CRICKET MATCH AT LORD'S

IT MAY SEEM SURPRISING TO the non-Harrovian reader that this cricket match should merit special treatment but it has played a powerful part in the history of the School. The Eton connection had begun with the appointment of William Thackeray as Head Master together with his Ushers William Cox and William Prior, all Old Etonians, in 1746. It was the beginning of Harrow's establishment as a fashionable school. Thackeray and his two Etonian successors, Robert Sumner and Benjamin Heath, created a network of influential individuals and families giving the School, in Christopher Tyerman's words, "a public reputation surpassing Westminster's and competing with Eton's as a seminary for the ruling classes in society, the state and the professions." As this association evolved, it developed into a rivalry, which found its expression in a cricket match.

"Rugby may be more clever, Harrow may make more row..." taunts the Eton Boating Song written by William Cory in 1863. "And all allow but one thing now/ The cup of life can sweeten/If we can say on Saturday/That we have beaten Eton", sang the Old Harrovians in 1891.

A postcard (right) and ticket (below) for an Eton Harrow match at Lord's

COMPLIMENTARY TICKET.
H
123
ETON v. HARROW,
JULY 14th and 15th, 1939.
Admit
MEMBER OF HARROW SCHOOL.
TO MEMBERS' ENCLOSURES—BLOCKS C, D, E, F, C,
AND THE ROOFS OF LUNCHEON ROOMS (BLOCKS, O & P.)
This Ticket does not admit at the Gate, but must be retained by the holder as a voucher for his seat, and must be shown at any time when demanded.

For over 200 years up to 1958, young girls from aristocratic or aspiring families, known as 'debutantes', were presented at court before embarking on the 'London Season', a social calendar that was to expose them to the delights of the English summer – and hopefully suitable husbands. The events included the Chelsea Flower Show, Trooping of the Colour, Henley Royal Regatta, Royal Ascot race week, The Royal Yacht Squadron Ball at Cowes – and Eton v Harrow at Lord's.

By the second half of the nineteenth century, the match had become a major event with all the national newspapers printing prospects in columns on the day and reports on the next two days. By 1870 a crowd of 10,000 was usual, rising to 15,000 by the early years of the twentieth century. Men wore top hats and morning coats, Harrow supporters sporting a cornflower button hole, Eton a white carnation tinted pale blue, and the ladies in summer hats and dresses – often featuring the colours of the school their escort was supporting. Many of the spectators would be in parked carriages round the ground: twelve hundred carriages were counted at the 1896 match. The lunch interval was host to a fashion parade across the outfield where the ladies could show off their hats and dresses, and people could see and be seen.

The crowd was sharply divided between those that cared passionately about the outcome and the large majority who had no interest in the cricket at all, let alone which side might win. Of the passionate minority, many seemed to take leave of their senses. A Harrovian described it as the "supreme rite when one identified oneself with every member of the side, suffered in their failures, exalted in their triumphs." In 1910 after an unexpected twist had brought victory for Eton, a contemporary report described how a prominent politician was seen "weeping, laughing and dancing on a Harrovian flag, and portly citizens in Bond Street were yelling the news

In 1939, when Harrow won for the first time for thirty-one years ... the supporters of the two schools set about each other in an appalling display of tribal ritualism.

to strangers with the light ribbon on them who had quitted the ground in despair an hour before."

In 1939, when Harrow won for the first time for thirty-one years, the ensuing scenes beggared belief. After the 'chairing off' of the victorious batsmen, the supporters of the two schools set about each other in an appalling display of tribal ritualism. The main target seemed to be the opposition's hats, which were first knocked off then trampled – although trousers supported by Old School braces were also said to be fair game. In some cases fighting broke out. It was not an episode of which either school should be proud, but it was followed not by disciplinary action but by a real war – World War II – during which the match was played in a much lower key at the two schools.

How did this all start? In the days before organised games, inter-school matches were rare, and few before 1800 were representative in the sense that we know today. However there is evidence of informal contests being played, probably scratch sides raised by the initiative of particular individuals often in the school holidays. Score sheets were rarely kept. So the early

The lunch interval at Lord's 1907. Nowadays spectators are requested to "keep off the playing area"

Nowadays the match is played before some three or four thousand people, mostly alumni of the two schools, together with current pupils and parents.

A view from the tavern of the 1928 match. Many of the spectators would be in parked carriages around the ground: 1,200 carriages were counted at the 1896 match

history of the match is restricted to casual references in the memoirs of some of the players. It was in just such a memoir that a record of the 1805 match has survived because Lord Byron, the poet, was a participant. The match was played on Thomas Lord's first ground, now Dorset Square, next to Marylebone Station. Byron seems an unlikely choice as he had a club foot. Arthur Shakespeare, a contemporary, wrote in his reminiscences: "Lord Byron insisted upon playing and was allowed another person to run for him, his lameness impeding him so much." John Arthur Lloyd, who captained the Harrovians, is quoted by Dean Merivale in his *Recollections* as saying: "Byron played in that match and very badly too. He should never have been in the XI if my counsel had been taken."

Byron himself wrote: "...We have played the Eton and were most confoundedly beat; however it was some comfort to me that I got 11 notches in the first innings and 7 in the second, which was more than any of our side except Brockman and Ipswich could contrive to hit." It was no surprise to find that the score sheet, discovered some years later, credited Byron, never one for self-effacement, with scores of 2 and 2.

It is said that the idea of a match taking place in term time was opposed by the two Head Masters because they feared for the behaviour of their spectator pupils. This seems to have been a wise judgement, as Byron's memoir goes on to describe how "after the match we dined together and were extremely friendly, not a single discordant note was uttered by either party. To be sure we were most of us rather drunk and went to the Haymarket Theatre, where we kicked up a row as you may suppose, with so many Harrovians and Etonians met at one place. I was one of seven in a single Hackney Coach, four Eton and three Harrow fellows; we all got into the same box, the consequence was that such a devil of a noise arose that none of our neighbours could hear a word of the drama, at which not being highly delighted they began to quarrel with us and we nearly came to a battle royal..."

Up to the First World War, of the 89 matches recorded, just 18 ended in draws but between the wars there were 13 draws in 21 years. The reasons for this were probably improvements in both the standard of school batting and the quality of the wickets at Lord's, reputed to be "pretty rough" in the early years. This did not seem to dampen the enthusiasm of the spectators, but everything changed after World War II. Not only were these the 'austerity years' but they seemed to have bred an altogether more defensive attitude to cricket. 'Lord's' was now too important a match to lose and the supposedly weaker side invariably adopted over-cautious tactics. By the late 1950s, the crowds had begun to disappear, morning coats and top hats became a rare sight, the 'debs' were no longer, and ground development had left space for no more than a handful of coaches. Twenty-two of the next 31 matches ended in draws until they were reduced to 'one day' in 1982. The hope that this might lead to more attacking and therefore interesting cricket proved unfounded, with only three out of the next 18 matches resulting in a win for either side. Unfortunately the only remaining spectators were the partisans, the very ones for whom a draw was better than a loss. Eventually a less parochial attitude began to prevail and in 2000 the match adopted the format by then accepted in almost all one-day cricket, that of each side being allotted a limited number of overs.

The pressure on the Marylebone Cricket Club, which owns Lord's and hosts not only Middlesex but also two five-day Test matches and several finals, is immense. Somehow Eton v Harrow has survived although the wicket is pitched at the 'Tavern' edge of the square – and sometimes even off it – making for a very short boundary on one side.

MCC played their part in the celebrations for the 200th anniversary in 2005. There was an exhibition in the Lord's Museum, a dinner for all the former players, at which the guest of honour was John Major; the toss was made with an 1805 sovereign, MCC produced a handsome commemorative scorecard – and Harrow won.

Nowadays the match is played before some three or four thousand people, mostly alumni of the two schools, together with current pupils and parents. Spectators are concentrated in the Mound and Tavern stands and the boxes. Support is often noisy and there is much goodnatured if rowdy banter between the rival factions, but incidents of drunken or boorish behaviour are extremely rare – at least among the boys.

Action from Lord's

HARROW
KEA

RUGBY FOOTBALL

THE INSTIGATOR OF RUGBY Football at Harrow was Dr Cyril Norwood, who arrived from Marlborough as Head Master in 1925. Although the School had dabbled in rugby in the early years of the century, it was in 1927 that it was adopted as the major game of the Autumn term; Norwood appointed Mr IRB Stuart, an Irish International, to run it.

In many ways it was a political decision. There was concern in the Public School world that soccer was becoming socially compromised by professionalism. The well-known but unattributed quip about rugby being a hooligan's game played by gentlemen probably originated around this time. Many "soccer schools" converted to rugby in the 1920s but at Harrow the question was whether either game should be introduced to replace one term of Harrow football and, if so, which. Dr Norwood, who was in no doubt which way the decision should go, arranged a demonstration rugby match in which several internationals took part and then held a 'whole school' referendum. Rugby won the day.

Early fixtures were against club sides but in 1928 the first school matches were played against Tonbridge and Rugby. AR Ramsay, who played in the XV at this time, later wrote: "I watch a fair bit of rugby around the world but it is a far cry from the funny game we used to play in the mud at the bottom of the hill". There appeared to be a strong emphasis on dribbling and forward rushes – a clear influence of Harrow football.

Haileybury was added to the fixture list in 1929 and Stowe in 1930. The first victory, amid great excitement, was 14–0 over Rugby in 1929.

Mr WH Stevenson, a Scottish International, took over in 1931 and the standard of play began to improve, if not the quality of the grounds. Some good players began to emerge, notably CD Laborde, who later returned to teach at the School, and PM Studd. Studd's side of 1934 lost only to Stowe (0–5) but the sides of the 1930s were competent rather than outstanding, rarely managing to win more school matches than they lost. Merchant Taylors' and Mill Hill were added to the opponents in 1933.

In 1939 there were great hopes of resurgence with a new Sixth Form Ground ready for use and a new master-in-charge, the Cambridge 'blue' and Scottish International, Mr RB Bruce Lockhart. But war broke out almost immediately, the first four matches were cancelled and Bruce Lockhart was called up to the Army.

Amazingly, in spite of petrol rationing and the other difficulties, the matches against Tonbridge (except 1943) and Haileybury continued to be played through out the war years. Rugby, Stowe and Mill Hill (who were evacuated) were replaced by Dulwich and University College School.

The immediate post-war years began promisingly with wins over Tonbridge and Merchant Taylors' in 1946, and over Stowe, Haileybury and Tonbridge in 1947. Mill Hill returned to the fixture list in 1948 and Wellington was added in 1949. However this period proved to be the nadir of Harrow rugby. An outbreak of polio could explain a dismal season without a win in 1948 but worse was to follow: the 1949 team scored not a single point and a lone victory in 1950 could hardly be described as a revival. Curiously these XVs included two future Internationals, Gurth Hoyer-Millar of Scotland and Peter Ryan of England.

In 1950, Mr AL Warr, an Oxford 'blue' and England International, became master-in-charge. The fixture list took on a more modern appearance with the number of club opponents being reduced to three: a pipe opener against WH Stevenson's XV, a 'teaching' match against a St Mary's Hospital team brought by Dr TA Kemp and a finale against the Old Harrovians. The revival was on the way. Mill Hill, Tonbridge and Stowe were beaten in 1951; Wellington, Rugby and Merchant Taylors' in 1952. The best sides of the decade were those of 1954

Rugby at Harrow

Dr Norwood, who was in no doubt which way the decision should go, arranged a demonstration rugby match in which several internationals took part and then held a 'whole school' referendum. Rugby won the day.

and '55, the '54 team under Rex Neame being the first Harrow XV to record an unbeaten season.

But Tim Warr realised that even good Harrow teams at home on Harrow clay were often run ragged on the sandy soil at Wellington or the chalk at Tonbridge. He persuaded the Governors to lay a new Sixth Form Ground on Julian 1, which was opened in 1957. It was a disaster.

For whatever reason – although the most likely was unquestionably contractors' incompetence – a whole series of misfortunes was to mean that "Warr's Folly" as he liked to call it, was not to be the nirvana for which so many had hoped. First, play had to be abandoned when cinders started appearing through the topsoil. Then further ground works compacted the soil and prevented satisfactory drainage. For many years the new ground fell far short of those at other schools – except in one respect, which had nothing to do with the quality of the playing surface: the New Sixth Form Ground was one of the best school grounds in the country for the spectators. The bank on the south side where the ground used to rise to the level of the athletics track provided a splendid viewing gallery and with the autumn sun shining from behind, the scene across the fields, especially on a block fixture day, was a joy indeed.

Mr John Rae, later to be Headmaster of Taunton and Westminster Schools, assisted by Mr Stephen Smith, a Cambridge 'blue' and England International, was master-in-charge from 1961 to 1965, a period of steady improvement. The fixture list at this time was WH Stevenson's XV (now effectively an Old Harrovian side), Merchant Taylors', St Edward's Oxford, Rugby, Tonbridge, Mill Hill, Haileybury and Wellington.

Sir Alan Outram, an Old Marlburian, who had served a five-year period of apprenticeship running the Colts, produced some fine XVs between 1966 and 1974. The 1967 side, captained by John Higginson, a shrewd tactician and outstanding fly half, partnered at scrum half by Peter Webster, later a Cambridge 'blue', suffered only one defeat 3–6 away at Rugby. The 1970 side, captained by Euan Clarke, later an Oxford 'blue', also only lost once, this time to Radley. But Sir Alan's great triumph was Harrow's first all-victorious team, the 1974 XV captained by James Baron and featuring an exceptional pair of half-backs in Matthew Fosh, later a Cambridge 'blue' and Malcolm Rutherford, playing in the first of four years in the 1st XV. The fixture list had now been expanded to include Bedford and Radley.

These years also saw a further improvement in the grounds with the Julian Fields and the Park Ground levelled and drained to form five pitches to be called the New Fields. For the first time Harrow Football was not played on these grounds in the Spring term.

From 1975 Mr Edward Gould, a former Oxford 'blue', and Mr Malcolm Bruce Lockhart, son of 'Rab', each ran

Harrow XV, 1927, the year that rugby became a major game

Facing page (top to bottom, left to right) Rugby: Harrow v Eton, 1927; Harrow v Rugby, 1930; Harrow v Rugby, 1954; Harrow v Wellington, 1955; Harrow v Haileybury, 1956; Harrow v Rugby, 1958

This and facing page: Rugby: Harrow v King's College School, Wimbledon, 2009, played on the Sunley Field, created in 2005 on the site of the former Parade Ground

the 1st XV for four-year spells. It was Mr Bruce Lockhart's misfortune to inherit some particularly weak teams and only one match was won in the seasons 1980 and 1981.

By this time Mr Ian Beer, a three-year Cambridge 'blue' and England International, had become Head Master. He appointed Mr Roger Uttley, former England Captain and British Lions player, to be Director of Physical Education and master-in-charge of rugby. These two were an attractive lure for the parents of rugby-playing boys and it was not long before the effects were felt. Another all-conquering side appeared in 1985. The Captain, Andrew Butler, missed much of the season through injury, but his influence was huge. The star of the side was an English Speaking Union scholar from Canada, Gareth Rees. Rees went on to play for Wasps after the end of the School season and ended up as the only non-International in the back line of the side playing in the Pilkington Cup Final against Bath at Twickenham. He later represented Canada in four World Cup competitions, a record for any country.

By now Epsom, Oundle and St Paul's had been added to the fixture list and safety rules had excluded the remaining adult opposition, the Old Harrovians. Another good side in 1987, led by Damian Hopley, Cambridge 'blue' and England International, only lost to Oundle and Wellington. This was followed by the School's first major rugby tour, a three and a half week trip to Australia for a party of 44 players, four Masters and assorted hangers-on. This tour to the southern hemisphere whetted the appetite for further adventures overseas. In the 1990s School teams toured South Africa, Japan and South Korea, and Argentina and Uruguay in 2004. Each tour provided a unique experience and memories for those involved, and clearly underlined the sporting and educational benefits of this type of expedition.

The best team of the 1990s was the 1993 XV, captained by Will Devas, which included Fraser Waters, who later played professionally for London Wasps and England. However, it is the 1999 XV that holds the accolade for a record number of points, the huge total of 344 points in what was otherwise an undistinguished season (won seven, lost six).

Throughout this decade, Harrow frequently hosted touring sides after the end of the School season. Ampleforth College, Rossall School and Belfast Academy offered testing competition from other areas of Britain, while Jeppe High School (South Africa), Peterhouse (Zimbabwe), Palmerston North (New Zealand) and a Provincial side from Western Australia were among opponents from overseas.

Mr Uttley was master-in-charge for twenty-five years, but the period was not been without its distractions as he was England Coach from 1987–1991 (when England were losing finalists in the World Cup Final) and England Manager from 1997–1999.

In 2002, the XV under the captaincy of Nick Defty was all-victorious – only the second time this has been achieved in the School's history.

Major ground improvements in 2003–5 led to the Sixth Form Ground moving to the Sunley Field on the site of the former Parade Ground, the levelling and drainage of the Julian and Upper Redding fields and the creation of two astro-turf pitches. The transformation of the "funny game played in the mud at the bottom of the hill", remembered by Arthur Ramsay, was complete. Mr Jesse Coulson became master-in-charge in 2008 and introduced many innovations including ice baths and 'conditioning'. The modern facilities at Harrow have attracted the All Blacks and Pacific Islanders to train at Harrow in recent years.

ASSOCIATION FOOTBALL

HARROW HAS HAD A most unusually fitful relationship with the game known to most of the world as 'football' but known here as 'soccer', to distinguish it from Harrow football, as it is in the United States to distinguish it from American football. Harrow was in at the start, played a big part for fifty years, gave up playing completely for another fifty years and then returned gradually to embrace the game once more. Soccer is now the major game of the Spring term.

In the first half of the nineteenth century, organised sport was beginning to take a hold in public schools and universities. Oxford and Cambridge had been playing cricket against each other since 1827 and the first boat race was in 1829, but football presented a problem since all the schools had been playing to different rules. Rugbeians, whose code allowed handling and running, could not agree with Harrovians, who could catch the ball but not run with it and Etonians and Wykehamists who could do neither. In order to try to avoid games being confined to Old Boys of the same school, two Old Salopians at Cambridge, Henry de Winton and John Thring, called a meeting in 1848, at which representatives of Eton, Harrow, Rugby, Winchester and Shrewsbury were present, to draw up a set of common rules: The Cambridge Rules. No copy of these rules has survived but a revised version was presented to the newly formed Football Association in 1863.

Soccer v St John's Leatherhead, 2010

The Old Harrovian Football Club was one of the earliest to be formed in 1859. One of their number, Charles Alcock, played in the first official Association Football match, London v Sheffield at Battersea on March 31, 1866, when he was the first player ever to be ruled offside. He became Secretary of the Football Association in 1870. The first FA Cup tournament was played in 1871 and it is said that Alcock based this knock-out competition on the inter-House competition he had played in at Harrow.

Alcock captained his team, the Wanderers, founded in 1860, to victory in the first FA Cup Final at the Oval on March 16, 1872. His side contained no fewer than three other Old Harrovians, RC Welch, MP Bett and WP Crake. Wanderers won 1–0 – which would have been 2–0 if Alcock had not notched up another "first", the first goal disallowed (for hand ball) in a Cup Final.

It is interesting to note that when the Football Association celebrated the centenary of the FA Cup in 1972 they invited the Old Harrovian AFC to represent Wanderers, then no longer in existence, by leading a parade preceding the Final at Wembley Stadium.

The School had a brief flirtation with the idea of converting to the Association code in 1864, but wisely realised that there was no sensible alternative at that time to Harrow footer on Harrow clay. However soccer was played on an occasional basis from 1880 and was introduced in 1896 as the official game of the Spring term. Old Harrovian soccer continued to flourish and the OHAFC was a founder member of the Arthur Dunn Cup Competition in 1902.

The soccer/rugger/footer debate rolled on through the early years of the twentieth century with various attempts to introduce one of the national codes foundering in the Harrow mud. The arrival of Dr Cyril Norwood from Marlborough as Head Master in 1925 provided the decisive blow in favour of rugger – partly, no doubt, for social reasons as soccer, by then predominantly a professional game, was seen to be lurching towards being a purely working class activity. Rugby football was officially adopted as the major game in the Autumn term the following year. By 1930 the OHAFC had also lapsed.

No official soccer was played at Harrow for the next fifty years although devotees were always to be seen kicking a ball about in House Yards, on five-a-side pitches and in the Sports Hall. Still, some continued to see it as a threat, especially when enthusiasm increased following England's World Cup victory in 1966. Some referred to soccer as 'Kev-ball' – a derogatory term – and it was described in a House Masters' meeting in 1967 as a "seeping and insidious threat".

The draining and levelling of the New Fields in the 1970s brought fresh demands for soccer and, as the game gained in national and international popularity, increasing pressure was put on the authorities to reintroduce it in the second half of the Spring term. The first official match of the new era was played in 1977.

Much credit for the reincarnation of soccer at Harrow goes to Mr David Elleray, master-in-charge, who later became House Master of Druries and a top international referee. His involvement with the world of professional soccer, culminating in his taking charge of the FA Cup Final between Manchester United and Chelsea in 1994, did much to raise the status of the game at Harrow.

The construction of two artificial pitches and the dramatic pitch improvements of 2005 had a dual effect on Spring term games: soccer spread over all the newly drained and levelled pitches and Harrow football withdrew to the Sheepcote and Hemstall fields where mud could still be found. Soccer achieved major game status in 1998.

The quality of play has reached a high level in recent years and the 1st XI has been more than a match for "two term" soccer schools such as Westminster and Brentwood. A short tour to Holland took place in 2000, the first since Mr Elleray's tours to US in 1982 and 1986, and a return trip to the US took place in 2009.

The Old Harrovian Association Football Club had been revived in 1963 due to the efforts of a group of enthusiasts, notably David Buik, Alex de Grunwald and Fred Woolley, supported by the then master-in-charge of Harrow Football, Mr Don McNeill. By 1966 they were fielding two regular teams in the Arthurian League, of which they were to become Champions in 1978. In 2007 they became the first 'Lent Term Soccer School' to win the Arthur Dunn Cup. At last Harrow soccer is fulfilling the promise that Charles Alcock and his fellow pioneers would have wished for.

The School Association football XI of 1922

HARROW FOOTBALL

The Harrow football XI, 1867

Facing page: The Queen examining a Harrow football on her visit in 1957; also in the picture (left to right) are John Wells, John Strover, Mr Charles Laborde and Head Master, Dr James

BEFORE THE ADDITION OF the east wing of the Old Schools, football was played in the School Yard. The bases (or goals), instead of facing each other, were on the same line, with the building round which the ball had to be kicked, in between. The ball appears to be about half the size of a football. When the east wing was built, 'fug' football (as it was known) was played at the west end of the Yard and in the cloisters then existing under Old Speech Room. This space was later enclosed to become the Armoury, then the School Office. From 1803 to 1850 football was played on what is now the Sixth Form Cricket Ground and then, when the School acquired some land on the east side of the Hill, a formal game began to evolve.

Most games arise out of the conditions of climate and terrain that prevail at the time. Harrow football is no exception. Like most of northwest London the Harrow grounds are solid clay, a material which in summer months is cracked with heat but in the winter becomes a slippery, miry marsh. It was in these unattractive and discouraging conditions that Harrow football was born. The rules of the game were codified in 1865 by Mr Edward Bowen, later House Master of The Grove, who used football allegorically in his lyrics of *Forty Years On* in 1872.

It is difficult to imagine the state of the grounds in the nineteenth century. Contemporary reports suggest six inches of mud but that it had often been up to a foot deep before the drainage had been put down in 1889. Conditions may have been dreadful but there was huge pride in the game: Mr EW Howson, later House Master of Druries, wrote two more football songs, *Three Yards* in 1885 and *Play Up* in 1887.

Harrow football is played eleven-a-side: four 'centres', two 'wings' on each side and three 'backs'. The purpose of the game is to kick the ball through the opponents' base, a space between two vertical posts but unlimited in height. It is essentially a 'dribbling' rather than a 'passing' game, the ball being propelled through the mud by the centres, punctuated by occasional dashes up the drier fringes of the field by the wings. The offside rule requires a player to be behind the ball (i.e. nearer his own baseline than his opponents') to be allowed to play the ball. If the ball is kicked in the air, it may be caught by an onside player from either side; after a fair catch and a shout of "Yards!" the catcher may carry the ball for three running yards and then has a free kick. A typical sequence of the game would therefore be for the centres to dribble the ball to within kicking distance of their opponents' base, perhaps with the help of the wings, and then to "give yards" i.e. to turn and kick the ball for one of his teammates to catch – ideally the centre back who will be lurking in a likely

A Harrow football is a large and, when wet and muddy, ponderous lump…In 1999 a football was found in the rafters of Stirling Castle, supposedly above Mary Queen of Scots' chamber…

position. The "yards" taker will then attempt to punt the ball through the base. Bases may also be scored from open play: "soccer bases".

One or two other features of football are worth mentioning. One is "fouling" which means "playing an opponent or the ball with the shoulder" – a perfectly legitimate act, not having the later meaning of the word. A player, who is onside, may "foul" an opponent whether or not he has the ball. This is useful to stop him following up his own kick; of course, this is not allowed once the fouler is put offside.

When the ball goes out of play on the side, it may be thrown in by any method, the most effective being an overarm bowl. A good thrower may be able to throw right into the mouth of the base from the touchline in places, so conceding a throw is a serious disadvantage – gaining a throw by kicking "in off" an opponent is a cunning ploy.

On the other hand kicking the ball over one's own baseline and conceding a "corner" is not such a serious matter as "corner" is a misnomer. In fact the ball then has to be thrown in perpendicular to the base line, so is less dangerous for the defenders – unless of course it happens near the base when it should be lethal.

If the attackers kick the ball over the baseline, a "base kick" is awarded. This is a kick-out three running yards from the base line. A base kick may not be handled nor does the offside rule apply directly.

Heading a Harrow football is unwise for anyone who intends to take further part in the game, but fouling is very effective. This is because a Harrow football is a large and, when wet and

... the Sheepcote and Hemstall Fields, previously the preserve of the farm cows, have come to the rescue. They provide a satisfactorily muddy, uneven surface on which all Harrow football is now played.

Football on Hemstall Field, 2010

muddy, ponderous lump. Its outer case comprises two circular pieces of leather stitched to a central rectangular piece curved to form a cylinder. This is a neat way of forming a near spherical shape with just three components. In 1999 a football was found in the rafters of Stirling Castle, supposedly above Mary Queen of Scots' chamber. It was formally identified by the National Museum in Edinburgh as being 430 years old and therefore the oldest surviving football. The interesting thing is not that Her Majesty may have been playing football in her chamber but that the construction of the ball is exactly the same as the Harrow ball, although considerably smaller. The Harrow ball is nearly a foot across at its widest. Also its spheroidal shape makes kicking it straight more difficult than it looks.

Up to 1930 cricket was played into the Autumn term finishing with the Goose Match at Michaelmas. The first football match was then played on Founder's Day at the beginning of October and, until 1896, football continued for the rest of the winter.

Various attempts to introduce soccer and rugby were unsuccessful largely because of the nature of the grounds, but Head Master Cyril Norwood finally achieved the adoption of rugby in 1927 – although it would appear that some of the characteristics of the Harrow game were carried over. One of the choruses of *The Song of the Forwards,* written by Norwood in 1933, "Feet, feet, feet, feet, one rush and together, let drive and let fly…" does not have much resonance with modern rugby.

Ironically, substantial ground improvements over the years have dealt a series of near mortal blows to Harrow football; it is not a good game on a dry, smooth, flat field. However the Sheepcote and Hemstall Fields, previously the preserve of the farm cows, have come to the rescue. They provide a satisfactorily muddy, uneven surface on which all Harrow football is now played. It remains a popular House sport, played largely in the month of January, but its devotees in the Sixth Form game now play matches throughout the Spring term. Recent developments have included away matches, some cross-fertilisation with the Eton field game and even overseas tours. Edward Bowen and John Farmer might have felt inspired to write another song!

Football under drier conditions, 2004

ATHLETICS

RUNNING RACES WERE ONE of the recreations enjoined by John Lyon on the scholars of the School but nothing is known of any organised athletics before the middle of the nineteenth century, when contests were held at the end of the Easter term on the football fields near the Watford Road. The sprints took place along the Watford Road, then known as Sheepcote Lane. The longer races: the mile, half-mile and quarter-mile were run first on 'Long Mile', now Eastcote Lane, at Northolt and later along the Pinner Road starting from outside the Roxborough Arms. ED Laborde quotes a contemporary report: "One feature of these races on the road was a conflict for precedence between the school and ordinary cart traffic; a second feature was that the road often had to be re-laid with heavy stones a few days before the race came off."

The pole vault in the School sports, 1938: note the smart turn-out of the Master officiating and the boys in hats

In 1884 a field was hired behind Ducker and MG Glazebrook, a Master and former Oxford athletics 'blue', undertook to organise The Sports properly. From 1886 to 1911 the events were held on the new Recreation Ground on Pinner Road. They included flat races over 100 yards, 200 yards, quarter-mile, half-mile and mile; 120 yards high and low hurdles; high jump, long jump, throwing the cricket ball, putting the weight; sack race, three-legged race and tug o' war. By this time each House was holding its own Sports with a similar sort of programme, although some of the events were handicapped. Then, when the School Parade Ground was constructed between the Julian Fields and the Park Lake in 1912, the opportunity was taken to build a running track round it, and the sports were moved to the new site. In 1933 a bequest was used to build the Boyer Webb pavilion near the running track, providing changing rooms for visiting teams.

The athletics (now the accepted generic term) continued to be held in the last two or three weeks of the Easter term up to 1963. A more sophisticated form of competition was devised whereby boys were split into age groups with set times and distances being ascribed to each event meriting a 'standard' or 'credit'. House points were awarded for standards and credits with a House cup for the highest average score per boy. Those with credits could then enter for the heats leading to finals for each event at each age group, all successes scoring more points for the House aggregate.

In 1947 athletics became an option for those who wished to pursue athletics in the Summer term. Coaching was offered by four Masters, Mr JDJ Havard, The Rev PHM Bryant, Maj EF Housden and Mr MC Noakes, and the two sergeant-majors on Monday and Friday evenings. About twenty boys took this up and they had two 'friendly' matches

against South London Harriers and London Athletic Club. In March 1948 Guy Butler (OH), an Olympic Gold Medallist, gave an illustrated lecture in Speech Room and this combined with the London Olympics that summer, gave a huge boost to athletics in general, but to the School in particular. Athletics became an official Summer term activity under the title of "Harrow Beetlers".

The 1949 Sports was a much higher profile affair: weight, discus, javelin and pole vault were added to the usual events. *The Harrovian* published a list of Records at the time; unfortunately the conversion to metric units in 1971 means that comparisons make little sense.

In 1963 School athletics was moved from the end of the Spring term to the Summer term, with the finals taking place in June "the first summer Sports Day since before the war". *The Harrovian* correspondent regretted that it was not a truly representative day as cricketers had not been available. By then the Beetlers had fixtures against Eton & Winchester, City of London & St Dunstan's, John Lyon, Charterhouse, Wellington, and Sandhurst & Henlow.

The cinder track of 1912 had become unfit for school athletics by the 1990s: quite apart from the quality of the surface, it was not only not level, it was also around 400 yards in perimeter. As a further indication of the lack of awareness, Harrow athletes had been running round their track clockwise while the rest of the world had long agreed on anti-clockwise circulation. By 2000 the track was obsolete with School records not validated at AAA level and opposition schools refusing to compete at Harrow.

The Tartan track was built as part of the Sports East Fields development and came into use in 2005. This resulted in another surge of enthusiasm for athletics: in 2009 up to sixty-five boys were in training under the direction of seven Masters and three external coaches; about fifty compete on any one day. The modern season consists of a series of meetings at which a number of schools compete, including two eight-school meetings at Harrow. This format means that every year the School is in direct competition with the leading schools in the south of England. There are also the Achilles Relays held at Iffley Road, Oxford, which attracts a nationwide entry, and the Oxford City Relays at Radley. In 2009 thirty-one boys competed in the Borough Championships, sixteen went forward to the County Championships. Of these three (in 400m, 100m hurdles and discus) became County Champions and were then selected to represent Middlesex in the English Schools Championships. Harrow athletics is in good heart. Long ago are the days in which *The Harrovian* reporter could say (perhaps with tongue in cheek), "There were some good times recorded this year but that may have been because Custos's watch had a habit of stopping unexpectedly."

The hurdles on the School Tartan track in 2009

BADMINTON

AS A SCHOOL SPORT, badminton is a comparative newcomer to Harrow, the first matches being played in 1991. It was therefore something of a surprise to find that Cyril Andrewes, a member of the School rackets pair of 1901, had become Canadian badminton doubles champion as long ago as 1928. A talented sportsman, he also played hockey for England and lawn tennis in Canada's Davis Cup team of 1925.

The modern game of badminton emerged from the very old game of battledore & shuttlecock, which was popular in China, Japan, India and Siam, where it had been played, more as a pastime than a competitive sport, since the sixteenth century. The game was brought to Britain in the 1860s and took hold at Badminton House, the Gloucestershire home of the Duke of Beaufort (an Old Etonian). The first formal rules were written at Poona in India in 1873 – by the British, of course.

Badminton became an increasingly popular sport in the east, particularly Malaysia, although it only achieved Olympic status in 1992. With the arrival of the new Sports Hall at Harrow in 1986, the game began to be played as a recreational sport. In the autumn term of 1991 the enthusiasm of a group of boys led by CCW Chu prompted the arrangement of fixtures against University College School, Merchant Taylors' and Haberdashers' Aske's and the following term against Aldenham. About fifteen boys formed the squad and Colts matches were also played. All the coaching was done by the captain with supportive help from the secretary PA Mosiman but, as the captain said in his report for *The Harrovian*, there remained one basic problem: there was no master-in-charge and so organisation of fixtures, coaching, transport for away matches and all the tasks which in other sports are done by the master-in-charge, fell to the boys themselves. Three years later another inexperienced team under the captaincy of J Leong played matches against Eton and Wellington. Since then Messrs John Medlicott, Chris Barry, Simon Page, Father James Power and Mrs Lotje Smith have taken on the responsibility of running the badminton, and the game has official status. The award of ties was sanctioned in 2000. The fixture list was extended to include Oundle, Eton, John Lyon and Wellington and there were also larger tournaments at Oratory and Abingdon. About ten boys were regular players.

In September 2006 Stephen Willis took on the coaching. It is much to his credit and to Mrs Lotje Smith's, the master-in-charge, that numbers have increased dramatically over the last four years and currently twenty-six players attend practice on Tuesday and Thursday afternoons. The representative teams are selected from a squad of eight to twelve players and there is a match most weeks. The squad continues to be dominated by Malaysians and boys from other eastern countries, who arrive at Harrow with good experience of badminton, but by no means exclusively. Regular opponents are Eton, Radley, Latymer, Haberdashers' Aske's, John Lyon, Haileybury, Wellington, The Oratory, Bradfield and Abingdon.

Nowadays minor games 'flannels' are awarded to players who reach an outstanding level, judged by national standards. It is most unusual for a player of a game so recently established at Harrow to receive such an honour but, in 2007, Russell Kueh, the captain, was awarded 'flannels'. He played against Middlesex and Hertfordshire county players on a regular basis with a high rate of success. In a very close match against the England number nine player, Kueh lost 21–19, 21–18.

The first Five Schools Invitation Tournament took place at Harrow in February 2008. Harrow won it in that year, followed by Haberdashers Aske's in 2009 and Eton in 2010.

Badminton, 2010

BASKETBALL

BASKETBALL IS AN AMERICAN game. Although it had been played for some time on a recreational basis in the Old Gymnasium and in some House yards, where baskets and backboards had been put up as an alternative "yarder", it was never part of mainstream Harrow games until the mid-1970s. The first captain of School basketball was DMS Narayn, appointed in 1974. However it was an influx of Americans, encouraged by Messrs Petherick and Crisp of the PE department that really put the game on the map. *The Harrovian* described it as an outbreak of basketball fever with cries of "box out" and "arc it", echoing round the gymnasium in unfamiliar accents. In fact the senior team that year contained not a single Englishman and much credit for its popularity must go to Mark Dancer and Richard Morrissey, who were largely responsible for this craze. Victories were recorded over The John Lyon School, Wellington and Salvatorian College against a defeat by Marlborough. Very popular House and Torpid competitions were also arranged. And craze it might have been with only NY Zahid returning the following year.

Basketball v Eton, 2010

However popularity increased and some matches were arranged for junior teams. The continuing supply of English Speaking Union students from North America around this time ensured a steady flow of seniors familiar with the game. Already the Spring term was beginning to become overcrowded with sporting choices and there were moans about the best players not being available.

When Mr Roger Uttley arrived as Director of PE in 1982 he found a flourishing sport. Although no basketball player himself, he immediately saw the game could be used to improve hand/eye coordination and fitness amongst senior rugby players. It quickly became established as a popular Spring term minor game and the inter-school fixture list was expanded. Fixtures were played on Thursday afternoon with practices on Tuesdays after the major game sessions. Initially there was just a senior team but demand from younger players and the arrival of the new Sports Hall in 1985 meant that a senior and junior team could be run effectively.

Regular opponents included Winchester, Marlborough, Wellington, Haileybury, Radley, and Stowe. The standard particularly amongst the seniors reached a very good competitive level and allowed individuals other than the regular sports stars to make their own mark. In addition the matches versus the OHs generally played on Founder's Day and Speech Day produced some great clashes and helped to maintain the sport's popularity.

For a number of years there was a fiercely contested House Competition: the most successful were The Park, Newlands and West Acre. External coaches started to be employed from 2005 and have really helped to cement basketball's place in the School's sporting options.

ETON
14

BOXING

THE STRIP OF GROUND just below the School Yard on the west side has long been known as the Milling Ground, 'milling' being a slang word for 'fighting'. It seems that this was the place where two boys would go to settle their differences by a physical fight – the puerile equivalent of settling a dispute by duelling. There was certainly a similar sort of ritual about the contest, with each side having seconds and supporters. In the 1840s records show two pots of water and a lemon being procured from the Crown & Anchor for the participants. "By a rule of the School, fights always took place in public. This was a wholesome rule, ensuring impartiality and fair play, which might have been jeopardised in the partial atmosphere of a boys' house." Certainly the fights attracted a good, if bloodthirsty, crowd. Reports of the ferocity of the fighting vary: there were times when the loser was carried back to his lodgings senseless and there were others when according to Percy Thornton, "Custos would, after a short skirmish, dissipate the pugilistic gathering by means of a kindly chaff which rendered his pacific efforts palatable alike to principals, seconds, and on-lookers." During the Head Mastership of Dr Vaughan (1845–60), Custos, Sam Hoare, was looked upon as the guardian of the Milling Ground.

Not surprisingly it is the poet Byron about whom many stories have been woven – not least by him. He portrayed himself as the champion of the weakling and the bullied. Byron is reputed to have matched the bullies and he claimed to have lost only one of seven bouts, enabling him to become admired and respected among his fellows – but one is never quite sure how much he exaggerated his heroics. There are theories that he was spurred on by his need to overcome the disadvantage of his club foot. Clearly he was a good boxer as, after he had left school, he used to spar with 'Gentleman' John Jackson, the former Champion of England – often for an hour at a time – when he was at Cambridge.

The introduction of padded gloves, called mufflers, came about in the middle of the eighteenth century and the first code of rules for fist-fighting was formulated by Jack Broughton in 1743, but this allowed holding, throwing and wrestling; fights at this time were little more than organised brawls. Bare-knuckle prize-fighting was popular until the Anti-Prize Fight Act of 1861. The Queensbury Rules, the basis for modern boxing, were devised in 1865.

At Harrow the fights on the Milling Ground seem to have ceased by 1875. An article in *Harrow Notes* of 1885 reports the "disuse of Milling Ground with regret" although "high spirits, courtesy and manliness have not declined". This coincided with the building of the Gymnasium in 1874. For many years Boxing, as it came to be known, was grouped with gymnastics (and sometimes fencing) as a 'gymnasium activity'. The instructors, usually ex-military physical training instructors, were the same for both.

Boxing became a popular activity in the Autumn and Spring terms of the first half of the twentieth century, but the choice of sports in those days was limited to football, fives, gymnastics, fencing, shooting and rackets for a few. An outstanding boxer in the early 1900s was John Hopley (OH), who was the Public Schools Heavyweight Boxing Champion of 1901–02. He boxed for Cambridge University and won his first fight against Oxford, knocking out his opponent in the first round, but such was the power of his punching that it took a long time for the unfortunate victim to recover. He even sparred against the World Heavyweight Champion, Tommy Burns, and knocked the Champion out. It is said that soon after this he decided not to continue boxing because of his fear of causing serious injury to his opponents.

The Park Champion House Boxing Team, 1951 (left); Champion Boxers, 1894 (right)

In 1924 *The Harrovian* reported that 135 boys had taken boxing and fencing lessons, more than ever before. There was an annual competition in nine weights; House and Individual Cups were awarded. For the first time that year the competition was split into a senior and a junior section, to avoid large young boys being mis-matched with light older boys. In 1925 there were eight weight divisions in each of the senior and junior sections. The first inter-school matches appear in 1933 when matches were arranged with Eton, St Paul's and Stowe, the latter two being replaced by Berkhamsted and Charterhouse later in the decade; there were ten or eleven bouts in each match.

In the 1950s boxing reached its zenith in most of the leading public schools. Harrow, under the direction of the master-in-charge, Mr David Christie-Murray, who had captained the Cambridge University Boxing Club in 1941, was among the best. He was well supported by the two instructors, Messrs Radford and Gorringe. Harrow's opponents were Wellington, Haileybury, Eton, Dulwich, Mill Hill and St Paul's. Harrow lost most of its matches with St Paul's but turned the tables with its unbeaten team of 1955, captained by JM Parker.

A number of Harrovians of this time continued boxing after leaving school, at university and at the well known Belsize Boxing Club, the oldest amateur boxing club founded in 1880. Most of its performers were former public school boys. Boxing was also a popular activity at the Harrow Club in Latimer Road and several Old Harrovians gave time to training the boys there. The Harrow Club was prominent in the creation of the National Association of Youth Clubs championships which continue to this day and, in the 1960s the Club, with the tuition from some Old Harrovian boxers, produced a number of National Youth Club Champions.

The successes of this period coincided with a concerted anti-boxing campaign led by the Labour MP Edith (later Baroness) Summerskill. Her book, *The Ignoble Art*, pointed out the physical dangers of boxing and the psychological undesirability of watching it. The former at least was supported by the British Medical Association. Safety precautions were introduced, mainly the sensible, more careful, matching of opponents by age, weight and skill but the campaign had its effect: fewer boys were choosing to box, fewer matches were being arranged. Its decline was not without its mourners: Dudley Savill (OH) a distinguished amateur boxer and an Amateur Boxing Association judge, wrote to the Head Master in 1964, deploring its decline. "I owe the moulding and structure of my character to the sport which I regard as a means of expression."

In fact Savill's lament was a little premature. Just when boxing had been apparently counted out, there began a resurgence. 1967, with matches against Eton, Dulwich, Haileybury and Highgate, was the third year without defeat. In 1971 there were eighteen School boxers, the highest for many years, and 100 entries for the inter-House Boxing Competition. In 1976 *The Harrovian* described the standards in the House Competition as "much higher than in previous years". And then nothing... there was no Captain of Boxing appointed for 1977 and no mention of it again. There was no knock-out blow; the sport which Head Master Norwood had considered to be an integral part of public school athletics simply disappeared into the archives. Boxing was never actually abolished: it just faded away.

B. S. B. WOOD R. S. EMERSON H. W. WOLLASTON

A. DREW A. H. HENDERSON G. R. W. STAINTON

ETON FIVES

THE GAME WAS INTRODUCED to Harrow by Mr EM Young, an Old Etonian who became a Master in 1863. Eton Fives is a handball game played in a three-walled court with a step, buttress and ledges, the design of which is based on the area at the foot of the steps to the Eton College Chapel; the first courts there were built in the 1840s. In those days accurate dimensions were not considered to be of great importance and the earliest Harrow courts seem not to have been very good replicas of those at Eton. They were described some years later as "peculiar rather than pleasing".

The earliest real patron of the game at Harrow was Mr GM Hallam, an Old Salopian who taught at the School from 1870 to 1906. As a result of his enthusiasm, four more courts were built in 1880.

It is clear that, from the earliest days, Fives was always in the shadow of its elder court-games sister, rackets. There are rackets reports several pages long in *Harrow Notes* and *The Harrovian* and regular features in *The Field.* Indeed Fives appears to have been controlled by the Rackets Committee.

The first School Fives match was played in 1885 against a visiting pair from Eton. This was an important development as there were no inter-school matches in any sport at this time. Apart from the cricket match against Eton at Lord's all other matches were against clubs or scratch sides. Even in Rackets all the play was "in school" except for the Public Schools Championships.

Eight more courts were built between 1889 and 1893, but the matches against Eton continued in "an even tenor of defeat" until 1897. An 1898 report in *The Harrovian* blamed the "demands of Harrow Football". A win at Eton, however, did come in 1900 when AH Crake and FB Wilson won both at Harrow and at Eton.

The first match against Charterhouse was played in 1900, ("We beat them in their own court which to a Harrow player is even more puzzling than the Eton court.") and the fixture continued annually, becoming home and away from 1903. At this time Harrow had an outstanding pair, EH Crake and RE Eiloart, who for three successive years won all their matches, home and away, against Eton and Charterhouse. Their only conquerors were the Masters' pair, EM Butler and G Townsend Warner, and it is to these two that the surge of Fives at Harrow at this time can be credited. Butler was the son and grandson of Harrow Head Masters. He was a classical scholar, captain of football and cricket at school, went on to Cambridge where he won 'blues' for cricket, lawn tennis and rackets. Amateur Rackets Champion in 1889, he was the archetypal school hero. George Townsend Warner, also the son and grandson of Harrow Masters, was an exact contemporary. A talented historian, he was a scholar and Fellow of Jesus College, Cambridge. Both Butler and Warner returned to teach at Harrow in 1891.

In 1922 George Townsend Warner was described as "the man to whom all Harrow Fives players of the last twenty years are indebted for such proficiency as they acquired." EH Crake, writing at the same time, says "The two masters of the game when I was at Harrow were George Warner and Teddy Butler and though both were approaching forty at the time, Eiloart and I only managed to beat them twice while we were there, and we used to play them every Friday of each Easter term. George Warner had the best first cut I have seen in the game and his reach was tremendous, while Butler was absolutely safe and a genius in the art of placing. We could not have had better teachers of the game."

In 1910 a Fives-playing Head Master arrived at Harrow from Repton: Dr Lionel Ford. His arrival had a dramatic effect and in 1911 six of the courts were

Facing page: The Newlands fives team, 1933

Boys playing Eton Fives

The 1930s were a golden age for sport in general and, at Harrow, fives played a full part. The Public Schools' Competition, begun in 1929, was dominated by Harrovians…

roofed and eleven new ones were built, eight of them being covered. Upwards of twelve pairs were being played in the Masters' match, and a three pair match against Old Harrovians was played in 1914.

There were long articles in *The Harrovian* at this time showing the increased interest in Fives: "…it would be a good thing for the Easter term to be looked upon as the Fives term, but co-operation of House Football captains is needed."(1913) "Anyone found playing any other games except Fives in Fives Courts will be fined 2s 6d." (1914). At this time there were twenty-four courts, seven of which were uncovered, but then came the Great War; afternoons were taken over by OTC parades and fives was crowded out. School matches and fixtures with Aldenham and Highgate were new ventures.

The 1930s were a golden age for sport in general and, at Harrow, fives played a full part. The Public Schools Competition begun in 1929 was dominated by Harrovians. Among them was the very talented – and possibly arrogant – KC Gandar-Dower, who also won the rugby fives competition. When asked if he knew the rules, he replied, "No – but I will by the semi-finals."

Fixtures against other schools were increasing. More than fifteen pairs regularly played against the Masters. There was now a House Three-pair as well as a One-pair and a Torpid (under-16) competition and all these are chronicled in *The Harrovian* with a match report for each School match and House Final together with full details of names and scores.

Again a World War interrupted: Fives continued to be played but in a very low key. Miraculously, considering the School's proximity to London, little damage was incurred in the Blitz but numbers at the School were down and petrol-rationing restricted travel.

In the 1950s recovery, Harrow did produce one outstanding pair: MJ Shortland-Jones and DJS Guilford, both of Druries, and both later to become Eton Masters, who individually and as a pair were to feature in no fewer than eight Kinnaird Cup Finals between 1953 and 1970. But Fives was being squeezed not only by Rugby, Football and Rackets but now by Squash, which enjoyed a boom period in the 1970s. Increasing demands on boys' time meant that the good games player was less inclined to combine other sports with Fives, except in a few Houses where there was a tradition or House Master's encouragement. So the Fives teams of the 1950s and 1960s were dominated by Druries, Moretons, The Head Master's and Rendalls.

Towards the end of the decade much-needed work was done on the courts: first, the top six courts were re-floored and lit, and when the second Rackets court was built in 1965, a Fives changing room was added. These top six courts then became the match courts.

Further roofing improvements were made in 1975 to restore the number of rain-proof courts to thirteen. A resurgence of interest about this time produced the first Harrow pair to reach the Schools Final for twenty-five years, AFH Bell and NMJ Hewens in 1977.

Since then progress has been even more marked. The arrival on the staff in 1981 of PG Dunbar, a former Schools' finalist from Highgate, injected much enthusiasm for the game which was rewarded by a victory in the Schools Championships of 1988 for MB de Souza-Girao and NR Chellaram, the School's first victory in this competition since 1936. They were not to have to wait so long to repeat it; JG Fleming and HD Duncan won in 1991, the year when de Souza-Girao added his name to the list of Kinnaird winners. RMW Norris and NR Shaw won again in 1994. Since then, Mr Dunbar's two sons, TG and PR, have become a formidable pair winning the Schools Championships in 2000 and the Kinnaird Cup three times.

However these successes should not mask a general decline in the numbers playing Fives. The Sports Hall and New Ducker, the modern glass-backed Squash courts, the extension of Soccer throughout the Spring term, the laying of two artificial pitches and the introduction of Hockey have combined seriously to erode Fives. And rackets remains the first choice for the talented court games player.

The 1961 School fives team: the first pair were awarded (and wore) 'flannels' (left); the 1982 School fives team (right)

FENCING

THE EARLIEST FENCERS AT Harrow took lessons outside the School, and in those days it was still possible for some of them to put their skills to practical use. The playwright and statesman Richard Brinsley Sheridan was one of the last men to fight a duel in England with swords. After that the contestants used smooth bore pistols, which were so inaccurate that the field of honour became much safer.

Sheridan took lessons from Domenico Angelo, the greatest master in England at the end of the eighteenth century. Angelo taught at Eton and made so much money from his salon in London that he was able to send his son Henry to the school. In 1805, after leaving Eton, Henry became the first fencing Master at Harrow. From then until 1886 the fencing Masters at Harrow were all Henry Angelos: father, son and grandson.

In the early years fencing took place wherever space could be found. After the building of a Gymnasium, however, fencing became one of the sports that shared it, and in 1887 Captain Erskine Tudor-Risk, who was in charge of the Gymnasium, presented the School with its first fencing cups. Soon afterwards, when the sport of fencing began to be organised on a national level, Harrow featured prominently. In 1890 the first Public Schools Championship was won by a Harrovian, J Openshaw. Two years later it was won by another, Winston Spencer Churchill.

In the early Public Schools Championship the contestants competed only at foil. A sabre cup was not introduced until 1897, and it was another twelve years before FWW Baynes won it for Harrow. Three years later, in 1911, KA Stewart became Harrow's third foil champion.

The duelling sword, the epée, was not introduced into the competition until 1933, and for this Harrow had to wait even longer for a winner. During the 1980s, however, coached by John Parkins, Harrovians featured regularly among the medal winners, and in 1988 the Championship was at last won for the School by Hugo Poncia.

Back in 1950 John Parkins had taken over at Harrow from his father Alfred, who also coached at the Lansdowne Club, where he trained Britain's most recent world champion (an Old Etonian called Bill Hoskyns). When the School gave up boxing, the fencers moved into the boxing loft above the gym, and this has been their exclusive home ever since. When the new gym was built and the old one converted into squash courts and a drama centre, the *Salle d'Armes* above them remained the same – much-loved, as dingy as always and encumbered by beams so low that it is impossible to fence sabre properly.

John Parkins died suddenly from a heart attack in 1995, which denied him his only unfulfilled ambition: he wanted to coach continuously at Harrow for over fifty years and surpass the record established by the cricket coach, Lord Bessborough. In John's memory, beaks, parents and Old Harrovians took a collection and equipped the loft with what was then the latest electronic scoring apparatus.

John Parkins was succeeded by Polish Olympic medal winner Ziemek Wojciechowski, who left a few years later to become British Olympic foil coach. After that fencing at Harrow declined. By 2007 there were barely a dozen fencers in the School, few of them regulars. But the standard at the top was still high. In that year Tim Hillgarth represented Great Britain in the under-17 World Championships, and in 2008 he came second in the under-18 British Championships.

2008 also saw the arrival of new brooms. Dr Andrew Worrall, who had helped to run fencing at Tonbridge, took over as master-in-charge, and James Chambers (OH), a former captain of the British epée squad and Harrow's only president of the British Fencing

Facing page: Fencing 2010; A hundred and twenty years after the first Public Schools Foil Champion was a Harrovian, the title returned to Harrow

When the School gave up boxing, the fencers moved into the boxing loft above the gym and this has been their exclusive home ever since.

Association, took over as coach. Since then numbers have increased, standards have risen and the School has attracted several seriously talented young fencers. In 2010, after ninety-nine years, the Public Schools Foil Championship title was brought back to Harrow by Christopher Nagle.

GOLF

THE SCHOOL HAS HAD a much longer association with the game of golf than the School nine-hole golf course, which opened in 1977. The Old Harrovian Golfing Society has had a steady following from its foundation in 1924 and the club has won the Halford Hewitt Competition for Public Schools Old Boys' teams eleven times and has been losing finalists ten times in the seventy-nine years in which the competition has been in existence.

There has also been a long golfing tradition among Masters at the School: Masters were involved in the foundation of the Chorleywood Golf Club in 1890 and the Sandy Lodge Golf Club in 1910. Indeed the Sandy Lodge Club's appropriate motto, *In Arena Virtus*, is recorded as having been written by "a Harrow Classics Master."

However great the enthusiasm for golf among Masters may have been, there was little encouragement given to boys. Northwick Park boasted a golf course but it was 'out of bounds' and, should a boy ask to go off for an afternoon's golf, his House Master would surely be able to think of 'something worthwhile' for him to do. Pat White, a Cambridge 'blue' 1932–33, was nominally in charge but, as golf was not an 'official School sport', opportunities for play were rare and matches unheard of. Golf would not have qualified as 'an hour's eccer' when that was the daily requirement.

When Mr Sandy Smith took over in 1967, the beginning of a reign lasting, in two spells, for twenty-five years, golf was seen as a threat to cricket. Whether this was because many of the best players were also cricketers, and golf was considered likely to contaminate their off-drives, or whether it was restrictions of time and place, is not clear. Trips to Sandy Lodge, where some practice followed by a round were the staple fare, were restricted to the Spring term – when the weather was likely to be at its worst. Group lessons from a visiting pro on an unused corner of the Phil ground were viewed with suspicion, and much time was spent guiltily replacing divots.

It was the OHGS's desire to encourage golf amongst Harrovians, and thus provide lifeblood for future generations of Halford Hewitt teams, that provided the initiative and financial support to build the School course. It was built on the former Farm Fields, running from the bottom of the Park garden to the edge of the Clementine Hospital grounds, flanked on the upper side by Newlands, the nature reserve, Kennet House and Herga Court, and on the lower side by the Farm and the Park Lake. It is a nine-hole course, short in length but not short of interesting features.

The creation of the School course gave a real fillip to golf and it was not long before regular matches against other schools began to be played. However these matches were played on club rather than school courses, partly because school courses all tended to be short and partly, no doubt, because playing at clubs with all the infra-structure that they provide was more fun. Arthur Vivian (OH), a stalwart of Moor Park, was particularly welcoming and hospitable. Matches were also played on courses such as Sandy Lodge, Huntercombe, Frilford Heath, Denham and Walton Heath – usually a course mutually convenient to the two schools was chosen.

Gradually a fixture list was built up and golf became an acceptable sport in the other terms. Junior school matches began to be played regularly on the School course and Harrow was a joint founder of the Middlesex Schools Golf Association, which continues to hold its junior tournament on the Harrow course in June.

The organisation of golf at the School is different from other sporting activities in that there is a club that boys must join if they wish to play. The first

Harrow School Golf Club Officers were Messrs Mark Warman (Chairman), David Fothergill (Secretary), David Sumner (Chairman of Greens Committee) and Sandy Smith. Thereafter another Master, Mr Andrew Bishop, took a particular interest in the Club and it is largely due to his efforts that it became the flourishing force it is today: 300 boys are registered as playing members and in addition there are 300 adult members, 100 of whom are Masters and members of School staff. The Club plays matches against twelve local clubs while a beaks' team plays annual matches as well as occasional tours. Opponents are Sandy Lodge, Chorleywood (both home and away), Denham, the Governors, OHGS, School Staff, Eton Beaks and Pinner Hill. Some forty beaks compete each summer for the Chorleywood Cup, presented to them by CGC in the year of their centenary 1990.

The School currently plays around fifteen matches per year against Wellington, Eton, Charterhouse, Bradfield, Epsom and the like. A team also enters the Head Masters' Conference Cup, the West Sussex Invitational and the Micklem Trophy. The latter is the main independent schools team tournament, which Harrow won in 1973 and 1974, and again in 1999 and 2000. An important recent development has been that Denham GC has extended junior membership to ten boys each year, which enables the team to play its home matches there.

The School Golf Course: ninth hole

GYMNASTICS AND PHYSICAL EDUCATION

ONE OF THE BENEFACTIONS of the Lyon Memorial Fund, launched to celebrate the School Tercentenary in 1871, was a new Gymnasium. This was the upper part of a building designed by Mr CF Hayward on a site just below the rackets court, and shared with a new workshop.

The new Gymnasium was fitted out at once and was opened in May 1874. It was used for gymnastics and fencing. Later a mezzanine floor was added for boxing and ju-jitsu. Swedish gymnastics and remedials for physical disorders were introduced in 1913 by Lieutenant BT Coote RN, when he was appointed Superintendent. The old equipment was replaced by Swedish apparatus, which was very avant garde at the time, and the facilities were said to be the best in any public school in the country at the time.

The principal use of the Gymnasium was for physical training, which became part of the curriculum under the tutelage of two ex-service Physical Training Instructors. The equipment available consisted of mats and wall bars, ropes, box and parallel bars. In the afternoons gymnastics was available for the specialist few.

In the first half of the twentieth century gymnastics flourished. The main competition was between House IVs with a School Gymnastics VIII being nominated each year. This did not seem to be directly related to the competitors selected for School matches. There were rarely more than one or two a year, opponents usually being from Eton, Berkhamsted, Mill Hill, Bradfield and Radley. Disciplines were usually mat, long box, broad box, and parallel bars although rings were included occasionally.

Moretons, Champion House Tug o' War team, 1897

Gymnastics in the second half of the century was becoming increasingly marginal. From reports in *The Harrovian*: in 1959 there were entries "from four Houses only"; in 1963 there were moans about Harrow's "outmoded apparatus"; in 1971 a low entry for the House Competition was explained by "rugger monopoly". A brief resurgence was stimulated by the arrival in 1979 of Mr RE Arnold, British Champion Gymnast 1977 and silver medallist at the Commonwealth Games 1978. In 1981 matches v Bradfield and Wellington led to entries for the Public Schools Gymnastics Championships, where ES Jume'an was an individual winner. Whether or not the demise of gymnastics was accelerated by the unexpected and untimely death in 1979 of Mr Norman O'Driscoll, a popular instructor, or by the departure of Mr Arnold in 1981, is not clear. It seems that it was largely kept going thereafter by a steady influx of prep school gymnasts.

Mr Roger Uttley, who came to Harrow to be master-in-charge of rugby, was appointed Director of Physical Education, and PE continued to be taught on the timetable to boys in the first two years (Shells and Removes). When the Sports Hall was built in 1985 there were no wall bars, ropes or rings, but gymnastic activity continued on the box and mat, with the addition of trampolining. Gradually pressure from other subjects began to make inroads until in 1999 PE was deleted from the Lower School curriculum, although it was then offered as an A-level option in the Sixth Form. Enthusiasts carried on with gymnastics out of school hours, although there were

no longer school matches; increasingly it was used by many for fitness and agility training.

It is interesting to note that Jonathan Rutland came to Harrow from Port Regis Preparatory School in 1986, not because of any opportunities at the School but because of its proximity to Hendon Gymnastics Club. Rutland trained every day at Hendon and was a Gold Medal winner in the British National Championships (under-19). Later, as a member of the Senior National Squad, he also competed internationally. At Harrow Rutland's achievements were recognised by his election to the Philathletic Club.

Champion gymnasts, 1901

HARROW

HOCKEY

THERE HAVE BEEN SEVERAL young hockey players arriving as Masters at Harrow over the years – Mr Michael Pailthorpe, an Oxford 'blue', in the 1950s and Mr John Strover, a British Olympic player, in the 1960s spring to mind – but the idea of playing the game at Harrow was out of the question. Harrow footer on Harrow clay it was, and long destined to be. However several boys had enjoyed playing hockey at their prep schools and there was an interest in the game smouldering below the surface: first Mr David Parry and later Mr Martin Smith organised some hockey on the Parade Ground. It was not an ideal surface and falling over was unwise but it was hockey of a sort.

Mr Ian Hammond, a Cambridge 'blue' arriving in 1999, fanned the embers of interest into flame and arranged for some boys to play on the Elmfield's five-a-side Astroturf in the following year. Through his contacts he arranged a few informal matches – away from home, of course – and when the School artificial pitch was built in 2005, some proper hockey began to be played. In 2005 there was a Senior team and a Yearlings team, and by 2006 there were two teams at each level and eight Masters coaching.

In 2008 the First XI won the Middlesex Championships and went through to the regional stage, but for the most part the School, with just one pitch, is unable to compete with the established hockey schools such as Tonbridge, Wellington and Bedford, where the game is 'ringfenced'. Good surfaces have been prepared on Ducker 6 and the outfield of the Sixth Form Cricket Ground but matches on grass are looked down upon by schools such as these. Harrow's opponents have included Eton, Radley, Bradfield, Pangbourne, Haileybury, Merchant Taylors', Mill Hill and St Alban's.

Nowadays soccer is the main sport of the Spring term and with the court games (rackets, squash and Fives) also anxious to recruit good ball games players, Mr Hammond is happy for the School to play hockey in the second league – at least for the time being. Hockey is well suited to cricketers and there is a steady supply of coaches among the Gap students, South Africans in particular. At Harrow it is becoming an increasingly popular game.

Hockey v Merchant Taylors', 2008

Facing page: Hockey v Eton, 2009

LAWN TENNIS

WHEN SPENCER GORE (OH) BECAME the first winner of the Gentlemen's Singles at Wimbledon in 1877, the Championship lasted for a week, but was suspended over the weekend so as not to clash with the Eton v Harrow cricket match at Lord's. That says as much as anything about the status of the two games at that time. For many years tennis was considered to be no more than a recreational sport at Harrow. The Harrow Lawn Tennis Club (HLTC), founded in 1880 and formerly situated at the bottom of Peterborough Road, claims to be one of the six oldest lawn tennis clubs in the world; there were also courts in the garden of The King's Head Hotel until the flats at Leigh Court were built in the 1960s. Boys used occasionally to play on these courts. There were also a number of hard House courts, but tennis was not recognised as a School sport.

The first cracks in the cricket wall appeared in 1964 when about thirty-five boys "who do not play school cricket" signed up to play tennis. A young Master who had taken up their cause asked the Head Master if he could arrange a match against another school. Dr James's reply, after a pause, was, "All right, but it mustn't go on the calendar; I don't want the cricketers to know about it."

For the first two years School matches were played on the HLTC courts but in January 1967 three "superb" Tennis-Quick courts were laid at the southern end of the Parade Ground. Professional coaching was introduced once a week and matches arranged against Cranleigh, Wellington, Haileybury, Merchant Taylors', Marlborough, Masters and Harrow LTC. Success came quickly and 1968 was an unbeaten season. For the first time the School entered the inter-Public Schools Cup at Wimbledon. The Nehru Trophy for inter-House Doubles and the Nicholson Cup for Junior House Doubles were introduced.

There were only small changes to this fixture list over the next decade: Aldenham and Eton were added and Marlborough dropped; the Marlborough match had probably been arranged by Sir Alan Outram, master-in-charge and an Old Marlburian, and was later dropped on grounds of distance. Every year the School entered for the Youll Cup and Thomas Bowl (for under-16s) at Wimbledon: they achieved consistent success without ever winning.

The Harrow team at this stage comprised a 1st VI, Colts and Junior Colts. Reports in *The Harrovian* complained of the number of boys having to be turned away due to shortage of courts, and in 1974 four 'Grassphalte' courts were laid. In 1976 the arrival of an American scholar in the VIth Form, GT Rossetter, described as the "best player on the circuit" did much to raise interest and standards. DJG Thomas and MWJ Ruffell won the Thomas Bowl at Wimbledon that year.

1978 was an unbeaten year for the 1st VI, although a new fixture against Bedford exposed some players to grass for the first time. By 1980 there were two Senior VIs, a Colts and a Junior Colts VI, each playing about seven matches a season. In 1985 five new En-Tout-Cas 'Playdek' courts replaced the three Tennis-Quick courts and the Grassphalte courts were renovated; a practice wall was erected. Again the team was strengthened by two US foundation scholars, but this time the outcome was less happy: they found the restraints of an English boarding school too great an infringement of their freedom and left the School on Speech Day.

Following a fire at their clubhouse in 1979, Harrow LTC sold their premises at the bottom of Peterborough Road and transferred the Club to the School courts a year later. This has been a mutually beneficial arrangement. HLTC is a thriving club of over 300 members, with ten teams playing in the Middlesex League. The Club has use of the Boyer Webb pavilion.

In 1986 the first Parents & Sons Tournament took place; this soon became a hugely popular event and the

Murjani family presented a trophy along with trophies for School Singles and Doubles. By this stage there were two professional coaches and Yearlings and Junior Colts B teams had been introduced.

In 1988 five new courts were added. A minibus-load of boys travelled to the David Lloyd Tennis Centre at Heston for coaching and entered LTA national competitions. In 1990 James Prendiville won a scholarship to the Harry Hopman Tennis School in USA.

The greatest boost to tennis since its introduction at Harrow came with the Sports East development and the laying of the Beckwith Courts in 2006. This massive project involving the re-siting of the VI Form rugby and soccer ground, the laying of a Tartan athletics track and the upgrading of the other football pitches also included twelve new courts on the site of the old VIth Form ground. Of the twelve new courts named after Peter and John Beckwith (OHs), who jointly funded them, six are acrylic and six are 'Kushion-Kourt'. In addition, one of the Astroturf multi-purpose pitches provides another twelve courts. The lower bounce means that these courts are used mainly by Yearlings. Where, previously, eighteen boys could play in a home match, now forty-eight can. The improvements were immediately reflected in the number of boys playing tennis and in results. The School entered the sixteen-team Public Schools League for the first time. There are now four Senior and eleven Junior teams. An important event is the 'Radley-Harrow-Wellington-Marlborough Tournament', which involves the top eight boys in each year group.

Meanwhile many of the House tennis courts have been converted to five-a-side football pitches.

The Beckwith Lawn Tennis Courts were laid on the site of the former Sixth Form rugby ground and opened in 2005 (above); lawn tennis on the Beckwith Courts (left)

MARTIAL ARTS

MINOR SPORTS ARE ALWAYS dependent on the enthusiasms of individual Masters – although sometimes the boys themselves have the drive and determination to start or resurrect an activity. This remains true even when there are outstanding visiting coaches. Judo was the first of the martial arts to come to Harrow: it started in 1976 under the direction of coach Keith Renfry, a Great Britain Silver medallist in the Montreal Olympics. There were matches against Eton and Aldenham in 1977.

The School Karate Club started on the arrival of Mr Richard Burden in 1979 and trained in the Wado Ryu school of Karate. Activity centred around a nucleus of about twenty boys, at least two of whom have continued after leaving the School and attained 3rd Dan: Julian Howells, a doctor, and Charles Falk, a barrister, are still training today. When opposition could be found school matches were arranged and certain keen boys were members of the Harrow local club, attending training in the evenings. In the 1980s and first half of the 1990s some very good Japanese teachers visited including Tatsuo Suzuki 8th Dan, the world recognised authority of Wado Ryu. Through Mr Burden's contacts the boys had regular access to the top Japanese sensei.

On the arrival of Dr John Cullern, the Karate Club began to veer towards ju-jitsu but then, with his departure to Winchester, the Club fell dormant. Nowadays many boys arrive at Harrow with prep school experience of some sort of martial art and are keen to continue. So the arrival of Dr Matthew Glossop in 2008 prompted a welcome revival. He is 3rd Dan in Shaolin-tsu Kempo, not one of the traditional Karate styles popular in the UK but more like an ancestor of modern Karate and descendent of Chinese Kung Fu. At the beginner level the basic training does not vary too much between

The karate team, 2010

styles: they all involve a whole range of striking and kicking techniques, as well as throws and locks. In the early days the main focus of the Club was on traditional martial arts training and on recruiting boys with no experience of Karate. However there is an emphasis on self-defence drills with partners and the more advanced boys (sometimes referred to as step sparring).

School matches are always an attraction for boys but Karate has many more variations on possible competition rules than Judo, so matching is a complicated process. It seems that many schools, such as Eton, offer a range of martial arts, which depletes numbers in any one. This is not the case at Harrow, where Karate and Judo each has about twenty-five boys, with only a few boys doing both. There is also a dedicated Dojo.

Judo has always run in parallel to the Karate Club. Jim Duigen, a sports hall instructor, taught the boys in the late 1970s and 1980s when Miss Judith Affleck became master-in-charge. The club continued to flourish under the tutelage of Paul Ajala, a 3rd Dan and former British Champion, who also teaches regularly at the Budokwai Centre in Fulham. Then in 2007 Mr Ivan Stroud, a brown belt 1st Kyu, took over judo, while Paul Ajala continued to coach. Dr Glossop is also a 3rd Dan in judo and former President of the Oxford University Judo Club, and his wife, Lauren, is also a black belt 1st Dan, so the School has a wealth of expertise available. There are matches with Winchester (very active), Eton (not quite so active), St Paul's and Westminster. The School also competes in the Independent Schools' Championship every year.

In 2009 two Japanese Judo 'greats', Katsuhiko Kashiwazaki (former World Champion), Shinji Hosokawa (former World and Olympic Champion), direct descendents of Jigoro Kano (Founder of Judo), visited the School and gave both boys and coaches useful advice. So long as these distinguished enthusiasts remain on the teaching staff, the martial arts look as if they will remain an active part of Harrow life.

Judo Masterclass

POLO

THERE HAVE LONG BEEN boys at Harrow with polo in their blood but it was not until the 1990s that a regular school team emerged. In 1991 the first of a series of annual matches against Eton was played. To provide some practice leading up to the main event, other matches were arranged and so the polo programme expanded, albeit in a piecemeal fashion. The growth of polo at Harrow coincided with an increasing interest in the sport at many schools. Indeed it is a curious fact that at a time when Britain seemed to be following an increasingly egalitarian path, such a seemingly elitist sport should gain ground – yet that is exactly what happened.

Polo is an unusual school sport in the sense that the School provides very little in the way of facilities and equipment. It is an expensive game and everyone involved is very dependent on parents for ponies, livery, coaching, transport and picnics. Indeed the initiative for the School to start the game came from the boys and their parents. The first polo team was very strong and several of the boys of 1991, notably Jack Kidd and the Dickson brothers, went on to become professional players. It was not surprising therefore that Harrow triumphed in the first match against Eton, played at the Guards Polo Club at Windsor. However the balance of power quickly shifted and Eton began a run of victories that was to last twelve years. Yet there was no lack of commitment on the part of the small group of young players and their parents, who took up the reins after the departure of the 'pros'. For many years the driving force was Mr Charles Betz, a leading figure in the world of school and university polo, whose two sons represented the School between 1994 and 2000. Of the polo-playing schools, only Millfield and Rugby have their own field and Eton have Windsor close at hand, so Harrow forged links with several polo clubs, notably West Wycombe, Ham and Kirklington near Oxford. This enabled the School to play matches against Stowe, Radley, Wellington and a few others. Also, during the 1990s, the School was fortunate to have the support of HRH Crown Prince El Hassan bin Talal of Jordan (OH), who hosted memorable pre-season tours to Jordan.

Initially polo was categorised under equestrian activities in general and so Dr Glyn Jenkins became the first official master-in-charge. In 1996 Mr Ross Beckett who had retired as House Master of Elmfield the year before, took on polo as a sport in its own right, handing over to Mr Nick Page in 2001. By this time the number of boys wanting to play was growing, encouraged no doubt by the acquisition of a wooden horse and the construction of a polo pit, enabling boys to practise their stick work during spare moments on the Hill. The engagement of several top professional coaches led, not only to

Polo: The A team, winners of the Eton v Harrow match at The Guards' Polo Ground, 2009

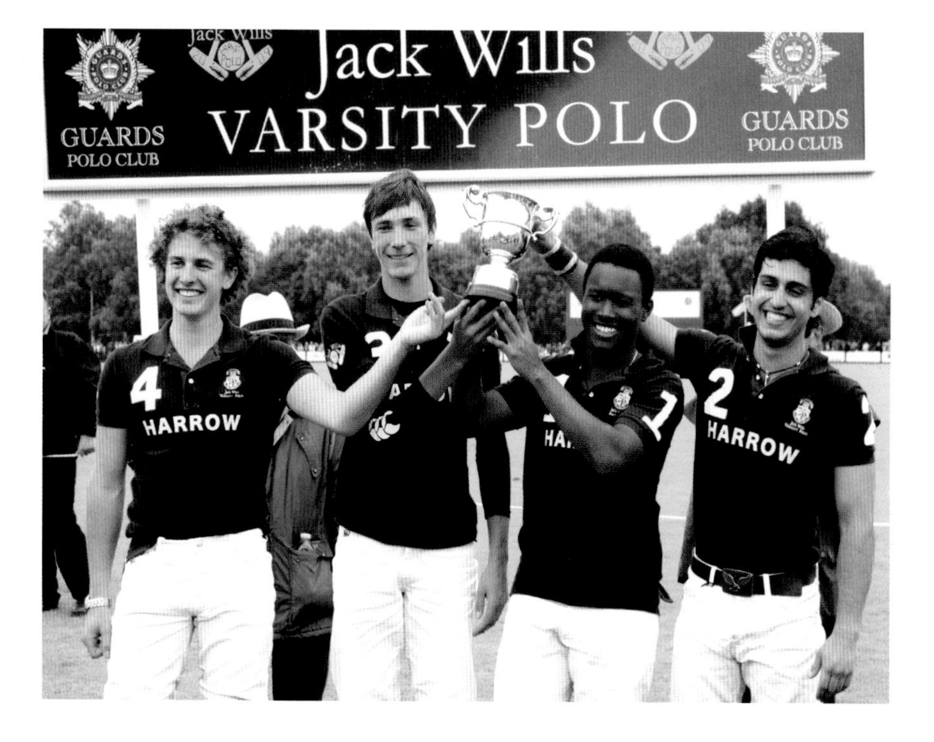

improved individual technique, but, crucially, better tactics and teamwork on the field. Also significant was the wholehearted backing of Head Master, Mr Lenon, who openly displayed his enthusiastic support by sporting his HPS tie on a regular basis and by unfailingly attending the Eton match at Windsor.

When at last Eton was defeated in 2004, it was the beginning of an unbroken run of victories for the next five years. Eton v Harrow has become a notable fixture in the polo calendar as it is always scheduled on one of the major match days at the Guards Club in June, and consequently attracts a large crowd of spectators and generous sponsorship. It is also the custom for the parents of the players from both schools to lunch together beforehand – a social event to rival the cricket match at Lord's.

Yet there is more to the polo season than a single match. Harrow polo expanded to embrace five teams playing at appropriate age groups and standards. The 'A' team became very strong and was led by two exceptional players, Lord Richard Le Poer and Jack Richardson. Mr Page was been fortunate in the appointment of several female members of the teaching staff who provided enthusiastic and knowledgeable support. In fact the master-in-charge for the extremely successful 2007 and 2008 seasons, when Harrow won the top division of the National Schools Tournament, was his successor Mrs Vicky Smit.

Polo at The Guards Polo Ground

RACKETS

RACKETS BEGAN IN THE Fleet and King's Bench debtors' prisons in the mid-eighteenth century, but Harrow was the first school to play the game. This is not thought to have been caused by any particular link between these two institutions. The basic requirement for rackets is a piece of flat land and a high wall. Prisons were able to oblige in these two respects, as was the School after the enlargement of the School Yard in 1821. Originally the Sixth and Fifth Forms played against the west wall of the Old Schools, while the rest of the School used the high south wall of the Yard that backs onto Druries. Early prints show the protective netting fitted to the top of this wall, which was pulled down in 1889.

The 'courts' for this primitive game played in the Yard had all sorts of hazards such as chimneys, drain pipes and net-covered windows, requiring some complicated rules, and the absence of side and back walls was compensated by 'rackets fags' who were designated ball-stopping and collecting duties. The game was played with cut-down ('real') tennis racquets and leather-covered balls referred to as 'best fives', sold by a Mrs Arnold, known to the boys as "Old Polly".

Public Schools Rackets Champions 1971: John Prenn and Mark Thatcher with Roger Crosby, rackets professional

In 1850 two new courts, known as the Shell and V Form courts, were built just below the Milling Ground. Both were 'open', the V Form court having just one side wall. Sam Hoare, Custos, took over the supply of balls and became an unofficial rackets coach.

An Old Harrovian, Sir William Hart-Dyke, was the first rackets champion to have learnt the game outside the debtors' prisons and he was largely responsible for the construction of the closed and covered court in 1865. The court adjoined the V Form court down the hill on its west side. Although its dimensions are slightly larger than those that later became 'standard', it is still in use today. Hart-Dyke later recalled that the front wall service line was rather higher than in modern courts, necessitating a 'squash-style' lobbed serve and, as drop shots were common, early rackets pairs played "one up, one back". There were long rallies and the game was conspicuously slower than it is today.

The Public Schools' Championships was first played in 1868 at Prince's Club, at Lord's in 1887 and thereafter at Queen's. Harrow dominated in these early years.

Percy Ashdown was Amateur Singles Champion in 1890 and seven times Doubles Champion. It was at this time that the Crawley family burst upon the rackets scene, Ernest winning in 1883, Eustace in 1885 and 1886 and Stafford in 1895. They were to be followed a generation later by Kenneth, Aidan, Leonard and Cosmo and two generations later by Randall and Andrew.

There were further successes in the 1940s and 1950s when Roddy Bloomfield won both the Singles and the Doubles with Chris Strang in 1954. Geoffrey Simmonds, a winner in 1947, was the instigator of an appeal to build a second court at Harrow in 1965, a project not without its difficulties as there had not been a rackets court built for over fifty years and

none of the skilled craftsmen, particularly plasterers, had survived.

John Prenn, a Schools' winner with Mark Thatcher in 1971, went on to become World Champion for most of the 1980s and Harry Foster also became World Champion in 2005. In all, a Harrow pair has won the Schools Doubles Championships thirty-one times, including five times in the last ten years. Eton has achieved twenty-three victories and is second to Harrow in this regard.

The tradition of employing a rackets coach goes back to the earliest times and is compatible with the perceived need for professional coaching in cricket: difficult games require proper instruction. Nowadays it is also an essential for safety reasons: a rackets ball can be a lethal missile among unsupervised pupils. Harrow has been fortunate in its pros: the Crosbys, father Fred and son Roger, occupied the post for seventy years. The first official 'pro' was George Smale, appointed in 1871, but in the following year he was succeeded by Walter Gray of the famous Cambridge cricket family. Then Judy Stevens came from Prince's in 1885. Charles Williams, who was pro from 1909–22, achieved fame by surviving the sinking of the Titanic while on his way to contest the World Championship in New York. (The Titanic had a squash court and Williams was working his passage by coaching during the voyage). He didn't win but he must have had a few yarns to tell in the pros' room in later years. Charles Williams later became World Champion from 1911–1913 and again from 1929–1935.

The pros have a varied role: they need to ensure a steady stream – or at least a trickle – of talented ball games players: rackets is not a game for the coordinatedly challenged. But to justify their positions they need to provide a niche for those who enjoy the game without expecting to achieve representative distinction: realistically, two pairs per year will give regular matches to twenty-five boys at most. John Eaton, the current pro, has done well to avoid indulging *prima donna* tendencies, always a danger in individual sports.

From 1888 when MC Kemp, a former Public Schools and Amateur Doubles Champion, was appointed to the teaching staff, the School has been very fortunate in having some rackets-playing Masters to complement the pros. The most distinguished was Charles Swallow, twice unsuccessful Challenger for the World Championship. The present master-in-charge, Mr Peter Warfield, has ensured that the fine traditions of Harrow rackets have been maintained.

The School Yard, the original rackets court; note the protective netting above the wall (above); Fred Crosby, rackets professional, 1922-62 (left)

ROWING

FOUNDING A BOAT CLUB at a school situated on top of a substantial hill and some miles distant from a suitable stretch of water called for no little optimism and enthusiasm. In 1962 Mr Geoffrey Treasure, an Old Salopian, who had rowed with distinction at Oxford, formed a boat club from a small group of keen boys. Based on the Tideway, by courtesy of the Thames Rowing Club at Putney, the aspiring Harrovian oarsmen worked at technique and stamina in the Club's rowing tank and in tubbing sessions on the water; in the summer of 1963 an VIII was formed for the first time. By the following season a second VIII of novices had also appeared providing strength in depth and the brave (or foolhardy) decision was taken to turn this motley crew without any previous racing experience into a Harrow VIII good enough to appear at Marlow Regatta – an event second in prestige only to Henley in the eyes of the traditional rowing schools. To row at Marlow before a critical enclosure would be to establish Harrow rowing at one blow – but to fail would cast doubt over the whole project. In the event the Harrow VIII's first competitive race resulted in victory over the King's School, Worcester, but a narrow defeat at the hands of an experienced St Paul's crew. It was a performance good enough to satisfy the sceptics: the pioneers had shown what could be achieved against the odds and that Harrow rowing did have a future.

Rowing is an expensive sport and initially Harrow crews were obliged to borrow boats and oars and to depend on Masters and parents for transport. As well as support from Thames Rowing Club, help also came from Oriel College, Oxford, (Mr Treasure's college) and the OUBC itself loaned Harrow a set of appropriately coloured blades. Parents weighed in with an appeal for funds with which to purchase a boat, and a new base was found at the Rutland Boathouse at Hammersmith. Yet serious progress depended on the tenacity of the boys faced with three return journeys a week by underground railway from South Harrow to Hammersmith and upon Masters with the time, enthusiasm and expertise to coach crews in the tricky conditions on the Tideway. At this point Mr Treasure was appointed House Master at The Head Master's House and withdrew from the rowing scene but the day was saved by the arrival of Mr Edward Gould, an international oarsman and rugby 'blue'.

It was Mr Gould's decision to move from VIIIs to IVs, which are better suited to a small boat club, and also to enter as many regattas as possible during the Summer term to acquire experience before the national Schools Regatta, held in those days at Pangbourne. Success was achieved in 1969 when Harrow won the National Schools Coxed Fours Cup.

But underlying difficulties lurked. Although the Boat Club had acquired its own boats, oars and a rigid inflatable with a powerful outboard motor for coaches, the time spent travelling became increasingly a disincentive. A minibus, the gift of the father of the captain of the successful 1969 crew (and the first minibus to belong to the School) did much to help, and the early 1970s saw further successes at regattas across the south of England from Tonbridge to Gloucester. A move was made from Hammersmith to Twickenham Rowing Club in the mid-1970s but interest among the boys was already dwindling and the decision was taken to suspend activities.

Twenty years later – in spite of misgivings among senior Masters – the arrival of Mr Patrick Weir provoked a revival. There were echoes of the 1960s as a new group of enthusiasts, backed by equally enthusiastic parents, started all over again: funds were raised and equipment purchased. An important advance from the previous era was that sophisticated rowing machines and other fitness apparatus in the Sports Hall enabled oarsmen to

train on the Hill. The appointment of another Master with rowing experience and expertise, Mr Christopher Lee, added to the expectations. But a boat club still needs a suitable stretch of water and in its second life the Harrow School Boat Club became an adjunct of the Marlow Rowing Club – an unwitting reminder of 1964 and the Club's first serious race. For a while, rowing prospered again. The most successful season of the second era was 2007 when Mr James Hanson, by then master-in-charge, moved operations to Putney, the scene of the first tentative strokes taken over forty years previously. Boating on the Tideway in the Spring term was followed by a training camp in southern Spain in the Easter holiday. Due reward followed that summer with victories for Harrow crews in races at Marlow, various other regattas and the National Schools Championships. But, as with boys, Masters come and go; the departures of Messrs Weir and Lee, followed by the appointment of their successor Mr James Hanson to an administrative examinations post, were mortal blows. Rowing has once again disappeared from the Harrow scene.

It is interesting to reflect that two Old Harrovians, Charles Wordsworth and Charles Merivale, rowed in the inaugural Oxford and Cambridge boat race in 1829, and that a number of Harrovians, who did not row at school, have gone on to achieve rowing success later. In fact John Badcock, who represented Great Britain in the European Championships in 1959, was sent to Harrow by his oarsman father precisely *because* the School did not row, his theory being that rowing is such an all-consuming sport at a rowing school that many become disillusioned and never row again. Equally surprisingly, JAGH Stewart, who rowed in the 1984 Oxford boat, was a cricket 'flannel' at Harrow, appearing at Lord's in 1979 and 1980.

1st IV training in Seville, April 2007

SAILING

THE SAILING CLUB WAS formed in 1931 on the initiative of Mr Eric Gannon, a Modern Languages Master who had served with the Grand Fleet in the Great War. He was described as "dapper in appearance, reflecting a blend of the Spanish hidalgo and the piratical sea captain". He was known to the boys as "Sinbad". The original objective of the Club was to "encourage interest in practical seamanship". The focus of activity was at Bourne End, the headquarters of the Upper Thames Sailing Club, where members enjoyed the privileges of cadet membership. Visits were made on Tuesdays during the Summer term and a sixteen-foot half-decked boat was chartered.

In the first phase of the Club's life, up to the outbreak of the Second World War, there were lectures, occasional matches and the season's highlight, the Spring holiday cruise. The first match against Eton was raced in twelve-foot dinghies, borrowed from the Oxford University Sailing Club. There was also a match at Stowe on their lake.

The Spring Cruises were in different locations on chartered vessels: in 1934 a forty-eight-foot 'botter' type yacht was taken from Rotterdam to the Zuider Zee; in 1936 an eighteen-ton schooner was taken from Bursledon on the Hamble round the Isle of Wight. Five or six boys crewed on these cruises, which were extremely popular. In 1939 the Club was given a fourteen-foot dinghy by CA Minoprio. It was kept on Ruislip Reservoir and named "The Minnow" but the outbreak of war brought all activity to a halt.

The Sailing Club was relaunched with great enthusiasm after the war under the name of Harrow Argonauts. Mr H Cooper was President, GR Odey, Secretary. In 1946 completely new sets of sails were bought for each of the four twelve-foot dinghies. Rickmansworth Sailing Club generously provided moorings and a shed for rigging; they also presented the Rickmansworth Challenge Cup for the winner of the match against Eton. The Argonauts became affiliated to the Yacht Racing Association and, in keeping with the pre-war tradition, there were a number of lectures: for example "Dinghy Sailing" by Mr McConnell and "Naval Design & Construction" by Lt Cdr C Kingsley.

In 1952 the Odey Cup was awarded for the best individual helm. By 1953 there were five matches: against Charterhouse, Eton, Haileybury, Stowe and Aldenham and in 1955 the Old Harrovian Sailing Club was founded.

During the 1950s the Harrow Argonauts Sailing Club had six Yachting World Cadet dinghies, which were maintained, during the winter, by the members. The Cadet was an 11ft hard chine pram dinghy with three sails, main, jib and a small spinnaker. It was usually sailed two up but was also good to sail single-handed. It was a very good training boat but its place has now been taken by the single-handed, single-sailed Optimist.

Sailing took place on Aldenham Reservoir, about six miles away and members made their way there by bicycle. Most of the instruction in sailing was left to the more experienced boys. Matches were sailed both home and away. Eton and Radley both sailed on the Thames, Oundle on the Nene, Charterhouse on Frensham Pond, and Haileybury on the New River at Broxbourne. The matches were team races where the places of all three boats in the team are taken into account.

By 1960 there were no fewer than thirty-seven Argonauts; Gavin Anderson (OH), always a generous supporter, presented the School with Fireflies to replace the Cadets and the teams entered several sailing competitions. In 1963 Mr Alan Sankey took over as master-in-charge and the Argonauts entered the Public Schools Competition at Bembridge, sailing the Club boat, a twenty-foot Bermuda rig with keel.

In the fifty years since then, the Sailing Club's fortunes have ebbed and flowed. For reasons physical and political, the Club's base has moved from place to place. In 1975 the dam broke at Aldenham Reservoir, forcing a move to the Welsh Harp at Neasden. A further upheaval occurred in 1979 when an industrial dispute caused the Welsh Harp reservoir to be drained. In 1984 the Club acquired six new '420' dinghies. The 420 was the internationally accepted youth trainer, an ideal school boat, complete with spinnaker and trapeze. Unfortunately, Welsh Harp would only allow its affiliated schools and universities to sail the club classes, which at that time were the Firefly, GP14, and Fireball, so the School returned to the smaller Aldenham Reservoir. The following year the Public Schools Competition was sailed in 420s for the first time, and most schools by then had moved from Fireflies to 420s. Then, in 1986, sailing moved to Datchet Water. This has a much larger sailing area, with no tree-lined banks and, as it stands high above the neighbouring countryside alongside the M4 and M25, there are constant winds. This has remained the Club's headquarters ever since.

As in most minor sports that take place away from the Hill, sailing has depended on the combined enthusiasm of Masters and boys to keep its club afloat. Among the latter, MTO Stanley (1975) was a particularly good captain and his House, Druries, won the newly presented Kelsey Cup for inter-House competition. In 1980, under Mr Roy Murray, and an enthusiastic captain, WN Barton, new equipment was purchased and training courses were established. The Club by then had eight Firefly dinghies and forty members. The fiftieth anniversary was properly celebrated by an unbeaten season, repeated the following year but victory in the Public Schools' Championships at Itchenor remained elusive. External support is inspiring too: remembered long afterwards is a lecture from the Old Harrovian Olympic bronze medallist, Robin Aisher, who was four times captain of the British Admiral's Cup team – although he didn't sail at Harrow.

All school matches at this time were for six boat team racing matches, held under the British Schools Dinghy Racing Association (BSDRA) rules. In 1988, the team were finalists in the Hoad Trophy: this is the national schools' team-racing championships.

Mr Charles Baker took over in 1996; he was also National Secretary to the BSDRA. Each summer season a full calendar of fixtures was sailed against other schools including Eton, who shared the home water at Datchet. The Thames Valley Area Championship was hosted and run by Harrow at Datchet Water and always attracted six or more schools for a competitive day's sailing. A match against Old Harrovians and the Kelsey House Sailing Cup were also regularly sailed. In 2002 Harrow again qualified for the BSDRA International Team Racing Championships, held at Spinnaker Club in the New Forest, and finished creditably as runners-up in the Silver League.

Over this period a program of boat replacement was started: taking advantage of the economically priced Spanish-built 420s, which had been introduced with the schools market in mind, new boats were purchased every two years. Links with the RYA national 420 youth squad were developed and all the top helms spent one or two intense training weekends with them at Rutland Water in the winter months to improve their skills: team-racing requires physical strength (in high winds), technical skill, mental agility and the ability to work for a team win rather than personal glory. This acquired expertise was passed down to other members of the team. In 1998 Jim Saltonstall, the British Olympic and senior RYA racing coach, gave a lecture that did much to raise the profile of this 'minor game'.

Two or three afternoons each week in the Summer term spent away from the confines of the Hill, sailing on some beautiful inland waters, foster in boys enjoyment of an activity that they can pursue for years after they leave school. The many members of the Old Harrovian Sailing Association that take part in the Arrow Trophy at Cowes (named after the Harrow Silver Arrow and originally started as an Old Boys' match between Harrow and Eton) bear witness to this.

White Mischief at Itchenor, 2003

SHOOTING

NOT SURPRISINGLY, SHOOTING AT Harrow began life as an activity of the Harrow School Rifle Volunteer Corps, which was formed in 1859 as a company of the 18th Middlesex RVC. In 1908 it became the Officer Training Corps, renamed Junior Training Corps in 1940 and finally Combined Cadet Force in 1948.

In early days, shooting was at rifle butts in Rayner's Lane; as an adjunct to this, a Morris tube shooting range was built just below the Milling Ground. In 1904, this was replaced by a fifty-yard Morris tube screen range on the north side of Garlands Lane, which spent some years under the name Rifle Range Lane. In 1924 the screen range was pulled down and replaced on the same site by the miniature range that exists today. This is a twenty-five-yard range with eight firing points; its popularity led to an increase in competitions both within and outside the School.

In 1861 the Public Schools Shooting Competition was inaugurated, the team shield being presented by Lord Ashburton and the individual cup by Earl Spencer, both Old Harrovians. It was held at Wimbledon until 1891, after which it was transferred to Bisley. Since then Harrow has won 'the Ashburton' eleven times, equalled only by Charterhouse, and the Spencer Cup has been won by a Harrovian on ten occasions. Shooting was hugely popular at this time with large numbers of boys vying for a place in the School team. *The Harrovian* wrote, "The great object of interest in the Corps is the annual match at Wimbledon... Harrow has earned the admiration and envy of all the public schools for its excellence in shooting; and the Shield (the Ashburton) has become so identified with our School, that while others might be content with a high place in the Contest, we should regard anything short of the first place as a failure and a defeat." A song, *The Harrow Blue*, sadly not included in the present edition of the Song Book, commemorated the exploits of the Shooting VIII:

So the Ashburton Shield again they bore
To the wall where it loved to hang before,
A prize to their shooting due,
With a rush of triumph and wild young cheer
Which gladden the hearts of all who hear
And who love the Harrow Blue.

In 1867 a House Competition was inaugurated, entitled the 'Silver Arrow' in allusion to the former archery contest. By 1883 there were fixtures against outside opposition: 9th Middlesex RVC, Tower Hamlets RVC, Inns of Court RVC, Cambridge University & 23rd Middlesex RVC. When the range at Rayners Lane was condemned as unsafe and closed, practice was transferred to ranges at Welwyn, Runnymede and then Bisley.

After the Great War the main competitions continued to be shot at Bisley, including the House

Facing page: Harrow VRC Shooting VIII & Cadet Pair c1904 (above) and Harrow OTC Shooting VIII c1914 (below)

Shooting was hugely popular at this time with large numbers of boys vying for a place in the School team… A song, *The Harrow Blue* ... commemorated the exploits of the Shooting VIII

DISTce Yds
TARGETS
No OF ROUNDS
NAMES
HARROW V.R.C.
TOTAL EACH DISTANCE
GRAND TOTAL

competitions for the Silver Arrow, Ebrington Cup and the Pass and Recruit prizes. There were also 'away' fixtures v HAC at Pirbright and 1st Herts at Welwyn. To give boys greater opportunities with the service rifle, a thirty-yard range was opened beside Ducker in 1925. The VIII won the Eastern Command Cadet Challenge Shield that year but successes never matched up to those of the early years.

After World War II the School had the luxury of a full-time shooting coach, CSM Moores. This enabled all boys to have the experience of regular miniature range shooting. The weekly 'shooting detail' with the sub-text: "Do not run. Do not be late" regularly featured on House noticeboards. Long-range shooting continued with twice weekly visits to Bisley; the team in their Australian-style shooting hats, were a distinctive sight on the High Street on half-holiday lunch times. In 1958 the VIII won the Country Life Competition for the first time in its fifty year history.

The standard of shooting remained consistently high during the 1970s and 1980s under the enthusiastic direction of Mr Tony Crofts. The team were runners-up in the Ashburton – by one point – in 1984 and five boys in four years were selected for the British Cadet Rifle Team trip to Canada. In 1984 JE Ironside-Smith won a place in the final team for the Michael Faraday match.

In 1991, the status of shooting was given a boost when Mr Nick Bomford was appointed Head Master. He had captained the Oxford University Rifle Club and represented Great Britain in 1960.

Nowadays small-bore shooting takes place in the twenty-five yard range in Rifle Range Lane (recently renamed Garlands Lane). During a typical year, a squad of about fifteen boys will shoot regularly over the two Winter terms, leaving the summer clear for full bore at Bisley. Unlike some schools which have switched over to civilian rifles, Harrow still uses the old Lee Enfield Number 8, as this makes it possible to shoot competitively under the auspices of the CCF, and to enter the two major competitions around which the small-bore year is based. In the Autumn term the Stanniforth Competition tests deliberate shooting, and in the Spring term the Country Life covers a range of skills: grouping, rapid, snap and landscape. In addition the School shoots shoulder-to-shoulder against others, although nearby opponents are now getting rather hard to find, several of the School's old rivals having given up entirely or changed rifle. RGS Guildford, Epsom, Bradfield and Charterhouse now offer matches on a regular basis. The range is also used by the Stanmore Rifle and Pistol Club.

The full bore shooting team consists of twelve boys, who have been selected from their performances and skills learned in small bore shooting. The 'orbat' is that of a team captain, two teams of four and a team of eight; each boy will also have the chance to fire as an individual in most competitions. Among the annual competitions are the Sussex Cup, Sawyer Cup, Middlesex Trophy, Surrey Cup and Clayton Challenge. All these events are run at Bisley, normally throughout the summer months. However the main effort is directed towards two events: the Ashburton Shield and the Imperial Meeting, which attracts an entry field of up to 4,000 firers, some of whom represent their countries at international level. In 2006 the team came nineteenth in the Ashburton, enough to win cups for the Best in London District, the Grenadiers Cup and the Seymore Shield: competition is much tougher than it was in the nineteenth century.

Shooting pair, winners of the Silver Arrow, c1890

Facing page: Shooting at the miniature range.

SQUASH

THE GAME OF SQUASH rackets originated at Harrow. In the first half of the nineteenth century, organised games were beginning to take shape, but by 1850 the only organised games available – apart from archery – were football, cricket and rackets, and provision for rackets was woefully inadequate for a school of 450 boys and rising. Accordingly, the boys, ever resourceful, invented their own 'mini-rackets'.

In 1924 Lord Dunedin wrote in a letter to *The Times*, "I went to Harrow in 1863; at that time the covered [rackets] court did not exist. There were two regular racket courts, the Sixth form, a huge open rectangle just below the milling ground and the Fifth form just below it. Squash was played in the 'Corner'." This was an area of the School Yard, bounded by the west wall of the Old Schools, the adjacent wall of the present Vicarage and the Milling Ground wall, then considerably closer to the Old Schools than it is now. "Squash had been played there for a very long time – *ultra memoriam* as far as I could discover. The origin of the game was undoubtedly there… At that time, as far as I know, squash was not played at any of the other great schools. Of course we played with the old squash hollow ball with a hole in it…."

Dunedin goes on to say that most Houses used to have a suitable space where boys could play this miniature version of rackets, although "most of them made very poor courts."

Of course the game at that time bore very little resemblance to that played today. *The Badminton Library* illustration (facing page), entitled 'Squash-Rackets at Harrow School' shows two boys playing in the Head Master's House Old Side Yard, wearing tailcoats and straw hats! Most of the 'courts' had three or sometimes just two walls. In many there were hazards. For example, in the 'Corner', "there were two hazards for which you could intentionally play – the buttress line to the great window which returned the ball straight down and the pipe which might send it anywhere. The Corner was better for 'four' games than for singles." Of the House 'courts', "the best of these was indubitably Rendalls… The shape of the House formed a natural interior three sides of a square and it was full of hazards in the shape of windows, pipes, etc." It seems that the variety given by these hazards were desirable as they made the game more interesting.

A rackets ball, consisting of a core wound round with string and encased in a stitched leather cover, was hard and quite unsuitable for this alternative game played in a smaller space, and a soft rubber ball was found to be much more satisfactory. The "hollow rubber ball with the hole in it" was to give squash rackets its name – although not initially: in accordance with the School slang, "eccer" for exercise, "footer" for football, "yarder" for yard games, rackets became known as "harder", and the game later to be known as squash rackets was, for a time, "softer".

In 1864, when the covered rackets court was built, an unusual situation occurred: there was a surplus of funds, and so two Eton Fives courts and four Rugby fives courts were built. While the boys took to Eton fives, they preferred to play with racquets in the Rugby courts, which hence became squash courts. Later the old Shell rackets court was converted into a further four squash courts, but there were no agreed dimensions for a squash court at this time. In 1897 the four original (Rugby Fives) courts were thought to be too small for squash and were remodelled into three larger courts. It was not until 1922 that a sub-committee of the Tennis and Rackets Association laid down some rules and agreed on uniformity of ball and court dimensions. In 1929 the Squash Rackets Association was formed, a long overdue governing body for the game.

At Harrow the courts on the site of the old Shell rackets court were knocked down and replaced by two

plaster-walled wooden-floored courts in 1936 but the first School match was not played until 1940. "At long last," sighed *The Harrovian*, "the School has played a squash match: it is indeed encouraging that a game which is one of the most popular and widely played throughout the School has entered into competition with outsiders." In the 1960s four of the open fives courts were converted to squash courts; the four stone squash courts remained in place (but were rarely used) until the 'new' rackets court was built on the site in 1965.

Modern technology has hastened the development of squash perhaps more than any other court game. Fibre glass then titanium/graphite composition rackets, glass-backed heated courts, sprung floors and squash balls, still made of rubber but with a mind-boggling list of added ingredients, polymers, vulcanising agents, fillers and re-inforcers, have led to a fast, attritional game that bears little similarity to its ancestor in 'the Corner'. Two modern glass-backed courts were built as part of the Ryan Theatre development in 1995.

Squash at Harrow is a flourishing game, played by a School team with a full fixture list over the two winter terms. There are no longer drain pipes or window ledges to take into account but several Houses have their own courts and squash continues to be a popular recreational game at all levels.

Squash in The Head Master's House yard, one of the original courts. Image from the Badminton Library of Sports & Games, 1903

SWIMMING AND DUCKER

UNTIL THE EARLY YEARS of the nineteenth century the School had no bathing place, but many boys used to swim in the Old Duck Puddle, a pond situated on the northeast side of the Watford Road, roughly opposite the present gates to the School Farm. It was fed by a stream then known as The Dyke, later called Sheepcote Brook.

In 1809 the Governors rented a piece of land just southeast of the present Northwick Park Hospital, which was excavated and became the 'New Duck Puddle". This occupied the area between the iron bridge and the cottage of what later became Ducker. Like its predecessor, this pond was polluted and foul and many boys preferred the pond at The Grove or the Park Lake for swimming. However Duck Puddle gradually became more popular, although it was described in 1836 as "a confined pond of stagnant fluid, standing on a bed of deep soft ooze, much frequented by water snakes"!

Between 1845 and 1851 improvements were made by lining the sides and bottom with bricks and by building changing sheds and a towel house. In 1850 the Dyke was diverted and water was pumped into the pool from an artesian well at Sheepcote Farm. A caretaker was appointed and a cottage built for him.

Further improvements were made in 1881 when the pool was redesigned by John Fowler. It was trebled in size, becoming 170 yards long in an 'L-shape', and was lined with concrete. Several bridges were built, the slates around the edges were replaced by asphalt, and new sheds, seats and a wooden clock tower at the east end were added. Water was supplied from the Colne Valley waterworks. The new pool was ceremonially opened on 28 May 1881.

In the following hundred years, few changes were made: the old wooden cottage was replaced by a brick house in 1896. A water cleanser was installed in 1936. And the name 'Duck Puddle' in accordance with other Harrow names (footer, speecher, eccer, yarder, etc.) became Ducker.

For many years, Ducker was a very popular bathing place, celebrated in the eponymous School Song. Traditionally boys swam naked, the privilege of wearing trunks going to 'Dolphins' – those who had displayed their expertise by completing a five-length course using different strokes, overcoming obstacles, climbing out and diving in, all in nineteen minutes. Non-swimmers were confined to the shallow end.

Ducker was also much enjoyed by the families of Masters and other School staff, who were able to use the pool when the boys were otherwise engaged. This was especially so in the summer holidays when family picnics and parties were very popular.

In the cold winters experienced in the early part of the twentieth century, when the temperature dropped below freezing, Ducker was frequently half emptied and used for skating.

A combination of events led to the demise of Ducker in the 1970s. First, the ageing concrete lining was showing an increasing number of cracks, resulting in a steady loss of water; this proved to be beyond the scope of cosmetic patching. Second, advancing dates of the Summer term, cooler summers and demands for competitive swimming called for heating of the pool. A heating plant proved to be ineffective and costly. Third, other schools were increasingly covering and heating their pools or investing in new indoor heated pools, providing swimming all the year round. The days of Ducker were clearly numbered. Although inevitable, few decisions have provoked such an emotional reaction from Old Harrovians, Masters and staff. Ducker was finally closed when a new twenty-five-metre, state-of-the-art pool was built as part of the Sports Hall

Traditionally boys swam naked, the privilege of wearing trunks going to 'Dolphins' – those who had displayed their expertise by completing a five-length course using different strokes, overcoming obstacles, climbing out and diving in, all in nineteen minutes.

complex in 1985. The old pool remains derelict and neglected after the failure of several planning applications to develop the site.

The quality and attractiveness of the new pool did much to win over the sceptics. Since the establishment of the new Ducker, competitive swimming and water polo have became a major part of the School's athletic programme. The accurate and efficient electronic timing system has raised competitiveness to a new level, resulting in School teams that have been undefeated for six years.

The School team has won the Bath Cup – the 4x50m relay for independent schools – in both 2009 and 2010, breaking the record in 2009. Swimming lessons are offered throughout the year, ranging from beginners to advanced level. It has also allowed the Biathlon to become one of the highlights of the School calendar and the pool has provided an aquatic alternative to Long Ducker (the annual charity run to Marble Arch and back). Competitors need to complete 400 lengths in three hours – the equivalent of the 20 mile run.

Ducker is also, as it was in the past, a social and recreational forum for many boys simply to splash about and cool off during the hot summer months. Many Masters and their families, and members of the local community, use the pool too and it has become an important and intrinsic part of life at Harrow.

Old Ducker

Scenes from 'Old Ducker': Although the pool was closed in 1985, the site has never been developed; it remains a sad sight

Scenes from the new Ducker

THE HARROW RIFLE CORPS

FIFTY-FIVE HARROVIANS FOUGHT AGAINST Napoleon I at Waterloo so it was no surprise that Harrow responded to the call for volunteers during the French scare of 1859. France was again ruled by a Napoleon, the Emperor Napoleon III. He was regarded with considerable suspicion by many Englishmen as 'a mystery man with a deadpan face and a goatee'. The French were seen as a threat and the Queen and her Prime Minister, Lord Palmerston, were convinced that invasion loomed, particularly as the French had started to build a fleet of ironclads and were extending their fortified naval base at Cherbourg, seemingly in preparation for 'a midnight foray' across the Channel.

Despite the objections of the penny-pinching Chancellor, Mr Gladstone, an Etonian, the Harrovian Prime Minister, supported by his Sovereign, demanded £11million to strengthen coastal defences and enlarge the fleet. In addition the War Committee encouraged the formation of a Volunteer Movement to which Palmerston promised to supply the rifles. Queen Victoria and Prince Albert attended reviews in Hyde Park and at Aldershot, as well as shooting matches at Wimbledon. England was to be defended.

Corps Camp, 1911

Amidst a furore of "patriotic slogans, rousing sentiments and xenophobic suspicions", Harrow made its contribution to the national effort. A public meeting was held in Speech Room, under the chairmanship of Dr Vaughan, to discuss the formation of a Harrow Rifle Corps. There were speeches which expounded the duties of a rifleman, others which were calculated to arouse martial spirit by painting a vivid picture of the horrors of French rule, and so on until some humorous banter over the matter of uniform concluded the meeting. Finally on December 30, 1859, official sanction was granted and the Harrow Rifle Corps came into being as the 18th Middlesex Rifle Volunteers. The date is commemorated on the Rifle Corps cap badge.

The initial response to the call for volunteers was enthusiastic and in 1860 there were some 350 who joined. However, numbers equally quickly fell away and in 1863 Vaughan's successor, Dr Montagu Butler, presided over the reorganisation of the Rifle Corps and provided an armoury beneath the Old Schools. Butler also took a close interest in the uniform: grey-blue with dark blue facings and much braid. At one stage magnificent fur hussar hats with enormous white plumes were the order of the day.

Until the Boer War, the Rifle Corps "remained an eccentric and minority activity". Numbers fluctuated; for example in 1882 there were only around thirty rising to about 200 in the late 1880s before dropping back to just over 100. Frequent appeals for support were made in *The Harrovian*. Thus *The Harrovian* writes in June 1870, "no-one will ever be the worse in after-life for being able to 'form fours' and 'wheel' properly ... We

cannot help saying that we think the School is bound to back up the Captain of the Corps in his endeavours to improve its condition; and whilst tendering to him our deepest thanks for all his past efforts, we feel sure that as the members increase in number he will spare no pains to bring the Corps to the highest state of perfection." The same year the Rifle Corps was presented with what were grandly called 'Regimental Colours', by Lady Crabbe, in the name of her son, Eyre Crabbe. *The Harrovian* noted that "notwithstanding the inclemency of the weather, a large number of spectators had assembled to witness the ceremony... the School Corps after having performed sundry military evolutions under the command of their officers, were formed into square ... the colours were then duly presented to the Captain, who amidst loud applause, handed them over to the keeping of 'Ensign Newall'".

Drill was held weekly on Wednesday evenings so as not to interfere with cricket but it appears that both attendance and standard were patchy. Shooting was much more popular and a place in the VIII that competed for the Ashburton Shield was much coveted. For some volunteers, notably the young Spencer Churchill, the Corps, in particular 'field days', provided an exciting and, in his case, inspiring diversion from the drudgery of school life.

The Boer War began a period of change. An attempt was made to enlist all boys over the age of fifteen and drill parades were moved to mornings. In addition grey-blue uniforms gave way to khaki, although the black buttons of the rifle regiments were retained. In 1908 the Rifle Corps was, as at other schools, re-established as an Officer Training Corps as part of a series of reforms introduced by the then Secretary of State for War, Richard Haldane. The OTC with its junior division in the public schools and its senior division in the universities came into being to help overcome a shortfall in officer recruiting in both the regular and

Harrow Rifle Corps below the Chapel terrace, 1895

reserve armies. A new range was built below Garlands and in 1910-11 a parade ground was constructed beside the Football Fields. Yet the Corps remained voluntary, with just over half the School enlisting. General Sir Allan Adair, in his autobiography, recalls the Corps at that time with some fondness and humour, "Our OTC seemed to us as professional as some Territorial battalions". Field days were the highlight: "...our Corps, supported occasionally by a battery of Royal Field Artillery, or a troop of Hussars, or such schools as Eton or Wellington, attacked Territorial units or other schools at Richmond Park or Princes Risborough... The field days culminated in a grand supper in the evening at which a band played." Camps too were well supported: "discipline was good, maintained by our sentries with fixed bayonets until a squabble over jam led to a boy being bayoneted in a moment of over-enthusiasm" – no health and safety committee or detailed risk assessments in those days.

In 1912 the OTC was inspected by General Sir Horace Smith-Dorrien, who two years later was to save the BEF in the retreat from Mons by the action his Corps fought at Le Cateau. Smith-Dorrien congratulated the 'battalion' on its progress since the beginning of the OTC and expressed a hope that to be at Harrow would soon be synonymous with being in the OTC. It was also his hope that more Harrovians would join the Territorial Forces and Special Reserve in their country's hour of need. The same year King George V, on a visit to Harrow, inspected a Guard of Honour and remarked upon the good reports he had heard of the Harrow OTC.

After the outbreak of the First World War, OTC parades were increased to four a week, night exercises were introduced and field days were held four times a term. *The Harrovian* provided some gloomy accounts of those field days: "Against the Royal Military College, Sandhurst, the chief umpire was unable to give a decision beyond the fact that a large percentage of casualties would have been the toll of many of the units engaged." And again, "...after some miles of fighting in which we crossed hill, dale, wood and moor, we ended on the golf course with a charge, shoulder to shoulder, against an impregnable position, and were annihilated to the last man." All too close to the reality in Flanders and France.

Between the World Wars the OTC was a central feature of Harrow life, recognised as such by the Governors who decreed that it be compulsory for all boys over fifteen. Parades were held twice a week on Wednesday afternoons and on Friday mornings before lunch. As well as being compulsory for the boys, Masters were expected to join. Some who had been appointed before 1918 returned to teach after their war service and many of those appointed in the following years had also served. However, compulsory Corps was

The inter-House Assault Course competition, now known as the "Endurance Test"

not popular with all boys and Masters alike. 'Slacking at Corps' met with strong official disapproval. *The Harrovian* carried a lively correspondence in 1929-30 concerning the rights and wrongs of compulsory Corps and in particular complaints about Friday morning parades and drill on Sundays for some Houses. A petition in May 1930, *supposedly* signed by 400 boys, called the excessive number of parades "military torture" and demanded a "reduction to one parade a week". The row aroused considerable press coverage, not least in Germany, questions were asked in the House and Eton offered to send a platoon to the Hill to restore order. Nevertheless Friday parades continued.

In 1940 the Officer Training Corps became the more prosaic Junior Training Corps. This in turn became the Combined Cadet Force to reflect the tri-service nature of the organisation when Royal Navy and Royal Air Force sections appeared. Many of the Masters appointed between 1945 and the mid-1960s had either fought in the Second World War or done post-war National Service so there was plenty of military experience among the officers. The Corps also remained an important and compulsory element of Harrow life and, until the end of National Service in the late 1950s, many boys regarded the Corps as a necessary preliminary to their two years' conscription.

Maintaining a compulsory Corps where boys joined after three terms and remained until they left school became increasingly difficult once National Service had been phased out. Officers and NCOs had to be more imaginative, and in some cases ingenious, in an attempt to vary the routine of weekly parades and training. A large number of specialist sections sprang up, some to last longer than others. More attention was focussed on adventurous training, originally known as arduous training, which reflected official as well as local thinking. Nevertheless the bullet needed biting and in 1965 a process began which was to conclude with the introduction of a voluntary Corps in 1973.

"Echoes of Edwardian Harrow" is the verdict of a former Master on the Corps in the 1980s and '90s. In some ways he has a point. The re-adoption of the original title, Harrow Rifle Corps, is one. The fact is that the officers are once again amateurs, Masters whose own military experience, if any, is based on their own school CCF, university OTC or Territorial Army service. On the other hand, although voluntary, the great majority of Harrovians choose to join. Harrow's record in winning Scholarships to the armed services is second to none and the Rifle Corps provides a fruitful ground for regimental recruiters. The expertise provided by the permanent staff of ex-regulars employed to instruct (officers as well as cadets) and to administer the Rifle Corps is of paramount importance. Camps are varied and challenging. In recent years training has been carried out not only in the UK and Germany but also in Norway, France, Cyprus, Jordan and Brunei; all a far cry from the tented camps at Tweseldown.

Change continues steadily. The Armoury has moved from its original position in the Old Schools to a less public and more secure site. The grand 1910 Parade Ground has been replaced by a new and smaller one below the twenty-five-metre range. The Assault Course has been re-named the Endurance Event – a military rather than School initiative to signify its embrace of an increased range of activity. Yet one thing remains constant, the steady flow of recruits "to rally round the bugle-sound, and join the Rifle Corps".

The House Drill competition

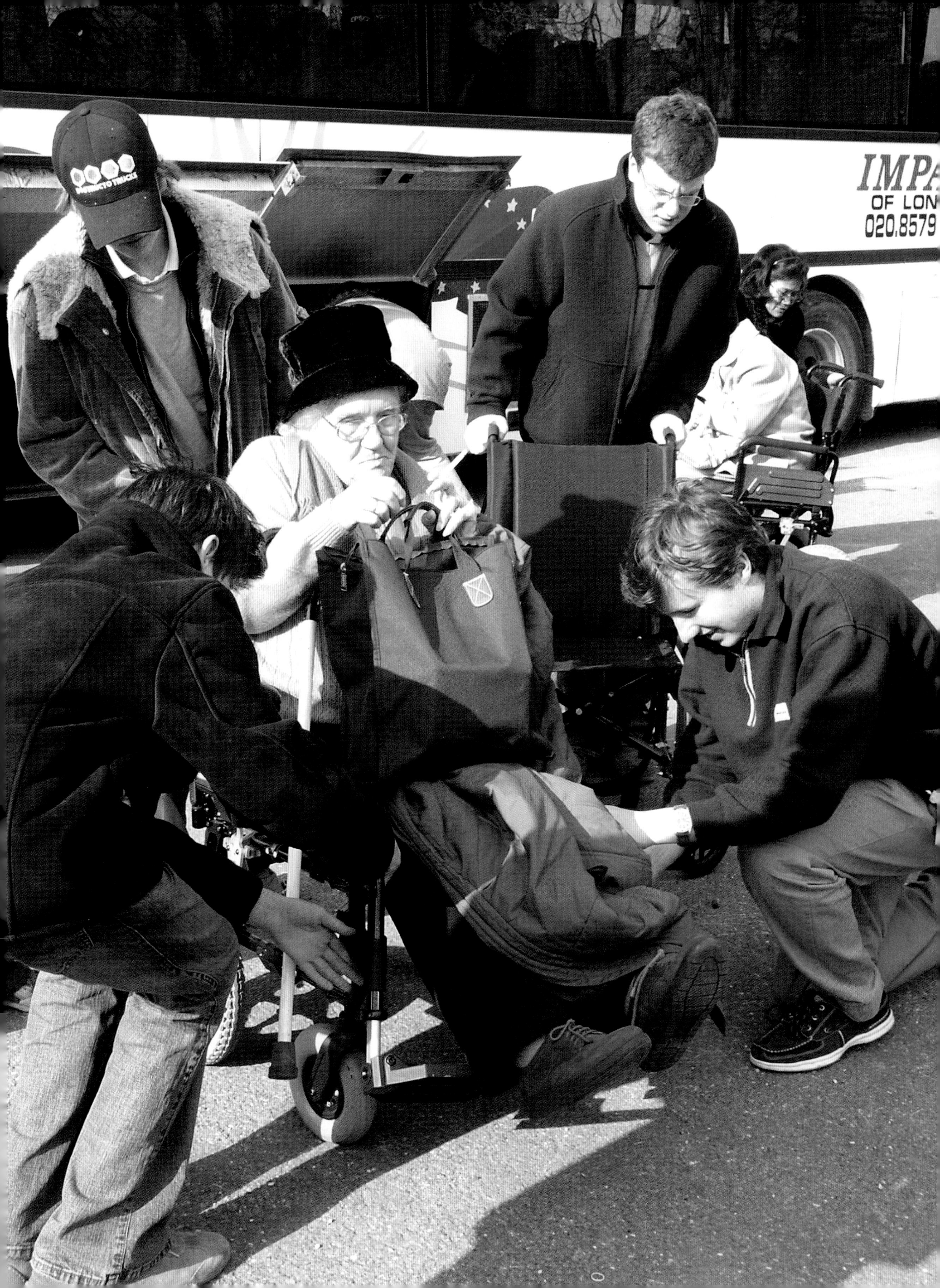
IMPA
OF LON
020.8579

COMMUNITY SERVICE

ALTHOUGH THE CONCEPT OF service to the community, especially those perceived to be in need of help, can be traced back at least to the founding of the Harrow Club (see page 252), Mr Charles Swallow must be credited with starting the community service (then known as 'social service') group in the area of Harrow, soon after his arrival in 1961. Its function was, and continues to be, to provide help for individuals and institutions in the neighbourhood of the Hill. It expanded rapidly from a few seniors in 1963 to about sixty boys by the time Mr Swallow left Harrow in 1973. But there was a dual purpose, the second and equally important part being an educational process for the boys concerned – and also for those not concerned but observers. Most Harrovians of that era had very little idea of how other people lived and their experiences were salutary.

When Mr Swallow left Harrow to teach at Bicester Comprehensive School (and later to be Headmaster of Mount Grace School, Potters Bar), he was succeeded by Mr John Rees who developed Community Service even further. As part of his educational philosophy, Mr Rees encouraged boys to form committees, to make judgements and take decisions. Committees learnt to handle real power and ran three lively fundraising events, bringing the School and the community two minibuses and financial support for various local charities. The fundraising was not intended to be an end in itself but was again seen as a way of educating boys as well as helping the deprived. The Eagles and an NSPCC playgroup called the Gumbies used School facilities; the mentally handicapped at Whittlesea School were visited regularly; there were camping expeditions and annual outings.

In 1979 John Rees was appointed as Headmaster of Blundell's in Tiverton, and Mr Andrew Lee took over; Mr Tim Hersey provided the continuity, vital in an activity where personal contacts are its lifeblood. The 1970s and 1980s were halcyon days for Community Service. 'Health and safety' restrictions were much less intrusive and criminal record checks rarely contemplated. As the privilege of using a bicycle, formerly restricted to School Monitors, was extended to Community Service volunteers, it was altogether easier for boys to move around the borough safely under their own steam. Furthermore the people with whom they worked were themselves less hidebound by the rules and regulations of their own organisations. The idea was prevalent that young people could be trusted, not feared, and that they are a source of idealism, ideas and initiative. For the independent schools as a whole there was a widespread movement in favour of 'voluntary services' and Harrow was prominent among them.

Gardening groups operated in South Harrow helping the elderly; boys assisted with 'Riding for the Disabled' in Northwood; participated in drama and swimming classes with disabled children in local schools and at the leisure centre; rooms were redecorated, furniture shifted for starter homes, and on one memorable occasion a garage-sized equipment shed was shifted from one playground to another at Whittlesea Special School – a job that nowadays 'health & safety' would have strangled at its inception. Boys helped with photography, IT and music in adult day centres and assisted at two after-school or 'latch key' clubs, one in central Harrow and another on the Rayners Lane estate. On two occasions a party took the NSPCC children on holiday in Devon, made possible by Blundell's School and Marks and Spencer's Community Involvement Department, who provided both adult volunteers and food.

After a brief period under Mr Jonathan Fosh, Community Service was taken over by Mr Richard Tucker in 1992. As the constraints of the school day and other considerations began to tighten, work

A Community Service outing

started to focus more on the elderly. Throughout this period Mr David Dawes provided valuable support both as a minibus driver and wise counsellor. He continued to help Mrs Loretta Moseley when she took charge in 1998.

Mrs Moseley has preserved and strengthened Harrow's links into the local community, particularly with the elderly, but also through her own local contacts as a governor of a local primary school. Nowadays around seventy-five boys from the Remove upwards are involved in the School's Community Service programme. All members have chosen this option voluntarily from the School's extra-curricular activities, and several boys do it as part of the Duke of Edinburgh Award scheme.

Although Community Service is timetabled as a Wednesday afternoon activity, older boys are able to do Community Service on any day of the week that suits them and many make their own way to and from their placements. On a typical Wednesday four Masters are involved, driving minibuses on routes through Central Harrow, Kenton and Sudbury Hill. Other boys are driven to placements in Eastcote, North Harrow and Pinner in individual cars.

For many years Field Day was used for some very successful day trips to places of interest. A coach full of the elderly and house-bound, accompanied by boys, set off to places such as Windsor Castle, Blenheim Palace, Bletchley Park, Brighton, Leeds Castle, Oxford, Woburn Abbey, Kew Gardens and Whipsnade Zoo. There were also trips on the River Thames both in and out of London. Unfortunately the recent reduction of Field Day to a half holiday has prevented this from continuing.

Another important activity that has become history was giving supper and chatting to the homeless in the winter night shelter in Harrow; sadly the shelter no longer exists.

'Visiting' is an important and valued Community Service activity. Visits are made to housebound elderly and disabled people in their own homes, and to residential homes, sheltered accommodation and a day care centre for the elderly. These visits include running errands, gardening and generally 'doing jobs that need to be done'.

Once a term, a tea party is held for the national charity, Contact the Elderly. In October 2008 the School was host for a tea party for over 100 local elderly people as part of this scheme. The event was sponsored by Waitrose who provided cakes; the School provided tea and sandwiches; there was live music, and also a "knitathon", encouraging people to knit woollen squares, which were then sent to Indian orphanages where they are made into blankets. The party from the Sudbury Neighbourhood Centre were so inspired by this that they continue sending squares almost eighteen months later!

Weekly visits are made to four local primary schools where boys' contributions include: assisting teachers in the classroom; helping with office routine; helping to run sports and art classes in the after-school programme; listening to children read; and mentoring children with social and behavioural problems on a one-to-one basis.

Boys work in local charity shops, collect money on Alexandra Rose Day in Harrow Town Centre, help with an annual drama day for mentally handicapped children, assist at a local Beaver Scout group on Tuesday evenings…. The litany of activities performed by Community Service is too long to list in full.

Boys planning to read Medicine, Veterinary Science or Dentistry need to show some evidence of Community Service to prove that they are able to communicate well with people of all ages and backgrounds, so there is a large demand for Community Service places in the Sixth Form. In the last ten years any boy applying to a university in the United States has been strongly advised to show evidence of Community Service as this has become part of the selection criteria.

The daytime traffic in modern Harrow and Brent makes access to all the places where Community Service needs to go altogether more difficult than it once was, and the tightness of the programme of the School day has reduced the time available. But this very successful School activity continues to play an important part in helping Harrovians to reflect on the wider society of which they are part. It continues to fulfil the dual role that Charles Swallow envisaged fifty years ago: an education for the boys, igniting a flame that has fired many to engage in civil society well after leaving Harrow; and a service to the community, surely something entirely consistent with the values of the School – and indeed those of its Founder.

Afternoon tea at The Shepherd Churchill Hall; boys providing musical accompaniment for a primary school choir in a retirement home (right)

Facing page: Some 'seniors' are entertained on the Hill

HARROW SONGS

THE TRADITION OF UNITING the School through its Songs owes everything to the happy collaboration of two remarkable men: Mr John Farmer, the pioneer of music at Harrow, and Mr Edward Bowen, Master and poet. To Farmer goes the credit for creating a musical culture that was truly inclusive. On his arrival in 1862, the challenge facing him was formidable. Finding a complete dearth of musical activity, and eager to engage as many boys as possible, he saw communal singing in the evening as the way forward. He faced much opposition, but remained undeterred, and with Bowen founded a tradition that has given generations of Harrovians tunes and lyrics that remain in the blood long after their departure from the Hill.

Of course, the Songs were not introduced for solely musical reasons. The Head Master in John Farmer's day, Dr Montagu Butler, realised their potential for promoting 'good fellowship among boys' and for helping pupils identify and understand the values that bound them together. Much has been written about the power of the Songs to draw the thoughts of Old Harrovians back to their schooldays. It is, however, wrong to believe that the Songs are part of a deliberate policy to brainwash boys with some kind of rose-tinted love for their school, although it is easy to see how such an assumption could be made. Infectious melody and memorable words that enter our consciousness whilst we are young will, inevitably, stay with us forever.

Mr Edward Bowen, author of Forty Years On and many other Songs (above); Mr John Farmer, composer of many Harrow Songs (right)

It is also erroneous to regard the Songs as 'sermons' that convey some uplifting 'message' of high moral purpose; indeed, to do so may be asking more of them than their words can bear. They are, first and foremost, an entertainment in the spirit of the romantic period, and it is perhaps no coincidence that their creator, John Farmer learnt his musical trade in Germany and had worked with Wagner. Two of the most important vocal forms to come out of Germany are the Lutheran Chorale (with its didactic Protestantism) and Lieder (so wonderfully exemplified by Schubert and Schumann). Lieder in particular were conceived as musical entertainment for the home or the salon, enabling people come together to sing solo or part Songs for enjoyment. In this way, they could establish friendships, further their musical education, and consolidate or elevate their social standing. Given his musical training, it is, perhaps, not too fanciful to see Harrow Songs as a product of a genre that John Farmer brought back from Germany, and established here on the Hill.

Many of the earlier Songs are, in effect, a 'call to duty'. School and country become synonymous, and in their yearning after selflessness and high endeavour, the Songs reflect the spirit of 19th century romanticism. Yet, they are unique because they are almost exclusively about Harrow. Their themes touch upon retrospection, love, nature, the insidious encroachment of industrialisation and urbanisation, the struggle of the individual versus the crowd, journeying (physically or spiritually), evolution, conflict, loss, and even the supernatural. This list reads like a resumé of the libretti from a Schubert Song Cycle, or a Byron poem. The themes are quintessentially romantic, and appeal to teenage boys

because they see themselves, of course, as Romantic heroes! The harsh reality of scholarship is meagrely represented in Harrow Songs; it is, after all, hardly a romantic concept, and not necessarily alluring to a typical teenage boy.

John Farmer created a wonderful foundation of Songs, upon which others could build. In the current edition of the Song Book, there are fifty-three Songs. Over thirty are from the pen of Farmer; twenty-nine have lyrics by Bowen. More than twenty of all the Songs are sung regularly by the whole School; others are solos or are revived from time to time by the School XII. Most of the Songs were written before 1920, and the names of Farmer, Faning, and Buck figure large among their composers.

The earliest known Harrow song is *Io Triumphe!* – a hymn of praise to the School in Latin, with a text by Mr BF Westcott (later Bishop of Durham). More Songs in Latin followed, even some in four parts, before John Farmer first collaborated with Bowen in 1867 to produce a song in English about cricket, *Willow the King.* Farmer and Bowen formed an ideal partnership: Bowen's ability to pen lyrics that combined humour, sentimentality and gentle didacticism with a 'boyish' turn of phrase, complemented Farmer's skill as a composer of catchy melodies. Farmer's early experience in Germany shows itself in his work. *Forty Years On, When Raleigh Rose* and *Five Hundred Faces,* have something of a German chorale about them, and there is more than a trace of Schubert in the melodies and accompaniments of many of his other Songs. At the same time, there is something intrinsically British about Farmer's work. Although the Songs of Bowen and Farmer tell of sport and full-blooded endeavour on the playing field, giving robust snapshots of Harrow life, they contain some wonderfully poetic passages too.

Farmer left Harrow in 1885 but before doing so, he collaborated with Bowen to produce one final

Winston Churchill with Dr Moore, Head Master, at Songs in Speech Room, 1942

Churchill Songs at the Royal Albert Hall, 2009

offering that is simply entitled, *Songs.* It is evident that by this date, Songs were fundamental to the corporate life of the school. John Farmer, against the odds initially, had succeeded in establishing a great and potent tradition.

Farmer collaborated with other writers before leaving, most notably with Mr Edmund Howson, to give us *Five Hundred Faces.* After Farmer's departure from Harrow, the task of composing the music fell to Mr Eaton Faning, with texts by Howson and Bowen. The writing is now tauter and less lyrical and the music more martial, perhaps less graceful, but even so, some of the Songs from this time remain firm favourites with current Harrovians. Even the more lyrical *Ducker* and *Here Sir!,* ever popular with the boys, have a more hard-edged, late-Victorian (almost Edwardian) tone. *Left! Right!* is a rousing recruiting song from 1897 that playfully recounts young Brown's progress from cadet to Major General, something more than a few Harrovians of that generation would achieve.

Between 1901 and 1927, Mr Percy Buck (knighted in 1937) was the Director of Music. During these years, more Songs were added, but only the two composed by him are still sung. One of these is a solo song called *You?* with a text by Mr G Townsend Warner. This, the first song to be added to the collection after the Boer War for which young Brown had been recruited, has a poignant and stark opening; Buck's late nineteenth century harmonies, so unmistakably English, point up the sombreness of a text that deals with grief and loss. Percy Buck's *The Silver Arrow,* composed in 1910, remains one of the School's favourites. It has the evocative power, like some stirring piece by Elgar or Holst, to conjure up a sense of nostalgia and patriotism, and raise a lump in the throat of all Englishmen, even if Maltby's text does not quite match the quality of the music.

After the First World War, we have to wait until the 1930s before there are any new Songs. The composer is now Reginald Thatcher, with a new Head Master, Cyril Norwood, writing verses in a style reminiscent of that of Bowen. Indeed, Thatcher's music is closer in style to that of Farmer, and Norwood's verse, echoes, and sometimes quotes from, earlier Songs. Perhaps this retrospection, whether deliberate or not, was an attempt to reassure the School and the nation that the turbulent years were over, and that all would be well again. In a song of 1931 called *The Twentieth Centur-ee,* we are told that today is no worse than yesterday, but just different. *John Lyon's Road* (1932) promises that, despite modernisation and encroaching suburbia, Harrow will remain fertile ground for intellectual growth. Faith in Harrow's permanence is further highlighted in a song of the seasons, *East is East.* Dr Norwood, an educational reformer, was not afraid of instituting change whilst at Harrow. Perhaps his most significant innovation was the introduction of the game of rugby. This did not have an easy passage and controversy over whether or not the game should be played at the School reached the pages of the national press. Thatcher and Bowen then produced a song that places rugby at the heart of life at Harrow; their *Song of the Forwards* is dedicated to the XV of 1932. The last song of these years is *Leavers*, and the Songs themselves are the subject of this unashamedly romantic, nostalgic and sentimental piece. One wonders if Bowen and Thatcher knew that this would be the last Harrow song for some time. Certainly the steady stream of Songs now stops. Perhaps, with the world close to war once again, anything that smacked of untrammelled nationalism was becoming uncomfortably suspect.

In recent years, only a few Songs have been added, and these have usually marked special occasions or events. For example, there is *The Centenarian* with music by Richard Drakeford and words by Mark Warman and Jeremy Lemmon. Several Songs by Richard Walker, in collaboration with Tom Wickson, have been added to the collection. The last song in the current book is one of theirs and it commemorates the refurbishment of the Vaughan Library. That it should do so is a nice irony, for who can say now that our Songs do not celebrate intellectual curiosity?

We all know how good it feels to sing our favourite hymns, many of which were written at the same time as the best-loved Harrow Songs. Why do we enjoy giving voice to such music? Is it that the communal activity of singing with those who share our beliefs and values binds us together more closely, strengthens our resolve, deepens mutual understanding and fosters well-being? Perhaps, but what really matters is that singing is simply good fun, and Harrow is fortunate to have preserved a tradition that gives such pleasure to so many. Boys come together in House, at least once a term, to sing our Songs. The School gathers three or four times a year to sing them to invited guests, especially for Churchill Songs, which celebrate the memory of Sir Winston, who returned to the Hill in the dark days of 1940 to let the Songs lift his spirits. Occasionally, the whole Harrow community of boys, parents and former pupils fills the Royal Albert Hall, to sing the old favourites. As Churchill himself said *....they shine through the memories of men.....They cheer and enlighten us......and I think they are, on the whole, the most precious inheritance of all Harrovians.'*

Harrow Songs are heard the world over. Many schools think that *Forty Years On* is *their* school song, even if they have no idea what the 'tramp of the twenty two men' means; one imagines this line must cause alarm, or perhaps excitement, in those girls' schools that claim the song as their own! Shackleton reported that on his Antarctic Expedition in 1916, the singing of a couple of Harrow Songs had helped to keep up morale, even though there were no Harrovians in his group. In the 1920s, the playing of *Forty Years On* was even used successfully to quell a prison riot.

Thanks to Farmer and Bowen's vision, singing remains an irrefutable force for good at Harrow. What matters above all is that the boys love and cherish Songs that remain with them for the rest of their lives. The Songs have been criticised for being too cultish and demonstrating an unwholesome "grip of the old school at its tightest." Tribalism, however, also has many strengths and in an age when social cohesion and a sense of community seem of secondary importance, may not actually be such a bad thing.

Successive governments have bemoaned the lack of singing in schools, but the finger of accusation cannot be pointed at Harrow. This remarkable, and in many ways unique, choral tradition is both nurtured and sustained.

THE HARROVIAN

THE HARROVIAN IS ONE of very few – possibly the only – *weekly* newspaper published in a British public school. It describes itself as "both an organ of record and a forum for comment, debate and the expression of individual opinion within the School."

It was first published in something like its present form in 1888, rising out of a series of precursor publications such as *Harrow Notes* and *The Tyro*. The School was growing in numbers and in fame and there was a need for an outlet for the pupils' creativity and an urge to record events around them and in the wider world. It was just one example of a school that had found a sense of identity and confidence in itself.

The Harrovian became a weekly publication in the 1930s, under the leadership of Mr Ronnie Watkins, who established a format and style that has continued to this day and has since been copied by other schools. Indeed the fortnightly *Radley Chronicle* – similarly printed on A4 buff-coloured paper – was founded by Luke Bartlett (OH) as recently as in 2004.

In common with other journalistic enterprises, the primary aims of *The Harrovian* are twofold. To begin with, it is a chronicle: there is a conscious effort to capture accounts of important events in the life of the School. There are therefore reports on the big features of the School year. It prints the Head Master's speech on Speech Day, – sometimes verbatim, sometimes in summary; it tries to give a flavour of the atmosphere at Churchill Songs and names the Guest of Honour; it lists the Old Harrovians who played football against their Houses on Founder's Day; it gives a full report and scores of the Eton match at Lord's and so on. Future generations will want to be able to chart the relative fortunes of soccer and rugby sides, as well as finding out as much as possible about which minor sports are flourishing at the time, and which are in decline or dormant. The same principle applies to events in the cultural life of the School. There is an impressive calendar of art exhibitions in the Old Speech Room and Pasmore Galleries; there are many Rattigan Society and House plays, and an impressive programme of concerts and other musical events week by week. *The Harrovian* tries to give as broad a coverage of School activities as possible. It is not just that many of these events are unrecorded elsewhere; they need to be recorded in an easily accessible form, all in one place, where people expect to find them.

The Harrovian also provides information on staff, writing brief notices about new Masters and rather longer ones at their departure. These notices also extend to departing members of the support staff who, either by length of service or force of personality, have made a notable impact on the School.

A caveat on all this is that the editors are heavily reliant on the enthusiasm and efficiency of Masters and others responsible for submitting reports. The reader only has to look back at past numbers to see examples: rugby reports published the following June, a spate of lengthy articles on fly fishing or full bore shooting, no farewell notice for a distinguished and respected leaving Master. Sometimes the long reports are reflections of genuinely flourishing activities, at other times it is the whiff of the printer's ink that has lured the correspondent. Needless to say, the quality of articles varies hugely: the ones that describe in minute detail the menu for breakfast on an expedition are only of interest to the participants – unless they are quite beautifully written.

The second primary aim of *The Harrovian* is to provide a platform where boys may express their own ideas, opinions and views in the dignity of the printed word. A notable feature of the paper is that articles remain anonymous. The maintenance of this tradition ensures that even the most timid writer can express

THE HARROVIAN.

No. 1.] THURSDAY, FEBRUARY 2ND, 1888. [SIXPENCE.

individual views without fear of public personal attack – though they will often have to read criticism of controversial ideas, or ill-thought-out lines of logic, in the following week's edition. The master-in-charge always – and the Editors generally – will know who has written any particular article, but names do not appear on articles in print. Until the mid-1990s, letters could appear under pen names, but today all correspondence must appear above the name of the writer. This has resulted in some reduction in the quantity of correspondence, but generally improved its quality – though it may well be blander than in some past generations.

The Harrovian is edited by a committee of boys who meet each Tuesday evening to put together the edition that will appear on Friday – though still with the traditional publication date of the Saturday. The Editors are a self-perpetuating oligarchy that recruits new colleagues by inviting likely members of the School to write test pieces. If the Editors like these, the writer is asked to join. There is no set number of Editors, but there are usually six to eight. The press of events in current times means that it is rare for all the editors to manage to attend any individual meeting. In recent times there has been a conscious effort to inculcate in the minds of the School that writers write, while Editors edit – thus attracting writers from a wider constituency of School opinion and countering the impression of *The Harrovian* as something only for an intellectual elite.

The Harrovian has been printed in-house since 1992, initially by offset lithography, and currently photocopied. Articles are sent in, usually by email, from a wide variety of sources and made up by Harrow School Desktop Publishing into the galley proofs for the Editors. The finalised pages are printed in the School Office.

The advent of the internet and computer technology has inevitably changed considerably many things about such a venture as producing a school newspaper. The typesetting and page-making are much expedited by modern hard- and software. All boys now have access to a computer and articles are always typed by the writer, rather than presented in manuscript. Several important aspects of the current process have been added though – such as the regular appearance of photographs. While there have long been photographs, even photographic inserts, in the paper, it only with the advent of specialist design software and wide use of digital cameras that photos have become an essential part of the mix, week by week, page by page.

The Harrovian has appeared online since 2006, first via the Harrow Association website and now via the Harrow School website, too. This proves a popular way of looking at the content and has had at least two significant effects: the numbers of paper copies printed weekly has been reduced from over 1,100 to 600, as many boys prefer to read a full-colour version on their computer screens than the black and white version on the buff paper. Also, there are now readers worldwide – many Old Harrovians and parents, but some not, as the email responses prove. The name and fame of Harrow creates its own interest in our doings. Copies of the paper edition are still supplied to the national reference libraries: the British Library, the national libraries of Scotland and Wales and the Universities of Oxford and Cambridge.

Inevitably the feel of *The Harrovian* has changed over the years, reflecting current interests and issues, but also depending upon the style and the enthusiasms of each generation of writers. A strength of the publication is the way it can in turns be serious or trivial, social or philosophical, sporting or artistic. The master-in-charge must always motivate but moderate, and the Head Master exercises a role as censor of last resort.

Perhaps it is a sense of history that motivates many of the current writers. The fact that researchers so often turn to back numbers of *The Harrovian* to find out what previous generations were thinking and doing, places a responsibility on the editors beyond that of the weekly essay. What the future knows of us will be derived firstly from pages, so often hurriedly written, but ultimately a record of contemporary thought and comment: steps along John Lyon's Road, "a path… that never should be undone."

Masthead of the first of the new series of The Harrovian, *published in 1888*

THE SCHOOL FARM

IN A PAPER WRITTEN around 1945, Mr DM Reid, the Senior Biology Master, explained the genesis of the Farm. It sprang out of his belief in the need for fieldwork in his teaching. Reid was 'anti-games' and he opens his paper with an extended whinge about the extra-curricular arrangements for boys at the time. "Most boys are countrymen", he claimed and deplored the fact that "purely artificial, non-country pursuits such as highly organised games, in which all were compelled to indulge to such an inordinate extent, could not really satisfy more than a small proportion of them." His first attempts to persuade the Head Master (Dr Vellacott) of this gained him a plot of land below the Music Schools for experimental purposes, but his ambitions went well beyond just that.

The prospect of war in 1939 and the possibility of food supply shortages gave Reid another opportunity and he proposed to the Head Master (by then AP Boissier) that he should attempt to cultivate and raise crops on some of the School's waste land: he was given "the unwanted lower part of the Park garden." The ground was too poor to yield any worthwhile crops, although they did grow some swedes and potatoes, which they sold. Part of the soil was spade-turned – a laborious task; he acquired a pony plough (but no pony), which the boys returning from footer were persuaded to haul through the clay with a long rope. By this time Reid had about a dozen 'regulars', but "the work was so hard and the rewards so meagre that I often wondered why they stuck it, especially as implements were so scarce (due to lack of money)."

Reid's next move was to take over an old pigsty in the Park garden; it was too small for a cow shed but Reid managed to buy two Dexter heifers – a small breed which could be accommodated there. He also acquired an old tractor and a cut-down horse-mower and was given the use of the Deynecourt field for hay. This little patch of grass was supplemented by scythe-cut grass from the orchard of the Head Master's house.

Beset by obstacles at every turn and what he perceived as lack of cooperation from the three Head Masters of this period, Reid next bought a Dexter bullock. "Two boys and I went off in a lorry to a Dexter breeder and bought a calf – a tiny fellow – for thirty-five shillings".

His eye then lit on three fields below Kennet End where there was an old steading, belonging to the School but let for a nominal sum to the Vicar for grazing two ageing horses. The Head Master was unwilling to remove the Vicar's horses but Reid pointed out to him that the War Agricultural Committee was likely to requisition the fields and so once more he got his way. Boy labour was again used to hedge and ditch and eventually bring the land under control.

With this achieved, two more Dexter heifers were added and a few home-bred calves, a dozen head of poultry and some pigs; the area did begin to resemble a farm. By this time the war was in full swing "with bombs dropping all around us on many nights." With the arrival of Dr Moore as Head Master, he felt he was at last getting some support: he was repaid some of the money he had personally spent and was lent some of the Head Master's gardeners to help with the milking (boys at that stage not being allowed out of their Houses to help). Later Moore agreed to the employment of a cowman and following the purchase of some "full-size" cows a milk round was started and some income gained at last.

For Reid, teaching by day, fire-watching at night and farming early mornings and late evenings made for a demanding schedule. "I was now feeling the strain," he wrote, "of so many activities and combating so many difficulties that my health began to suffer and sometimes I had to spend an hour or two in bed in the afternoon. It was during one such period that the

There are about forty head of longhorn cattle and a flock of the same number of Shetland sheep. They are reared both for slaughter and for breeding.

Head Master telephoned to say that he had two visitors who wanted to see over the Farm. "I went and met the Headmaster of St Columba's College, Dublin, and a young master of his staff. As we sauntered back across the fields, I discovered that the younger man knew all about farming, that he taught mathematics and that he would be delighted to come to Harrow on the Hill. So it was that Sidney Patterson was added to the stock of what was now Harrow School Farm."

Mr Sidney Patterson was appointed Director of the Farm in 1944. In due course Perrins Farm on the Ducker Road, amounting to 155 acres including the football fields, was repossessed by the School. "It has turned into a great educational asset", wrote a Governor, Sir Lancelot Royle, in 1949, "and the School as a whole has come to accept agriculture as part of its activities; at present there are no fewer than eighty boys that are expert in the use of milking machines and are accustomed to the management of cattle and pigs."

The stock by then had grown to a herd of 37 Dairy Shorthorn Milch cows, two pedigree bulls, 24 calves, a herd of 69 pedigree Essex pigs, 300 head of poultry and a flock of 34 sheep. There was a farm committee of four Masters and fifteen boys; there were also two full-time farm dairymen. Houses took turns to send a team of volunteers at 5.40 each morning to help with milking and routine jobs; many also helped in the afternoons. Old Harrovians were generous in donating money for buildings, including a new pig-house and much of the other construction work was done by boys. However the profit of £22 on the year was a poor return on the Governors' investment of £10,000.

Some of the longhorn cattle on the School Farm

In addition to the Farm there was also a Farmers' Club which had its own small room on the first floor of The Hill (the School tuck shop at the time) with comfortable chairs and farming magazines to read. Meetings were also held there with talks from outside speakers and boys.

This period was probably the peak time in the Farm's life, in activity and in educational benefit. The only thing it did not do was to make any money. Even boys who had nothing to do with the Farm would be aware of its existence, either by having to dodge their way through the herd on the way to Ducker or by experiencing an unexpectedly soft landing following a tackle on Sheepcote 1.

When Mr Patterson became House Master of The Grove in 1958 he was succeeded as Farm Director by George Parrott. This was a poisoned chalice: the Governors could not decide whether they wanted the Farm to be educational or to make a profit. They ended up by doing neither: gradually the grazing area was reduced, as football fields were up-graded and the creation of the golf course, begun in 1973, reduced it further. The herd was also reduced, supplying less milk. The pigs and chickens went and Mr Parrott's milk round became a delivery of yogurts and orange juice to fewer and fewer houses. Mr Parrott, besides teaching Biology, busied himself with other country pursuits: angling, fly-tying, clay pigeon shooting and riding, before leaving in 1980 to take over an inherited estate in Scotland.

The Farm Committee, 1954

Facing page: Early morning work at the farm

Mr Andrew Hunter took over as caretaker but, as an amateur, relied heavily on the expertise and experience of Tom Loftus, who had been herdsman for thirty-eight years. Some of the old football fields were regained for hay and 10,000 bales were cut in 1981, 4,000 of them by volunteer boys in the summer holidays. The herd was increased to thirty-five milking cows producing 184,000 litres of milk and home grown heifers were introduced.

Mr Peter Harries arrived as the new manager in 1982 and a new herdsman, Mr Tom Perkins, a year later. He injected new life into the Farm. A new pasteuriser was acquired and eighty gallons of milk were sent to the Shepherd Churchill Hall each day. Among innovations were a large tractor and muck-spreader and a new winter shed. Although Mr Harries only stayed for four years, he did much to implement modern farming techniques at Harrow. His successor was Charles Lesley. A new herring bone milking parlour was installed, the herd increased to sixty head and bull beef was also expanded. But this was a time of political turmoil: Mr Lesley left to return as a tenant farmer, but faced continuing problems. Improvements to the Upper Redding field removed a valuable source of silage and reduced his winter forage by 20%. He disposed of the School's milk quota – unfortunately at the bottom of the market – and the herd was sold off too. Tom Perkins introduced proper animal husbandry, and the turkeys, Gressingham ducks and the new stock, which included some rare breeds, created a great deal of interest. However the Farm continued to make a loss and Charles Lesley departed.

Tom Perkins took charge of the Farm in 2002 as an employee of the School, combining the job with that of forester. Mr Perkins's research into 'alternative farming' came to the inevitable conclusion: the School farm could never be a commercial proposition. In 2003 it became a 'conservation area' operating a grazing programme to manage grasslands under the direction of Natural England. There are about forty head of long horn cattle and a flock of the same size of Shetland sheep. These are reared both for slaughter and for breeding. The animals are also taken to graze two areas at Ruislip Woods and Horsenden Hill under the scheme. The acquisition of some laying hens was a disaster: some were taken by a fox and the rest by human predators. Security of both equipment and livestock is a serious problem.

All new boys visit the Farm as part of their introduction to School activities but regular farmers are far fewer than in earlier years. Some go as a Duke of Edinburgh Award activity; others as work experience before applying for a veterinary course; few boys, it seems, are planning a career in farming. But working with animals is therapeutic and the Farm is an escape from the pressures of the School life, a haven of informality and tranquillity; and it is just ten miles from Marble Arch: an asset indeed.

CONTIO LATINA

THE 1670s, WITH HINDSIGHT a momentous decade in Harrow's history, saw the origins of three traditions central to the ethos of the School. First, the revival of archery was greeted with great enthusiasm and marked before the turn of the century by Sir Gilbert Talbot's gift of the Silver Arrow "to be shot for by twelve young Gentlemen". Second, the creation of the post of Custos (Adkins being the first), and, third, the first 'Oration' or 'Contio Latina', delivered in 1674 by John Dennis. Each of these traditions in some way reflected the wider appeal of the classical ideals and imagery that were so fashionable in Europe following the Renaissance (consider the paintings of Poussin or Claude). Though films like *Gladiator* and *Troy* perhaps fail to carry enough weight as to amount to a classical revival, nevertheless the Contio has survived, more or less intact, to the present day and shows no signs of dying off anytime soon.

From the outset, in an age when Head Master Hide in the 1650s had encouraged oratory in Latin among his scholars, the Contio was first and foremost a demonstration of linguistic flair and oratorical ability. It was only in the nineteenth century that the Orator was required to be the Head of School and until then prowess as a classical scholar would be the main criterion for selection. Thus John Dennis went on to study at Caius College, Cambridge (for two years at least – he was later sent down for sword-fighting). The earliest Orators would receive payment for their efforts: the second Orator, Woodcock, received ten shillings for a pair of gloves. From the time of Head Master Heath in the 1770s the Orator received a classical text from the Chairman of Governors, much as present day Orators are presented with a book.

Although it is no longer the custom to stand in silence to hear the Contio, as was still expected as late as the 1920s, the ceremonial aspects of the event remain pretty much unchanged. The traditional elements of the Contio are that it should be a record of the events of the year, both within and beyond Harrow, that it should be held on the second Saturday in November to coincide with the Governors' meeting, which was originally the official 'annual audit meeting', and that it should be delivered in Latin.

Not all Governors or Head Masters have accepted these fundamental tenets, however. In the 1720s one of many gaps in the tradition occurred, this one being a result of the Governors' decision to move their audit meeting for social reasons to Lady Day, which fell in the Easter holiday. In 1895 Head Master Welldon, a vigorous reformer, suggested abolition but was sternly rebutted and in 1924 under Head Master Ford (who was unjustly blamed for the controversy) the Chairman of Governors, Walter Long, also expressed his intention to abolish the tradition. Although there was no Contio that year, a compromise was agreed for the following year: the Contio was delivered in English. This never happened again and 1926 saw the tradition restored in all its Latin glory.

A cursory glance at the list of 'Oratores' that appears in the opening pages of the Contio, would be enough to dampen the zeal of any future reformer that might consider ending the tradition. There are some stellar names to be found here. Many of the great Harrow families adorn the list: five Drurys in the nineteenth century, together with a famous scion of that family, Herman Merivale, who was Professor of Political Economy at Oxford in the 1830s and a distinguished civil servant; GO Trevelyan, father of the more famous historian, GM Trevelyan, but a distinguished statesman and author in his own right, gave the Contio in 1857; JE Bourchier, who later founded four annual prizes "for the encouragement of the Study of Modern History and English Literature," gave the Contio in 1863; of the Butler family, future Head Master Henry Montagu Butler (son of George Butler, Head Master

1805–1829) delivered the Contio in 1851; his son, the historian Sir James Butler, was Orator in 1907 and FER Butler (no relation of the foregoing, now Lord Butler of Brockwell and author of the Butler Report on the Iraq War) composed his own Contio in 1956.

Although it is no longer a requirement that the Head of School should compose his Contio, that honour falling instead to members of the Classics department, a considerable number in relatively recent years have. As well as Lord Butler, there have been PAG Stilwell (1964), later House Master of The Grove, WGS Massey QC (1971), currently a Governor, and, most recently, S-DR Liddle (2003), who went on to win the top First in Classics at Oxford in 2009. WGS and PWE Massey (2000) belong to another very select list: fathers and their sons who have both delivered a Contio.

It is quite clear that the grandeur and longevity of the Contio now carry a weight which renders any suggestion of its abolition half-hearted at best. Anyone who has witnessed Contio would testify to the austere magnificence of the occasion. The whole School wear tails. The Orator himself is resplendent in evening tail coat, wing collar and white-tie. The original function of the event, to avail the Governors of the year's events, is reflected in the ritual distribution of copies of the Contio to the Governors by the Head of School. The speech is also greeted with a formal vote of thanks from the Chairman of the Governors. For many in recent years the preference has been to respond in English, though lately the Chairman has revived the graceful tradition of responding in Latin.

The text of the Contio also follows a fairly routine pattern: it begins with the rhetorical device known as *recusatio*, a sort of disingenuous apology-in-advance for its own meagreness, often accompanied by marks of respect directed to previous Oratores; the official welcome to the Governors is then followed by summaries of foreign affairs, key events in the UK and the principal academic, sporting and cultural achievements of the year at the School. Sometimes these sections occur in sequence; at others the events are mixed together (usually when they are subsumed by the requirements of some Classical theme). It is customary to quote classical authors, to make mythological and historical classical allusions and to pun mercilessly and badly.

In the golden age of classical learning it is very likely that some Governors and Masters were able to translate the Latin (and the occasional bit of Greek) more or less effectively without the aid of a translation. Nevertheless there is little doubt that the event has regularly been met with the pretence of understanding in those with little Latin and less Greek. In the days when all boys studied Latin at least up to O-level (now GCSE), it was an expected practice that the text would have been translated in school. For many years that has not been the case and, fortunately for all involved, since the early 1980s the Contio has been printed with an English translation parallel to the Latin text. In addition, the role of explanatory footnotes has expanded over the years. In the early twentieth century they acted as a roll of honour, giving names of scholars, successful Oxbridge applicants, retiring Masters and new appointments. Now the tendency is towards more extensive footnotes to explain references that cannot be made in the body of the text because they would place too much strain on the Latin. However, the relationship between the Latin text and the English translation is often quite (sometimes very) loose. In recent years Heads of Classics have tended to cite authors and texts currently being read by Harrovian students of Latin and Greek, to keep them on their toes. Other innovations are the inclusion of images and one Orator who managed to weave a Bob Dylan number into his Contio, accompanying himself on the guitar.

While these developments have served to keep the event engaging and to make it more digestible, most Harrovians and Governors, upon witnessing the Contio for the first time, remain impressed by the solemnity of the occasion, by the novelty of hearing an extended piece of spoken Latin and by the perspective it gives on the rich heritage and tradition of the School.

Contio, 2008: HMM Turner, Head of School

THE PHILATHLETIC CLUB AND THE GUILD

SCHOOL SPORT IN THE early part of the nineteenth century must have been rather informal. It was not until 1865 that the laws of football were actually written down. Even that champion of games, Mr Edward Bowen, author of many School Songs with a sporting theme, thought that Masters should interfere as little as possible in the running of games. To introduce a modicum of order, in 1852–3 the Head Master, Dr Vaughan, devised the Philathletic Club to organise school sport. The Club, comprising the leading games players in the School, was thus responsible for appointing captains of games, for the draws for House matches and competitions, for resolving disputes and for electing new members. The captains of the major sports (cricket, football and later rugby) were *ex officio* members. The captains were responsible for arranging fixtures, selecting teams and awarding 'flannels'. Elections were made by a committee of five, consisting of the President (Head of School *ex officio*), the captains of the three major games and a 'minor games representative'. Voting was by secret ballot, one black ball to exclude.

The Guild, 2003

As the sporting hero cult began to take hold, members of the Phil became increasingly powerful. With their distinctive black bow ties and their right to walk down the middle of the street, a privilege abandoned only with the arrival of motor traffic, they acquired a status superior to that of the School Monitor. They also held considerable authority as they were allowed to punish offenders – and not only on issues concerned with sport.

In the 1930s the Head Master had begun to appoint some distinguished sportsmen to the teaching staff, largely for their coaching skills. Inevitably they began to take control of the organisation. By the 1950s the increase in the number of fixtures and the complexities of the calendar began to place demands for organisational skills and analysis on the captains, qualities not necessarily enjoyed by the young men with those responsibilities, and Masters began to play an increasingly important part. Under Dr James the position of the School Monitor was progressively enhanced, leaving the Phil as a purely consultative body. By the 1960s there were already questions being asked about its very existence, but Dr James, after consulting two Masters who had themselves been members of the Phil, decided against abolition with the risk of infuriating some influential Old Harrovians.

There had no doubt always been an element of corruption in a boy-run organisation where feelings could run high over such an emotive issue as games at a time when they were considered to be so important. There was often a suggestion that members might be electing their chums rather than strictly on merit. That is not to say that Masters were any less corrupt. One House Master at this time was known to have excused his fast bowler from morning school so that

...in 1852-3 Head Master Vaughan devised the Philathletic Club to organise School sport ... in 1987 Head Master Beer formed The Guild, a parallel club for those who had made a conspicuous contribution to School life outside sport.

he could rest up and be fresh for the House match in the afternoon!

Matters came to a head in 1987 when the Phil committee refused to elect the Captain of both Rackets and Tennis and again in 1991 when they refused the Captain of Football – presumably because they just didn't like them. At this point Head Master Beer intervened: again the future of the Phil was questioned and again abolition was proposed. This time Mr Beer decided on a different tack: he clearly thought the Phil was harmless and that abolition would cause more upset than it was worth. He was happy to allow the Phil to remain honorific but he was also aware that the age of the cult of games was passing and that he could do something to redress the balance. He formed the Guild, a parallel club for those who had made a conspicuous contribution to School life outside sport. Thus the leading musicians, actors and artists became members but service to the Farm, for example, was also recognised.

Mr Beer also removed the responsibility for election from the members. Nominations from Masters in charge of games and other activities were to be made to the Second Master, who would decide on recommendations to be made to the Head Master.

The Guild could wear claret ties with the School lion crest in School dress and claret waistcoats on Sundays. They were given use of a room in the War Memorial building; it might be airless but honour was satisfied. It was another twenty years before the much coveted bow tie was extended to the Guild.

The Philathletic Club, 2004

THE JOHN LYON SCHOOL

WHEN ELIZABETH I GRANTED A charter to John Lyon in 1572, it was for a free grammar school for the boys of the parish of Harrow, and it is this feature that led to the foundation of the later institution, The John Lyon School, the only school in the Harrow Foundation to bear the original benefactor's name.

Over the centuries, as Harrow School developed, prospered and sometimes retrenched, it grew further from Lyon's initial intentions and from the terms of the official charter. By the nineteenth century, obtaining a place at the School had more to do with wealth and title than need and proximity. In an early and pleasing example of parent power, Harrow's most impressive of Head Masters, Dr Vaughan, had his life made uncomfortable by the volume of local complainants against the admissions policy. His response was to suggest to the Governors that they should overcome the objections by establishing a separate school and paying its master. This the Governors refused to do, so Vaughan, to his credit and at his own expense, started the English Form the following year, in 1853.

The English Form comprised up to thirty neighbourhood boys taught by Mr Hutchinson, nephew of the poet Wordsworth, in a converted shed known, with proper honesty, as 'The Barn'. It stood on the High Street and had its own gated grounds and climbable tree.

Dissatisfaction in Harrow, however, was not unique. Complaints about the policies and behaviour of charitable schools came from many quarters and in 1861 a Commission, headed by Lord Clarendon, launched an investigation. This led to the 1868 Public Schools Act, requiring such schools to regularise their structures and activities. Harrow School's response was not to change, but to make such adjustments as allowed it to continue the tenor of its ways in as unchanged a way as possible. The concession was to turn the English Form into an actual school, at first given – with arresting condescension – the name of the 'Under-School of John Lyon'. This soon became the 'Lower School of John Lyon' with the opening in 1876 of a designated building, now and for generations known as the Old Building, in Middle Road.

The Lower School, which even then frequently referred to itself as The John Lyon School, shared its Governors with Harrow and in time shared use of several of the same facilities, but it operated as a separate entity with its own staff. From 1889, answerable to the Governors and including two of them, it had its own Committee of Management. It was a six-day-a-week school and the curriculum neatly bridged the requirements of everyday commercial life and university admissions: English, Latin, Modern Languages, History, Geography, Maths, Natural Science and Writing. Seventy-five years later, apart from Natural Sciences, which had early broadened into Chemistry, Physics and Biology, the curriculum had hardly changed. Much else had.

The thirty boys accommodated in The Barn (who were clearly accepted as Old Lyonians once the School was established) had increased to over a hundred by the 1890s and a measure of academic success at the highest level was not long coming. In the same decade, HA Cram, who was Head Boy, came second out of nearly 5,000 in the Cambridge Physical Geography examination while, around the same time, a boy called Bartlett sat sixteen science and arts examinations at one go and passed the lot, gaining a National Science Scholarship.

Though not in the original prescription, sport featured significantly from early in the school's life with Association football being adopted as the winter game. The first record of football colours being awarded occurred in 1894, the same year that the cricket team

The John Lyon School

played eighteen matches. Earlier still, in the days of The Barn, the boys informed Mr Gregg, their then Headmaster, that permission had been given for them to play cricket on Harrow's VI Form Ground and he joined them there for the game. In fact no permission had been given and poor Gregg found himself embroiled in the almighty row that followed.

As the twentieth century began, numbers at John Lyon were reduced from 145 to no more than a hundred, owing to the financial pressures felt by the Harrow Governors. Not much later, however, they rented the Baptist chapel on Byron Hill to allow numbers to increase once more. A keen cycling club, regular extra-curricular lectures on a wide range of topics especially foreign lands, and visits to places of interest from the gasworks to Fishmongers' Hall, were added to the opportunities available to the boys. Drama, music, a rifle club and a scientific society, as well as monthly detentions, feature on the school calendar as 1910 approaches and fees were raised to £10 a year for parishioners, £12 for those from further afield. One of the latter, a boy called Stillman, travelled daily back and forth from Hounslow and the school calculated that he covered 4,700 miles a year doing so.

The Old Lyonian Association, separate from the OL Football and Drama Societies, and with extensive facilities on the Hill, came into existence in 1902 – six years before the formation of the Harrow Association.

The Lower School of John Lyon, 1894

The Great War took a toll of young Lyonian lives as it did of thousands of others across Europe. Both the brilliant Cram and the much-travelled Stillman were among the more than fifty former pupils killed.

In the decade following the war, changes occurred. The school magazine, a commercially-run affair sold for twopence, increased its price while reducing its regularity from eight times a year to five times; the Governors increased their annual sponsorship from £400 a year to £600 a year and fees to parents increased, this time to £15 a year; for the first time Speech Day was held, not in the Public Hall on the High Street as previously, but in Harrow's Speech Room; and the schoolyard, clinker until now, was finally asphalted.

In 1926 EH Butt retired as Headmaster. For the first century of its life, there was notable continuity (or introspection, depending how you regard it) in the Lower School's leadership. Gregg continued to teach at the school long after he had been superseded by Young. Butt arrived while Gregg was still at the helm and served through the whole of Young's headship. And OA Le Beau, a polymath with arts and science degrees and a Fellowship of the British Astronomical Association, conferred on him at the age of sixteen when he discovered a new star, succeeded Butt in 1926, having already taught at the school for fifteen years. Le Beau was to serve as Headmaster for the next quarter of a century and to continue to teach astronomy at Harrow until his death in 1975.

Early in Le Beau's headship, the next major development occurred with the construction of the New Building, comprising a large assembly hall, doubling as a gym, science labs and further classrooms. It was opened in 1930.

By then the school uniform was well established: navy blue blazer with crest on the breast pocket, white shirt, diagonally striped blue and maroon tie and grey trousers, short or long according to age. Monitors and those with sports colours wore a larger and more impressive pocket badge, the rampant lion and outline of the shield in gold and a bar across the lower part of the shield bearing initials for whatever honours were denoted: M for Monitor, F for football colours, B for boxing and so on. Those senior boys awarded House Colours for their services substituted a single colour tie, denoting their House, for the usual school one. And Prefects, lower than Monitors and consequently often stricter, marked their importance with a small red lion worn on the left lapel of their blazer. This uniform and its variations remained in force until the 1990s, with school caps – the first item of uniform ever stipulated – abolished for sixth formers in 1956 and for all boys, thirteen years later. Sixth formers gave up blazers, and impressive badges, for suits in 2000.

As the New Building opened, the Governors announced that ten acres of land at Sudbury had been acquired for the John Lyon Sports Ground and money-raising began to build the first pavilion, since twice replaced. Until then, boys had used the Philathletic Ground, the large field on the other side of Lower Road from the school, three afternoons a week for games and from 1933 they regularly used the Harrow School 'Bowling Shed' for cricket practice.

Pressure for places at John Lyon continued to increase and more space was urgently needed, answered in 1935 by a substantial extension to the New Building.

Throughout the 1930s the School Cadet Force retained the countywide Lucas-Tooth Championship for combined physical and parade ground drill and among several other competitions won, it took first place in the country in the Lady West Competition of 1937.

Two years later the Headmaster was elected to the Head Masters' Conference; and with the outbreak of war found "almost daily Old Boys in the services spend an hour of their leave with us". The first of many boys to be lost, most of them only a year or two out of school, was a young pilot killed in December 1939. They, and their comrades killed in the First World War, were to be commemorated by a fine new Memorial Library, opened with touching solemnity in 1950.

School numbers increased to around 400 and, under the new Headmaster, Boyd Campbell, who took over in 1951, further physical expansion was undertaken. A small building housing a Biology lab, a classroom and rooms for the Cadet Force and the Ambulance Section – all first aid in the school was in the hands of boys trained by St John Ambulance – had just been erected; and later a new pavilion at Sudbury was opened by Sir Stanley Rous, Chairman of the Football Association. Around the same time the Red House, across the road from the school, was acquired and here the Headmaster and Secretary, Sixth Form and First Forms were moved. In the garden an octagonal chamber for music and drama was built. Drama had featured, often with a play performed in French, at successive Speech Days until the war, and in 1954 had been revived by the boys themselves. Music, always popular in the school, advanced with personal tuition in a range of instruments, then further by the development of a Motet Choir of international repute which sings and has sung in cathedrals and halls across Europe, the States and the UK. From 1960, boys started participating in the Duke of Edinburgh Award scheme, which became a useful and challenging alternative when, to the regret of many, the Cadet Force was closed down in 1976.

Gymnastics had been taken to a new level by sports master and then current Olympian, George Weedon, with the John Lyon team frequently winning the Schools' South of England Championship.

The closure in 1959 of the Mercers' School in Barnard's Inn, Holborn, brought a number of boys and one staff member to The John Lyon School. The story of the latter, which formally took the name in 1965, is of steadily increasing growth in numbers, facilities and breadth of syllabus and activities.

As numbers increased, so did construction. Oldfield House, on the site of a former large house at the end of Crown Street, and built to house all the lower forms, opened in 1981; the Lyon Building, containing several more classrooms and the Boyd Campbell Hall for assemblies and some performances, opened in 1990. Its one drawback was that it obscured for ever the panoramic view from the schoolyard westwards across neighbouring counties.

Next, during the Headship of Tim Wright, came the splendid Sports Centre development with its indoor pool, volleyball and basketball courts and much else besides. This was opened in 1997 by the Duke of Edinburgh, his presence being a recognition of the fact that at ceremonies where the awards in his name were presented, the largest contingent, usually more than half of the total, came from The John Lyon School.

Further extension to the New Building, renamed the Main Building, now unrecognisable to those who knew it originally, was completed in 2008. It provides state-of-the-art science laboratories and two drama studios, as befits a school which, according to those league tables we all so dislike, is number one in the country for Drama.

In 2010 The John Lyon School remains an all-boy, day school; it has six hundred pupils, now of wide ethnic origins, drawn from across northwest London; it is highly academic, but includes some outstanding sportsmen, artists, musicians and actors. It is known for its pastoral care and generation after generation has commented on the pervading atmosphere of friendliness. The school is managed by its own Governors; the number of teaching staff has grown from the four with which the school began to sixty-three and in 2009 it was the first boys' independent school in Britain to appoint a female Head, Miss Katherine Haynes.

HARROW INTERNATIONAL SCHOOLS

HARROW INTERNATIONAL SCHOOL Bangkok was founded in 1998, Harrow International School Beijing in 2005 and Harrow International School Hong Kong is due to open in August 2012. Those are the bare facts, but behind the facts lies a story of determination, fortitude, faith – and luck.

The seed for Harrow International Schools was sown in 1989 when the Bursar, Michael Liddiard, was on a visit to the Far East in connection with the Summer School. The initial interest came from Japan and Korea, but after protracted negotiations the decision was taken to open a school in Bangkok, backed by Japanese business interests. The concept of the English Public School was well established in Thailand where there was a long tradition of the princes being educated at Harrow. Although there were international and British schools around the world, the idea of a British independent school establishing a satellite school in the Far East, using its name and 'brand', was almost unheard of, and there was much soul-searching among the Governors: there were fears of "diluting the brand", concern about being able to transfer Harrow standards to a foreign culture, and, most importantly, doubts about the financial wisdom of the proposal. Sir John Akehurst, Chairman of Governors at the time, must be credited with having the belief to take the idea forward.

Harrow International Schools: Principal, Dr Mark Hensman (below left) and Proprietor, Mr Daniel Chiu (below right)

Facing page: Harrow International School, Bangkok

Having gained the agreement of the Harrow Governors to open a school in Bangkok, a Head Master, Mr Stuart Morris, was appointed. Eight intrepid pioneers, Stuart and Sue Morris, David and Sue Foster, Mike and Caroline Elmitt, Matthew Farthing and Carole Ann Eastgate, arrived in Bangkok in January 1998. The timing was unfortunate: an economic recession was taking grip in Asia; the Japanese backer did not have the financial resources to withstand it, the site selected for the school proved to be unobtainable as the owner of one small plot of land in the middle would not sell, and the fledgling school was left stranded. A potential disaster loomed.

The enterprise of Stuart Morris saved the day: gaining support from the small group of founding parents, he identified a condominium as a suitable site and opened a language centre. And then came a lucky break: one of the founding parents was Mrs Chiu, whose husband was a well known and successful Hong Kong entrepreneur. Mr Daniel Chiu liked what he saw and agreed to provide financial backing for a school. Within thirty days two floors of the condominium block were converted, capital was made available, teachers were able to be paid and Harrow International School Bangkok opened in September 1998 with around 100 pupils.

By 2002 the number of pupils had increased to 800 and the school had outgrown the premises, which had always been considered temporary. A permanent site was purchased in the northern part of the city and a beautiful new school was built in ten months. Stuart Morris left

Harrow International School, Beijing

the school to found Shrewsbury International School in Bangkok and Dr Mark Hensman was appointed Head Master, a post he held for the next seven years. During those years the school became established at its new site as a day school of 1,200 students, with a significant boarding element. The school's remarkable growth in the early years reflected a sudden increase in demand by Thais for places in international schools in Thailand. Consequently the school started with a high proportion of Thai students and even today, 68% of the students are Thai. The next largest nationality is British with 12% with the remainder comprising 32 other nationalities. In recognition of its Harrow School origins, the day houses were named Churchill, Byron, Nehru and Sonakul (after Chatu Mongul Sonakul, a distinguished Thai OH) and the boarding houses, The Knoll and Bradbys. At the new site it was possible to broaden the scope of the co-curricular activities, particularly in sport and music.

The school celebrated its tenth anniversary in 2008. The emphasis has been on high academic performance, broad co-curricular opportunities and strong pastoral care. The success of the academic programme has been borne out by excellent university placements, mainly in Russell Group universities in the UK. It is not possible – or even desirable – to replicate the customs and practices of a UK 'all boy' secondary boarding school in a day/boarding school of pupils aged 3–18 on the other side of the world. It is possible, however, to replicate excellence, achievement and style. In August 2009, Mr Kevin Riley, previously Head of The John Lyon School in England, was appointed Head Master of Harrow Bangkok, while Mark Hensman became Executive and Chief Operations Officer of Harrow Schools International.

Encouraged and emboldened by the success of Harrow Bangkok, the Governors and Mr Chiu turned their eyes towards mainland China where Mr Chiu already had considerable business interests. China is a country with huge opportunities for international schools and Beijing was an obvious choice for a Harrow school. Mr Matthew Farthing, one of the original intrepid pioneers and Director of Studies in Bangkok for seven years, was appointed Head Master. His first challenge was to convert an old, dilapidated Chinese Middle School into a modern attractive campus. This took some doing but in August 2005, an 11–18 co-educational day school opened with about fifty pupils. It was the birth of Harrow International School Beijing. Since then, a primary school was opened in 2008, and the roll has grown to 350 pupils. Under Chinese law, Chinese nationals are unable to enter an international school unless they have a foreign passport. As a result, the proportion of Chinese students at Harrow Beijing is less than the proportion of Thai students in Harrow Bangkok: approximately 20% are Chinese, 16% British, 14% Korean and the remainder a mix of thirty-six other nationalities. The plan is that, eventually, a new campus integrating primary and secondary schools will be built on this site. As in Bangkok, reflections of Harrow School can be seen with pupils wearing bluers and straw hats. Also as at Harrow Bangkok, high academic standards leading to excellent university placements, a broad co-curricular programme and strong pastoral care networks are in evidence.

In 2009 the Hong Kong government made available a site for a boarding school in the New Territories. Against strong competition, the bid was won by Harrow School and in August 2012 a new school, Harrow International School Hong Kong, will open. The Head Master will be Mr Mel Mrowiec, currently Deputy Head Master of Harrow School in the UK. Many students from Hong Kong have come to Harrow over the years and this latest collaboration is entirely appropriate.

After a nervous, tentative start, interaction between the International Schools and the 'mother' school have become both cordial and mutually advantageous. Sadly Sir John Akehurst did not live to see the seed he planted come into full bloom. The placement of two Harrow School Governors on each of the International School Boards has brought two-way benefit. While Harrow International is a franchise, and the financial benefits to Harrow UK demonstrable, Harrow UK has done much more than lend its name. Former Chairman of Governors, Mr Peter Siddons, has attended virtually all the Bangkok and Beijing Governors meetings. His financial expertise, honed at PriceWaterhouse Cooper and already proven at Harrow UK, has been invaluable. Other Governors with educational experience, notably Mrs Anne Longley, former Head Mistress of Roedean, and Mr Edward Gould, former Master of Marlborough, have visited the schools and given their advice.

Mr David Dawes retired from Harrow UK in 2003 and has taught Mathematics at both the Bangkok and Beijing schools. Mr Gordon Montgomery came to Bangkok to teach Mathematics and Physics five years ago and is now a Head of House (House Master); three of Bangkok's teachers spent a year on the Hill two years ago and one of them, Miss Sarah Mackrory, joined the Harrow UK staff. In addition Gap Students from the Hill have come to both schools most years. The Head of Drama from Bangkok, Mr Severin Herbert, spent 2007/8 in Beijing setting up a new department, and a combined ICT group from all three schools meets annually. Dr Hensman and Mr Farthing use Harrow UK as a base for their annual staff recruitment and appointment interviews.

There have also been pupil visits to Harrow: several students from the International Schools have, over the years, attended Harrow's Summer School and last year a group of senior students from Beijing came for university placement advice.

One of the most special Harrovian visits occurred in January 2009 when NASA astronaut and OH Dr Nicholas Patrick visited both Bangkok and Beijing schools. His impact was remarkable – the depth and breadth of his knowledge about a myriad of things, his passion for knowledge and his ability to communicate it to children of all ages, and his charismatic personality, endeared him to all. He returned to the Space Station in January 2010 and carried with him banners from HIS Bangkok, Beijing and Hong Kong.

The establishment of the International Schools has provided a top grade opportunity for young people living in Thailand and China who want a British-style education; it has increased awareness of Harrow School in the Far East; and the bottom line is that the revenue received by Harrow UK has enabled the School to extend its awards of bursaries to those unable to afford the full fees.

The school celebrated its tenth anniversary in 2008. The emphasis has been on high academic performance, broad co-curricular opportunities and strong pastoral care.

THE MUSEUM OF HARROW LIFE

SUCH IS THE INTEREST IN the School from the world outside that nearly 10,000 people join one of the School tours each year. The standard tour takes about an hour and a half and includes the Fourth Form Room, Speech Room, Chapel, the Shepherd Churchill Dining Hall, the Sports Hall and the Museum of Harrow Life, but the itinerary can be varied to accommodate special interests. Many visitors come to see a school that is an example of an education system admired and emulated around the world. Some come to see the architecture, others the gardens. There is a significant body of interest, led by the Churchill Society based in the US, that wants to explore the association with Sir Winston; for them, Speech Room (where there is a Churchill portrait by Salisbury and which was the scene of his memorable visit for Songs in 1940), the War Memorial with the recent Churchill display boards, Fourth Form Room (where his name is carved), possibly the Fencing Salle (Churchill was Public Schools Foil Champion in 1892), The Head Master's House (Hall, name boards and House group photographs) and Chapel is an appropriate tour.

One of the exhibits in the Museum of Harrow Life

Recently a group of sixth formers studying "the influence of English Public Schools on the development of sport" visited. Their tour featured the School Yard (home of rackets), the rackets courts, the Head Master's House Yard (example of an original squash court) and an introduction to Harrow football.

However most come for curiosity: they find the hats "quaint", the Fourth Form Room a "wow", the sporting facilities "stunning" and the atmosphere of bustling activity in spectacular surroundings both novel and stimulating in a way that those who live, work or study on the Hill often do not appreciate. Many visitors are surprised to find an "oasis of tranquillity" just ten miles from central London – of course they haven't been inside the boarding houses.

Tours of the School were started in a small way in 1979 to meet a growing demand from tourists visiting London. The idea came from Mrs Jean Leaf, wife of John Leaf who was brought up as the son of the House Master of West Acre, was a boy in Elmfield, later returned to teach and became House Master of Druries. The tours became increasingly popular and requests rapidly increased as groups such as the National Trust, historical societies, NADFAS, retirement fellowships and local schools

all took advantage of the opportunity. There are now, additionally, numerous visits from overseas school children, especially French, German, Dutch and Scandinavian, but also including Japanese, Koreans and Chinese. The organisation required for all these visits is considerable and this has been taken on by Mr and Mrs Leaf, who between them set up the structure for booking, greeting, guiding and collecting payments. There are about a dozen approved guides, several of whom can offer foreign languages. Mr and Mrs Leaf are also responsible for the creation of the Museum of Harrow Life, situated on the lower floor of the Old Music Schools. The Museum houses many objects of interest: some had previously remained unseen in the School Archive; others have been donated by Old Harrovians. The interior is broadly divided into sections: Early Times, Customs, Games, Wartime, Giants of Old, Songs, Speech Room, Science and two boys' rooms. Many visitors ask if they can see a boys' House and more particularly a boy's room. Clearly this would be an unacceptable infringement of privacy and so one of the earliest aims for the Museum was to show a replica of a boy's room. There are two in the Museum: a modern room and one from about 1890. The modern room is equipped with furniture and fittings that have become standard since the House refurbishment programme of the 1980s and 1990s, whereas the Victorian room, in strong contrast, has a gas light, coal fire, put-up bed, leather-bound books and a fine roll-top desk. Wax figures bring life to the displays. Mr Leaf has also produced *An Illustrated Guide to Harrow School,* the images for which are the work of two other Old Harrovians, Geoffrey Shakerley and the late Patrick Lichfield.

The income from tours was initially used to stock the shop in the Museum but this was repaid in eighteen months. Thereafter funds were set aside to create the Museum. In 1997 a suitable site became available and the Museum opened in May 1998. The cost had been covered entirely from the accumulated funds. However the prime purpose of the tours is not to make money but rather to provide a structured opportunity for people to see the School.

The Old Music School now houses the Museum of Harrow Life

THE HARROW CLUB AND THE MISSION CLUB

IN THE SPRING OF 1883 the Head Master, Dr Butler, wrote to all Old Harrovians informing them of the decision to start a School Mission in Latimer Road in Notting Dale. Notting Dale was one of the drabbest and most squalid districts in London. The station at Latimer Road was known as Piggery Junction "from the miserable and unwholesome establishment for the feeding of those animals which then occupied the site of our Church and Mission Room." The men of the area that were employed were mostly brick makers, costermongers and casual labourers while the women, the real breadwinners, worked mainly in steam laundries away from their homes and children. It was an area of London that rivalled the worst of the East End for poverty. "Rich inhabitants there were none; the moderately poor were scarce." "The purpose of the Mission," wrote Dr Butler, was "to minister to the wants of the poor and the neglected, and in so doing to bring together classes of our fellow countrymen who know far too little of each other."

The first Missioner was The Reverend William Laws, an Old Harrovian and senior curate at St Mary Abbots Church in Kensington. Masters and boys at the School undertook to pay his salary for at least seven years. They, together with charities and members of the newly formed Harrow Mission Association, would also be responsible for other expenses, such as the purchase of land and the construction of the buildings. From the earliest days the School was deeply involved with its new Mission: as well as financial and administrative support, there were many visitors to Latimer Road.

Revd E Stogdon, Vicar of Holy Trinity, Latimer Road, the Harrow Mission church

On Trinity Sunday 1884, the Mission Room was opened and in 1887 the foundation stone of the Church was laid by the Duchess of Albany: ninety boys from the School provided a guard of honour. The architect of both Mission and Church was Norman Shaw.

William Laws described the work of the Mission as spiritual, philanthropic, educational and to provide entertainment. Progress was rapid: a kitchen provided penny dinners for children whose mothers worked in the laundries. The meticulously kept records show that, in its first seventy days of opening, the kitchen had served 9,507 dinners of which 1,702 were free. By 1888 Clubs for men and youths and boys were established and Laws was calling for a girls' club. From the start sport played a prominent part in Club life and a sports field was purchased in 1887. In 1893 a children's holiday fund was set up to enable younger members to go on fortnight holidays in Hertfordshire and Essex. This was the beginning of the camps organised by the Mission which took place annually until a property was purchased in 1985 in the Forest of Dean. In 1902 a day nursery was established, with the Princess of Wales as Patron.

By the 1920s cracks in the relationship between the Church and the Clubs were beginning to appear and in 1931 the Council of the Mission appointed a Harrow Master as the first Manager of the Club. By 1939 the Mission's responsibility for the Parish of Holy Trinity had ended. By 1953 the role of the Club had changed completely. Originally the need had been for a centre where people could receive the necessities of life like good food and adequate clothing, but in the seventy years that followed, social conditions had improved, poverty and disease had declined and the Clubs became less a centre of relief and more a centre of community life. However, there was still a need for fostering human welfare in other than material ways.

In 1963 approval was given for the Club to take over the old Mission Church, now no longer in use, and planning began that culminated in the opening of the new premises of The Harrow Club W10 in 1967. The luxury of a huge sports hall opened up many possibilities. However, the sheer vastness of the new premises threatened to destroy the intimacy of former years, while the cost of running and maintaining them became so great that the Club was unable to live within its means. In 1970 the Club decided to sell its sports ground in North Wembley, which it had purchased in 1922. This was a valuable site and meant that the Club suddenly found itself with large funds available. The space in the new premises allowed for a great increase in the activities it could offer, while the acquisition of first the vicarage and then the bakery allowed for the setting up of new enterprises. The first change was the name: what had in turn been called the Harrow Mission and the Harrow School Clubs became 'The Harrow Club W10'. The second change was that the Club membership admitted both boys and girls. But the most dramatic changes have been in the geography of the area. In the 1960s the neat Victorian terraces of Notting Dale were replaced by the tower blocks of the Silchester and Edward Woods estates. The construction of the A40 link road and Westway severed the Club completely from the White City area and, in 1997, a boundary change moved the Club from Hammersmith and Fulham to Kensington and Chelsea. The area is now one of the most densely populated in the UK: some thirty different nationalities occupy public housing, while the gentrification of the remaining older properties has made parts of the area fashionable. As the end of the century approached, it was clear that the Church building and its facilities were inadequate. The expectations of young people were changing and with it the notion of a youth club. Advertising, style, fashion, television, computers, mobile phones, iPods, the internet, ease of travel and the increasing profile of sport have all influenced modern life. Harrow Clubs recognised the need for change.

In 1996 there was a break in the succession of Harrow Masters chairing the Management Committee, with the appointment of Mary Tuck, a distinguished civil servant and local resident. Under her guidance, a £2 million building appeal was launched and the comprehensive redevelopment of the buildings began. With the support of Octavia Hill Housing Trust and the De Paul Trust, the old Vicarage became a hostel for homeless young people.

Throughout its history the successful evolution of the Harrow Club has relied on many Old Harrovians. In 1897 a hostel was acquired to accommodate Old Harrovians willing to lend a helping hand. This involvement has continued. School Monitors also played an important role in the management of the Clubs, particularly during the Great War.

Since the 1970s a succession of liaison Masters at the School have continued the close connection with the Club. The creation of the Nottingdale Urban Study Centre led to the emergence of the Nottingdale Technology Centre, and, following a visit by the Minister of Technology in 1981, the Government pledged a £20 million programme to set up information technology centres throughout Britain; Nottingdale was the consultancy unit behind the programme. Although the Urban Study Centre was closed in 1995 when much of its work had become part of the mainstream school curriculum, the Nottingdale Technology Centre thrives. In 2000 The Prince of Wales attended the official reopening of Harrow Club W10 as a 'community centre for the twety-first century'.

The Mission buildings

Worth Press and the Harrow Development Trust gratefully acknowledge and thank those listed below for their generous support, without which this book would not have been possible.

SPONSORS

Adeson, Mrs Linda
Baldwin, Roger
Barclay, Alistair
Beecham, Edward
Blair, Hew
Bond Gunning, Heyrick
Bond Gunning, Rufus
Brankin Frisby, Jonathan
Brown, Andrew
Brown, Fraser
Butler, Douglas
Byford, Colin
Campbell, Colin
Carew, Lord
Cecil, Dr Mark
Chow, Dr Jason
Chow, Mr & Mrs Teck
Cilley, David
Cilley, Judith
Cliff, Clive
Clifford, Murray
Cohen, Hugo
Cohen, Oliver
Compton, Richard
Craig, David
Demierre, Pascal
Dick, Robert
Eady, Anthony
Feggetter, Jeremy
Fiallos, Alexander
Firth, Nigel
Fortune, David
Freethy, Simon
Friedman, Sandy
Goddard, Philip
Goodenough, Alexander
Goodliffe, Peter
Gordon, Martin
Gower, Christopher
Greenstock, Sir Jeremy
Guthrie, General Lord
Hamilton, Guy
Hassan, Faisal
Hassan, HRH Princess Sumaya Bint El
Hedley Lewis, Mervyn
Hermon-Taylor, Christopher
Houston, Andrew
Howes, David
Ivison, David
Jeffares, Timothy
Jones, Dafydd
Joseph, Richard
Keatley, Robert
Krywald-Sanders, Mrs Sandra
Kurtz, John
Lalude, Dr Tunde
Lambourne, Christopher
Latham, James
Leather, Mark
Lee, Sanha
Lewczynski, Mark
Lithgow, Mrs E
Lockett, Jeffery
Lotery, James
Love, Andrew
Love, Anthony
Maxey, Henry
Maxey, Richard
McLauchlan, Nigel
McMullen, Fergus
Miller, James
Minne, Eric
Minoprio, Charles
Minoprio, Stephen
Mitchell, Paul
Moi, Gideon
Nicholson, Frank
Nicholson, Sir Paul
Nordhagen, Jan
Ovia, Mrs Kay
Parr, Adam
Parr, Glenn
Phillips, Leighton
Phillips, Simon
Picot, Dr Christopher
Powell, Guy
Proctor, Julian
Quilter, Guy
Raper, Brian
Reid, Hubert
Rowbotham, Adam
Rowbotham, Mark
Ryan, Peter
Savill, Paul
Savill, Dudley
Savory, Michael
Scawn, Mrs Elaine
Scawn, Michael
Scott, Alistair
Shah, Mrs Sweta
Siddons, Peter
Simmonds, David
Simmonds, Craig
Simmonds, Geoffrey
Slipenchuk, Grigory
Smith, Zikomo
Smouha, Richard
Stafford Allen, James
Stanes, Richard
Steinart, Alexander
Stevenson, Mrs Libby
Stevenson, Paul
Sunley, John
Taralrud-Bay, Norman
Tenison Mosse, Lewis
Theobald, Peter
Tonks, Henry
Trotter, Rupert
Virgin, James
Walduck, Alex
Walduck, Richard
Walduck, Nicholas
Wallace, David
Warren, Peter
Wells, John
Wellwood, James
Wiggin, David
Wightman, James
Williams, Edward
Wisskirchen, Marcus
Wong, Winston
Young, Alex

SUBSCRIBERS

Adams, Richard
Addison, Mark
Advocaat, Alexander
Alauddin, Tunku Naquiyuddin
Aldous, Thomas
Alen-Buckley, Michael
Alireza, Abdullah
Anderson, Anthony
Anderson, James
Archer, Paddy
Armitage, Stephen
Ashton, Richard
Ashwell, Mrs Susan
Astaire, Mark
Astaire, Mrs Susan
Aulak, Sukjinder
Babtie, William
Back, Nigel
Baines, David
Baker, Charles
Baker Wilbraham, Sir Richard
Bankes, Charles
Barattolo, Pier
Barclay, Joseph
Barkes, Bryan
Barrs, Michael
Barton, Tom
Bates, Roger
Bayliss, Jeremy
Beckett, Ross
Beer, Ian
Benn, Michael
Beresford, Anthony
Beresford, Nicholas
Beresford, Richard
Beresford, Toby
Birri, Simon
Blad, Edward
Blad, William
Blenk, Peter
Bloomfield, Roderick
Blosse-Lynch, Henry
Blount, Charles
Bois, Stephen
Boissier, Roger
Bolingbroke-Kent, Noel
Bomford, Nick
Bond, John
Bott, Charles
Boushehri, Sohrab
Boxhall, Richard
Bradkin, Brandon
Bradley, Brendan
Bredin, Terence
Breeden, Guy
Brewster, Mrs Annie
Broadhead, Mrs Jill
Brooks, Richard
Bruce, Robert
Bruce-Lockhart, Malcolm
Brunault, James
Brunault, Matthew
Buchanan-Jardine, Sir Rupert
Burn, John
Butler, Lord
Cable, Anthony
Caldecott-Smith, David
Campbell, James
Cannon, Mrs Angela
Capon, Andrew
Carden, Peter
Carr, Paul
Carrington, Roger
Carris, Norman
Carter, The Rev Mark
Cartwright, Peter
Cellier, Peter
Chalmers, Ian
Chalmers, John
Chambers, James
Chant, David
Cheales, David
Chelsea, Lady
Chinvaravatana, Aroon
Choi, Jason
Chopra, Arjun
Clemett, Mrs Juliet
Clive, John
Cobb, David
Collinge, Victor
Collins, John
Collins, Robert
Connell, Sir Michael
Cooke, Marcus
Cooke, Nicholas
Cooke-Priest, Patrick
Coyte, David
Cregeen, Peter
Crofts, Tony
Crump , Ernie
Currie, Dr Edward
Dastur, William
Davies, Robert
de Broe-Ferguson, James
de Klee, Mrs Fiona
de Lukacs Lessnar, Andrew
de Rosiere, Vicomte Roland
De Rougemount, Clive
de Zoete, Timothy
Deane, Nigel
Demeure, Achille
Denison-Smith, Lt Gen Sir Anthony
Dettmer, Simon
Dick-Cleland, John
Dickson, Alistair
Donnelly, Michael
Du Boulay, Robin
Du Sautoy, Nicholas
Dubash, Ardeshir
Dutton-Forshaw, Graeme
Eadon, Simon
Edwardes-Ker, Charles
Eiloart, Mrs Joy
Ellis, Roger
Elsey, Alexander
Farnham, George
Farquharson, John
Findlay, Jeremy
Fosh, Jonathan
Fosh, Matthew
Foster, Neil
Fowler-Watt, Donald
Francke, Donald
Francke, John
Frankel, Andrew
Franks, Timothy
Gajland, John
Galgey, William
Gall, Francois
Garrett, Simon

Gasson, Dr George
Gaunt, David
Gaussen, Colonel Samuel
Georgallides, Maximilian
George, David
Gibbens, Declan
Gibson-Wynes, Kim
Glasspool, Mrs Jules
Glynn, Robert
Golby, David
Graham, Andrew
Graham-Jones, Michael
Grant, James
Grant, Richard
Green, Richard
Gregson, Dr Richard
Griffith, Robert
Gwynne, Desmond
Hadon, Pen
Haldane, Andrew
Haldane, Mark
Hall, Michael
Hamilton, Peter
Hamwee, Nick
Hanson, James
Haria, Dhruvkumar
Harrild, Brian
Harris, Mrs Gillian
Harris, Simon
Harrison, Alastair
Harrison, Dr Stephen
Harrison, Paul
Hart, Adam
Hart, Peter
Hartley, Robert
Harvey, Mrs Sophia
Hastings, Howard
Heber-Percy, Algernon
Helmer, Gavin
Henderson, Shamus
Hersey, Tim
Hewens, Nicholas
Higgins, Eugene
Highley, Henry
Highley, Sam
Hirdaramani, Mrs Mona
Hoare, Toby
Hoban, Mrs Jasmine
Holmes, Mrs Anouchka
Hopkins, John
Houghton, Edward
Hume, Stephen
Hunter, Peter
Hurst, Christopher
Ingledow, Ben
Ingram, Ian
Isbister, Simon
Ivison, Marcel
James, David
James, Dr Richard
Jefferis, Tim
Jensen, Niels
Johnston, Max
Jones, David
Kane, Michael
Keighley, Graham
Kemp, Christopher
Khayat, Antoine
Kilner, Thomas
Kininmonth, James
Kinsella, Dr Lawrence
Kirk, The Rev Andrew
Laing, John
Lander, James
Lane, Nicholas
Lanning, George
Lau, Paul
Lawrence, Alistair
Lawrence, Sebastian
Lawrence, Stephen
Lawson-Cruttenden, Tim
Leaf, John
Leat, Mrs Ann
Lee-Jones, Dr M
Lehrell, Peter-Carlo
Leigh, Paul
Lemmon, Jeremy
Lemos, Mrs Ireni
Lesser, Joe
Lewis, John
Liddiard, Michael
Little, Edward
Llewellyn, Evan
Lonsdale-Hands, Horatio
Loughbridge, Gordon
Lowe, Mrs Jane
Lydiard-Wilson, Jonathan
Lyons, Toby
MacGregor, Colin
Mackie, Alec
Macpherson, Mrs W D
Maloney, Justin
Mann, Christopher
Maydon, Robert
Mazet, Mrs Ann
McBeath, John
McClelland, Michael
McCorquodale, Glen
McGuinness, Fraser
McKinnon Holmes, Dr Charles
McMullen, John
Mee, John
Mehta, Nilesh
Mercer, Peter
Micklem, Mrs Jane
Miles, Mrs O M
Miller, Jock
Minoprio, John
Minoprio, Richard
Misra, Mrs Shalini
Montgomery, Michael
Morrison, Graham
Morrison, Hamish
Moss, David
Mucklow, John
Murray, Roy
Murray Lee, Denzil
Narayn, Mark
Nash, Jeremy
Nevill, Captain Richard
Nichols, Peter
Norman, Jeremy
Northcott, Montague
Northcott, Richard
Norton, Michael
Ogilvie-Harris, Mrs Sheila
Olesen, Thomas
Outram, Sir Alan
Parsons, Sir John
Parsons, Toby
Patel, Dr Nalin
Patel, Mrs Sadhna
Patrick, John
Pearson, Charles
Pearson, David
Pearson, Martin
Pearson, Martin
Pearson-Jones, Mrs Sandra
Pelham, Henry
Pelham Burn, Angus
Percival, Mrs Serena
Pernas, Alvaro
Phillips, Anthony
Philips, Nigel
Phillips, Henry
Picton-Evans, Dr Angela
Pinkstone, Dennis
Pitcairn, Julian
Pittalis, John
Powell, Michael
Powell, Robert
Power, The Rev James
Preece, Cdr Richard
Prenn, John
Prior, Andrew
Prior, Mrs Sarah
Proger, David
Proger, Tim
Purcell, James
Rafique, Tariq
Ramsbotham, James
Readman, Peter
Rees, Thomas
Reid, Charles
Reynard, Charles
Rich, Mrs Victoria
Richards, Mrs Deborah
Richardson, Howard
Ritchie, Major Alastair
Ritchie, Richard
Ropner, Jonathan
Rowlandson, Richard
Royle, Godfrey
Royle, Peter
Sadeghifar, Farbod
Samuel, Bill
Sanderson, Lance
Sayers, Michael
Scully, William
Seligman, Charles
Seligman, Hugh
Seligman, William
Serrell-Watts, Sebastian
Sharp, Mrs Brenda
Sheaf, Andrew
Sheridan III, Robert
Shirley-Smith, Richard
Shoji, Maroi
Sichel, Donald
Siddons, John
Sims-Hilditch, Hugh
Singer, Forbes
Smith, Elliot
Smith, James
Smouha, Brian
Spiro, Robin
Staley, Mrs Suzannah
Stephenson, James
Stephenson, Timothy
Stevenson, Geoffrey
Stidston-Nott, Callum
Strachan, John
Straker-Smith, David
Stayt, John
Streeter, John
Swan, Christopher
Target, Mrs Samantha
Taylor-Restell, Ian
Thomas, Sir David
Thompson, Myles
Thompson, Nimble
Thornton, Edward
Thurlow, Ed
Thurlow, Max
Thurston, Robert
Thwaites, Christian
Trevor-Jones, Hugh
Trower, Hugo
Tso, Shiu
Turner, Glenn
Usher-Smith, Julian
Van Namen, John
Vargas, Ashley
Vermeir, Raphael
von Bohlen und Halbach, Arnold
Wake-Walker, George
Wake-Walker, Michael
Walden, Richard
Walduck, Stephen
Walker, Dr David
Walker, Mrs Cece
Wall, Nicholas
Wallace, John
Waller, Sam
Waller, Toby
Walton, Ian
Walton, Luke
Walton, Max
Ward, Timothy
Ward, Graham
Warner, Nicholas
Warren, Christopher
Warren, James
Wathen, Julian
Watson, Ronald
Watson, Sir Simon
Webb, Charles
Weedon, Mark
Weir, William
Welman, Ted
West, Graham
White, Mrs Gretchen
Whitehead, Mark
Whitehouse-Vaux, William
White-Thomson, Ian
Whitmee, Mrs Gillian
Wickson, Tom
Wieloch, Hastings
Willis, Henry
Wills, Richard
Wilson, Albert
Wilson, Andrew
Wilson, John
Winlaw, Antony
Winner, David
Wong, Michael
Woodhouse, Charles
Woodhouse, George
Woodhouse, Sam
Woolley, Fred
Wyatt, Neil
Wyman, James
Wynn-Williams, Rhydain
Yannaghas, Michael
Zetland, The Marquess of

REFERENCES

Tyerman: *A History of Harrow School*
Harrow: Portrait of a School ed Dudley
Thornton: *Harrow School & its Surroundings*
Howson & Townsend Warner: *Harrow School*
Shymansky, Lichfield & Golland: *An Illustrated History of Harrow School*
Laborde: *Harrow Yesterday & Today*
The Harrovian 1888-2010
Harrow School Register, editions 1-8
The Harrow Almanack 1865-1939
Pevsner: *The Buildings of England*

ACKNOWLEDGEMENTS

The author is grateful to:

The Keepers and Governors of Harrow School and the Head Master for permission to use material from the School Archive and current photographs of the School.

Rita Boswell for her assistance and patience in responding to a stream of requests for photographs and other material from the Harrow School Archive.

Dr Christopher Tyerman for permission to quote extensively from *A History of Harrow School 1324-1991*, published by Oxford University Press, 2000.

The following, who have provided material for the book ranging from short notes to complete essays: Andrew Alban, George Attenborough, Charles Baker, James Baron, Simon Berry, Peter Bieneman, Brendan Bradley, Michael Burrell, James Chambers, Rob Collins, Sir Michael Connell, Patrick Cooke-Priest, Richard Corthine, Dr Bill Dalton, Major Adrian Davies, Graham Dunbar, John Eaton, Michael Etheridge, Charles Farrar-Bell, Dr Iain Farrell, Mark Greenstock, Steven Griffiths, Ian Hammond, Mark Hensman, Peter Hunter, Bryan Hurl, Alan Jaggs, John James, Dr Patrick Kaye, John Leaf, Carolyn Leder, Andrew Lee, Jeremy Lemmon, Keith Metcalfe, James Morwood, Loretta Moseley, Roy Murray, Graham Palmer, Tom Perkins, The Rev James Power, Andrew Reed, Dudley Savill, Roy Seymour, Ben Shaw, Sandy Smith, Martin Stead, Andrew Stebbings, Peter Stilwell, Derek Swift, Chris Tolman, Martin Tyrell, Roger Uttley, Tom Wickson, Antony Winlaw, Gary White, David Woodcock and others.

James Hanson, Nick Marchant, Brett Prestidge, Graham Riley, Minnie Walker and Tom Wickson for modern photographs.

Rob Dudley, Kirsty Shanahan, Ross Beckett for advice on text and proofreading.

The publisher Kenneth Webb (Newlands 1951[3]) wishes to acknowledge and thank:

Harrow School for the use of images from the School's archive.

Nicholas Marchant for supplying numerous photographs and Robert Dudley (The Head Master's 1957[3]) for his advice.

Special gratitude goes to the author, Dale Vargas (Druries 1952[3]), for whom the publication of this book is the culmination of several years of work and research. In spite of his intimate knowledge of the School, the sheer mass of factual information that needed to be collected for the 440 years of the School's history would have daunted many. The selection of the images was another monumental task; the compilation of the text was almost an adjunct. That he should have embraced the challenge with such enthusiasm has been both a joy and a relief to me: the result is a book that I hope will give pleasure to its readers, and of which we can both be proud.

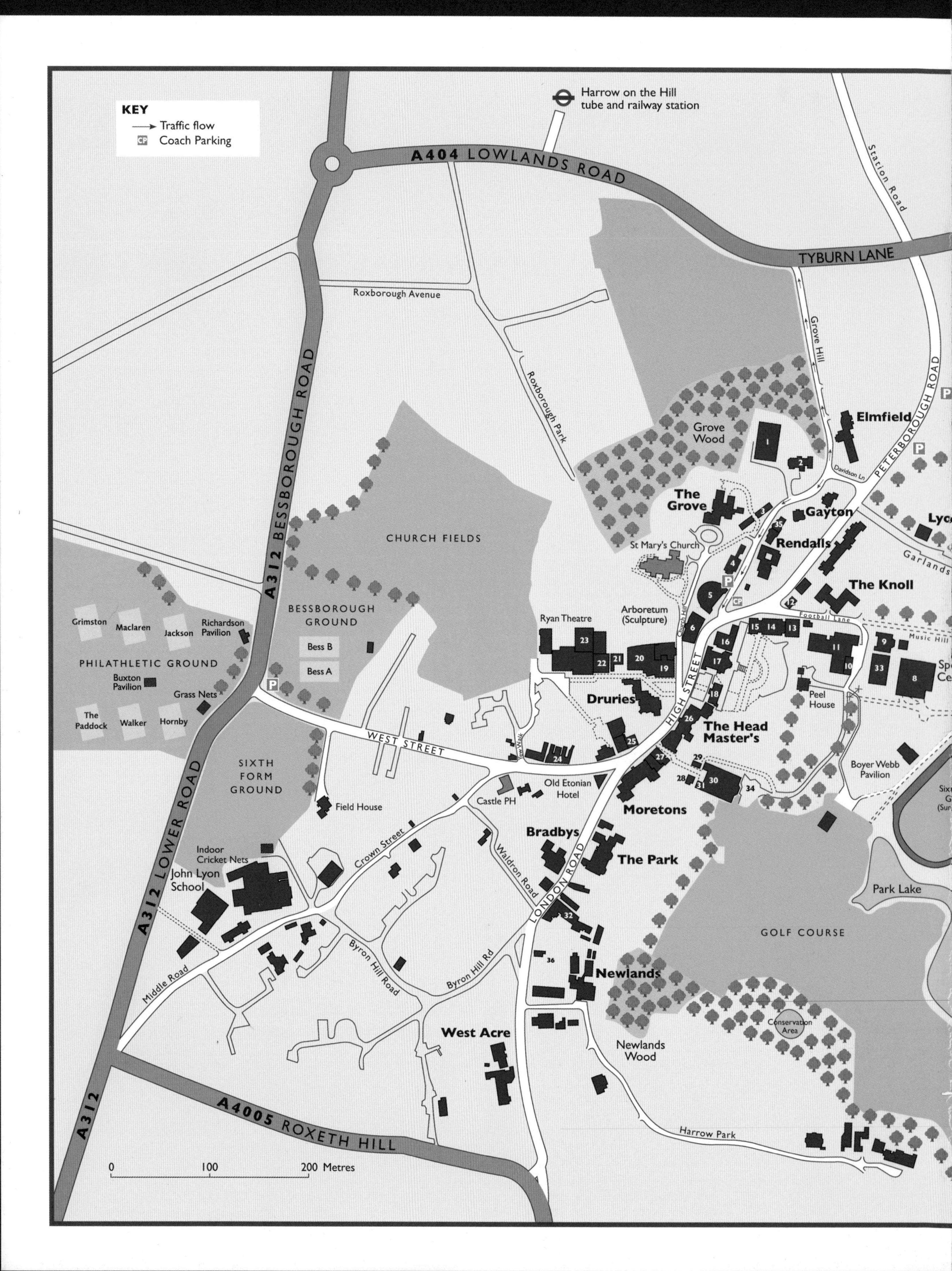
KEY
Traffic flow
CP Coach Parking
Harrow on the Hill tube and railway station
A404 LOWLANDS ROAD
TYBURN LANE
Station Road
Roxborough Avenue
Roxborough Park
Grove Hill
PETERBOROUGH ROAD
A312 BESSBOROUGH ROAD
A312 LOWER ROAD
A312
A4005 ROXETH HILL
Grove Wood
Elmfield
Davidson Ln
The Grove
Gayton
Rendalls
St Mary's Church
The Knoll
Garlands
Football Lane
Music Hill
CHURCH FIELDS
BESSBOROUGH GROUND
Bess B
Bess A
Grimston
Maclaren
Jackson
Richardson Pavilion
PHILATHLETIC GROUND
Buxton Pavilion
Grass Nets
The Paddock
Walker
Hornby
SIXTH FORM GROUND
Ryan Theatre
Arboretum (Sculpture)
Church Hill
HIGH STREET
Druries
WEST STREET
Peel House
The Head Master's
Boyer Webb Pavilion
Old Etonian Hotel
Castle PH
Field House
Moretons
Bradbys
The Park
Indoor Cricket Nets
John Lyon School
Crown Street
Waldron Road
LONDON ROAD
Park Lake
GOLF COURSE
Middle Road
Byron Hill Road
Byron Hill Rd
Newlands
West Acre
Conservation Area
Newlands Wood
Harrow Park
0
100
200 Metres